A Political Theology of Nature

This book argues that the modern separation of humanity
from nature can be traced to the displacement of the triune
God. Locating the source of our current ecological crisis in this
separation, Peter Scott argues that it can be healed only within
theology, through a revival of a Trinitarian doctrine of
creation interacting with political philosophies of ecology.
Drawing insights from deep ecology, ecofeminism, and social
and socialist ecologies, Scott proposes a common realm of
God, nature and humanity. Both Trinitarian and political, the
theology of this common realm is worked out by reference to
Christ and Spirit. Christ's resurrection is presented as the
liberation and renewal of ecological relations in nature and
society, the movement of the Holy Spirit is understood as the
renewal of fellowship between humanity and nature through
ecological democracy, and the eucharist is proposed as the
principal political resource Christianity offers for an ecological
age.

PETER SCOTT is Senior Lecturer in Theology in the
Department of Theology & Religious Studies at the University
of Gloucestershire. His previous publications include *Theology,
Ideology and Liberation* (Cambridge University Press, 1994) and
the *Blackwell Companion to Political Theology* (co-editor, 2003).

Cambridge Studies in Christian Doctrine

Edited by
Professor COLIN GUNTON, *King's College London*
Professor DANIEL W. HARDY, *University of Cambridge*

Cambridge Studies in Christian Doctrine is an important series which aims to engage critically with the traditional doctrines of Christianity, and at the same time to locate and make sense of them within a secular context. Without losing sight of the authority of scripture and the traditions of the church, the books in this series subject pertinent dogmas and credal statements to careful scrutiny, analysing them in light of the insights of both church and society, and thereby practising theology in the fullest sense of the word.

Titles published in the series

1. Self and Salvation: Being Transformed
   DAVID F. FORD

2. Realist Christian Theology in a Postmodern Age
   SUE PATTERSON

3. Trinity and Truth
   BRUCE D. MARSHALL

4. Theology, Music and Time
   JEREMY S. BEGBIE

5. The Bible, Theology, and Faith: A Study of Abraham and Jesus
   R. W. L. MOBERLY

6. Bound to Sin: Abuse, Holocaust and the Christian Doctrine of Sin
   ALISTAIR MCFADYEN

7. Church, World and the Christian Life: Practical–Prophetic Ecclesiology
   NICHOLAS M. HEALY

8. Theology and the Dialogue of Religions
   MICHAEL BARNES SJ

9. A Political Theology of Nature
   PETER SCOTT

Forthcoming titles in the series

Worship as Meaning: A Liturgical Theology for Late Modernity
GRAHAM HUGHES
Remythologizing Theology: Divine Action and Authorship
KEVIN J. VANHOOZER

A Political Theology
of Nature

PETER SCOTT

CAMBRIDGE
UNIVERSITY PRESS

PUBLISHED BY THE PRESS SYNDICATE OF THE UNIVERSITY OF CAMBRIDGE
The Pitt Building, Trumpington Street, Cambridge CB2 1RP, United Kingdom

CAMBRIDGE UNIVERSITY PRESS
The Edinburgh Building, Cambridge, CB2 2RU, UK
40 West 20th Street, New York, NY 10011-4211, USA
477 Williamstown Road, Port Melbourne, VIC 3207, Australia
Ruiz de Alarcón 13, 28014 Madrid, Spain
Dock House, The Waterfront, Cape Town 8001, South Africa

http://www.cambridge.org

First published 2003

Printed in the United Kingdom at the University Press, Cambridge

Typefaces Lexicon No. 2 9/13 pt and Lexicon No. 1   *System* LaTeX 2$_\varepsilon$ [TB]

A catalogue record for this book is available from the British Library

ISBN 0 521 64165 9 hardback
ISBN 0 521 52717 1 paperback

For Harry Jonathan and Esther Katelyn, in great hope

Boundless intemperance / In nature is a tyranny.

MACBETH ACT IV, SCENE III

Contents

Preface xi

Part I **God, nature and modernity**

1 Nature in Christian theology: politics, context and concepts 3

2 The common realm of God, nature and humanity 30

Part II **The politics of nature**

3 Deep ecology: the return of nature 63

4 Ecofeminism: the reproduction of nature 89

5 Social ecology: the dialectical emergence of nature and society 109

6 Socialist ecology: the production of nature 136

Part III **The triune God and un/natural humanity**

7 The worldly Christ: common nature 169

8 Life in the Spirit: un/natural fellowship 201

9 *God–body*: un/natural relations, un/natural community in Jesus Christ 233

Bibliography 259
Index 271

Preface

Always I have linked Christian living with issues of power, theological existence with politics. Even when I have struggled with my baptism – and I have struggled quite a lot! – the shaping power of my religious formation has always included a political aspect, although I have changed my mind on the nature of that politics. This book encompasses these interests: it offers a theology of living before and from the triune God within the politics of ecology. I do not know whether sufficient time remains to overcome the injustices in our ecological relations with nature. Yet while there is still life in us, we keep on. That seems right and hopeful.

This book has been a long time in the writing. Through this process I have accrued many debts. I am glad to acknowledge these here.

First, I must thank my academic home through this period in the Department of Theology and Religious Studies at the University of Gloucestershire. I am especially grateful for the granting of several sabbaticals and the support of Stanley Rudman and Fred Hughes (past and present Heads of Department). The able administrative assistance of Patricia Downes and Annie Brocklehurst has given me much needed time for this research. Library staff, including Maggie Wheel and Sue Mills, have graciously responded to many requests for information. In the closing stages of the project, Scott Jordan and Chris Evans furnished vital computing support. Throughout this period, I have taught courses in ecological and political theology: I thank those students who studied this material with me for their theological seriousness. Perhaps some of their questions as to 'what I think' are answered here. Not least I thank members of the Theology Reading Group who remind me of the importance in theology of learning in community.

Sabbaticals in 1996 and 1998 were spent in the extraordinarily rich and creative environment of the Center of Theological Inquiry, Princeton, where I learned so much. I am grateful to the Centre's Director, Wallace M. Alston, and its Senior Scholar for Research, Robert Jenson, for encouragement and support. Through these periods members of the Centre made formative contributions to this project, including: Don Browning, Torrance Kirby, Bill Lazareth, Nancy Duff, George Hunsinger, Tony Ugolnik, Peter Ochs, Niels Henrik Gregersen, Victor Nuovo, Avihu Zakai, David Tracy, Frank Clooney, George Newlands, Wentzel van Huyssteen, Miroslav Volf and Rusty Reno. Our stays at the Centre were greatly enhanced by the active kindness of Mary Beth Lewis, Maureen Montgomery, Linda Sheldon, Cecelio Orantes and Kathi Morley.

I owe a considerable debt to those friends and colleagues who have read and commented on various chapters and whose contributions have greatly improved the book. Here I thank Niels Henrik Gregersen, Bill Cavanaugh, Melissa Raphael and Elaine Graham. I am very grateful one more time to my friend, Al McFadyen, for many arresting conversations, some of these not immediately theological. Debts of a more general kind I also have: to Denys Turner, who talked through with me some of my early ideas; to Luco van den Brom for an important conversation; and to Victor Nuovo and Avi Zakai who give me confidence where none exists. For theological–moral support and timely interventions I thank Peter Selby and, once more, Niels Gregersen.

Cambridge University Press, through Alex Wright, Ruth Parr and Kevin Taylor, has been a wonderfully efficient publisher. I thank Paul Northup for kindly compiling the bibliography at short notice and Gillian Maude for her careful copy-editing. The series editors, Colin Gunton and Daniel Hardy, have read the entire manuscript and I am grateful to them for their feedback and encouragement. Special thanks must go to the latter: years ago Dan Hardy read a brief prospectus for the book and responded almost immediately with a strong recommendation to pursue the ideas now presented here.

A paper written for the 1999 meeting of the Society for the Study of Theology, published as 'The Future of Creation: Ecology and Eschatology,' in David Fergusson and Marcel Sarot (eds.), *The Future as God's Gift* (Edinburgh: T. & T. Clark, 2000) represents a preliminary version of part of the present work. Chapters 7 and 8 are revised and greatly expanded construals of sections of this essay. I thank the Society for the invitation to present a plenary paper. Furthermore, I am grateful to Celia Deane-Drummond and Paul Murray for invitations to speak at various colloquia and conferences. Preparing for these has been the occasion of important moves along my cognitive path.

To my wife, Amanda Pitt, I owe more than my words can say. 'I am asham'd: does not the stone rebuke me / For being more stone than it?' (*The Winter's Tale* Act V, Scene III). And, further, I am grateful to my parents, Anne and Michael Scott, for their continued interest in my work and touching willingness to read every word of my theological prose.

When I first began work on this project neither of our dear children, Harry and Esther, had been born. So the book has been written through the many changes that parenthood brings and has, I hope, been improved by them. One of my deepest fears is that the ecological issues discussed through this book will barely be addressed by their parents' generation. If they ever ask me what I did through this period, I shall say that I brought them to Sunday School and wrote this book. I hope that they find wisdom in both. To them this book is dedicated, with measureless love.

Part I

God, nature and modernity

Nature in Christian theology: politics, context and concepts

The aim of this book: political theology of nature

The motivation for writing this book lies in my belief that Christian theology has an important contribution to make to the reinterpretation of the human habitat demanded by ecology and the reconfiguration of human social life demanded by the imperatives of environmental sustainability. Yet I am also convinced that a new type of theology of nature is now required.

In theological discussions of the environment, attention has been focused on the relation between theology and the natural sciences, on the one hand, and the 'value' of nature, on the other.[1] Yet the concentration on these two areas is to construe the concerns of environmentalism too narrowly. Environmental concern is not directed to some abstraction, called Nature. Instead, such concern is directed towards the quality and character of habitation, including the habitation of humanity. Questions privileged by environmentalism include: how do life forms interact? How might the quality of life be improved? How can life be sustained in the long term? With these questions come certain perspectives for interpretation (global, aesthetic) and commitments to simpler, more sustainable forms of life (recycling and decentralisation, for instance).[2]

Such questions, perspectives and commitments are not exhausted by inquiries in the natural sciences or into the 'value' of nature. A third area of inquiry emerges: the distortions of human sociality as enacted in the

---

1. These distinctions are Douglas John Hall's, as reported in James McPherson, 'Ecumenical Discussion of the Environment 1966–1987', *Modern Theology* 7:4 (July 1991), 363–71 (367).
2. On the contours of environmentalism, see Max Oelschlaeger, *Caring for Creation: An Ecumenical Approach to the Environmental Crisis* (London and New Haven: Yale University Press, 1994), p. 71.

relations of un/natural humanity with nature. Because environmental concerns may be traced back to a disharmony between humanity and nature, environmental strategies are founded in and directed towards the distorted sociality of humanity. Environmental strategies are thereby redirective. Such strategies seek the reconstitution of human social life towards *wholeness*, *diversity* and *integrity* in its transactions with its natural conditions and away from patterns of *fragmentation* and *disintegration*. As we know, such patterns of fragmentation and disintegration have their own dynamics, leading to the suppression of the importance (but not the actuality) of the natural conditions of human life; our interdependence in the delicate and reciprocal interactions with nature which constitute our un/natural humanity is obscured. Competition over resources (social and natural), insecurity and distrust at all levels (international and national, racial and ethnic, gender and familial), rapid consumption of natural resources and reduction in biodiversity and the quality of agricultural land are instances of such fragmentation and breakdown.[3]

This book sets out some of the contours of a new theological approach, which I am calling *political theology of nature*. Such an approach directs theological attention not to the natural sciences nor to the 'value' of nature but instead to the interaction between un/natural humanity and socialised nature. The theological problematic presented here is concerned with the question: what theological specification can be given to the varied and variable relations between un/natural humanity and socialised nature in such manner that neither are lost? More strongly, can a political theology of nature within a doctrine of creation offer a perspective in which human freedom and contingent nature might be related to secure their mutual affirmation and healing? And we should note the importance of the matter to the wider reaches of theology: if no satisfactory response to this last question can be given, the significance of Jesus of Nazareth is put in question. For who is Jesus Christ if not the action of God in such narrative concentration that an embodied life of human freedom and contingent nature is the saving presence of God?

A political theology of nature is a complex inquiry given the varied and variable relations between humanity and nature. There can be no general construal of such variability; attention must be paid instead to particular

---

3. For a useful discussion of questions of global security, etc., see part 1 of Alan Race and Roger Williamson (eds.), *True to this Earth* (Oxford: One World Publications, 1995).

issues. Yet these issues do not offer themselves in neutral descriptions. The theological task is thereby twofold. First, to offer an analysis and critique of instances of the relations between humanity and nature. Second, to offer a theology of nature which might serve as the 'prequel' to the life, cross and resurrection of Jesus Christ such that God's engagement with (and against) humanity in our relations with nature might be specified more clearly. In short, how might the practices of this society, in its relations with nature, be directed more fully towards the expansionary presence of the triune God?

A political theology of nature is thus an exercise in theological anthropology in a liberative key. Maurice Bloch has noted that 'the very enterprise of studying man [sic] is always a political exercise, and that anthropology has always either challenged or legitimised the society in which it occurs'.[4] One of the central claims of this study is that a political theology of nature is oppositional: it seeks the liberative transformation of nature's meanings. For what is required is both the liberation of theology and the liberation of the world: a political theology of nature invites both the transformation of theology itself and the presentation of a theological concept of nature which affirms the reality of the natural conditions of human life in ways which foster unity and solidarity between creatures.

Naught for your comfort: we are right to be suspicious of the concept of nature in that it has been used to defend that which is only conventional or artificial. Yet we are not convinced, rightly, that we are without nature. In my view, Christian theology is well placed to offer an oppositional reading of nature which specifies humanity in its un/naturalness. How does humanity relate to nature in the perspective of the triune God? – this is a revolutionary question. What do we know of the integrity and wholeness of un/natural humanity? How might such integrity and wholeness be enacted?

The argument of the book is thus to be found in two related ideas which, in theological perspective, form a single theme.

The first idea holds to the view that: 'The origins of the contingencies which are overwhelming us today lie in social contexts, and no longer

---

4. Maurice Bloch, *Marxism and Anthropology* (Oxford University Press, 1983), p. 131. In fact, 'challenge' does not quite cover the range of possible interactions of resistance. See my reinterpretation of the account of alternative, oppositional and specialising modes of resistance in the work of Raymond Williams in Peter Scott, *Theology, Ideology and Liberation* (Cambridge University Press, 1994), pp. 36f.

directly in nature.'[5] The balance of this statement is important: I do not hold to the view that nature is socially constructed *simpliciter*; the structures and processes of nature are real and 'excess to thought'. The engagement with that nature, through our socially formed discourses, is by a range of social practices in our habitation: knowledge of nature is always thereby perspectival and emerges in particular praxes.[6] Which means that the way in which social and political theory understands the natural conditions of life is central to this book. 'Economics, politics and social theory are reinterpreted [in ecology] from a central concern with human relations to the physical world as the necessary basis for social and economic policy.'[7] A political theology of nature offers such reinterpretation *in theology* concentrating upon human relations to the physical world in the politics of human habitation as construed by political ecology.

This book explores the issue of the presence of the triune God to political–ideological forms: how the core doctrines of Christian faith may be situated in the material processes of politics and ecology. It examines the 'symbolics of nature' as these inhibit or encourage views of material production, that is, the relations between the physical world and social humanity. The ecological claim of the centrality of human relations to the physical world is here privileged.[8] My account of nature is therefore an account of ecological nature as grasped within social and political theory. My concern is not with the scientific – natural or life – dimensions of nature, but instead with human relations to the physical world. What follows acknowledges that too often nature is interpreted as an abstract singular – my writing is an attempt in theology to make plural the singular.[9]

5. Jürgen Habermas, *The New Conservatism* (Cambridge: Polity Press pbk. edn, 1994), p. 204.
6. Of the four epistemologies identified by David Demeritt as 'constructivist' (David Demeritt, 'Science, Social Constructivism and Nature', in Bruce Braun and Noel Castree (eds.), *Remaking Reality: Nature at the Millennium* (London and New York: Routledge, 1998, pp. 173–93), my 'philosophical' position is closest to 'artefactual constructivism'.
7. Raymond Williams, *Keywords* (London: Fontana, 1976), p. 111.
8. In what follows, it will become clearer that I am less concerned with the institutional bases of these accounts of nature. Drawing on a distinction made by Perry Anderson, I am focusing not on the institutions which support such inquiries into nature (principally, academies) but rather on the issue of democratic extension: in what senses do these accounts of nature encourage greater participation by members of the *polis* in shaping the social and natural conditions of their lives? See Perry Anderson, *English Questions* (Cambridge: Polity Press, 1992), pp. 242–3. Cf. Oelschlaeger, *Caring for Creation*, p. 23: 'Religious discourse . . . is one possible way a democratic people might achieve solidarity – that is, create the political will to elect leaders who in turn would create public policies that lead toward sustainability.'
9. For the claim that theology has, by the construal of the natural order in relation to a single cause, tended to simplify nature, see Raymond Williams, *Problems in Materialism and Culture* (London: Verso, 1980), pp. 69–70.

The second idea which governs this book is that the mediation of nature by social contexts is graspable as concrete, not abstract, in theological interpretation. Reality is the sacrament of command, writes Dietrich Bonhoeffer.[10] The difficulty, as Bonhoeffer well knew, is breaking through in thought to reality. The central theological claim here, analogous formally to the Christological claim that in the career of Jesus of Nazareth we have God in concretion, is that through the operations of the triune God in creation we encounter the dynamics of the interaction of humanity and nature *in concreto*. In such concretion the distorted sociality of humanity-in-nature will appear on the interpretative horizon thereby allowing the issue of wholeness and integrity of un/natural humanity to be adequately considered. The theological issue is to hold to the presence of God as interwoven with the natural conditions of humanity as these emerge in human social life. What may we discern of this presence? How might the humanity–nature relationship be rethought and reconfigured towards being in the truth of the triune God?

Concrete, specific and particular are thus, for theological reasons, related to abstract, general and universal: it is no surprise that the core of the book is taken up with analyses of human–nature interaction. What follows focuses not on general issues in the interpretation of humanity and nature but instead on particular issues in political ecology to show their concretely liberative or restrictive character in and through their relations to the concept and actuality of the triune God.

Against the tendency to construe the ecological crisis as the context for theology or to respond to complaints of Christian collusion in the ecological crisis, I consider that attention must be paid to the way in which the concept of nature is present in theological theory in the context of the distorted sociality of humanity. As a contribution to this task, the next section seeks to locate the emergence of the modern meanings of nature in order to frame the present inquiry. It is not sufficient, in my view, to take the ecological crisis as evidence of the objectification of nature by humanity without attention to historical shifts of meaning. Nature, the most elusive term in our language, requires such circumspection.

Following that I give an account of some of the theological issues raised for a political theology of nature which serves also to locate my own work. Attention then moves to the relations between the terms,

10. Dietrich Bonhoeffer, 'A Theological Basis for the World Alliance', in John de Gruchy (ed.), *Dietrich Bonhoeffer: Witness to Jesus Christ* (London: Collins, 1988), pp. 98–110 (p. 103).

'creation' and 'nature'. Finally, I contend that Christian theology – in the form of the *political–ideological interpretation of nature* – is well placed to engage with its own history and contemporary debate towards the liberation of un/natural humanity in nature.

The disgracing of nature

'We shall continue to have a worsening ecological crisis until we reject the Christian axiom that nature has no reason for existence save to serve man.' Thus Lynn White concludes on the contribution of Christianity to the ecological crisis.[11] Briefly summarised, White's thesis is that modern science and technology, although now international, have their origins in the West. To this development, Christianity makes no small contribution particularly through its creation story which, according to White, decisively introduces the notion of historical development, stresses the transcendence of humanity over nature and, last, claims that nature has been created by God for the benefit of humanity. Thus Christianity makes an important contribution to the disgracing and subsequent mastery of nature.

A veritable industry has grown up in theology to respond to White's thesis.[12] The best way to join the debate is, it seems to me, to set out Christianity's case for the affirmation of nature across its many dimensions. Such – with a focus on the interdependence of social humanity and nature – is the purpose of this book. In this section, I want to affirm only part of White's thesis: the attempted mastery of nature in the West involves the separation – indeed, alienation – of humanity from nature, and, further, that Christianity makes a contribution to this alienation and yet also seeks to overcome it. Indeed, *theologically*, the issue of the alienation of humanity from nature is graspable only in terms of developments in the relation between nature and grace through modernity. It is simply not the case that the fate of nature as the object of the dominion of humanity can be traced to Christianity. Instead, Christianity, as the history of the relation between nature and grace in the modern period demonstrates, has its own difficult passage, making along the way both positive and negative

11. Lynn White, 'The Historical Roots of our Ecologic Crisis', *Science* 155 (1967), 1203–7.
12. Whatever the merits of White's case, it has, as James A. Nash notes, a wider public resonance thereby placing Christianity on the defensive in the discussion of environmental matters. See James A. Nash, *Loving Nature: Ecological Integrity and Christian Responsibility* (Nashville: Abingdon Press, 1991), p. 70.

contributions.[13] Yet, in keeping with the general thrust of the argument of this book, I see no way beyond the alienation of humanity from nature, except dialectically. If the nature/grace distinction informs the alienation of humanity from nature, the way forward is through the *theological* criticism of the political–ideological structures and processes which support this distinction in order to present again the interrelation of humanity and nature as creatures before God.

The story of the disgracing of nature is often told as part of the history of the modern natural sciences.[14] From a theological point of view, at issue here is the failure of Christianity to incorporate the new account of nature given in the natural sciences into its own thinking. As Louis Dupré writes: 'Having failed to incorporate the world picture presented by modern science, theological doctrine withdrew [through the seventeenth century] from one bastion after another without making new intellectual conquests.'[15] Moreover there is, on Dupré's view, a more fundamental point: in the failure to incorporate the findings of the sciences into Christian doctrine, 'theology gradually withdrew from its millennial task of defining the fundamentals of the world view'.[16] The separation of nature, humanity and God (which Dupré explores in terms of the contrast between nature and grace) is thus one form of the retreat of theology from the contestation of and contribution to public meanings and concepts. As Dietrich Bonhoeffer notes from prison, in its long march through modernity Christianity eventually becomes associated with the themes of metaphysics, partiality and inwardness.[17] These three are interrelated in that the construal of Christianity in terms of partiality means that Jesus Christ is Lord not of all of life, but only of part of it. The restriction of Christianity to a part of the world connects with Bonhoeffer's assertion that religion is to do with the individual, in his or her inwardness. The address to the individual is validated and stabilised in terms of a metaphysical God who 'appears' at the margins of the world in the form of a supernatural realm. Bonhoeffer traces the marginalisation of the theological account of the world partly to the failure of theology to address the issues posed by

13. See Louis Dupré, *Passage to Modernity: An Essay in the Hermeneutics of Nature and Culture* (New Haven and London: Yale University Press, 1993).

14. See John Hedley Brooke, *Science and Religion* (Cambridge University Press, 1991).

15. Dupré, *Passage to Modernity*, p. 247.   16. Ibid., p. 69.

17. The list of letters which gives credence to this summary is long, but see especially those, collected in Dietrich Bonhoeffer, *Letters and Papers from Prison* (London: SCM Press, 1971), dated 30 April 1944, 5 May 1944, 29 May 1944, 8 June 1944 and 16 July 1944, and the important sketch, 'Outline for a Book'.

the new cosmology of the sixteenth and seventeenth centuries: 'As in the scientific field, so in human affairs generally, "God" is being pushed more and more out of life, losing more and more ground.'[18]

Thus the theologian is faced with a double difficulty: the separation of humanity and nature *and* the marginalisation of God are aspects of the same tendency. The overcoming of the displacement of God requires the articulation of a world view. Or, better, attention to the presence of God requires the theological reconstruction of the concepts of God, nature and humanity. Paulos Mar Gregorios has suggested that the modern conception of nature as other than humanity emerged as the stress on nature as related to God's grace receded.[19] If so, the theological response must take the form of a public argument in favour of a *common realm* of God, nature and humanity.

We may agree, as a matter of historical record, that nature, meaning that which is *other* than humanity, emerges at the beginning of the modern period.[20] Unsurprisingly, Karl Marx captures modernity's objectification of nature in the hope of its mastery by humanity:

> Subjection of nature's forces to man, machinery, application of chemistry to industry and agriculture, steam navigation, railways, electric telegraphs, clearing of whole continents for cultivation, canalisation of rivers, whole populations conjured out of the ground – what earlier century had even a presentiment that such productive forces slumbered in the lap of social labour?[21]

Yet the theological way forward cannot be a strategy of mere reversal. If the modern period has stressed the *otherness of humanity to nature* ('the subjection of nature's forces to humanity'), a sound strategy cannot be a stress on the *proximity* of nature. For the displacement or eclipse of God remains in place for both strategies. Instead, the problem which needs to be addressed is to overcome the separation of nature and grace in such manner that the concept of God is constitutive of a liberative understanding of nature.

The disgracing of nature thereby involves the marginalisation of the concept of God from an account of humanity-in-nature. Thus when

18. Bonhoeffer, *Letters and Papers from Prison*, p. 326.
19. Paulos Mar Gregorios, *The Human Presence: Ecological Spirituality and the Age of the Spirit* (New York: Amity House, 1987; orig. 1978), pp. 19–20.
20. Even so, the emergence of modern meanings of nature has been a complex affair: the work of Keith Thomas suggests that in popular culture the divide between humanity and non-human nature has persistently been crossed. See Keith Thomas, *Man and the Natural World* (Harmondsworth: Penguin, 1983), pp. 80f.
21. Karl Marx and Friedrich Engels, *The Communist Manifesto* (London: Verso, 1998; orig. 1848), pp. 40–1.

Gordon D. Kaufman writes of the standard Christian metaphysical schema as God–humanity–world, we should not agree too easily.[22] Although Kaufman's account may be a true *description* of the Christian schema, it makes no reference to the interaction between these terms towards the formulation of a theological concept of nature.

Yet it is clear, as Louis Dupré has argued, that there is an intimate relation between nature, humanity and God. Indeed, Dupré contends that from the end of the Middle Ages and through the early modern period there is a profound alteration in the concept of nature on account of changes in its relations to God and humanity. The direction of this tendency has the theological accent falling on God and humanity. The origins of this stress are not to be found in the Reformation. Rather the Reformation is a partly modern attempt to reunite nature and grace. However, the attempt is not wholly successful, leading to a partial restriction in Protestant theology to the theme of *the-anthropology*.[23]

Yet this restriction has been long in the preparation. Louis Dupré argues that patristic Christianity took further certain tendencies present already in Stoic and Epicurean thought: 'The Christian doctrine of individual salvation further detached the person from the cosmic context in so far as it made each individual responsible to God. Each person stood in direct relation to God rather than to the cosmos.'[24] However the crucial pre-modern theological moment is late nominalism. In the fourteenth century, the concept of nature becomes decisively detached from its context in grace (as had been the position of Augustine and Aquinas, for instance). What nominalism sets in train is the unravelling of our three themes: God, nature and humanity. The distinction between the *potentia absoluta* and the *potentia ordinata* permits an interpretation of nature as given, yet without a specific theological context. The *telos* of nature, as given in the actions of the creator God, is hereby denied. Although there are a number of efforts to rejoin nature to grace – the Renaissance, the Reformation and Jansenism – none is persuasive. The way is then open

---

22. Gordon D. Kaufman, 'A Problem for Theology: The Concept of Nature', *Harvard Theological Review* 65 (1972), 337–66 (349).

23. For example, the weaknesses of Barth's account of non-human nature are carefully explicated by Santmire: see H. Paul Santmire, *The Travail of Nature: The Ambiguous Ecological Promise of Christian Theology* (Philadelphia: Fortress Press, 1985), pp. 148–54. A comment by the early Bonhoeffer confirms Santmire's reading of Protestantism: 'The inadequacies of nature and history are God's cloak. But not everything corporeal, not all nature and history, is meant to be sacramental. Nature as such does not symbolise Christ. His presence is confined to the forms of preaching and the two sacraments.' *Christology* (London: Fount, 1978), p. 54. For Dupré, see *Passage to Modernity*, chapters 7 and 8.

24. Ibid., p. 95.

to the development of the notion of technically graceless *natura pura* in the sixteenth century, the separation in Protestantism of philosophy and theology and the divorce between the sciences and theology.[25]

A specific account of the Christian involvement in the environmental crisis emerges. The objectification of nature, with the alienation of humanity from its natural conditions, is thus supported by the attention given in Protestant theology to grace in relation to humanity.[26] The result is the steady attempt to describe grace in terms of a salvation history from which, it seems, nature is excluded. Theological interest in nature recedes further, especially in the ambivalence over natural theology,[27] together with a steady withdrawal by theology from attention to the institutional and social processes of natural humanity.[28] Writing in 1933, Bonhoeffer notes that 'nature' is not often treated in studies on Christology: 'There has been little consideration of this question in Protestant theology in the past.' Later, in *Ethics*, he writes: 'The concept of the natural has fallen into discredit in Protestant ethics.'[29]

Given such developments, perhaps it is not surprising that Lynn White could write: 'Christianity is the most anthropocentric religion the world has seen.'[30] Yet, we must also note that the modern period in the West is

25. Ibid., pp. 174–81. The emergence of 'new' natural theology can, according to Dupré, also be traced to this juncture.

26. Of course, this account is intimately related to the claim that the development of the natural sciences is permitted, at least, by the disenchantment of nature: nature is transcended by God and yet is ordered. Nature thereby becomes available as an 'object' of human inquiry and systematic classification. For two rather different accounts of the drive of modernity towards the classification of nature, see Thomas, *Man and the Natural World*, ch. 2; Zygmunt Bauman, *Modernity and the Holocaust* (Cambridge: Polity Press, 1989; 1991 pbk.), pp. 66–72. The emergence of the natural sciences is, in fact, not the primary and determining moment of the separation of humanity and nature, for such emergence presupposes the separation of humanity and nature (Dupré, *Passage to Modernity*, ch. 3). The emergence of the contrast humanity/nature is, arguably, a wider anthropological development.

27. As Dupré points out, the different valuations placed on natural theology by Protestant and Catholic theology can be related to responses to the common factor of the separation of nature and grace in the late medieval period. See Louis Dupré, 'Nature and Grace: Fateful Separation and Attempted Reunion', in David L. Schindler (ed.), *Catholicism and Secularization in America* (Notre Dame, IN: Communio, 1990), pp. 52–73 (p. 61). Hence, although the rejection of natural theology reaches its greatest point of intensity in the twentieth century – see Karl Barth, *Church Dogmatics*, II/1 (Edinburgh: T. & T. Clark, 1957), pp. 128–78 – such a rejection had been a common theme in nineteenth-century Protestant theology. Indeed, such rejection is prefigured by the separation in Protestantism of theology and philosophy: see Dupré, *Passage to Modernity*, pp. 215–16.

28. Political judgments were, in Protestantism, derived from an approach which distinguished between Church and State together with an emphasis on 'orders of creation': see Dietrich Bonhoeffer, *Ethics* (London: SCM Press, 1955), pp. 254f., 271f. The natural conditions of human life are not important in this view.

29. Bonhoeffer, *Christology*, p. 64; Bonhoeffer, *Ethics*, p. 120.

30. White, 'The Historical Roots of our Ecologic Crisis', 1205.

the most anthropocentric period the world has seen. The important question is therefore whether or not a dialectical reading of Christianity can be sustained: given the context (including Christianity's contribution to that context), is a political theology of nature possible which might offer a liberative account of un/natural humanity?

God, nature, humanity

As a result of such a complex story, it becomes clear that the theological way forward cannot be the straightforward affirmation of a theology of nature as a way of correcting what is taken to be an overemphasis on the theology of history.[31] Why? First, because the relations are too complex to admit of such a reversal. Second, because in a straight reversal, which privileges nature over history and space over time, the issue of the presence of God is not attended to and thereby goes unresolved. A theology of the *common realm* of God, nature and humanity must rather show how the concept of God (re)establishes the concepts of nature and humanity. Overcoming the displacement of God is also the affirmation of humanity and/in nature.

We may now see how the two claims are related: the separation of nature from God and the privatisation of theology are part of the same tendency: the eclipse of God. Thus, although Dupré speaks in Catholic terms of nature, grace and transcendence, his account offers a precise history of the changing relation between *revelation* and *creation*, *salvation* and *nature*, *justification* and *world* that Bonhoeffer traces in Protestant theology. 'The displacement of God from the world, and from the public part of human life', writes Bonhoeffer, 'led to the attempt to keep his place secure in the sphere of the "personal", the "inner", and the "private".'[32] Such privatisation of belief can be tracked in the loss of significance attributed to nature as a theological topic. In a description of the state of the debate on the concept of 'the natural' in Protestant theology, Bonhoeffer writes: 'For some [the natural] was completely lost sight of in the darkness of general sinfulness, while for others, conversely, it was lighted up by the brilliance of absolute historicity.'[33] Thus, Bonhoeffer notes a tendency in Protestant theology to concentrate on humanity and God; nature is either obscured by sinfulness or occluded by reference to the 'historical' act of revelation. Hence two

---

31. As is noted by Rosemary Radford Ruether, *To Change the World: Christology and Cultural Criticism* (London: SCM Press, 1981), pp. 57–70.

32. Bonhoeffer, *Letters and Papers from Prison*, p. 344.   33. Bonhoeffer, *Ethics*, p. 120.

theological issues emerge: first, what theological account can be given of the *activity* of God *in concreto* to the reality of nature and humanity? Second, the problem of the *relevance* of the Christian God is also raised: can a theological account be given that engages with and learns from secular description of humanity-in-nature?[34]

An example of the close relation between the separation of nature, humanity and God and the privatisation of belief is technology. At first glance this seems unlikely: what has technology to do with God? Yet that is precisely part of the point: technology provides and supports a view of the world which appears to make God redundant. 'Nature was formerly conquered by spiritual means', Bonhoeffer writes, 'with us by technical organisation of all kinds.'[35] Yet in fact the concept of nature which permits technological development emerges in theology: only when the *telos* of nature is denied (as it was in nominalism), is it possible for a new *telos* of nature to be provided by humanity; nature is then available for appropriation by technology. As Dupré writes: 'But without a common teleology that integrates humanity with nature, the mastery of nature becomes its own end, and the purposes originally pursued by it end up becoming secondary . . . [Thereby] science was destined to give birth to the most comprehensive feature of modern life, namely technology.'[36] We see here again the double irrelevance of theological interpretation of the world: the emergence of technology is coterminous with the emergence of a grace-less nature; the development of technology contributes to the 'world come of age' which denies the relevance of transcendence.

In its reliance on the denial of the transcendence of nature, technology marks an aspect of modernity's displacement of God and the setting up of humanity *sicut deus* over nature. What are the consequences of such a denial for our understanding of humanity-in-nature? The denial of the transcendence of nature – that is, the denial that nature might receive its reality from outside itself and is thereby not sufficient unto itself – makes nature infinite. As Bonhoeffer noted, 'An infinite universe, however it may be conceived, is self-subsisting, *etsi deus non daretur*.'[37] Together with this notion of an infinite nature, comes the view that nature has to be given a *telos* by *human* action. Thus the presence and action of God are thrust

---

34. Often, it is assumed that Christianity has no contribution to make: see Val Plumwood's excellent philosophical book, *Feminism and the Mastery of Nature* (London: Routledge, 1993), which offers an incisive account of the philosophical history of the dualism of (male) humanity/nature, but omits any reference to the importance of *transcendence*.
35. Bonhoeffer, *Letters and Papers from Prison*, p. 380.   36. Dupré, *Passage to Modernity*, p. 74.
37. Bonhoeffer, *Letters and Papers from Prison*, p. 360.

outside infinite nature; the stress is now placed on a human *telos* that incorporates nature. Hence a new view of the future emerges, together with an affirmation of 'progress': 'Unlike the apocalyptic future, which would violently interrupt the passage of time and bring history to a close, the modern future appeared as the endlessly postponed terminus of a continuing history.'[38] From the perspective of humanity–nature relations, the future then comes to be seen as a human endeavour; further, because ontological priority is now given to the future, human achievements are to be secured in the shortest possible time. But the future is this-worldly, to be secured by the actions of humanity.

With the emphasis on an immanentist future comes the separation of humanity from nature. Paradoxically, the stress on a self-sufficient totality of nature leads to the separation of humanity from that totality. Hence there runs through modernity an increasing stress on the objectivity of nature: the classical and medieval onto-theological synthesis that held together nature, self and the transcendent, loses its power. Of course, differing interpretations of the synthesis have been given. Christianity secured an especially important demotion of the cosmos: the creator is transcendent over God's creation. Yet that did not, at first, encourage the view that cosmos and self could be separated. The modern period manages precisely this feat, however:

> Modern culture has detached personhood from the other two
> constituents of the original ontological synthesis. For Greek and
> medieval philosophers the person formed an integral part of a more
> comprehensive totality, yet ruled that totality in accordance with a
> teleology both immanent in its own nature and transcending it. The
> image of the person which emerged in the sixteenth century became
> increasingly more enclosed within itself. Eventually it narrowed its
> teleology to one of self-preservation or self-fulfilment, either social or
> individual. [39]

The implications for theology of the new teleology, which sees humanity as placed in an open horizon and as other than nature, are profound. For now humanity sees itself as at the leading edge of history (which in this temporal scheme is also the centre of the world). The theme of *creatureliness*, which might permit an account of humanity placed in the *middle* of the world as part of nature, is displaced by a view of humanity as superior to nature's contingencies. God's blessing, if it is appealed to at all, is

38. Dupré, *Passage to Modernity*, p. 156.   39. Ibid., pp. 163–4.

understood in terms not of living from the middle, but living at the scientific, technological edge.

Yet the actuality is different from the promise: although all stress is now placed on self-directed humanity, humanity's emancipation from nature is not humanity's emancipation from itself.

> Our immediate environment is not nature, as formerly, but organisation. But with this protection from nature's menace there arises a new one – through organisation itself. But the spiritual force is lacking. The question is: What protects us against the menace of organisation? Man is again thrown back on himself. He has managed to deal with everything, only not with himself . . . In the last resort it all turns upon man.[40]

Humanity is opposed to nature; nature and humanity are opposed to God. The view of humanity as at the leading edge of history obscures the presence of God, denies the rule of God and privatises belief. Further, the world is left as it is: humanity remains locked into the attempt to free itself from its own natural conditions. It is therefore no exaggeration to conclude that: *nature is the problem of modernity.* In the concept of nature are to be found the interrelated issues of a humanity which refuses to live out of the middle of its existence, a stress on the domestication of nature and the displacement of God.

Human freedom, natural contingencies

The theological task emerges more clearly: not to leave the world as it is. What might be the outline of a theological account which declines to leave the world as it is? The contribution of a political theology of nature is Christological: the common realm of God, nature and humanity has Christ as its centre. 'God is no stop-gap; he must be recognised at the centre of life . . . The ground for this lies in the revelation of God in Jesus Christ. He is the centre of life.'[41] This commitment to the Christological form of the presence of God supports the notion of a common realm. The presence of God returns humanity to *die Mitte.* What does this mean?

We have seen that the reduction of a stress on grace leads to the separation of humanity from nature and the objectification of nature. I have already noted that the attempt merely to reunite humanity and nature is theologically insufficient: it fails to acknowledge that the concept of God

---

40. Bonhoeffer, *Letters and Papers from Prison*, p. 380.   41. Ibid., p. 312.

too has been displaced in the separation of humanity and nature. Such displacement is no small matter. At issue is whether or not some justification can be given of the circumstance in which humanity finds itself: as free yet within a context that resists (to some extent) that same freedom. Philosophers influenced by the German idealist tradition gloss this problem in terms of freedom and necessity. So Dupré: 'The search for an adequate conception of transcendence appears far from finished. How does the necessary allow genuine contingency? How does the contingent affect the nature of necessity?'[42]

In line with the theological politics being advanced in this book, I shall speak less of dependence and autonomy and more of the hegemonic situation in which humanity is placed as opposed to social freedom, of the ideological forms of knowing contrasted with practical truth. Yet the basic point remains: how are the three figures of God, nature and humanity to be related such that the justification of the relation between these three can be seen? The issue is practical: without such a justification, history must bear its own burden. Hence the constant modern stress on the improvement of humanity's environment, the emphasis on progress and the constantly receding Siren of the 'good life' and the 'American dream'. Here we encounter the conditions in present human society of the 'limitless' exploitation and degradation of the environment.

We are confronted by a central problem of modernity: human freedom, *qua* freedom, cannot be dependent on any conditions. Otherwise that very freedom is contradicted. Such freedom is only operative (and, it is hoped, effective) in a particular context. Yet the context is given: as Marx noted, humanity lives from the dead labour of the past. Hence the attempt by humanity to dominate its environment in order to secure its basic needs runs into insoluble contradictions if humanity does not see itself as placed in that environment. Abstract freedom struggles against abstract nature. The contours of Western life as we have them today are, then, founded upon the distorted sociality of humanity and the destruction of the environment.

The claim that in theological understanding such issues are properly addressed needs to be made good. A theological account of the common realm of God, nature and humanity needs to show how, in conceptual form, the distortions of social humanity can be reframed towards an

42. Dupré, *Passage to Modernity*, p. 253.

extended account of freedom by, in and for nature. A theological interpretation of nature grants finitude to nature and to humanity, thereby
placing humanity in the middle of nature and history. A theological interpretation offers an account of the reality of the relations between humanity and nature. The combination of these two commitments – humanity in
the middle, the centrality of the relations between humanity and nature –
requires ontological specification.[43]

The theological justification of nature and humanity raises questions
about standard ways of reflecting on nature. First, postmodern emphases
which reject all ontology must themselves be rejected. Such critiques are
right to detect a problem in the relation between the freedom of the subject and the necessity of nature. Such critiques are right, in part, also to
reject the notion of the free subject. But there remains the matter of the reality of nature in its relations with humanity which needs to be addressed.
The dispute between the freedom of humanity and the necessity of nature
cannot be resolved by eliminating nature, as some seek to do. Consider
here the following comments: 'We made Nature and it just *is* our descriptions of it and the way we treat it. Nature is a cultural product.' 'Nature
has come to an end.' 'We have deprived nature of its independence, and
that is fatal to its meaning. Nature's independence *is* its meaning; without it there is nothing but us.'[44] It may be true, as these comments suggest, that the necessity of nature is not given in the order of things. Yet it
cannot thereby be ignored. How the partial freedom of humanity relates
to nature still needs to be specified.

Second, appeals to science in the form of a new creation story which do
not explore these ontological issues are equally suspect. Resolutions to the
problem of the alienation of nature and social freedom cannot be resolved
in favour of some 'natural' basis (learned either from ecology or the natural
sciences).[45] Simply stressing nature where once humanity was emphasised
does not address the vital issue: what is the relation between the sociality of humanity and the ecology of nature (which is after all the root of
the problem)? For theology, the attempt must be made to show how the

---

43. If the turn by the natural sciences towards the explanatory power of narrative offers a
clue, the boldness of my ontological endeavour is less out of step with the wider intellectual
culture than perhaps it would have been twenty years ago.
44. Don Cupitt, 'Nature and Culture', in Neil Spurway (ed.), *Humanity, Environment and God*
(Oxford: Blackwell, 1993), p. 35; Anthony Giddens, *Beyond Left and Right: The Future of Radical
Politics* (Oxford: Blackwell, 1994), p. 102; Bill McKibben, *The End of Nature* (New York: Random
House, 1989), p. 58.
45. Arne Naess, *Ecology, Community and Lifestyle* (Cambridge University Press, 1989), p. 39.

common realm of humanity, nature and God establishes the reality, inter-relations and liberation of humanity, nature and God.

Such commitments, stated briefly and baldly, hint at some of the theological principles operative in this book. In my view, the theological task is *reconstructive* rather than *constructive*. That is, I am committed to the basic shape of Christian doctrine in the theological consideration of nature. Such a decision involves judgments about natural theology, the doctrines themselves and the dynamic articulated by Christianity. Yet I do not think that some reconstructive theological proposals, which seek to reinvigorate the motifs of human dominion of nature or stewardship, are tenable.[46] Instead, the relation between humanity and nature requires fundamental reconsideration; the metaphors of dominion and stewardship are not central to my position. Rather, I offer here an extended attempt to specify, in theological perspective, the natural conditions of humanity. The relevance of the Christian schema is defended in and through a move into the doctrine of creation: the liberating dynamic of Christianity is reconstrued under the rubric, 'Christ and creation'.[47]

Yet, as can be seen from the opening section of this chapter, the theological task undertaken here focuses on the *polis*. Thus there is an important 'liberal' emphasis in what follows thereby to incorporate a theological account of the world. In support of this incorporation, in the next chapter I shall engage with the concept of nature by way of a philosophical theology which enjoys certain liberal characteristics. Yet the engagement will be thoroughly theological. For the political theology of nature presented here needs to be differentiated from the theologies of nature which lean more heavily upon philosophies of nature, usually derived from the natural sciences, which are alien to Christianity. With this openness to the natural sciences – often construed generally in terms of a common creation story – there remains the danger that the content of the natural sciences

---

46. This way of the attempted re-presentation of the relevance of standard Christian models of human responsibility for nature is rich and varied: see Thomas Sieger Derr, *Ecology and Human Need* (Philadelphia: Westminster Press, 1975) who continues to use the language of 'mastery' of nature; Robert Faricy, *Wind and Sea Obey Him: Approaches to a Theology of Nature* (London: SCM Press, 1982); Douglas John Hall, *Imaging God: Dominion as Stewardship* (Grand Rapids: Eerdmans and New York: Friendship Press, 1986); the early Bonhoeffer: Dietrich Bonhoeffer, *Creation and Fall: A Theological Interpretation of Genesis 1–3* (London: SCM Press, 1959; lectures given in 1933).

47. Further examples of work in this area include Jürgen Moltmann, *God in Creation* (London: SCM Press, 1985); Colin E. Gunton, *The One, the Three and the Many* (Cambridge University Press, 1993); Gregorios, *The Human Presence*; Santmire, *The Travail of Nature*; Nash, *Loving Nature*. In his stress on the ambiguity of modernity and his attempt to construct an ontology of communion of humanity and nature, Hall's *Imaging God* fits partly in this category.

is extended – reductionistically – to specify the context of theology. On this view, particular stress can be laid on the incarnational presence of God or the cosmic Christ in nature.[48]

I am more sympathetic to those theologies which address the *politics* of nature. Yet such accounts offer, often in subtle ways, a substantial and far-reaching alteration to Christianity. For instance, it is not always clear in this approach whether or not there is a determining place for Jesus Christ: the incarnation is transferred from Christology to the doctrine of God in order to account for God's presence in and to the world.[49] Furthermore, the stress on the natural sciences does not properly address the matter of the *interaction* between humanity and nature. Last, the appeal to the natural sciences is considered to be the way in which theology secures its credentials as a public discipline. Yet, in fact, the 'publicness' is specified by the natural sciences.

A political theology of nature, as I have described it, directs theological attention to the relations operative in the common realm of God, nature and humanity. The rationale of this attention is Christological. Yet there remains the important matter of the theological account of the 'world come of age' by way of a theological engagement with the 'secular' politics of nature. Setting out the contours of this double commitment – Christ and world – is the task of this political theology of nature.

Creation, nature

I have already advertised my commitment to the basic shape of Christian doctrine throughout this argument. In connection with the doctrine of creation, this involves a commitment to two rules of theological thinking. First, that creation is the free, unconstrained act of God. Creation is to be understood not as necessary but as contingent: traditionally, this rule has

48. Consider, for example, the work of process theologians such as John B. Cobb, *Is it Too Late? A Theology of Ecology* (Beverly Hills, CA: Bruce, 1972); David Griffin, *God and Religion in the Postmodern World* (Albany: State University of New York Press, 1989); Jay B. McDaniel, *Of Gods and Pelicans: A Theology of Reverence for Life* (Westminster/John Knox Press, 1989) (at least in the area of metaphysics) and, especially, Teilhard de Chardin, *The Phenomenon of Man* (New York: Harper, 1959), and *The Divine Milieu* (New York, Harper, 1960). James B. Gustafson's *A Sense of the Divine* (Edinburgh: T. & T. Clark, 1994) may also fit here.

49. Examples in this area abound: see Sallie McFague, *Models of God: Theology for an Ecological, Nuclear Age* (London: SCM Press, 1987) and *The Body of God: An Ecological Theology* (London: SCM Press, 1993); Rosemary Radford Ruether, *Gaia and God: An Ecofeminist Theology of Earth Healing* (London: SCM Press, 1994); Matthew Fox, *Original Blessing* (Santa Fe: Bear & Co., 1983); Leonardo Boff, *Ecology and Liberation* (New York: Orbis, 1994); Gordon D. Kaufman, *Theology for a Nuclear Age* (Manchester University Press, 1985).

been glossed as *creatio ex nihilo*. In other words, God creates out of God's freedom and will; there is no pre-existing material nor any resistance to God's will. Creation in its entirety is the result of God's action. 'God's relation to the world is like this: not a struggle with pre-existing disorder that is then moulded into a shape, but a pure summons.'[50] Creation is the free decision of the social God: a gratuitous action. God has no 'need' of creation; creating is rather an action of God's love. When God wills to be not-God, creation comes to be. Against pantheism, the world is contingent, that is, not necessary; it is thereby truly other to God.

Second, the order of creation is dependent on God's act. The act of creation is not to be understood as concerned only with a beginning but also with the middle and the end of the world. Creation is never to be understood as an immanent, creative process; the notion of *natura naturans* is, in line with mainstream Christian commitments, hereby rejected. In sum, the world is internally related to God: it exists, and continues to exist, on account of God's loving purposes. An account of creation that is externally related to God, as in deism's interpretation of creation as machine, is ruled out.

It is likely that this *creatio ex nihilo* has its source in Israel's understanding of the activity of God in the covenant. 'The cosmic order and origin were traced back to the God of salvation history, and thereby unlimited power came to be seen in God's historical action', argues Wolfhart Pannenberg.[51] Similarly, Rowan Williams traces the theme of creation out of nothing to Israel's return from Babylonian captivity:

> This deliverance, decisive and unexpected, is like a second Exodus; and the Exodus in turn comes to be seen as a sort of recapitulation of creation. Out of a situation where there is no identity, where there are no names, only the anonymity of slavery or the powerlessness of the ghetto, God makes a human community, calls it by *name* (Is. 40–55), gives it or restores to it a community. But this act is not a *process* by which shape is imposed on chaos; it is a summons, a call which establishes the very possibility of an answer.[52]

Moreover, in Christian tradition, there can be no discussion of covenant or deliverance except by reference to Jesus Christ (cf. John 1.1–18). Thus creation is always understood to be an event related to incarnation. For incarnation has to do with the liberation and transformation of creation.

50. Rowan Williams, *On Christian Theology* (Oxford: Blackwell, 2000), p. 68.
51. Wolfhart Pannenberg, *Systematic Theology* (Edinburgh: T. & T. Clark, 1994), II, p. 11.
52. Williams, *On Christian Theology*, pp. 67–8.

In other words, creation is understood to be a Trinitarian action; creation is the external action of the triune God.

Why, then, do I describe this book as an inquiry into the theology of nature rather than into the doctrine of creation? Further, what might the relation be between the concepts, 'nature' and 'creation'?

When, in conversation, I have tried to explain the thesis of this book on 'nature' to others, one of the most popular questions has been: 'what about *creation*?' How does the concept of 'creation' relate to the account of 'nature' proposed here? And interlocutors have become impatient when I have been unable to give them a clear answer. Yet, there are reasons, bound up with the history of the doctrine of creation, why people pose the question and why in the past I have been stuck for an answer. These reasons further complicate, as I hope to show, an inquiry into the theology of nature.[53]

First, one of the reasons why the question 'what about creation?' proves difficult to answer is that one interpretation of creation has been to see it as a context for asking questions of salvation. Such an approach is what Dietrich Bonhoeffer called 'methodism': the search for every opportunity to convict people in their sins. Thus to ask a question about creation is to ask about the context of the drama of salvation. What is being inquired after is the affirmation of the reality of free will, the ubiquity of sin and meaningfulness of human action. A question about creation is, it transpires, a question about the possibility of, the need for and the capacity to respond to, grace.[54] Or, in a more defensible version of the same approach, creation is construed as preparatory for the purposes of God. 'If theology is primarily concerned with the Trinitarian God as purposive', Daniel Hardy writes, 'creation is the condition for the realisation of the purposes of this God, and receives its reality from the realisation of these purposes'.[55] Attention to these purposes then becomes the primary concern rather than a direct inquiry into the conditions, possibility and potential of the world. In response to the concept of 'nature', people ask after 'creation' in order to draw nature within the reconciling dynamic of salvation.

Yet there is a further, none the less intimately related, use of the word 'creation' which has recently become popular: Max Oelschlaeger's *Caring*

---

53. In reflecting on this matter, my thinking has been clarified by the important essay, 'Creation and Eschatology' by Daniel W. Hardy, in *God's Ways with the World: Thinking and Practising Christian Faith* (Edinburgh: T. & T. Clark, 1996), pp. 151–70.
54. Precisely such a view of creation is operative in 'philosophical' forms of theodicy: see John Hick, *Evil and the God of Love* (London: Macmillan, 1966).
55. Hardy, 'Creation and Eschatology', p. 154.

for Creation is a good example.[56] This further sense again wishes to affirm a context. In this view, creation functions as the origin of a legitimating narrative and thereby as a normative basis for considering the environment. As Oelschlaeger suggests, the narrative of Christianity affirms the meaningful *telos* of history and offers a different story than the dominant narrative of modernity, that of utilitarian individualism.[57] But, as Daniel Hardy notes, the reading of creation is here always *indirect*: the attempt to understand the detail of creation as the gift of the creator God, which must involve an account of the creator and the creature and their interaction, is here avoided by attention to the pragmatic utility or function of such accounts. Which, we might add, in the long run harms the vitality of Christian faith as serious questions about the truth of Christianity are sidelined by concerns as to its relevance (as if the latter can be decided without reference to the former).[58]

I do not, in the first instance, inquire into creation as the condition of salvation nor as the origin of a legitimating narrative. In addition, I am not dealing with nature in the sense of 'all that is', a 'totality' – although the concept of *creation* does carry such a meaning.[59] Hence my description of this book as a theology of nature. Yet even the description 'theology of nature' is too general. For the reality of nature is various. My argument is predicated upon a direct inquiry into nature by the political and social sciences. I am concerned with a particular zone of creation: the interaction between humanity and non-human nature. That is, it is possible to treat nature in a number of dimensions: physical, evolutionary, social. The term 'creation' obscures such multiplicity. I intend to focus on only one zone: nature as it enters or impinges upon the social sphere, in political and social description.

Last, as part of an inquiry regarding the transformation of theology itself, we must look at the relation between creation and nature at the metatheoretical level. The conflation of these two concepts may also be

---

56. Oelschlaeger, *Caring for Creation*.

57. Rosemary Radford Ruether's *Gaia and God* is a further excellent example. In her opening chapter, Ruether summarises three accounts of different creation stories and inquires after the normative messages (concerning hierarchical relations and so forth) which can be read off such creation stories.

58. See, further, Wolfhart Pannenberg, *Toward a Theology of Nature* (Louisuille, KY: Westminster/John Knox Press, 1993); *Introduction to Systematic Theology* (Edinburgh: T. & T. Clark, 1991).

59. Hegemonically so, such that all discussion of Christianity and nature is presumed to be a dialogue between theology and the (philosophy of the) natural sciences. This book is intended to be a contribution to a dialogue, but in a different direction.

understood as the attempt by Christian theology to get some purchase on modern developments in the adventures of the concept of nature (outlined above, pp. 8–16). To ask the question: what is the relation between creation and nature? is to seek a way of drawing the concept back into the doctrinal shape of Christianity towards the maintenance of the relevance of Christianity. To work to subsume the concept of nature under the rubric of creation is to suggest that Christianity has some pertinent resources from its long history of thinking doctrinally about creation. The problem here, as noted above, is that – under the pressures of our decisively modern circumstances – it is not clear that Christianity enjoys easily available resources from its own traditions.[60]

From this conflation of 'creation' and 'nature', significant confusions follow. One way of interpreting the important work of Sallie McFague would be along such lines: because the Christian God is a creator God, Christianity must have something to offer concerning the redemption of nature; nature and creation are convertible terms. Yet, although McFague holds to this claim, she also stresses that our circumstances are novel ('I believe that our time is sufficiently different and sufficiently dire that theologians must not shrink from the task of thinking boldly and imaginatively'[61]). What is the result? The character of the Christian contribution is unclear. 'Creation' and 'nature', it transpires, are not convertible terms. Christianity is thereby found, despite its emphasis on creation, to be lacking resources in the face of the newness of our current problems in relation to nature. The conclusion follows inexorably: new models of God are required.

Furthermore, the theological imperative – based in the ancient traditions that speak of God's world-relatedness to which Christianity is both heir and contributor – to offer some insight into the ecological crisis prompts the turn to the 'creation stories' allegedly told by the natural sciences. Because such scientific explanations operate at the logical level of the 'universal' of physical nature, no attention is required to be paid to the *distinctiveness* of humanity. The important dimension of nature at the social level is obscured. Hence the reasoning behind the steady emphasis in McFague's work on the place of humanity *in* nature now becomes clear. Thus a reductionist emphasis (legitimated, but not warranted,

---

60. See Pannenberg, *Toward a Theology of Nature*, pp. 72–3; Louis Dupré, 'The Dissolution of the Union of Nature and Grace at the Dawn of the Modern Age', in Carl E. Braaten and Philip Clayton (eds.), *The Theology of Wolfhart Pannenberg* (Minneapolis: Augsburg, 1988), pp. 95–121.
61. McFague, *Models of God*, p. 29.

theologically) correctly stresses the continuities between humanity and non-human nature but marginalises the specification of humanity's otherness to non-human nature. Hence the meaning of humanity is underdetermined which, in turn, eclipses what is in urgent need of specification: the distinction between humanity and nature.[62]

I am thereby holding to the term 'nature' in order to stress that attention is here focused on direct inquiry of nature in social and political description. Nor do I wish or intend to offer a new legitimating narrative of nature: to treat creation stories as normative and subsume the relations between nature and humanity under such normativity. Nor do I assume that nature and creation are convertible terms. Instead, the theology of nature offered here, based on the assumption that theology is obliged today to produce new concepts to speak of the relation between nature and grace, is political–ideological, predicated upon a direct inquiry on nature.

The politics of theology: political–ideological interpretation of nature

A political theology specifies the liberation of the concept of nature towards the affirmation of un/natural humanity. To close this chapter, I offer more detail on the theological style of interpretation that I am calling *political–ideological* interpretation of nature. Such a theological style departs from the style most commonly found in the area of ecological theology which, in its focus on the significance of Christian symbols in the framing of a vision towards consciousness raising (which may also include the reinterpretation of these symbols themselves), is best described as 'symbolic–hermeneutic'.[63]

The influential work of Sallie McFague is a good example of such an approach: 'the world as God's body' is offered as the guiding idea and model for reconceiving the identity of God and human ethical responsibility towards nature. Especially in *Models of God*, McFague stresses that to speak of the world as the body of God is a heuristic strategy offering a 'picture' of the relation between the world and God in order to respond to an

---

62. No significance can be ascribed, on these non-theological premises, to the *imago Dei*. See McFague, *The Body of God*, p. 103: 'The first step in theological anthropology for our time is not to follow the clues from the Christic paradigm or even from the model of the universe as God's body, but to step backward and ask, Who are we in the scheme of things as pictured by contemporary science?'

63. Peter C. Hodgson, *Winds of the Spirit: A Constructive Christian Theology* (London: SCM Press, 1994), p. 43.

ecological sensibility.[64] The term 'picture' is also to be found in the sequel, *The Body of God*: 'My project', McFague writes, 'is to embody the picture of reality from postmodern science in a model that will help us to internalise its new sensibility in a way not just compatible with but enriched by Christian faith'.[65] The theological task is thereby the development of appropriate symbols, consonant with the dominant view of reality in the natural sciences, towards the acknowledgement of the 'organic' reality of nature.

Such a concentration on symbols is, I believe, a difficulty: theological attention is devoted to a new future yet how this future comes to us and how it might already be present is less clear. The theological construction seems close to a projection in that it is not firmly related to the political–ideological dynamics of our situation. In this book, I am interested in a political theology of nature rather than a theology of transcendent symbols.

Why? Because the articulation of a new vision informed by transcendent symbols may only serve to redouble the alienation of humanity from nature. As Norman Gottwald stresses in his account of biblical hermeneutics, 'The religious symbolism for such a project [drawing on the Jewish and Christian past] will have to grow out of an accurate scientific understanding of the material conditions we face.' Otherwise the projected freedom remains disconnected from contemporary circumstance (and the original liberating message). Furthermore, contributions in the area of practice and belief 'will be judged by whether they clarify the range and contours of exercisable freedom within the context of the unfolding social process'.[66] Thus any 'symbolic–hermeneutic' interpretation must begin from political–ideological analysis in order to explore, in this instance, the varied and variable relations between humanity and nature. The distinction between humanity and nature is not operative only in the realm of discourse. It has material dimensions also. The distinction between humanity and nature is not a mere idea; it supports, and is supported by, material processes.[67]

I would not wish to overstress the contrast between these two styles: holding to a different future is important. Yet I am arguing that the transformation of social relations will only be secured by way of political–ideological analysis. Theologically, such transformation can only be

---

64. McFague, *Models of God*, p. 78.   65. McFague, *The Body of God*, p. 83.
66. Norman Gottwald, *The Tribes of Yahweh*, cited in Oelschlaeger, *Caring for Creation*, p. 90.
67. See my *Theology, Ideology and Liberation*, esp. chs. 1 and 2.

secured by thinking through the relation of humanity–nature and God. Peter Berger captures part of the matter in the following comment on the institutional dimension of the ecological crisis:

> most of the threats to the planetary ecosystem are the results of habitual human ways of relating to the physical world, ways dictated by institutional arrangements. Inversely, our relations with nature – the way we have used land, materials, and other species – both reveal and shape the institutions through which we deal with each other.[68]

Yet these exchanges between humanity and 'nature' are not only institutional. Other processes are involved, which incorporate institutions. As fundamental as the concept of 'institution' to the study of society are those structures and relations which form political, social and economic processes. Hence, the task is to address those theoretical constructions which support the material basis of the distinction between humanity and nature. This is the task of the following chapters.

It is therefore much too simple to say, as Lynn White does, that, 'What people do about their ecology depends on what they think about themselves in relation to the things about them. Human ecology is deeply conditioned by beliefs about our nature and destiny – that is, by religion.'[69] What is required is the theological criticism of those constructions which support the distinction in order to get to the material basis of the society (its politics, economics and technology). For what we think about ecology is shaped by the actual social transactions between humanity and nature which determine, and are determined by, our religious outlooks. In such fashion, Berger's correct emphasis on the centrality of human social life to the interpretation of the crisis in human relations with nature may be addressed theologically.

Such political–ideological interpretation finds the categories of 'environment' and 'ecology' to be central to a theology of nature. 'Environment', referring to that which needs to be conserved or preserved, is a recent usage and has, in its turn, been supplanted by 'ecology'. Thus ecology is now the more common word as the (technical and nontechnical) description for the relations between social humanity and the physical world; it is the task of ecology to name these physical conditions. In this sense, environmental science is replaced by ecological science.

---

68. Peter Berger, *The Good Society*, cited in Oelschlaeger, *Caring for Creation*, p. 191.
69. White, 'The Historical Roots of our Ecologic Crisis', 1205.

Part of the reason for this development lies in the history of the term, environment. From the early nineteenth century, 'environment' signified the conditions of the setting of human action, both social and natural; thus human action was understood, as in naturalism, to be conditioned by its environment. Deliberately excluded were accounts of context in terms of agents and resources understood to be 'extra-environmental', for example, God. This earlier sense also implies the notion of critique: the salient features of the environment must be accounted for and, implicitly at least, their worth judged.

Thus environmental features were not to be occluded by reference to God or the spiritual. Precisely this sense of critique re-emerges in the 1950s and 1960s when environmentalism involves the criticism of the dominant world view and its will-to-exploitation of nature. (Environment, in this sense, cannot be studied without reference to wider cultural and political aspects.) Such an understanding of environmental *critique* has been taken over by ecology. Yet, 'environment' is a useful word in that it retains something of its earlier scientific sense by drawing attention to the locality in which an entity is placed; to specify an environment is not, except by implication, to specify the whole of nature. Further, the human environment is partly natural, partly social. Such reciprocal, dialectical interaction is specified nicely by the concept of environment.[70]

'Ecology' has the etymological sense of 'rigorous study of the household'. That is the sense in which I shall be using the term rather than the sense of the life-science academic discipline. The 'mission creep' of what C. S. Lewis calls the 'methodological idiom' is evident here: ecology has come to mean, 'that which is studied in the discipline called ecology'. Yet this is not its only meaning. I shall here hold to a rather more general reading: the sense of interconnection or interrelation between humanity and the natural order at all levels: interpretative, ontological, epistemological and ethical.[71]

To paraphrase Bonhoeffer: human life is now disunion with self, neighbour, world and God.[72] For a critical, political theology of nature the attempt to overcome such disunion resides in an analysis of human–nature

70. For 'environment', see Cupitt, 'Nature and Culture', pp. 33–45 (pp. 33–6); Donald Worster, *Nature's Economy* (Cambridge University Press, 2nd pbk edn 1994).
71. For 'ecology', see Carolyn Merchant, *Radical Ecology* (New York and London: Routledge, 1992); Carolyn Merchant (ed.), *Ecology: Key Concepts in Critical Theory* (New Jersey: Humanities Press, 1994); Williams, *Keywords*, pp. 110–11; Joseph Sittler, *The Ecology of Faith* (Philadelphia: Muhlenberg Press, 1961).
72. Bonhoeffer, *Ethics*, p. 5.

interactions in political–ideological interpretation. Our principal players are in place: God, nature and humanity. The theological task is the analysis, criticism and reconstruction of humanity–nature relations which obscure the visibility of the environment as the common realm of God, nature and humanity. A theological reading of un/natural humanity – the nature of social humanity, its natural and cultured relations to nature, its use of nature – is our aim. In this task, the liberation of nature, the liberation of humanity and the liberation of the promeity of God are at stake.

The common realm of God, nature and humanity

Common realm

According to Ferruccio Rossi-Landi, there is an important relationship between what he calls the natural sciences and the spiritual sciences: both have a tendency to work with a reified notion of the natural.[1] Both sciences, Rossi-Landi continues, are non-dialectical: one privileges space over time, the second interior space over the public realm. Both are 'static'. Here lies the difficulty and challenge for a theology of nature. For a connection, restrictive and damaging, may be noted between the non-dialectical theorisation of space and religious interiority. A theology of nature must present nature as temporal as well as spatial, thereby as engaged with and other than humanity. Likewise, the Christian faith must, through the engagement with non-theological disciplines, perform a constructive argument in the public realm towards an ontology of nature. The presentation of a conceptuality that would support a dialectical reading of nature and the public character of the Christian faith is the aim of this chapter.

The theological explication of the conceptuality of the *common realm of God, nature and humanity* requires an account of the creaturely relations of humanity and nature before God in engagement with other, non-theological, accounts of the interrelations of humanity-in-nature. Such a theological explication must consider carefully problems of definition, hermeneutical issues, method and metaphysical matters. That is, the way forward must be by careful attention to the definition of nature operative at any point in the argument, the understanding of modernity in which the argument is conducted, the relation between theology and

1. Ferruccio Rossi-Landi, *Marxism and Ideology* (Oxford University Press, 1990), p. 317.

non-theological disciplines and the continuities and discontinuities posited between humanity and nature.

The theological concept of the common realm of God, nature and humanity specifies a particular context of relations in which to interpret nature. First, nature here means that which is objectified and domesticated in modernity as other than humanity. The concept also makes clear that nature and humanity are both creaturely; that is, they are other to God. Thus the concept of the common realm permits a series of relations to be presented to theological attention: the presence of God which establishes – and is the source of – the reality of humanity-in-nature; and the separation of humanity and non-human nature. The concept of the common realm of God, nature and humanity is thereby an acknowledgement of our modern circumstances: the understanding of nature has become detached from humanity and God. The concept of the common realm of God, nature and humanity is thus a concession to the modern interpretation of nature: the physical world is usually understood as that which is other than humanity.

Second, the concept of the common realm claims that humanity and nature are understood properly only in mutual co-explication with the concept of God. This co-explication is difficult to achieve because one outcome of the modern separation of nature from God and humanity is the presentation of nature in various sorts of scientific description. These descriptions are culturally dominant, yet also somewhat indigestible theologically. So the common realm carries the commitment to theological engagement with non-theological, hegemonic interpretations of nature. As Carol Christ has noted: 'Because the disjunction of divinity, humanity, and nature is deeply embedded in the words, *God, humanity*, and *nature* ... [t]he three terms in the triad "God, man and nature" must be rethought together.'[2] Such a process of rethinking towards the healing of humanity

---

2. Carol P. Christ, 'Rethinking Theology and Nature', in Irene Diamond and Gloria Feman Orenstein (eds.), *Reweaving the World: The Emergence of Ecofeminism* (San Francisco: Sierra Club Books, 1990), pp. 58–69 (p. 61). Indeed, a close analogue to the common realm is to be found in ecofeminism: the stress on a web of life understood with reference to spirit or the sacred presses towards a notion akin to the common realm: see, further, Paula Gunn Allen, 'The Woman I Love is a Planet; the Planet I Love is a Tree', in Diamond and Orenstein (eds.), *Reweaving the World*, pp. 52–7; Starhawk, 'Feminist, Earth-based Spirituality and Ecofeminism', in Judith Plant (ed.), *Healing the Wounds: The Promise of Ecofeminism* (Philadelphia: New Society, 1989), pp. 174–85 (pp. 174, 182). In some cultures, human societies are understood by analogy with certain ecosystems: 'the forest as a community has been viewed [in Indian civilisation] as a model for societal and civilizational evolution', Vandana Shiva, *Staying Alive: Women, Ecology and Development* (London: Zed Books, 1989), p. 55.

and nature will thereby require attention to those disciplines which treat of nature in the modern sense.

In such manner, political–ideological interpretation in the theology of nature directs attention to the society of God, nature and humanity. The society of this common realm is the way in which God freely decides to be with God's creation. As co-participant in a common realm that encompasses the natural history of humanity, God is with and for humanity. Hence the concept of the common realm of God, nature and humanity embodies an important epistemological commitment: to the careful theological specification of the ontology of humanity. For the notion of un/natural humanity extends beyond human embodiment to theological consideration of the material world itself. The issue of the environment in which humanity finds itself is given its proper theological place. To speak of the common realm of God with humanity and nature is to insist that only through their co-explication – which, as the commitment to *creatio ex nihilo* reminds us, is mutual yet asymmetrical – can we arrive at theological judgments about natural, social humanity.

I have proposed the concept of the common realm of God, nature and humanity in order to acknowledge yet overcome the alienation of humanity from nature. Hence my preferred concept notes a modern movement towards the separation of nature and humanity and the displacement of the concept of God from the interpretation of nature. What follows may be understood as a theological attempt to overcome this double alienation of God from the world and humanity from nature.

Contemporary dilemmas: personalism and naturalism

In the previous chapter I argued that the political–ideological interpretation of nature requires a theological conceptuality to promote a direct inquiry into the theology of nature, humanity and God. The origin, methodological status and key words of this conceptuality are the subject of the final sections of this chapter. What dilemmas will such a direct inquiry encounter, however?

Difficulties in the interpretation of nature emerge in two general tendencies. Both theological and non-theological disciplines are caught up in a discussion on the duality of the concept of nature: should humanity be understood as part of nature or as other than nature? We can grasp the difficulty if we reflect on one of the root meanings of *phusis*: 'to dwell'.[3] What is the meaning of this reference to habitation? The sense could be that of the wider context in which humanity lives, that humanity *indwells* nature. Or the reference might be to how humanity *transforms* its dwelling in order to make it habitable. Or, to put the matter differently, does nature as habitat signify that which is inclusive of humanity or that which is other than humanity?

Here etymology shades into politics: for each tendency values the 'upper' part of the duality more highly than the 'lower'. For example, if humanity is understood as other than nature, then humanity is valued more highly with the consequent objectification and instrumentalisation of nature. The hierarchy also has certain epicycles: for instance, if humanity is defined in terms of the capacity to reason, such a capacity may be ascribed unequally between the sexes. The male is then understood to be more rational than the female; hence the female is 'closer' to nature. Thus the duality has a specific politics, natural and sexual. If, by contrast, nature holds the upper place, then humanity is itself 'denatured': for the specific profile of un/natural humanity is lost through its relocation in natural processes. Some interpretations in sociobiology–evolutionary psychology are good examples of this tendency. Again, we see that the duality has a specific politics, here social.

What forms does the duality take? If we follow Val Plumwood's analysis,[4] yet also incorporating certain modifications, we may note in theological perspective two tendencies: I shall call them *personalism* and *naturalism*. The first stresses humanity as other than nature, the second the place of humanity in nature. The tendency of personalism seeks ways of showing the difference of humanity from nature. Within such a tendency, two strategies are detectable: the claim of the *discontinuity* of humanity from nature and the claim that nature has no proper *autonomy*. Thus nature is either different from humanity or serves humanity.

Differences between these two strategies can be detected. The first strategy of personalism – discontinuity between humanity and nature – has the form either of the mere acknowledgement of natural conditions of life (nature as the stage of the human drama in the *theatrum mundi*) or

---

3. C. S Lewis, *Studies in Words* (Cambridge University Press, 2nd edn 1967), pp. 34–5. Lewis traces the meanings of the word 'nature' with reference to the Latin, *natura*, the Greek *phusis* and the Anglo-Saxon, *kind*.
4. Plumwood, *Feminism and the Mastery of Nature*, pp. 41–68.

their radical exclusion (certain forms of post-structuralist theory take this option, on epistemological grounds).

The second strategy in personalism seeks to deny the self-sufficiency or autonomy of nature. Nature may be thought to lack an essential quality (say, volition, rationality[5] or developed consciousness); it thereby needs to be 'completed' by humanity. Bill McKibben has proposed a new variant of this approach: because nature is no longer independent of humanity, it thereby lacks reality. Or nature may be primarily defined teleologically (see, for example, the work of theologian Thomas Sieger Derr or philosopher Reiner Grundmann) as that which is available for human use.[6]

With this stress on instrumentalisation often comes the claim that non-human nature is homogenous and thus all of nature can be treated in the same way. An Hegelian recently made precisely this point to me: all non-human nature is available, as lacking 'rationality', to humanity. In that all of nature shares in that lack, no pertinent (moral, ontological) distinctions can be made between the suffering of the higher and lower animals. Post-structuralist emphases on nature as 'flux' fit here also: nature 'is' a single quality, flux, to which no permanent significance – ontological, moral – can be ascribed. Indeed, at the epistemological level, it may be claimed that nature cannot be known. Nature thus becomes an issue and problem 'within' culture.

The tendency of naturalism reverses the priorities of personalism. Here the continuity between humanity and non-human nature is affirmed.[7] Indeed, humanity is understood as part of nature. As Luco van den Brom argues, on this view 'Humanity is thus subordinated to nature' and 'our place in the world is [understood as] monistic in the sense that it underscores the unity and overall balance of our world and our participation in it'.[8] Van den Brom dubs this the 'monistic model'. At its severest, a hard naturalism is proposed which insists that humanity must be in some sort of conformity with the 'laws' of nature which may take a neo-Stoic (as in deep ecology or Gaia, for example) form. In a series of further

---

5. Cf. Marti Kheel, 'From Healing Drugs to Deadly Drugs', in Plant (ed.), *Healing the Wounds*, pp. 96–111 (p. 105).

6. For the references, see McKibben, *The End of Nature*; Derr, *Ecology and Human Need*; Reiner Grundmann, *Marxism and Ecology* (Oxford: Clarendon Press, 1991).

7. See the accounts of hard and soft naturalism in Holmes Rolston III, *Science and Religion: A Critical Survey* (New York: Random House, 1987), ch. 6. The most sustained attempt known to me to develop a religious reading of hard naturalism is Willem B. Drees, *Religion, Science and Naturalism* (Cambridge University Press, 1996).

8. Luco van den Brom, 'The Art of a Theo-ecological Interpretation', *Nederlands Theologisch Tijdschrift* 51:4 (1997), 298–313 (304).

differentiations, nature lacks nothing, has value in its own right and enjoys a diversity to which humanity makes little contribution (again, as in the Gaia hypothesis).[9] Nature is sufficient, valued and diverse simply in its being. Furthermore, some theologians and philosophers propose a dynamic naturalism in which a 'resurrection of nature' is anticipated. In this view, nature is in bondage either to futility or to the oppressive effects of capitalism. With the resurrection of nature comes the resurrection of humanity with hopes for a new science and technology.[10] For all these views, humanity then becomes a problem 'within' nature.

The strength of naturalism is that it seeks to overcome the dualisms created by personalism. Against the denial of non-human nature, humanity's dependence on non-human nature is affirmed. Against the exclusion of nature from theoretical and practical consideration, the continuity of humanity with nature is maintained. Against the suggestion that nature is incorporated to human needs on the grounds that in itself it suffers from a lack, nature is to be understood as having its own story and identity. Against its instrumentalisation, non-human nature is a centre of needs, value and striving on its own account. Last, against the homogenisation of nature, its complexity and diversity must be affirmed.

The difficulty with this sort of approach, as Plumwood is quick to point out, is that the end result can be the affirmation of what was previously denied: the dualism is merely reversed. Hence personalism gives way to different sorts of naturalism.[11]

What is excluded from this critique is the concept of God which in turn means that the basic dualistic patterns cannot be addressed fully. As I have argued, the modern separation of humanity and nature is coterminous with the domestication of transcendence and the displacement of God from the world. Yet Christian theology too often remains caught in

9. For the references, see Bill Devall and George Sessions, *Deep Ecology: Living as if Nature Mattered* (Salt Lake City: Peregrine Smith Books, 1985); James Lovelock, *Gaia: A Look at Life on Earth* (Oxford University Press, 1987).

10. For a critique, see my 'The Resurrection of Nature? Problems in the Theology of Nature', *Theology in Green*, 4:2 (1994), 23–35.

11. In the interests of comprehensiveness, two further moves may be reported. One approach takes the form of trying to raise the lower side of the dualism to the upper side. In debates on ecology this takes the form of the affirmation of technological fixes, the promise of consumer goods for all: for, if the dualism has supported the unequal appropriation of 'nature's goods', then the resolution must be to spread goods more widely which in turn means greater reproduction. A different strategy, associated with postmodernism, dissolves all identities, those of humanity and non-human nature alike. The displacement of the modern subject does not yield an immutable natural order. Instead, it reminds us that all identities are constructed.

precisely the same dualism being outlined here. For Christianity – as we saw in the previous chapter – has tended to stress the otherness of God to humanity or has presented revelation as the contrast of creation, thereby turning human–nature relations into a matter of indifference. Although such views are correct in their maintenance of the transcendence, mystery and otherness of God, these are easily deconstructed into a stress on the continuity of humanity and nature, the value and subjectivity of nature, the personification of nature as Mother and the 'natural' identity of humanity in nature. However, the result is unfortunate: the affirmation of nature at the expense of the displacement of God.

A third strategy is required: neither the uncritical affirmation nor the dissolution of the difference of humanity, but rather the reconstruction of the identity of humanity as un/natural. For the denial and exclusion of nature in personalism, as we have seen, undercuts the reality of nature, whereas resistance by naturalism to the incorporation, instrumentalisation and homogenisation of nature denies the differences between the human and the non-human. So the theological reconstruction has to be dialectical: to affirm continuities against the first and affirm difference against the second. In doing this, Christian theology makes a renewed contribution to the criticism and reconstruction of the overarching modern story of the pre-eminence of humanity over nature. (Indeed, it may be that the reconstruction of the relation between humanity and nature requires not a story or narrative but instead a renewed 'economics' founded in the act of the creator God.) Van den Brom's summary judgment is right: a theological perspective proposes that 'the human being is not the whole of creation but a part of the larger system of creation' while yet understanding 'the human agent as a responsible being occupying a special place in the whole of creation'.[12]

The core theological issue here is the action of God: in what ways is God interacting with humanity–nature towards their liberation and interrelation? The concept of the *common realm of God, nature and humanity* has been formulated to address this issue. For we should note that the tendencies reported above – which stress either the manipulable otherness of nature or the place of humanity in nature – raise an important theological difficulty. Where you place the stress – either naturalism or personalism – has severe consequences for the doctrine of God. As Gordon

---

12. Van den Brom, 'The Art of a Theo-ecological Interpretation', 310.

Kaufman has pointed out, once nature (including humanity) is regarded as the action of the creating and conserving God, a problem emerges. On the one hand, the Christian God is described in terms of a moral personalism. On the other hand, the realm of nature is not easily explicated in terms of moral personalism.[13] That is, modern views of nature tend towards naturalism. Furthermore, in modern ecological thinking, nature is interpreted as without *telos*. Nature appears to name a process not best described in terms of 'dimensions of purpose, value and meaning'.[14] Hence there is a tension between a moral and volitional description of God and a processive, naturalistic description of nature.[15] It is not sufficient, then, to argue that the theological problem is the separation or disaggregation of humanity from nature and the world from God. We must also attend to the descriptive discourses of personalism and naturalism as these are applied to God and the world.

Of especial importance in this discussion is which of the descriptions is to be applied to humanity. For Kaufman claims that, in the history of Christianity, personalistic description has been applied to God *and* humanity. Thereby a tendency emerges in which humanity is understood as *other* than nature. God and humanity have moral, volitional capacities (albeit they have these differently) that nature does not share. Thus nature is that which is operated upon by God and humanity. There remains, of course, a crucial ontological distinction between humanity and God. Yet a secondary distinction emerges: between humanity and 'nature'. 'Nature is not conceived primarily as man's proper home and the very source and sustenance of his being', Kaufman concludes, 'but rather as the context of and material for teleological activity by the (nonnatural) wills working upon and in it'.[16]

I agree with Gordon Kaufman that the reductionism detected here – of 'nature' having its end in humanity – must be opposed. Yet I fear that Kaufman is proposing a reductionism in the other direction: humanity

---

13. Hence the far-reaching reconstruction of God in pantheism proves largely indigestible to Christianity: the construal of nature as infinite turns upon a naturalistic metaphysics. Even the important distinction between *natura naturans* and *natura naturata* cannot rescue pantheism from its naturalism. On this view, the continued popularity of deism – on the grounds of its capacity to operate within moral personalism – is at least comprehensible.
14. Thomas, *Man and the Natural World*, p. 170.
15. Even here, matters are not simple: it is of great importance to the naturalism under discussion from which 'level' of nature the naturalistic terms are derived: biology privileges categories of *life* and *vitality*; physics privileges *connection*, *energy* and *entropy*.
16. Kaufman, 'A Problem for Theology', 353.

as having its end in nature. Hence, I shall be arguing for, and developing a conceptuality which supports, the claim of the commonality, yet distinction, of humanity and nature. For reference to God does not, I shall argue, draw humanity into a metaphysics based on categories (cognitive, volitional, moral) derived from the description of the interhuman sphere which has, in turn, the unhappy effect of separating humanity from nature.

From natural theology to philosophical theology

At this point it will be objected that the *common realm of God, nature and humanity* is an exercise in neat natural theology and as such has no place in the theology of nature. Here we need to make some careful distinctions.

Natural theology is not a single theological approach, as Wolfhart Pannenberg has conclusively shown.[17] A form of natural theology that is worth defending takes its cue from core theological interpretations of the nature of God and the world. It is dedicated to that centrally important task of theology: the criticism of idolatry. Thus the following standard statement, by George Hendry, cannot be allowed to stand as adequate: if 'to establish a knowledge of nature in the light of God ... may be taken as a rough definition of a theology of nature', then the task of natural theology is to 'establish a knowledge of God in the light of nature'.[18] If such an account is inadequate, what is 'natural' knowledge of God?

To begin, we may note that theological tradition makes a distinction between *cognitio acquisita* and *cognitio insita*: that is, between knowledge which is publicly accessible yet needs to be acquired through philosophical reasoning, and natural knowledge of God which may be known through the conscience or some such. In what follows, I shall be defending philosophical theology as a form of *cognitio acquisita*. Before that defence, I

---

17. Pannenberg, *Systematic Theology* (Edinburgh: T. & T. Clark, 1991), I, ch. 2. For my account of natural theology, I am also drawing on Moltmann, *God in Creation*, pp. 57–60; David Tracy, 'John Cobb's Theological Method', in David Ray Griffin and Thomas J. J. Altizer (eds.), *John Cobb's Theology in Process* (Philadelphia: Westminster Press, 1977), pp. 25–38; Michael J. Buckley, *At the Origins of Modern Atheism* (New Haven and London: Yale University Press, 1987); Dupré, *Passage to Modernity*; Karl Barth, *Church Dogmatics*, I I /1 (Edinburgh: T. & T. Clark, 1957), pp. 128–78.

18. George S. Hendry, *Theology of Nature* (Philadelphia: The Westminster Press, 1989), p. 14. In *The Body of God*, p. 73, McFague offers a similar definition. And this approach is evident in the ecofeminist literature: see Brian Swimme, 'How to Heal a Lobotomy', in Diamond and Orenstein (eds.), *Reweaving the World*, pp. 15–22 (p. 20).

wish to acknowledge that two complaints made against natural theology must be accepted. First, natural theology should not claim to operate with an account of pure, objective, ahistorical reason. No such reason exists. Second, natural theology should not offer a philosophical metaphysics as a way of mediating between faith and the world – such a mediating position is often taken, as in the work of John Cobb, by process thought.[19] Natural theology is not a buffer between the Gospel and the world; natural theology does not offer a philosophical context in which Christian and modern world views are brought into conversation.[20] Nor, in the anthropological turn evident in some natural theology, am I here concerned with an account of the readiness of humanity to receive revelation.[21]

Instead, to quote Pannenberg, natural theology is concerned with the philosophical clarification of the word, God: for 'God . . . makes possible an ultimate explanation of the being of the world as a whole, namely, by creation.'[22] This type of inquiry, which is my subject here, I shall call philosophical theology. Such theology is concerned with the hermeneutics of the word, 'God': the protocols or rules that govern God-talk.

What is this discipline to which the theologian must adhere in the use of the term, 'God', in order to avoid idolatry (the confusion of God with some part of the world or the world itself)? How is philosophical theology helpful in the theology of nature? A philosophical theology offers not an alternative description of nature but an oppositional engagement. For the concept of nature in theology can both obscure nature and contribute to the eclipse of God. There is the danger that the attempt to stress God's relation to and involvement with nature legitimates nature as a new 'universal'. In this movement, what is lost is precisely those instances of humanity–nature interaction in and through which our environment is threatened. Such theoretical developments employ the term 'nature' but everywhere misunderstand it. What is obscured here are the

19. John Cobb, *A Christian Natural Theology Based on the Thought of Alfred North Whitehead* (London: Lutterworth Press, 1966).

20. McFague's view in *The Body of God* also comes close to this view: natural theology is the detection and articulation of congruencies between scientific and theological world views. For McFague, philosophy of science seems to provide both a world view and the context for the conversation between world views.

21. A modern variant of natural theology, sometimes called 'new style' natural theology (John Macquarrie) or fundamental theology (Gerard O'Collins) has an anthropological rather than a cosmological reference. The transcendental Thomism of Karl Rahner or the method of correlation of Paul Tillich can be understood as distinctly anthropological forms of natural theology (in which nature signifies *human* nature).

22. Pannenberg, *Systematic Theology*, I, p. 71.

particular ways in which nature is a problem for us. We do not, so to speak, assault nature all along the line. Instead, we have – to continue the military metaphor – local skirmishes of great intensity, which contribute to a general crisis. Against such a tendency, philosophical theology makes fluid the meanings of nature and foregrounds the issue of how the relations between humanity and nature are to be understood.

And the eclipse of God? It seems to me that too much ecological theology develops a conception of nature which is at best atheological and often antitheological. In short, the 'universal' of nature becomes the norm and basis for metaphysical construction of a system in which 'God' is named but whose agency is occluded and identity misrecognised. The stress on 'ecology' becomes a new way of offering a system to which theology must conform.

How does philosophical theology support a political theology of nature? Philosophical theology makes possible the grasping of the relationship between the unity of the whole and the concept of God. Furthermore, what is called into question, as I hope to show, is the restriction of the standard Christian metaphysical schema to God and humanity (with nature, as other and inferior to humanity, included under the notion of 'world').[23] Philosophical theology raises the issue of the unity of God in its relation to the unity of that which is not God. In other words, we must note an important epistemological point: the *concept* of God is conditioned by its relation to the 'totality of finite reality'.[24]

What does this mean? Central to the 'philosophical' problematic of the theology of nature is a conception of the whole which circumscribes the idea of God: an idol. How, then, for philosophical theology is the unity of the whole to be conceived in its relation to the idea of God in such fashion that idolatry is avoided?

In my judgment, the concept of God requires that we think of God in terms of a differentiated unity and of the world as a differentiated unity – although this unity and differentiation are held asymmetrically by God and the world. For, as the unconditioned ground or source of 'all that is', God is the source or ground of both differentiations and wholes,

23. For an account of the Christian metaphysical schema, see Kaufman, 'A Problem for Theology', 349; H. Paul Santmire, 'Toward a New Theology of Nature', *Dialog* 25:1 (1986), 43–50; and Santmire 'Healing the Protestant Mind: Beyond the Theology of Human Dominion', in Dieter T. Hessel (ed.), *After Nature's Revolt: Eco-justice and Theology* (Minneapolis: Fortress Press, 1992), pp. 61–5.
24. Wolfhart Pannenberg, *Metaphysics and the Idea of God* (Edinburgh: T. & T. Clark, 1990), p. 146.

including the unity which comprises 'the totality of finite reality'. In the perspective of philosophical theology, we cannot concentrate only on the differentiated 'parts' for otherwise how can we be sure that God is the source of the unity of the world, and not only of the parts?

Or, to put the matter the other way round, how can we be sure that the unity of the 'world' does not escape theological control and, functioning as an idol, become 'God'? Answer: by understanding the differentiated parts in terms of the unity of the whole, as a totality, in that God is the force of the unity. As Pannenberg puts it, God is the 'unifying unity' who secures the unified reality of the whole. In all its differences and determinations, nature, understood in terms of its unity and differences, has its source in the activity of God. The unity of God is thereby not assimilable to the unity of the world (which does not deny the immanence of God to the parts through the whole). Only in this way are the unity of God and the unity of the world secured.[25]

Already we see that an unqualified account of the notion of the unity of God is insufficient. In order to grasp the differentiation of the world in terms of 'difference' and 'unity', I have been obliged, following Wolfhart Pannenberg, to employ such terms as 'activity', 'ground' and 'force'. Failure to use such language ensures that, in relation to the idea of God, the particularity of the differences which form a unity cannot be thought. Thus, in order to use the word 'God' correctly – without confusion with the world and without confusion of the terms, 'difference' and 'unity' – some form of differentiation in God must be accepted. The conception of the world, Pannenberg writes, 'must be based upon a difference within God, one which typifies the relationship between part and whole'.[26] Of course, the difference is not that *of* part and whole; that would be for interpretation of the world to control interpretation of God. 'Activity,' 'ground' and 'force' emerge as important terms which show how the whole is dependent upon God and yet the differences are unified by the active force of God through the natural order. A key element of a theology of *creatio ex nihilo* – the original and continuing dependence of 'all that is' on God – is thereby secured.

What conception of nature is presupposed by this exercise in philosophical theology? We must note the differentiated unity of all natural processes in relation to the unity of God. We learn from this inquiry in

25. See further my 'Ecology: Religious or Secular?', *The Heythrop Journal* 38:1 (1997), 1–14.
26. Pannenberg, *Metaphysics and the Idea of God* , p. 144.

philosophical theology that extreme care will need to be exercised – on theological grounds – to settle or fix the meaning of the term, 'nature'. For the differentiated unity of God raises the question of which worldly unities and differences we are speaking. It follows that humanity's relationship to nature is unclear and will require thinking through from the theme of the world in relation to the concept of God. Metaphysical matters are placed in their true, theological, perspective: antitheses such as humanity and the natural, culture and nature are hereby ruled out. Instead, the unified totality of reality is privileged. Yet theological attention is directed to the differentiation of all reality and also holds to the view that, in its totality, reality relates to God. That is, reality in its totality and differentiation, is founded upon God. The task of philosophical theology is the explication of this claim.

The provocation of philosophical theology is to think through the relation of God to the world (including humanity). Nature is not to be treated as a new form of 'universal'. The creator God must be understood as encompassing the whole. Yet the differentiation of the unity of the world into differences is also to be found in the idea of God. It is of the intimacy of God's relation that God is immanent in differences and unities, parts and whole(s). Thereby the parts are secured as genuinely differentiated and the wholes as true unities.

The relation between unity and differences, whole and parts presupposes temporality and boundaries. That is, in the denial of the false universal, 'nature', the totality is placed in a new perspective: as formed and open to reformation in its relation to God. Wholes and parts must be understood in the perspective of the unity-in-difference required by the concept of God: such wholes and parts are not fixed, and cannot be fixed by thought. Only if the notion of the difference in God is denied, can such wholes and parts be fixed. Thus the ontology operative here (and required by the difference in God) is temporal: the organisation of differences and unities changes through time. The correlative account of boundaries must be equally critical: the reformation of parts and wholes is the reorganisation of boundaries between things.

Three important conclusions emerge. First, the differentiation of parts and wholes is given in the concept of God. Second, such differentiations cannot be fixed; all differentiations are temporal. Third, differentiations are given towards a certain continuity or stability. Can further specification be given to this claim that the unity and differences of the world are given in the concept of God (who is difference-in-unity)?

Becoming, unity, sociality and openness of God and creatures

In a remarkable section, 'Creation as Benefit', Karl Barth argues that the *philosophical* counterpart to his *theological* account of creation would be the concept of 'pure becoming'.[27] Theologically, creation as divine benefit means, for Barth, that the connection between creation and covenant cannot be weakened or broken. Creation cannot be known without the covenant; the covenant cannot be known without creation. Or, as Barth himself puts it, 'the truth of the covenant is already the secret of creation, that the secret of the covenant includes the benefit of creation'.[28] For notions of creation and creature are only intelligible in the light of the God who creates as benefit.

No world view, Barth continues, has managed to hold to this insight of creation as divine benefit. Yet he seems not to rule out the possibility of such a philosophical world view: 'The philosophical equivalent for the theological idea of divine creation would have to be that of a pure and basic becoming underlying and therefore preceding all perception and being.'[29] A little later, however, he appears to take back this openness to a philosophical counterpart: when formal consideration gives way to material matters, the (necessary) incapacity of philosophy to acknowledge 'creation as benefit because it is the work of God in Jesus Christ' is exposed. Nevertheless, Barth introduces an important category: *becoming*. Indeed, he declares that the philosophical account of pure becoming will only be acceptable to theology if 'this pure becoming is pure divine benefit preceding all knowledge and being and underlying all knowledge and being'.

As was argued in the previous section, I propose a closer rapprochement between philosophical theology and reconstructive theology than Barth would allow. But, in my judgment, the concept of *becoming* permits an important theological correction. The world and God are to be understood in terms not of *being*, but of *becoming*: the reality in which all creatures participate is not 'static' but dynamic. Indeed, with this correction, come further corrections to transcendental categories.[30] For the categories of

---

27. Karl Barth, *Church Dogmatics*, III/1 (Edinburgh: T. & T. Clark, 1958), pp. 330–4. I thank George Hunsinger for drawing this section and its significance to my attention.
28. Barth, *Church Dogmatics*, III/1, p. 333.   29. Ibid., p. 340.
30. In the discussion that follows on transcendentals, I am drawing on Norman Kretzmann, 'Trinity and Transcendentals', in Ronald J. Feenstra and Cornelius Plantinga (eds.), *Trinity, Incarnation and Atonement: Philosophical and Theological Essays* (University of Notre Dame Press, 1989), pp. 79–109; Daniel W. Hardy, 'Created and Redeemed Sociality', in *God's Ways with the*

one, true and *good* are replaced by *unity, sociality* and *openness*. In such a way is *becoming* to be understood as divine benefit.

What are transcendentals? 'By transcendentals', writes Colin Gunton, 'I mean those notions which we may suppose to embody "the necessary notes of being", in the pre-Kantian sense of notions which give some way of conceiving what reality truly is, everywhere and always'.[31] Transcendentals are therefore concepts with general reach; their aim is to give, at the most general level, an account of all reality. *Being* is the most obvious example of a transcendental. Attempts to interpret transcendentals require further categories and concepts which seek to 'draw down' the meaning and significance of such transcendentals; I offer some further concepts in the next section. Yet I have already made a theological correction: *becoming* is the key transcendental; it precedes all attempt at interpretation. Thereby, as Barth notes, the transcendental, *becoming*, applies also to God because the divine gift or benefit of creation as *becoming* precedes all knowledge and ontology. For, as a transcendental, *becoming* transcends all attempts at interpretation; thereby it applies also to God, who cannot be known except in self-disclosure. Thus the 'essence' of God, in philosophical description, is *becoming*.

Other terms have been favoured in theological tradition as transcendentals. These I have already listed: *one, true* and *good*. However, I propose a more modest set of transcendentals that coheres better with the transcendental of *becoming*: *unity, sociality* and *openness*. Such transcendentals are general terms which, 'before' knowledge and ontology, specify the general characteristics of reality. Thus, to select any thing is to say, prior to all other specifications, that in so far as a thing is, it is *one, social, open* and *becoming*. I do not claim that these transcendentals are ways of making all reality present. When John Milbank writes that 'One cannot look at this process [sc. of worldly reality] as a whole, but one can try to imagine what it means, its significance', the four transcendentals do not resist such a claim.[32] The four transcendentals proposed here do not map the entirety

World: Thinking and Practising Christian Faith (Edinburgh: T. & T. Clark, 1996), pp. 188–205; Gunton, *The One, the Three and the Many*; Dietrich Bonhoeffer, *Sanctorum Communio: A Dogmatic Inquiry into the Sociology of the Church* (New York and Evanston: Harper and Row, 1960); Dietrich Bonhoeffer, *Act and Being* (London: Collins, 1961); Clifford Green, *The Sociality of Christ and Humanity: Dietrich Bonhoeffer's Early Theology 1927–1933* (Missoula, MT: The Scholars' Press, 1972).

31. Gunton, *The One, the Three and the Many*, p. 136.

32. John Milbank, 'Postmodern Critical Augustinianism', *Modern Theology* 7:3 (1991), 224–37 (226).

of reality. Rather, they specify the basic or fundamental features of that reality 'of which we are a part and in which we live'.[33]

A simple example will serve to illustrate this point. Consider the university as an institution: in so far as it is a single legal, corporate entity it enjoys a unity; in so far as it relies upon a series of inputs of energy (to run the light, heat and computing systems) and interactions (between administrators, Faculty and students) it is social; in so far that it is susceptible to changed inputs and interactions immanently and in relation to its environment, the institution is always open; as such the institution is not in a state of being, but rather in a process of becoming. (It should be noted that there are degrees of unity, sociality and openness: for instance, a university which closes down, lays off all its workers and dismisses all its students, still maintains a certain degree of openness: security, protection of buildings, etc. Even if these services are discontinued, and the institution is abandoned, minimal patterns of openness still occur: the abandoned institution still occupies land and is susceptible to the benign actions of homeless people seeking shelter and the less benign action of vandals, wind and rain.)

It does not follow from this perspective that the entirety of the institution is amenable to conceptual analysis. As David Ford has pointed out, following the work of French sociologist Pierre Bourdieu, there is much social action which is hard to discern.[34] Support for transcendentals therefore does not lie solely in their explanatory power but also in a commitment to read the world in a certain way. Thus, for instance, in a certain situation – sexual abuse, for instance – it may be difficult to discern open and social aspects.[35] Yet these features are present, even if only counterfactually.

Why these transcendentals? First, I wish to stress that arguments in the theology of nature turn upon an implicit account of transcendentals. Consider, as a good example, the discussion of creation and covenant in *Loving Nature* by James Nash. What does the fact of God's creation tell us about the world? Nash presents us with the basic feature of *relationality*:

> Since God is the source of all in the Christian doctrine of creation, all creatures share in a common relationship . . . This affirmation of relationality is, moreover, enhanced by the theory of evolution, which

---

33. Gunton, *The One, the Three and the Many*, p. 145.
34. David F. Ford, 'What happens in the Eucharist?', *Scottish Journal of Theology* 8:3 (1995), 359–81 (360–1).
35. See the extraordinary book, also in this series, by Alistair McFadyen, *Bound to Sin: Abuse, Holocaust and the Christian Doctrine of Sin* (Cambridge University Press, 2000).

> describes humans as related to every other form of life through our
> common beginnings in one or more living cells and through our
> subsequent adaptive interactions. We evolved relationally; we exist
> symbiotically . . . we are interrelated parts and products of a world that
> is continually being made and nurtured by God.[36]

Given such an affirmation, it is hard to know how to describe relationality except as a transcendental. Although he himself does not explicitly say
so, Nash clearly means to draw to our attention *the* most fundamental feature of physical reality. This claim is reinforced by the appeal to evolutionary science and in light of the subsequent affirmation that God's presence
to relational reality is the basis of Christian ecological ethics. Later, Nash
insists that the covenant tells us of 'a rational order of interdependence –
which Christians also see as a moral, purposive order of relationality and
ecological integrity – that appears to be universal and that demands re-
spectful adaptability from moral agents'.[37] A new word is now added –
integrity – and sharp consequences are drawn: the human task is to
adapt to its environment. And the order is rational, intelligible. As doubly
grounded – in creation and covenant – 'relationality' functions as a transcendental. Yet because this claim is not set out in any detail, difficulties
arise. Writing later on the *imago Dei*, Nash opines:

> The image of God (including dominion), then, is . . . a special role or
> function – a vocation, calling, task, commission or assignment.
> Applied ecologically, the image concept recognises a basic biological
> fact: humans alone have evolved the peculiar rational, moral, and
> therefore, creative capacities that enable us alone to serve as
> responsible representatives of God's interests and values, to function as
> the protectors of the ecosphere and self-constrained consumers of the
> world's goods. The image is as much a responsibility as a right
> ecologically.[38]

Ambiguities emerge: the *imago Dei* acknowledges a 'biological fact' which
in turn suggests that care of the environment by humanity is located in biology. Thus it seems that basic biological facticity somehow undercuts the
cultural interests of humanity (which is rapacious of nature). Yet, if it is a
biological given, how is it that human beings manage to avoid this biological imperative so successfully? Further, amidst this biological givenness,
what is the role of cultural artifice in addressing the ecological crisis?

A related difficulty can be traced in the work of Sallie McFague. In
The Body of God, there emerges a strong commitment to a rapprochement

---

36. Nash, *Loving Nature*, p. 97.   37. Ibid., p. 100.   38. Ibid., p. 105.

between theology and the common creation story. For McFague, two ontological characteristics of the common creation story are of interest to theology: the 'radical interrelatedness and interdependence of all aspects' together with the emphasis on the multilevelled character of the universe with the 'higher', more complex, levels dependent on the lower, 'simpler', levels.[39] Further, McFague extends a philosophical transcendental to encompass God: a procreative–emanationist account of creation permits the universe to be grasped as the body of God; God is present through all parts of the universe.[40] Thus, although McFague does not say so, the transcendental of relationality applies also to God.

On what grounds should we accept such a view? McFague offers several: clues from embodied knowing, faith traditions and compatibility with scientific reality are all important. Yet there is also a fourth reason: 'it helps to make things better'.[41] A world view is to be adopted because it makes a contribution to the improvement of our circumstances, for both humankind and otherkind. Yet here McFague's transcendental inquiry is at its weakest: for her theology offers, in effect, a theological legitimation of a scientific cosmology. How such a move contributes to the humanisation of our circumstances is not clear. For what is occluded in this account is a view of human practices which need to be redirected into more sustainable patterns. Thus an abstract cosmology supports an abstract anthropology. The root of the abstraction is the transcendental of relationality which does not permit the identification, analysis and criticism of the anti-nature configurations of social humanity.

This short excursus in two theological ecologies is directed towards making only one point: in ecological theology, the issue of transcendentals cannot be avoided. The theme of relationality in Nash and McFague, I have argued, can be seen as a quasi-transcendental category. Yet, because the status of such transcendental thinking is unclear and the transcendentals not fully articulated, ontological commitments get confused with transcendental commitments. Thus, for both Nash and McFague, there is a tendency towards seeing humanity as compelled to conform to 'laws' of nature. The way of drawing humanity into nature is in terms of such relationality; attempts to deny this move are then thought to imply the denial of continuities between humanity and nature.

This debate thus has a certain *politics*: it does not clearly articulate how the presence of God requires the reconsideration of humanity in

39. McFague, *The Body of God*, pp. 105, 106.   40. Ibid., pp. 151–7.
41. Ibid., p. 88.

nature except in terms of the relationality suggested by the natural sciences. In that the content of the natural sciences specifies the context of theological work and the political argument turns upon an account of the laws of nature which are assumed to be benign, the case made is neither theological nor oppositional.

Yet why have I turned to the transcendentals of *unity, sociality, openness* and *becoming*? And are these transcendentals too political? These transcendentals are related to the philosophical theology already presented. In the previous section, I argued it was important to see how difference is common between God and creatures (although, of course, it is not the same difference). Such differentiation in God is secured in philosophical theology. Thus, transcendentals apply to God as well as to creatures. Differentiation in God points towards the notion of becoming. So these considerations are preparatory for the claims made in this section.[42]

However, there is a certain 'politics' of transcendentals. When Norman Kretzmann writes, 'The *transcendentals* are . . . *general* in the sense that all of them express modes in which being occurs in absolutely everything, another respect in which their place among our most fundamental concepts is natural', he is right and wrong.[43] Absolutely right is the claim that transcendentals are general, but it does not follow that the transcendental terms are obvious or beyond dispute. Transcendental inquiry may indeed be natural but the terms are not given. Hence, from a theological perspective, the terms must carefully articulate God's self-statement in the flesh of Jesus Christ.

For the root, foundation and rationale of the characterisation of the transcendentals is Christological: the resurrection of Jesus Christ. The resurrection of Christ, requires, in my judgment, the interpretation that in the return of Christ to the world by God the Father, which is praise of Jesus by the Father in the Spirit, we have a Godly judgment on sociality. That is, the breach in sociality – the solidarity of human beings to be for one another – does *not* concretely in and for Jesus of Nazareth end in death. I have drawn out the implications of this for praxis elsewhere.[44] Yet by this claim I do not mean only that, as David Nicholls has conclusively shown, there is a persistent relationship between images of God and the

---

42. And it does not hurt that such notions at least chime with the claim of the end of metaphysics understood as the presence of being, so often announced these days. For an account, see Hodgson, *Winds of the Spirit*, pp. 53–66.
43. Kretzmann, 'Trinity and Transcendentals', p. 90.
44. See Scott, *Theology, Ideology and Liberation*, ch. 6.

polity.[45] I intend rather a theological point: God, nature and humanity are *social* concepts which are intelligible fully only if their social intention is drawn out. 'For the concepts of person, community and God', writes Dietrich Bonhoeffer, 'have an essential and indissoluble relation to each other.'[46] That is, only in sociality are the concepts of self, society and God properly explicable; these concepts presuppose and explicate sociality.

Here I wish to build on this argument by introducing an important amendment: for the resurrection of Jesus Christ is God's promise to the covenantal character of social humanity *in nature*; humanity and nature share the important feature of the transcendentality of sociality. Thus the promise of the continuation of solidarity even through death pertains also to nature. The promise of God the Father in Jesus Christ grants a future to that which is social. For nature also is social. Hence, if the act of election by God the Father in the resurrection of Jesus Christ is the election of *social* humanity, then that same act of God is the election of *social* nature.

It is important to note the logic of this claim: nature participates in the resurrection of Jesus Christ on account of the sociality that it shares with social humanity. Nature is redeemed in the vicarious action of Christ not on the grounds that it forms the natural conditions of human life but because it is *social*. Yet its social character is different from humanity; hence nature is redeemed from its curse, not reconciled from its sin.[47] In the raising of Jesus Christ as the proleptic anticipation of the resurrection of social humanity, the resurrection of nature is also anticipated: the social character of reality is both affirmed and reordered.

What requires attention, in my view, is the relation between the resurrection of Jesus' embodiment and the social character of reality rather than the relation between Jesus' embodiment and non-human nature. Jürgen Moltmann adopts a form of the second argument in *The Way of Jesus Christ*: 'With the raising of Christ, the vulnerable and mortal human nature we experience here is raised and transformed into the eternally living, immortal human nature of the new creation; and with vulnerable human nature the non-human nature of the earth is transformed as well. This transformation is its eternal healing.'[48] Yet, despite Moltmann's best efforts, it seems that creation is drawn into the resurrection of Christ on the grounds only that it is the *condition* of the covenant. Although

---

45. David Nicholls, *Deity and Domination* (London: Routledge, 1989).
46. Bonhoeffer, *Sanctorum Communio*, p. 22.   47. See Bonhoeffer, *Christology*, pp. 64–5.
48. Jürgen Moltmann, *The Way of Jesus Christ: Christology in Messianic Dimensions* (London: SCM Press, 1990), p. 258.

Moltmann insists on the 'naturalness' of humanity, he is unable to articulate the notion. Thus, in the end, that which is other than human achieves its place in the covenant on account of Christ's embodiment. A more fruitful theological way, I shall be arguing, is to affirm the sociality of all reality, human and natural.

Openness has the same root as sociality: the resurrection of Jesus Christ. For, presupposed by the resurrection of Jesus Christ, yet knowable only by it, is the claim that the ontological order, conditions and possibilities of the world are such as to permit the crossing by the becoming God into the world in incarnation, and a reordering of that same order, conditions and possibilities into concrete actuality by the resurrection of Jesus Christ. Philosophically, the world must be interpreted – in a formally identical claim – as absolute becoming. All ontology and epistemology must be oriented towards and proportioned by this becoming. Hence changes in social relations – that is, as founded in the transcendental of *openness* – are given in the resurrection of Jesus Christ; hence openness is actuality. As Jürgen Moltmann writes: 'It is theologically necessary to view created things as real promises of the kingdom; and it is equally necessary, conversely to understand the kingdom of God as the fulfilment, not merely of the historical promises of the world, but of its natural promises as well.'[49] And the promise of the Kingdom is made known, of course, in the history of Israel, culminating in the resurrection of Jesus Christ.

What of *unity*? The transcendental of unity has already been addressed in the previous section: parts, as unities, participate in the transcendental of *unity*; the whole which is comprised of the parts is also a unity and thereby participates in the transcendental, *unity*. Such an account is related to the older notion of the *one* as transcendental; yet the notion of oneness is too static to relate easily to the transcendental of creation as pure becoming. The unity of the world has its eschatological origin and destiny in the resurrection of Jesus Christ. Of course, this is a serious theoretical problem for Christian faith: how is the unity of the life, death and resurrection of Jesus Christ to be related to, indeed qualify, the unity of the expanding cosmos, on the one hand, and be the fullness of God, on the other?[50] This issue, in various guises, has been a central feature of Enlightenment critiques of Christology. I shall return to this point in part III.

49. Moltmann, *God in Creation*, p. 63.   50. Colossians 1.15–20.

My argument creates an obvious difficulty: are these transcendentals of *becoming*, *unity*, *sociality* and *openness* to be ascribed to *God*? I have argued that these transcendentals are general 'notes of being'. I have also argued that their root and foundation can be traced to the resurrection of Jesus Christ. Yet an argument of that sort suggests that transcendentals are properly ascribed or appropriated to the persons of the Trinity. Is this true?

The test case here is whether or not sociality may be ascribed to the second person of the Trinity. I believe it can. First, a general argument might be made, some of the contours of which have been visible through this section, that the association of Word and Son with sociality is appropriate: these terms (Word, Son) emerge from the contexts of communication and relationships and are thereby social.

Second, although the transcendental of sociality applies to God in God's essence-as-becoming and to all creatures, yet sociality is enjoyed by God and creation differently. God, we may say, has sociality perfectly. A further reason now emerges as to why sociality is to be ascribed to the *Logos*. God is unitive, social, open and becoming perfectly but creatures participate in the transcendentals asymmetrically, for the cause of these transcendentals in creatures is God. Thus the sociality of the world is caused by God and is the form of God's presence in the world. Nature (including humanity) is thereby invited to imitate the perfection of the sociality of God.

However, although the insight into the sociality of God is given in the witness to the resurrection of Jesus Christ, the practice of such sociality is ambiguous and opaque. For we cannot claim that we know clearly how to enact such sociality. The appropriation of the transcendental of sociality to God and to creatures is thereby strict: divine sociality, creaturely sociality. Yet, on account of Jesus Christ, we may attribute creaturely sociality to the Godhead *metaphorically*. The asymmetrical character of the relationship between God and world means that the attribution cannot be strict. To seek to escape such a metaphorical application would be to speak of that which cannot be spoken: the perfect sociality of the God-who-is-becoming. Nevertheless, the metaphorical ascription to the Word/*Logos* acknowledges that the world is revealed to be social. Sociality is real not abstract, actual not potential: it is to be ascribed metaphorically to the *Logos*. However, we must remember, because the ascription of sociality to God is strict, sociality cannot be read off the immanent Trinity.

What is basic to human and non-human life is sociality. We should expect nothing else, for sociality is the counterpart in philosophical theology of the turning of God's face towards humanity and nature in Jesus Christ.

Politics of nature: ecosocial ontology

I have argued that the concept of the *common realm of God, nature and humanity* provides a useful way of tackling the two problems with which a political theology of nature must engage: the overcoming of the double alienation of God from the world and humanity from nature. The concept of the common realm insists on the reality of nature and yet also insists on its interaction with humanity. Nature is neither entirely cultured nor simply given. Indeed, the conception of the world as totality and as difference generated by philosophical theology affirms, in theological perspective, such a claim: the otherness and the proximity of nature must be respected. Inquiry by transcendentals is also imperative in the search for a conceptuality directed towards the fundamental features of the world. In this section, I wish to develop further the conceptuality which supports this claim to the liberative potential of these transcendentals towards the concept of the common realm of God, nature and humanity.

At this point, the argument moves from the generality of transcendental argument. Now a further level of inquiry emerges: an *ontology of the ecosocial*. This ontology is an attempt to draw down the transcendentals: to offer 'categories of existence' dedicated to the exploration of that which exists.[51] The addition of the term, *eco*, stresses that interaction occurs between humanity and nature. Of course, such an ontology cannot breach the transcendental protocols set out in the previous section.

What are the key concepts of this ecosocial ontology? *Sociality*, *spatiality* and *temporality* of nature affirm the reality, otherness and proximity of nature in relation to un/natural humanity.[52] These concepts are derivable from the revelation of God: temporality, sociality and spatiality can be traced in the life, death and resurrection of Jesus Christ. What is more, these three concepts are also present in the adventure in philosophical theology we followed above (pp. 43–52). That section stressed the transcendental features of the world. The concepts of sociality, temporality

---

51. Allan A. Gare, *Postmodernism and the Environmental Crisis* (London and New York: Routledge, 1995), p. 119.
52. The theme, but not the concept, of contingency also runs through these remarks: as authored in the activity of God, creation is contingent.

and spatiality seek to capture in more detail such a theological description. How do they do this?

Sociality offers the pledge of a theological theory that stresses the interrelation of humanity and nature. Indeed, strictly, the concepts of temporality and spatiality are complementary ways of setting out the basic insight of the social character of all reality. Sociality spotlights the transactions between humanity and non-human nature. How in our social life are the natural conditions of human life grasped in the exchanges between human and non-human nature? How does the social freedom of humanity oppose oppressive and restrictive accounts of nature, in which the contingency of nature is denied? These questions can be answered only by reference to sociality.

The theological commitment to interpreting sociality as the key feature of an ontology of the ecosocial requires further elucidation. For sociality is not a concept which explicates itself. What does it mean to say that all reality is social? For Dietrich Bonhoeffer, whose important and creative innovation it was to foreground the concept of sociality, the central social relation is I–Thou; the central interaction is thereby between persons.[53] On these grounds Colin Gunton rejects the notion of sociality as transcendental: for, Gunton asks, how can the notion of sociality, which turns upon the interaction of persons, apply to all of reality? For non-human nature is not personal and thereby not social. Hence sociality is not a transcendental.[54] However such a claim is only true if the basic social relation is I–Thou, if the basic social category is person.

What if the basic social relation was to be interpreted differently? What if the basic social relation is itself best understood as work, labour, reproduction? A social ontology thereby specifies exchanges, transactions, interdependencies and interactions. This may be set out in various ways: personal communication, technological appropriation, economic and communal interaction and reproductive processes. Although work may function as the basic social relation, this is no foundationalist category. We must acknowledge different zones of interaction: ecoproduction, reproduction, communication and political authority – with nature as a fundamental condition of all these.[55] And we must acknowledge different

---

53. Bonhoeffer, *Sanctorum Communio*, *passim*.
54. Gunton, *The One, the Three and the Many*, pp. 219–23.
55. Here I am drawing on Len Doyal and Ian Gough, 'Human Needs and Social Change', in Carolyn Merchant (ed.), *Ecology: Key Concepts in Critical Theory* (New Jersey: Humanities Press, 1994), pp. 107–11 (p. 109).

sorts of work: interpersonal, political, economic, voluntary and cultural actions – all with natural conditions. Nature is *in nobis*; we are in nature.

We can, of course, make some important distinctions: the sociality of non-human nature is a condition for the sociality of humanity. Yet we must also note that nature's sociality is genuinely its own sociality; it is not imputed to it by the actions of humanity. Hence there remain important discontinuities as well as continuities between the social nature of humanity and the social nature of nature. Given these continuities and discontinuities, can any further points be made regarding this social ontology? I think that they can. I offer two further concepts.

Spatiality refers both to the reality of nature (including humanity) and its givenness by God. In the politics of nature, it refers both to the circumstance in which humanity finds itself to be placed – the social field of exercisable freedom – and the non-necessary character of humanity's place in its environment. The natural conditions of human life are part of the givenness of the blessing of God to un/natural humanity. This circumstance is always in dialectical relationship to God. Spatial nature is thereby not necessary nature. No claims can be made that God validates, at the social or political level, certain configurations of humanity or nature as 'natural'. The world could be other than what it is. Yet nature, as contingent, remains God's blessing: it is ordered towards the preservation of the creatures of God and is itself that ordering. Thus, as the social character of life makes clear, the contingency of God's order has elements of continuity and stability. In this stability and continuity – in its spatiality – the unity of the created order is prefigured and anticipated. Hence, humanity is placed by God into a real, natural context; the natural conditions of human life are real (however much they may be ignored in practice). The stability of nature is *extra nos*.

Temporality insists on the historicity of nature at all levels: cosmological, biological, social. In a limited sense, therefore, I am holding to the Jewish–Christian notion of temporal unfolding.[56] (The sense is limited in that the stress on sociality and spatiality are reminders of the synchronic character of the world, as is the stress on unity as a transcendental; straightforward linearity is not warranted theologically.) Nature cannot, at the political level, be understood without reference to the history of humanity-in-nature. Although non-human nature is an important part of God's blessing of continuity and stability, interruptions, expansions

56. Dupré, *Passage to Modernity*, pp. 145–52.

and contractions are nevertheless possible. Temporality indicates that specific differentiations and determinations can emerge and disappear within God's ordering of the world. Of course, no appeal can be made to specific determinations or orderings as validated by God. Yet there are such relations. In such fashion, humanity may transform its context into a habitat; it may also poison or destroy its habitat. The temporality of nature is *pro nobis*; it is a condition of human freedom (and, contingently, sin).

How is this position related to the gracing of nature and humanity in the perspective of the triune God? All three, as we have seen from the argument of the previous sections, are theological. Each of the concepts emerges as the result of theological argument. All specify important aspects of the gracing of nature. *Sociality* stresses the continuities between humanity and non-human nature. *Spatiality* indicates that nature is 'given': real and present. The *temporality* of nature acts as a protocol against those who wish to stress the space of nature over time.

Praxis and transcendentals: liberating nature and theology from idolatry

Through this chapter, an important difficulty in the consideration of nature, within theology and without, has been presented. Should one speak of the end of nature or its resurrection, of anthropology or cosmology, of freedom or naturalism? Where should one put the stress in the following: *Nature-includes-Humanity-which-is-other-than-Nature*? On the first occurrence of Nature or Humanity or on the second occurrence? The philosophical theology presented here contributes to the articulation of the *common realm of God, nature and humanity* by insisting on the commonality of God, nature and humanity, yet on the absolute difference between God and creatures. Furthermore, as regards the politics of nature, I have presented an ontology of the ecosocial which features the reality, stability and openness towards humanity of nature. Yet the nature of nature (including humanity) is, as given by God, social and contingent.

Too abstract? The common realm of God, nature and humanity specifies as *transcendental* features the conditions, actuality and potential of the world in terms of its unity, openness, sociality and becoming. These transcendental features cannot be breached in interpretation. Ruled out is any attempt to claim that the *becoming* of the world is *only* disorder. Ruled out is the claim that God validates a *specific* order. The practical consequences which flow from this are immediate and considerable. Already we glimpse the movement away from the fragmentation and disintegration of the world towards its integrity and wholeness. The fixity of nature and the pre-eminence of humanity 'over' nature are to be denied with equal force.

Both fixity and pre-eminence – examples of the misconstrual of the world as 'being' – are hereby rejected in favour of its becoming: the world is ordered, relational and temporal. Appeals to nature as requiring completion by humanity or as without stability must be rejected. Yet neither can the fixity of nature be accepted. It is not only that these positions cannot be ascribed to God. *Theological criticism requires their rejection.* For the sake of the freedom of God and the creatureliness of creatures, order and mastery are to be rejected. But in this rejection of the domestication of transcendence, the presence of God is not denied. (In a strange way, the theology of Sallie McFague ends in such a denial: although her new models of God are immanentist, these models have no ground in God's own life and so the stress on the new models of God in fact only highlights the absence of God from McFague's world.) Rather the emphasis on the transcendentals conceptualises the present action of God towards nature and humanity.

Becoming, unity, sociality and *openness* are my preferred terms for transcendental inquiry. Such terms reveal that the relational, temporal order of the world, given in the concept of God, is predicated upon exchange and transactions. The basic model offered here is of *(re)production, work.* Work is not only that which occurs between human beings, as I hope to show. Further, the stress upon labour or work also allows that the relations are alterable: such relations can 'expand' or 'contract'. As the direction of the world can be understood as expansion or contraction, an orderly alteration of the natural conditions of humanity in one of two directions is presupposed: towards their enhancement or towards their diminution.

A Christian imperative subsequently emerges: imitation of the expansive sociality of God by humanity, and the enabling and permitting of humanity's environment also to imitate God, require adequate conceptualisation. The ontology of the ecosocial – *sociality, spatiality, temporality* – is dedicated to this task. Again, the question will be: too abstract? I do not think so. What emerges at this point of the inquiry is a way of exploring and giving an account of the proximity and otherness of nature. We saw that it is precisely the failure in the dialectical presentation of otherness and proximity which marks so much modern theorising on nature. We will, of course, be required to indicate the specific responsibilities towards their environment placed on human groups in certain regions.[57] Transcendental inquiry is not an alternative or substitute for such attention but rather its vital precursor. None the less, what is required is a secure way of characterising human–nature relations in order to show how the transformation of its habitat is constitutive of human nature.[58] What we need is a theory, tested through analyses, offering an account of *Nature-inclusive-of-Humanity-which-is-other-than-Nature* which requires that all three nouns be accented.

These analyses are the subject of part II. Yet it is my claim here that only in a theological account can the stress on the proximity, stability and otherness of nature, its temporality and unity, be successfully articulated. For what is required is a theological conceptuality which supports the *direct* analysis of un/natural humanity as this is obscured in contemporary practice (the issue of political–ideological interpretation) towards the affirmation of the actuality of the common realm of God, nature and humanity.

Towards a political theology of nature

So far, I have argued for a philosophical theology of nature in a political–ideological key. The transcendentals of *becoming, unity, sociality* and *openness* articulate the common realm in which God, nature and humanity are mutually yet asymmetrically related. As part of the same argument, homogeneity is ruled out: difference in God requires differentiation of the world; worldly distinctions require the concept of a self-related God. The terminology of 'ground', 'activity' and 'force' emerged as important at this point.

The world has its *ground* in the activity of God. Following a Christological clue, I have interpreted such a ground in terms of sociality: the stability of the world resides in its social, yet always contingent, relations. The irreducible interrelationality of all things is best worked out within a conceptuality of the social. To further explicate the social ground of the world in God, I draw on the categories of temporality and spatiality. This theme, construed Christologically as dynamic encounter, is the subject of chapter 7.

---

57. Gare, *Postmodernism and the Environmental Crisis*, p. 161.
58. Joel Kovel, 'On the Notion of Human Nature: A Contribution toward a Philosophical Anthropology', in Stanley B. Messer, Louis A. Sass and Robert L. Woolfolk (eds.), *Hermeneutics and Psychological Theory: Interpretive Perspectives on Personality, Psychotherapy, and Psychopathology* (New Brunswick and London: Rutgers University Press, 1988), pp. 370–99.

The *activity* of God both differentiates and yet holds together: God is both *alpha* and *omega*. This activity of God is a *force* for alteration: the renewal of the social. Thus the activity of God is to be understood in terms of movement and dynamism towards the intensification of true dependencies. This theme, construed pneumatologically as fellowship, is the subject of chapter 8.

The movements of the social, temporal and spatial are to be described as the un/natural relations of the common realm. What does 'un/natural' mean? The term 'un/natural', which accrues developed theological content in part III, operates as a contrasting term to 'natural' and 'non-natural'. Against reductionist tendencies to interpret humanity as conforming to nature or as separate from nature, I offer here a richer ontology of the ecosocial. And this ecosocial ontology is richer because it is an ontology shaped in response to the activity of God as ground and force.

I anticipate here a certain type of pragmatic and sceptical response: how does the discourse of sociality, temporality and spatiality assist in thinking about un/natural relations? For example: if, struck by its beauty, I gaze at a starry night sky – how is this reaction to 'nature' analysable by the conceptuality I am offering through this book? In response, I should say that my argument moves at the level of fundamental theological categories. But such an answer, although necessary, is not sufficient.

So consider this: what account of un/natural relations is presupposed by an aesthetic reaction to a natural occurrence? Is a sense of insignificance occasioned by looking at the night sky a more appropriate reaction than regarding myself as a microcosm faced by a macrocosm? A curious song lyric by Sting makes my point: 'I took a walk alone last night / I looked up at the stars / To try and find an answer in my life . . . Something made me smile / Something seemed to ease the pain / Something about the universe and how it's all connected.'[59] On what grounds is this reading of the universe as source of solace to be preferred to the universe as source of alienation? What sorts of social relations engender such different aesthetic responses and are reproduced through them? We probably think that such responses are 'timeless' – but are they? Do they have a precise history in culture, religions and theory? How do such responses assist in the identification of the material processes by which Western humanity employs non-human nature (and other humans)? Is there a liberative connection between such a sensibility and praise of the triune God?

59. Sting, 'I'm so Happy I can't Stop Crying', from the album *Mercury Falling* (1996). Lyrics and music by Sting. Lyrics copyright Magnetic Publishing Limited.

To answer such questions we enter a third level of analysis: below the transcendental and the ecosocial, we have the level of *ordering* or *organisation*. How are we to think of the ordering or organisation of creatureliness? How do temporal, social and spatial orders emerge? What modes of determination shape un/natural relations? Here three categories of *historico-natural emergence* are of especial importance: *movement, structure* and *tendency*. The temporal, social and spatial is a realm of *movement*: of the temporal 'unfolding' of distinctions and determinations. Such movement is always by way of *structures*: orderings of becoming. Such orderings are subject to a range of *tendencies*: death or ending, of course, but also expansion, increase in richness or variety, and the enhancement of interaction, mutuality and fellowship.[60]

To return to my example of gazing at the night sky: what sort of *movement* between humanity and nature is evident here? If we say that this common way of interacting with nature leaves aspects of our Western un/natural relations untouched and unaffected, such sky-gazing could be interpreted merely as an escape from the ruthless ways in which we use up nature. Or such star-gazing could be a substantial criticism of other, dominant, ways of construing and interacting with nature. How shall we decide between these two opposed readings? One way would be to attend to the conditions of such movement: what are its supporting *structures*? Such reactions to a sky are learned rather than innate. But where do we learn them? When Don Maclean sings, in praise of Vincent Van Gogh, 'Starry, Starry Night', where does such a sensibility come from and what material interests does it support?[61] Are the interests that emerge in such a structure of feeling, to borrow from Raymond Williams, oriented towards the wholeness of human–nature relations or their disintegration? Lastly, is the *tendency* of such star-gazing that of personalism or naturalism? Interacting with the sky at night could be interpreted in affirmative ways: a vast universe that ends in a self-conscious part – humanity – might be understood as purposive and oriented towards the human. Or the same vastness might be read cosmocentrically. Human beings are in this manner decentred: 'nettles in a beautiful universe', as a student once put it to me.

Standing in your garden at midnight and watching the starry sky turns out to be a complex phenomenon patient of a range of interpretations. To test those interpretations theologically, we need to ask fundamental

---

60. The issue of historico-natural emergence is picked up again in chapter 8.
61. Don MacLean, 'Vincent (Starry, Starry Night)', from the album *American Pie* (1971). Lyrics and music by Don McLean. Lyrics copyright Songs of Universal, Inc. and Benny Bird Music.

questions: what are temporal, social and spatial orders and how do they emerge? How are movements, structures and tendencies to be thought in a political theology of nature? Through the next part of this book, ways in which the movement, structure and tendency of un/natural relations may be understood are considered. I offer a critical yet dynamic articulation: an interaction between the theological commitments of the common realm of God, nature and humanity and various political theories of ecology. The aim is the testing of these theological commitments, and their development and clarification.

Part II

The politics of nature

3

Deep ecology: the return of nature

Introduction: ecocentric and anthropocentric approaches in political ecology

The issue for a political theology of nature is how to give an account of the content of the ecological relations operative in this world of creatures. The opening narratives in Genesis offer us, at a minimum, an account of the creation as a sequence of forms which culminates in a world of creatures. These are narratives of *creation*: the world of creatures emerges as a 'consequence' of divine action. However, holding to creation is not the same as articulating in theological form how the human creature is related to other creatures. Christianity knows, I think, of the deep and intimate relations that govern this world: the contingency and dependence of creatures on their God. The matter is to develop a rich Trinitarian ontology in ways that draw strength from, and clarify and correct, the situatedness of the human: a social creature in a common realm, oriented towards the triune God.

In the previous chapter, the tendencies of personalism and naturalism in ecological discourse were noted. The categories of existence and historico-natural emergence that I proposed are designed to move the present inquiry beyond the practical and theoretical differences within these tendencies. Such a move is by way of a critical yet dynamic articulation of Christian theology with various political ecologies. In this chapter, then, attention shifts to the political discourse of deep ecology which has sought a hearing in the last thirty years or so. This discourse articulates, it claims, a fresh understanding of the place of humanity in nature. (Although some argue that these ways are not so new as some of their proponents would have us believe.) The aim of this chapter is to attend to the ways in which deep ecology understands nature in order to develop and sharpen the account of un/natural relations already presented. To test, in other words, these theological commitments and seek their development and clarification.

There are two dominant tendencies, I have said, in the consideration of nature. Both are reductionist: one seeks to reduce humanity to nature, the second reduces nature to a function of humanity. These two tendencies strongly inform the politics of nature. The first moves in an ecocentric direction; the second is anthropocentric.[1] It is, of course, possible to offer a rather more differentiated typology. John Rodman, for example, offers four sensibilities which can be identified in the environmental movement. These in turn can be divided into two unequal lists: 'resource conservation', 'wilderness preservation' and 'moral extensionism' are, as Rodman points out, to a greater or lesser extent anthropocentric. Only the fourth type, 'ecological sensibility', makes a full break with anthropocentrism.[2] In a similar and exhaustive analysis, Warwick Fox suggests that the litmus test is anthropocentric versus non-anthropocentric views. This anthropocentric/non-anthropocentric or ecocentric binary schema structures the debate in political ecology.[3] We are returned to the fundamental division between the tendencies of personalism and naturalism.

Ecocentric tendencies, as Richard Sylvan points out, locate value, good and worth in nature.[4] Thus nature, in which humanity is placed, is regarded as primary: it is the *locus* of the emergence of human beings, of intrinsic value (that is, has value in its own right) and embodies a pattern of wisdom which humans are obliged to respect (or suffer the consequences). Consequently, the promotion of difference between humanity and the rest of nature is regarded with suspicion. Although such ecological wisdom is not always held to be older than the mainstream Western religions, it is superior. Such ecocentric positions are also deeply critical of the mechanistic view of the cosmos promoted by 'Enlightenment science'.

Anthropocentric approaches, in contrast, resist the ascription of worth, value and good to nature. Here the search for wisdom tends to focus on the

1. Here I am drawing on the typologies offered by David Pepper in his *Modern Environmentalism: An Introduction* (London: Routledge, 1996), pp. 34f.
2. John Rodman, 'Four Forms of Ecological Consciousness Reconsidered', in George Sessions (ed.), *Deep Ecology for the 21st Century: Readings on the Philosophy and Practice of the New Environmentalism* (Boston and London: Shambhala, 1995), pp. 121–30.
3. Warwick Fox, *Toward a Transpersonal Ecology* (Dartington: Resurgence, 1995), pp. 22f.
4. Richard Sylvan, 'A Critique of Deep Ecology,' part I, *Radical Philosophy* 40 (1985), 2–12.

relations within humanity which affect or constitute relations between humanity and the non-human world. Such views may, in a liberal extension of the legal concepts of 'rights' and 'interests',[5] be prepared to grant rights to nature or accept that nature 'enjoys' certain interests. However, these moves are 'legal fictions' framed for the purpose of bringing to human attention the importance of habitat or environment for human survival. John Rodman calls this view 'moral extensionism': 'humans have duties not only concerning but also directly to (some) nonhuman natural entities, and these duties derive from rights possessed by the natural entities, and . . . are grounded in the possession by the natural entities of an intrinsically valuable quality such as intelligence, sentience or consciousness'.[6] On epistemological grounds, valuing is considered to be solely a human act. Nevertheless, although the ascription of value, worth and goodness of nature is always an act of *human* measurement and judgment, it is important to extend the range of human sympathies to include some aspects of nature. By such a procedure, important issues about the alienated and exploitative character of human social life are brought into sharper relief and thereby highlighted. This view has its critics: John Rodman notes that 'all the variants of this position are open to the criticism that they merely "extend" . . . conventional anthropocentric ethics'.[7] Such an extension, Val Plumwood notes, has a particular rationalistic, abstract form: 'the extension of . . . abstract moral rules to nature itself'.[8]

There is also a further sub-set of political theories which, although acknowledging certain environmental difficulties, remains *strongly* anthropocentric. Such views encompass those of free-market political parties and the like who argue that the innovations of the market will secure unending growth or that through careful negotiation the worst effects of environmental degradation can be mitigated (and maybe avoided altogether). David Pepper calls such views 'technocentric', Arne Naess suggests the term 'shallow', Rodman prefers 'resource conservation'. In a discussion of this 'technocentric' environmental politics in Europe, Pepper argues that faith is placed in the management of environmental demands or salvation by science or market forces. According to opinion poll evidence he reports, such a technocentric view is held by at least 65 per cent of the European

5. See Thomas Birch, 'The Incarceration of Wildness: Wilderness Areas as Prisons', in Sessions (ed.), *Deep Ecology for the 21st Century*, pp. 339–55 (p. 340); Michael S. Northcott, *The Environment and Christian Ethics* (Cambridge University Press, 1996), pp. 97f.

6. Rodman, 'Four Forms of Ecological Consciousness Reconsidered', p. 124.

7. Ibid.

8. Plumwood, *Feminism and the Mastery of Nature*, p. 170.

population.[9] In other words, this 'technocentric' view will be the position held – implicitly – by many of the readers of this book.

The focus of this chapter, however, is on deep ecology, an avowedly and self-consciously ecocentric approach. What is deep ecology and what does a political theology of nature have to learn from it?

What is deep ecology?

It would be tempting to describe deep ecology as another political ecology. However, at any rate in the view of its chief proponents, deep ecology is not least a movement of ecosocial activism. Prevalent as a theoretical movement in the USA, Canada and Australia, its chief practical contribution has been in the United States where it has been associated with the creative and influential Earth First! environmental movement. Formed in 1980 by five American conservationists, of whom Dave Foreman is the best known, Earth First! was convinced that the conservation of the environment could not be achieved by the usual political means. Its protests, known as 'monkey-wrenching', after the 1975 Edward Abbey novel, *The Monkey Wrench Gang*, have included damaging contractors' plant used in developments that encroach on wilderness and taking action in protection of non-human nature (for example, tree-spiking).

Earth First! in the States has had its internal conflicts. Martha Lee has pointed out the tension between apocalyptic and millennial forms of environmentalism in the movement. A tension can be detected, she argues, in radical environmental ideologies: on the one hand, there is the affirmation of the equality of nature with humanity; on the other, there is the strong ethical stress on human action in the present. On her interpretation, this tension in environmentalist ideologies emerged in the Earth First! movement in the form of a split. One group stressed ecocentrism – that human beings are not to be understood as enjoying greater value than non-human nature and therefore enjoy no consequent superiority – and thereby posited an apocalypse of nature in which it was not clear whether human beings would or should survive. A second group stressed instead millenarian aspects: the importance of ecological education towards the avoidance of apocalypse and the continuation of the human race.[10]

9. David Pepper, *Eco-socialism: From Deep Ecology to Social Justice* (London: Routledge, 1993), p. 34.
10. Martha F. Lee, 'Environmental Apocalypse: The Millennial Ideology of "Earth First!"', in Thomas Robbins and Susan J. Palmer (eds.), *Millennium, Messiahs and Mayhem: Contemporary Apocalyptic Movements* (New York and London: Routledge, 1997), pp. 119–37. Cf. Martha F. Lee, *Earth First! Environmental Apocalypse* (Syracuse, NY: Syracuse University Press, 1995).

We may note the paradox: immersion in nature can issue in a *voluntarism*. Such immersion issues in a form of transcendence in which the reconstruction of the human place-in-nature is required and action is thereby demanded. Deep ecology is, we might say, a profoundly moral movement. Whether or not these deep ecology commitments continue to permeate the Earth First! movement is doubtful, although Dave Foreman was strongly attracted to such views early in the movement's history. There is some evidence that the British variant of Earth First! was also initially influenced by deep ecology but there has been little sustained theoretical engagement in Britain.[11] The leading deep ecologists are American, Canadian and Australian, including George Sessions and Warwick Fox. None the less, the founder of the philosophical movement is usually taken to be Norwegian philosopher, Arne Naess, whose book, *Ecology, Community and Lifestyle* (an indirect translation from the Norwegian of *Økologi, samfunn og livsstil*, 1976), is regarded as an important statement of the philosophical basis of deep ecology.[12] Deep ecology has attracted the fiercest criticism: it has been charged with misanthropy and racism, not least by leading social ecologist, Murray Bookchin, whose work is the subject of chapter 5. Arguably, the environmental movement in the USA has been damaged by these choleric, testosterone-fuelled disagreements.[13]

How deep is 'deep ecology'?

What, then, are deep ecology's basic philosophical commitments? Deep ecology holds to the 'universal' aspect of nature. To amend Margaret Thatcher's dictum a little, nature cannot be bucked. However, this is nature not in its particularity and variety but in its 'universal' aspect. One of its leading exponents, George Sessions, summarises deep ecology thus: 'The crucial paradigm shift the Deep Ecology movement envisions . . . involves the move from an anthropocentric to a spiritual/ecocentric value orientation. The wild ecosystems and species on the earth have intrinsic value and the right to exist, and are also necessary for the ecological health of the planet and the ultimate well-being of humans.'[14]

11. Derek Wall, *Earth First and the Anti-Roads Movement* (London and New York: Routledge, 1999), pp. 40ff.
12. Arne Naess, *Ecology, Community and Lifestyle* (Cambridge University Press, 1989).
13. Andrew Light, 'Bookchin as/and Social Ecology', in Andrew Light (ed.), *Social Ecology after Bookchin* (New York: Guilford Press, 1998), pp. 1–23.
14. Sessions (ed.), *Deep Ecology for the 21st Century*, p. xxi.

Yet deep ecology is no single tendency, philosophically or as a political movement. A good place to start is to ask: what is meant by 'deep'? Although of course the adjective is contrasted with 'shallow' in its original formulation by Arne Naess[15] (and subsequently partly withdrawn) and thereby has pejorative overtones,[16] the principal meaning, as Warwick Fox has conclusively shown, refers to a formal method of 'deep questioning'.[17] This method, formulated by Naess, seeks to ask questions at a profound level about environmental degradation. 'Deep' refers to the profundity of social change yet it also refers to a formal method of questioning.[18]

Such a formal method has been used rhetorically by its proponents to privilege, at least since 1983–4, deep ecology as the only way of reflecting seriously and rigorously on human incursions into nature. However, this is not to say that deep ecology comprises a single tendency in the political theory of nature. Both Sessions and Fox are reframing deep ecology by attention to largely neglected aspects of the work of Naess. (In the process Sessions has disavowed some of his earlier work with Bill Devall.[19]) Such reframing concentrates upon the theme of the philosophy of self in deep ecology largely by drawing on the philosophical commitments of Naess's own writings.[20]

Such a development is more ambiguous than at first appears. Naess, the originator of 'deep ecology', has stressed the importance of grasping deep ecology as a 'platform'. That is, the appeal of deep ecology can unite a range of people with differing philosophical and religious views around a common platform. Recently, Naess has stressed this point as a way of keeping the environmental movement strong: the deep ecology platform unites by abstracting its position from basic principles. (For example, Naess has his own philosophical position, which he calls

15. Arne Naess, 'The Shallow and the Deep, Long Range Ecology Movements: A Summary' (1973), reprinted in Sessions (ed.), *Deep Ecology for the 21st Century*, pp. 151–5.
16. Pepper, *Modern Environmentalism*, p. 37.
17. Fox, *Toward a Transpersonal Ecology*, pp. 91f.
18. Naess, 'Deepness of Questions and the Deep Ecology Movement', p. 204.
19. See Sessions (ed.), *Deep Ecology for the 21st Century*, pp. xiii–xiv.
20. This strategy seems to be working. A recent collection of critical essays on deep ecology focuses almost exclusively on the work of Naess: Eric Katz, Andrew Light and David Rothenberg (eds.), *Beneath the Surface: Critical Essays in the Philosophy of Deep Ecology* (Cambridge, MA and London: MIT Press, 2000). A further development is the presentation of all ecocentric inquiries as having their home beneath the deep ecology umbrella – such a tendency can be detected in the eclectic nature of the contributions in the recent collection of essays edited by George Sessions, *Deep Ecology for the 21st Century*. Val Plumwood, 'The Ecopolitics Debate and the Politics of Nature', in Karen J. Warren (ed.), *Ecological Feminism* (London and New York: Routledge, 1994), pp. 64–87, has commented interestingly on the way that focusing on deep ecology may have inhibited ecological discussion.

'Ecosophy T'.[21] Yet to participate in the deep ecology movement is not necessarily to subscribe to this position.) While tactically advantageous, we shall see later that this move creates serious difficulties for the theologian.

Although it is a travesty of the position to claim that deep ecology privileges nature over humanity, the platform has moved in an ecocentric direction. Of course, the deep ecology movement has always been critical of 'anthropocentrism': part of the original rationale for setting out the deep ecology position was to stress how the environmental movement is not concerned solely with 'better' management of the environment. In 1973, Naess proposed seven points to describe the deep ecology position.[22] In 1984, this position was amended to eight (with the notable elimination of the concept of 'class').[23]

The 1973 platform begins with an ontological claim: the notion of humanity-placed-in-its-environment must be supplanted by 'the relational, total-field image'.[24] In this context, 'relational' refers to the philosophy of internal relations in which relations are treated as mutually constitutive. Humanity is therefore constituted by its relations with its natural conditions.

From this basic ontological claim, judgments of value follow. For Naess contends that, given such ontological commitments, all forms of life have an equal right to live. With this view is associated the preference to maintain the maximum diversity of species. The ontological commitments support the view that diversity, and its promotion, are central to a true understanding of the myriad forms of life. Four 'lesser' principles now follow: these set out certain requirements in human behaviour. To begin, the deep ecology platform, in this earlier version, includes the overcoming of class divisions (for it is easy to see how the affirmation of a straight diversity could include the affirmation of the 'diversity' of class). With this we are treated to principles of resistance to pollution and resource depletion and the commitment to complexity and decentralisation. These last can be seen to derive, in a loose way, from the first axiological principle: the affirmation of the right to life. To stress the right to live is also to proscribe the conditions which are inimical to life: among these are the depletion of resources, an overconfidence in the face of the complexity of the web of nature, and overcentralisation.

21. Naess, *Ecology, Community and Lifestyle*, ch. 7.
22. Naess, 'The Shallow and the Deep, Long Range Ecology Movements', pp. 151–5.
23. Arne Naess, 'The Deep Ecological Movement: Some Philosophical Aspects' (1986), reprinted in Sessions (ed.), *Deep Ecology for the 21st Century*, pp. 64–84.
24. Naess, 'The Shallow and the Deep, Long Range Ecology Movements', p. 151.

The 1984 platform, concentrating on matters of value and practice, is subtly different. (Indeed, the earlier platform is not much commented upon now – their author claims that these seven points 'smacked too much of the special metaphysics of a younger Naess'.[25]) Much of the position is set out in the first two points: an affirmation of the well-being of forms of life which are understood as having value in their own right. With this emphasis comes again a stress on the importance of the diversity of life forms – a diversity which has value in its own right. From here, six points of practice follow: that human beings should wherever possible respect this diversity, that a smaller human population is required to respect such diversity, that human interference in nature is excessive, and that it must therefore change, that the emphasis must be upon quality of life and that those who support the platform should act in support of it.

Commonalities between these two versions suggest, despite subsequent changes in emphasis, that deep ecology comprises (1) a new metaphysics (embracing both cosmology and world view) and (2) a philosophy of (an expansive) self. The implications of the new metaphysics and account of self require (3) a new anthropology and (4) a new ethics, both of which are 'ecocentric'. The new anthropology stresses the place of humanity in nature – 'Nature knows best', as Barry Commoner noted – and the new ethics insists on the intrinsic value of nature. Some commentators begin with the 'new' theory of value: for instance, John Rodman argues that what is distinctive about the ecological sensibility (which includes deep ecology) are the themes of value, metaphysics and ethics.[26] I consider that this is no longer accurate. The most recent work in the philosophy of deep ecology stresses metaphysical aspects – the situation of the self – in which a theory of value is grounded. I comment further on this below.

To return to the presentation of the two platforms in deep ecology, several differences should give us pause for thought. The omission of class in the later formulation is interesting – although its significance is difficult to assess.[27] Furthermore, the second version moves away from a *specific* metaphysical formulation and thereby from the *particular* account of intrinsic value which attracted so much criticism in the first version. However, if we highlight these differences between the two different versions of the platform, the only way of addressing the tensions is by attending

25. Naess, 'The Deep Ecology "Eight Points" Revisited', p. 221.
26. Rodman, 'Four Forms of Ecological Consciousness Reconsidered', p. 126.
27. In Naess, *Ecology, Community and Lifestyle*, pp. 208f., there is further discussion of class.

to the *philosophical* basis of deep ecology. If there are difficulties or inconsistencies at the level of the political platform, the only place where these can be addressed is by attention to the philosophical basis of deep ecology which is the root and guarantor of the political platform. As we have seen, it is just this move that Naess has resisted. For, as he correctly surmises, there is less chance of agreement on the philosophical basis than on the political platform.

Despite the founder's view, other deep ecologists, primarily Warwick Fox and Freya Mathews, have stressed that what is distinctive about deep ecology is its philosophical basis.[28] What is constitutive of deep ecology, for Fox, is not the platform – which is general – nor the formal method of questioning – which is false – but rather the philosophical basis. Further, Fox makes his own proposal – a 'transpersonal psychology' – as the basis for deep ecology. Freya Mathews also has pointed out that deep ecology requires a 'metaphysics of connectedness' and has as yet failed to supply one.[29] (It is thus somewhat ironic that the later 1984 platform jettisons all references to metaphysics.) This development towards metaphysics within deep ecology is helpful for the theologian. For I am interested here in the ways in which deep ecology may as a metaphysics obscure or reveal the common realm of God, nature and humanity.

Before moving to the theological analysis of the philosophical basis, I wish to note the significance of this shift of attention from deep ecology's political platform to its philosophical basis. Some commentators have suggested that deep ecology is becoming less amenable to Christian restatement.[30] At one point, in which there was agreement that deep ecology was above all a political platform, a Christian version of deep ecology was presented as a genuine possibility. Thus deep ecology, suggest Devall and Sessions, 'attempts to articulate a comprehensive religious and philosophical world view'.[31] Later they proposed Francis of Assisi and Giordano Bruno as Christian sources for the development of deep ecology. Naess has also accepted that there could be a variety of normative philosophical and/or religious systems which form the philosophical basis of the political platform.[32]

28. Fox, *Toward a Transpersonal Ecology*, part 3.
29. Freya Mathews, *The Ecological Self* (London: Routledge, 1993), p. 148.
30. I think that this is part of the point made by Katherine Dell, 'Green Ideas in the Wisdom Tradition', *Scottish Journal of Theology* 47:4 (1994), 423–51 (423–5).
31. Devall and Sessions, *Deep Ecology*, p. 65.
32. Naess, 'The Deep Ecological Movement', p. 79. See also, for a discussion of the biblical themes, Naess, *Ecology, Community and Lifestyle*, pp. 183–9.

The more recent development – which explicitly seeks to articulate the philosophical basis of the movement – is clearly more precise regarding the presuppositions of deep ecology. In the sense that a certain 'looseness' seems to be disappearing from the theory of deep ecology, the theologian will find it more difficult to affirm deep ecology. Or, more carefully, the resources being employed by deep ecologists towards the formulation of the philosophical basis, are not, I think, amenable to theology. The theoretical substructure of the platform, we might say, is being *politicised*. In the name of theoretical clarity and distinctiveness, deep ecology is seeking to present itself as a political *philosophy* as well as a political *platform*.[33]

Given that the formal method of questioning is to be rejected, as Fox recommends, I see no logical reason why the Christian theologian cannot engage with deep ecology in a discussion over philosophical fundamentals. Of course, deep ecologists are now proposing philosophical bases that are not Christian. But I do not see that this rules out – as a matter of method – a Christian basis.[34] Indeed, for the purposes of the current inquiry, it is easier to engage with the movement: the understanding of nature, rather than the environmental platform, is now privileged. However, even allowing for the possibility of a Christian metaphysics as the basis for deep ecology,[35] the dominant tendency in the political philosophy of deep ecology is – in my view – towards the development of a metaphysics of self which is not tractable to theological interpretation.

We are now in a position to note the structure of deep ecology: for Naess, it comprises four levels and a method. The method of deep questioning has been rejected by Warwick Fox as distinctive of deep ecology. That leaves the levels. One of the levels is the political platform of deep ecology which is preceded by the level of the philosophical basis of deep ecology. 'Above' the platform are two further levels – which do not concern my argument – of 'general normative principles' and 'particular rules and

---

33. Naess's political philosophy is subjected to sustained scrutiny in Katz, Light and Rothenberg (eds.), *Beneath the Surface*.
34. Here Dell, 'Green Ideas in the Wisdom Tradition', confuses levels: she considers that the philosophical basis of the later deep ecology is both given and inimical to Christianity. If the first point is granted, the second is certainly true. However, I dispute that the movement has in fact settled on a philosophical basis. Indeed, even if it did so, there remains no logical reason why the basis has to be accepted. If it were the case that the philosophical basis was arrived at by a process of logical deduction from the (agreed) platform, then Dell would be right. But, in fact, deep ecology does not move by way of logical deduction. Instead, it seeks weaker congruencies between the platform and the philosophical basis.
35. Should it come as any surprise here that deep ecology discusses – even if it cannot accept – the metaphysics of process theology? See, *inter alia*, Fox, *Toward a Transpersonal Psychology*, pp. 179f.

decisions adapted to particular situations'.[36] For Fox, although he notes the platform, and rejects the method, deep ecology is fundamentally an ecological *philosophy*. Hence Fox concentrates on the first level: the philosophical basis. What then is 'nature', in this view? What is the 'place' of humanity?

Into the depths: philosophies of deep ecology

To answer these questions, I turn to the writings of Fox and Mathews, drawing on other sources where appropriate.[37] I wish also to stress that both these writers are concerned – directly or indirectly – to move deep ecology away from discussions of value and towards metaphysics and thereby to rescue deep ecology from an identification with value theories in ethics. There is a sense in which the matter of the value of nature has never been Naess's primary concern. This clue is developed explicitly by Fox and is treated in a rather different manner – and from a greater distance – by Mathews. From ethics to cosmology: the reinvention of deep ecology continues. And we should note that this reinvention is partially obscured by the reception of deep ecology: ethical treatments – see Michael Northcott's important book *The Environment and Christian Ethics* – continue to treat deep ecology as in part a theory of ecocentric value.[38] The direction deep ecology seems now to have set for itself is slightly different. Ontology precedes ethics: 'It is … important … to *move from ethics to ontology and back*.'[39] The elaboration of an appropriate ontology for deep ecology is now its central concern.

In his critique of deep ecology, Richard Sylvan notes that deep ecology's value theory can be maintained only through a turn to epistemology and metaphysics. For deep ecology raises questions – in the form of internal critique – as to how value inheres in natural objects. Is such value given? How do we know this? Responding to these demands, Fox and Mathews seek to offer a basic ecophilosophy consonant with the platform of deep ecology. Both are indebted to the work of Arne Naess; both approach the matter by way of a philosophy of the self. Here the similarity ends: Fox draws upon modern psychology, Mathews on the philosophy of the modern natural sciences in the construction of their respective

36. Naess, 'The Deep Ecological Movement', p. 77.
37. Fox, *Toward a Transpersonal Psychology*; Mathews, *The Ecological Self*.
38. Northcott, *The Environment and Christian Ethics*, pp. 105–16.
39. Naess, *Ecology, Community and Lifestyle*, p. 67; italics in original.

ecophilosophies. Different notions of self are operative here. In short, these accounts represent the two ways of approaching the philosophical basis of Deep Ecology: either by way of philosophical psychology or cosmology.

Drawing on the work of Arne Naess, Fox proposes a reinterpretation of the concept of self in the direction of transpersonal psychology. Fox claims that Naess has been influenced strongly by Spinoza and Gandhi's Hinduism. Although Fox moves in a different direction, he claims the authority of Naess's writing in support: 'Naess's philosophical sense of deep ecology obviously refers to a psychologically based approach to the question of our relationship with the rest of nature as opposed to an axiologically based (i.e., a value theory based) approach.'[40] In other words, Naess has never been concerned with moral extensionism but with empathetic extensionism. Fox turns to 'transpersonal psychology' – with its account of a relational self – to make his case. The aim here is 'the realization of a sense of self that extends beyond (or that is *trans-*) one's egoic, biographical or personal sense of self'.[41] Although drawing especially on the work of Abraham Maslow, Fox insists that the introduction of a philosophy of the self is no foreign import into deep ecology. He goes to some lengths to show that transpersonal psychology can be pressed in non-anthropocentric directions *and* that the majority of adherents to deep ecology are concerned to present this notion of an enlarged or expansive self.[42]

Further, Fox claims that axiological approaches to deep ecology – which argue over the intrinsic value of nature – are in fact concerned with providing moral imperatives which *presuppose the existence of an atomistic, volitional self*. In short, being 'moral' requires an account of the 'responsible self' which transpersonal ecology seeks to overcome.

What, then, is the self proposed by Fox? More precisely, how is this an expansive, 'post-moral' conception of self? A transpersonal self expands or increases through three levels of identification: personal, ontological and cosmological. Of the three, Fox finds the last to be decisive. Yet there are problems with all the levels, as we shall see.

On personal identification, Fox claims that: 'Personally based identification refers to experiences of commonality with other entities that are brought about through personal involvement with these entities.'[43] Fox notes several areas of personal identification: family and friends,

40. Fox, *Toward a Transpersonal Psychology*, p. 197.   41. Ibid.
42. Cf. Naess, 'Self-realization: an Ecological Approach to Being in the World,' pp. 225f.
43. Fox, *Toward a Transpersonal Psychology*, p. 249.

locale, clubs and societies, even one's own culture and country. Putting to one side whether or not this is a helpful list, we should note that Fox claims that this is the least *trans*personal form of identification. Indeed, he insists that deep ecology usually focuses on the ontological and cosmological forms of identification because of the weaknesses inherent in personal identification. What are these weaknesses? Primarily, Fox has in mind the duality operative in this form of identification: attention to my immediate circumstance can, of course, be the basis not of my identification with others but rather my assertion of my own, allegedly narrow, interests.[44]

At first sight, this seems to be rather an odd reservation. Is it not central to an ecological politics to bring into view people's sense of their habitat or locale in oppositional ways? For instance, is not the relationship established between city dwellers and the built environment important in the formation of ecological politics? As I look up from typing this on my word-processor, my gaze passes through my window to the municipal park, Horfield Common, which abuts the end of our small garden. It is not much: a small patch of green in the middle of the city of Bristol. Yet local people feel strongly about it (as do I). In 1992, the supermarket chain, Tesco, sought to build another of its stores on land adjacent to the common. The local community was galvanised and sought (unsuccessfully) to resist the building of this new store with its giant car park on Golden Hill. And the store has gradually intensified its presence: it successfully applied in 1996 to open on Sundays despite an agreement – made at the time of the application to build the store – to open only six days a week. Tesco then made a further application to extend its weekly opening hours from 7. 30 a.m. to 10 p.m. When I hear or read reports that Tesco has now overtaken Sainsbury as Britain's leading food retailer (whatever that means), I know that this was achieved in part through decisions taken far away which have allowed a substantial intrusion into the locality of Horfield.

There are, of course, weaknesses with identification with one's locality. But some of us did learn through the summer of 1992 of the power of big business, of the deep relations between business and central government and of the part cravenness, part powerlessness of local elected officials. Interpreted thus, I consider such 'personal identification' to be deeply oppositional. Such impulses towards identification reside in the patterns of friendship of city dwellers towards their built environment. Here we can

44. See ibid., p. 262.

trace one of the crucial theoretical weaknesses of this form of deep ecology: its lack of politics.

What are the roots of this lack of politics? The problem resides in the concept of identification promoted by this variant of deep ecology. For identification, as Richard Sylvan has noted, suggests identity.[45] Yet the deep ecology position resists identity with one's locality. For such an account of identity, it argues, tends to support selfishness and reinforce egoism. Thus what one identifies with has to be 'at a distance'. Thus deep ecology wishes to hold to a strong reading of identification but draws back from the implications of this at the 'local' level. So it remains unclear what 'identification' means. Given that deep ecology is a form of transpersonal *identification*, such a lack of clarity indicates a weakness.

A different way of approaching this same issue would be to consider the world view projected by deep ecology. With what should a deep ecology world view help one to identify? Not with the local of course. For an ecological perspective must encourage people to 'think globally'. But deep ecology fails to see that people's local identifications may help them to 'think globally'.[46] An ecological world view must assist people to come to a sense of their place in the scheme of things precisely by attention to their own place. A world view operates through a number of levels, from the local to the global. However, it is the first level that is eschewed by deep ecology. Yet this leads to a very thin description of the urban, built environment where most people live. Nor should it come as any surprise that deep ecology does not issue in a political theory, precisely an ecological politics.[47] In such fashion, deep ecology contributes – like other political styles, as Timothy Bewes has shrewdly argued – to its own de-politicisation.[48] One should not, so the argument goes, entertain personal commitments of identification; rather one should encourage 'natural', 'spontaneous' (the words are Fox's) levels of identification beyond the personal. But this suggests not so much an ecological politics as an ideology of 'the natural'. Thus there persists, as Michael Northcott and Val Plumwood have pointed out, a problem of abstraction and rationalisation here.[49] Instead of highlighting how

45. Richard Sylvan, 'A Critique of Deep Ecology', part 2, *Radical Philosophy* 41 (1985), 10–22 (10).
46. Of course, it may be important to act and think locally as well as act and think globally: see Rosemary Radford Ruether, *Gaia and God*, p. 272; James O' Connor, *Natural Causes: Essays in Ecological Marxism* (New York: Guilford Press, 1998), p. 300.
47. Sylvan, 'A Critique of Deep Ecology', part 2, 14.
48. Timothy Bewes, *Cynicism and Postmodernity* (London: Verso, 1997), pp. 186–7.
49. Northcott, *The Environment and Christian Ethics*, pp. 116–18; Val Plumwood, 'Nature, Self and Gender: Feminism, Environmental Philosophy and the Critique of Rationalism', in Robert Elliot (ed.), *Environmental Ethics* (Oxford University Press, 1995), pp. 162–4.

economic forces inform a local situation, Fox's forms of identification seem rather to ape the 'at a distance' actions of economic forces in such a fashion as to deny, in a rationalising, abstract manner, the importance of place and particularity.

Writing in the 'foundations of Deep Ecology', Freya Mathews's position is better placed to engage with the problem of locality. She notes that a central problem for deep ecology is whether or not the affirmation of the cosmos as a self-realising and maintaining being invites careful attention to place and habitation. As long as matter continues, why worry about the precise form? Is not a strip mine merely the alteration in the material of a landscape? As long as the cosmic self persists in the pursuit of its conatus, why worry about temporary forms of matter amidst the long-term flux?[50] Such a view could be consonant with the destruction of selves and entities. Mathews turns the argument around by insisting that identification with the cosmic self invites the affirmation of the forms of life below the level of the cosmos; my relation to the cosmos is thereby mediated by these other teleological configurations of life. Such spiritual affirmation invites us to view the actually existing systemic selves as important and not as vortices in the flux of matter. She could also add, I think, that her position insists on biocentric egalitarianism (the equal right of all selves to flourish on account of the omnipresence of 'background value'), the affirmation of the diversity of species and the stress on respect for the vital needs (including the requirement to survive) of selves.[51]

Nevertheless, what is missing from this account is a discussion of the interrelation of the selves. Consider the argument that societies are self-realising systems and are thereby to be described as selves (and so have intrinsic value). Ecological problems do not arise solely from the fact, as Mathews claims, that our cosmology or world view does not permit us to see the reality of ecological interconnectedness. They also reside in the fact that a society has active relations with non-human nature towards the securing of inputs of energy. These inputs are largely associated with agriculture, natural energy resources and information. None of these are, in Mathews's analysis, selves. Thus it is hard to know whether they should be respected or not. Deep ecology abandons notions of hierarchy by affirming the equality of all selves but at the price of sharp political analysis. In other words, what needs philosophical attention is not merely the co-constitutive movements between humanity and nature but also the

---

50. Mathews, *The Ecological Self*, p. 160.   51. Ibid., pp. 126, 127, 128.

structures and tendencies of these processes. What Mexican indigenous people wish to know is how their commitment to an 'identification with their native earth' in defence of a 'sustainable ecology'[52] is clarified by deep ecology's critique of local identification. What Welsh miners wish to know is how such interconnectedness illuminates their transformation of a landscape even to the detriment of their own health, and how the turn to other sources of energy will acknowledge their commitment to the provision of coal. What Indian workers at the Union Carbide 'plant' in Bhopal need to know is how the stress on interconnectedness can give an account of the structures by which their bodies were treated as instrumentalised nature. How does a naturalist stress on interconnection highlight these issues? None of these, in my judgment, are open to analysis by the conceptual apparatus proposed by Mathews.

We come now to the second level. Fox proposes, as we have seen, three levels of identification: the personal, the ontological and the cosmological. In the second, ontological, level identification refers to 'the fact . . . that things *are*'. This facticity impresses us so strongly that we have a sense of the actuality of things in contrast to the nothingness that might have been.[53] So here Fox is concerned with what Paul Tillich once termed 'ontological shock'. It is Hamlet's question: to be or not to be? Why is there something rather than nothing?[54] Elaborating on this theme, Fox argues that this way of experiencing the world builds 'a deep but impartial sense of identification with all existents'. Fox readily grants there is no logical connection operative here: ontological shock is not the cause of ecological awareness. He argues, however, that sustained spiritual discipline in the acknowledgment that there is something rather than nothing can contribute to a commitment to acknowledging the presence of things. We might say, perhaps, that we have here a sense of the graced presentness of things.[55]

There are two difficulties with such a view. First, we should note that there is an ambiguity in Fox's admission that there is no logical connection between a sense of the mystery of presence and ecological awareness. For, as the history of existentialism shows, a sense of the mystery of being

52. James Petras, 'Latin America: The Resurgence of the Left', *New Left Review* 223 (1997), 17–47 (43).
53. See Fox, *Toward a Transpersonal Psychology*, p. 251.
54. Paul Tillich, *Systematic Theology* (London: SCM Press, 1987), I, p. 14; cf. Martin Heidegger, *An Introduction to Metaphysics* (New Haven and London: Yale University Press, 1959), p. 1.
55. Joseph Sittler, *Essays on Nature and Grace* (Philadelphia: Fortress Press, 1972), p. 88.

can be interpreted in negative, as in the existentialism of Jean-Paul Sartre, rather than positive ways. Although Fox concedes that this 'negative' reaction is a logical possibility, he does not show why it is a reaction that ought to be avoided. Additional reasons need to be offered to interpret the presence of being 'positively' rather than 'negatively'. And, as John Macquarrie has shown, these reasons are neither obvious nor compelling.[56] In short, such an inquiry forces a question about meaning. It is not obvious what the answer to this question should be: either courage in the face of anxiety over meaning or an affirmation of absurdity and the descent into nausea.[57]

Second, the concept of identification is here unclear. How does the act of identification relate to the passivity of meditation? One aspect of Heidegger's work invites a sustained meditative attitude towards the world as the key way of overcoming the technical mindset which treats the world as 'standing reserve' – as available for human use.[58] Yet such a stress on meditative receptivity does not fit well with the matter of identification. This problem is, in fact, noted by Fox: those deep ecologists influenced by Heidegger stress 'openness', he writes, rather than identification.[59] But openness is not identification. It is receptive, not expansive. It suggests a givenness to the 'environment' of the self; it suggests religious themes of the graceful givenness or gift character of the world. To join up with the previous point, openness suggests paying attention to the local and the particular. Although there are the most severe difficulties with Heidegger's view, that does not at all diminish the problem of relating 'openness' to 'identification'.

The politics of deep ecology

The third level of identification is 'cosmological'. Fox treats this as the most important level (while granting that those influenced by Heidegger will find the ontological level to have priority). What is cosmological identification? Coming to a 'realisation of the fact [sic] that we and all other entities are aspects of a single unfolding reality'; acquiring 'a sense of commonality with all other creatures'; developing an 'impartial identification

---

56. John Macquarrie, *Studies in Christian Existentialism* (London: SCM Press, 1966), pp. 16f.
57. The terms refer of course to the early work of Albert Camus and Jean-Paul Sartre.
58. See my 'Imaging God: Creatureliness and Technology', *New Blackfriars* 79:928 (1998), 260–74 (264).
59. Fox, *Toward a Transpersonal Psychology*, pp. 250–2.

with all particulars'.[60] The implications of this position are bolder than is obvious at first sight: for the key relationship of friendship is secured through this identification. Yet the friendship is construed in such fashion that it is possible that we, as a species, shall be required, through our sensibility of identification, to give up our interests in survival. If our interests lead to the diminution or termination of the realisation of other entities, then our interests are called into question.

In a pertinent criticism, Michael Northcott suggests that this notion of cosmological identification requires 'incorporating the other into self'. Rather than privileging the importance of limits in human interaction with nature, this notion of an expansive self effectively abolishes such limits – and encourages such abolition. Such a position erases key aspects of difference between humanity and non-human nature (here Northcott draws on the work of Val Plumwood) and thereby has the appearance of challenging the Western obsession with the concept of the self. Yet, in fact, such a view *perpetuates* the Eurocentric affirmation of self by incorporating all that which is not self into the expansive self.[61]

We can go further: the logic is totalitarian, the politics that of identity, the totality that of the 'whole' of the expansive self. The deep ecology position, as presented by Fox, is now seen to be a form of 'act-based' idealism whose roots lie in the work of Rousseau and Fichte (rather than Spinoza and Gandhi). The expansive 'natural self' forms the core of the theory. Yet, of course, such a self never meets resistance for it operates with no genuine account of otherness or difference. Such a self is precisely self-enclosed. It is never broken and remade through its encounters for its mode of relation is assimilation. Thus this self never negotiates but rather incorporates. In this precise sense, its logic is totalitarian. If an established and well-founded democracy, as Adam Przeworski suggests, may be defined as 'a system in which the politically relevant forces subject their values and interests to the uncertain play of democratic institutions,'[62] the deep ecology position has no conceptual place for the democratic play of negotiation. In short, we begin to approach the theoretical roots of a point made earlier: deep ecology lacks a political theory and lapses unwittingly into authoritarianism.

60. Ibid., pp. 252, 258, 256.   61. Northcott, *The Environment and Christian Ethics*, p. 115.
62. Cited by John Markoff, 'Really Existing Democracy: Learning from Latin America in the Late 1990s', *New Left Review* 223 (1997), 48–68 (59).

Of course, Arne Naess has strongly resisted the charge that deep ecology is fascist.

> The Deep Ecological requirement of "wide" ecological sustainability (protecting the full richness and diversity of Life on Earth), however, limits the kinds of Green societies that would be acceptable. Because the intrinsic value, respect and support of deep cultural differences are viewed ... on a par with attitudes to richness and diversity of non-human life forms, and social or political trends of the fascist or Nazi kind runs [*sic*] counter to the requirements of full ecological sustainability.[63]

Yet we have seen that the attitudes towards the richness and diversity of life forms are not securely grounded in the otherness and difference of those forms. So it is not reassuring to learn that respect for human groups and cultures is secured by analogical reference to the failure to secure natural differences. In this sense, deep ecology yearns for a utopia which is not securely based in some form of democratic ideal.

Freya Mathews's position is also open to objections along these lines. If a green society may be, on her account, understood to be a 'self' pursuing its own conatus, what is the relation between the *telos* of the social system and that of selves within that society? Mathews can, of course, appeal to the affirmation of diversity and the participation of all forms in intrinsic value. Yet, if it can be shown that the society in question has a natural cosmology and culture – that is, a culture which stresses the ecological relatedness of that society – on what grounds are the needs of selves of which no account is being taken or whose existence is actively threatened to be defended? Is not the self-realising system or society which Mathews proposes at least – to put it no more strongly – *compatible* with non-democratic political arrangements?[64]

However, despite some discussion in the literature, I do not wish to suggest that deep ecology in any way exhibits fascist tendencies. For example, Michael Zimmerman has pointed to what he regards as two worrying trends in the American environmental movement: a tendency towards neo-Malthusian arguments and a decrying of some of the gains of modernity. His analysis has been challenged by Val Plumwood who argues that

63. Naess, 'The Deep Ecology "Eight Points" Revisited', pp. 219–20.
64. In making these comments, I do not wish to base my arguments on the flimsy argumentation proposed by Luc Ferry, *The New Ecological Order* (University of Chicago Press, 1995), especially pp. 59–90. For a refutation of Ferry's argument, see John Clark, 'Aujourd'hui l'écologie?,' *Terra Nova* 1 (1996), 112–19.

the principal political danger is that deep ecology will become captive to the political, liberal, right rather than proto-fascist forces.[65] Clearly, there is an important issue here: by which political forces may deep ecology be suborned? However, in my view, none of this discussion points to the conclusion of a convergence of deep ecology and fascism. According to Roger Griffin, fascism may be defined as 'a palingenetic [to do with rebirth] form of populist ultra-nationalism'.[66] Given such a definition, deep ecology is not accurately described as fascist. Of course, some overlap may exist: fascism also, in part, opposes modernity and is authoritarian, but its core commitments lie elsewhere. What perhaps is more pertinent in the critical consideration of deep ecology is its authoritarianism, especially with reference to democracy.

That deep ecology operates with an account of the politics of identity is easily traced with reference to the concept of commonality. Fox repeatedly argues that cosmological identification invites a view of human commonality with the rest of the natural order. But what is the basis of this commonality? How is it known? As we have seen, the basis lies in the realisation of the self. We must move, Fox insists, beyond consideration of *similarities* between humanity and otherkind towards the consideration of *commonality* (always in the singular).[67] Fox resists the suggestion that this is identity thinking: in considering the commonality between myself and a tree, Fox claims, I do not consider myself to be a tree.

That, however, is not the only possible reading of identity. In rejecting simple identity, Fox fails to see that what he calls identification must mean identity by incorporation. That is, the deep ecology position reduces the otherness of that which is not (my)self to a single quality – 'we and all other entities are aspects of a single unfolding reality' – towards incorporation. The multiplicity, variety and particularity of otherness is obscured through the claim that all things are basically the same and can thereby be incorporated into my expansive self. So, although Fox insists, against Sylvan, that identification does not mean identity, this is – given the wider theoretical commitments of deep ecology – merely an assertion.

65. Michael E. Zimmerman, 'Ecofascism: a Threat to American Environmentalism', in Roger Gottlieb (ed.), *The Ecological Community* (London and New York: Routledge, 1997), pp. 229–54; Michael E. Zimmerman, 'Possible Political Problems of an Earth-Based Religiosity', in Katz, Light and Rothenberg (eds.), *Beneath the Surface*, pp. 151–94; Val Plumwood, 'Deep Ecology, Deep Pockets and Deep Problems', in Katz, Light and Rothenberg (eds.), *Beneath the Surface*, pp. 59–84.

66. Roger Griffin (ed.), *Fascism* (Oxford University Press, 1995), introduction, p. 4.

67. Fox, *Toward a Transpersonal Psychology*, p. 231.

We should note also an important epistemological commitment: the capacity for identification is known by the monological voice which incorporates the variety of the world into itself. It is knowledge by power: the construal of sameness towards its incorporation. (The appeal to 'intuition' as the basis of cosmological identification merely serves to obscure this point.)

To be fair to deep ecology, Freya Mathews has noted this problem of the relation between self-realisation (the 'expansion' of the human self) and other selves. Approaching the matter by way of the concept of the cosmos rather than the concept of self, Mathews proposes a metaphysics of substance monism derived from the philosophy of the natural sciences and related to the metaphysics of Spinoza. The detail of her position need not detain us here. She does, however, claim that in the post-Einsteinian universe we need a new account of individuation. If the new scientific cosmology rules out 'substance' as the principle of individuation, how is the individual to be established? Mathews's answer draws on systems theory and Spinoza: the new definition of the individual is the systemic, conative self. Thus the definition of substantiality is that of systemic selfhood in which the self seeks its own realisation or maintenance. An entity which has some of the marks of the system – stability, homeostasis, feedback loops, etc. – and the marks of self-realisation – *telos*, self-interest, agency, self-evaluation – may be counted as a self. The most obvious instance of a self is, of course, the organism. In addition, although it does not enjoy the feature of systemic openness, Mathews proposes that the cosmos itself is a special instance of self.[68]

Such a set of commitments allows for the development of the position maintained by Fox. For Mathews can show how it is that, from her position, the self which is the human organism can see itself as part of the metaphysics of interconnectedness and can thereby register in awe and wonder its place in the whole. Her position demonstrates its real strength, however, in the face of a different issue: for the notion of self-realisation only makes sense if the cosmos is the sort of place which supports such realisation. What if the cosmos was itself inert and devoid of meaning? What if the cosmos was as much destroyer as creator? The claim to the cosmos as self allows Mathews to insist that self-realisation on the part of the human organism is part of a wider, cosmic self-realisation. Whereas Fox's position tends to look like an act of aggrandisement by the self, Mathews can appeal

68. Mathews, *The Ecological Self*, pp. 91–116.

to a wider cosmological context of self-realisation in which the conative will-to-exist of the systemic self is placed.

Yet now the politics of identity resurfaces at a different level. Whereas Fox's transpersonal self incorporates other selves, for Mathews my aim of self-realisation unites me with the cosmos:

> It is through my conatus that I, and other selves, achieve oneness with the ecocosm ['the universe seen as a self-realizing system']. Recognition of the fact that my conatus unites me with the ecocosm, which is thus seen to be my greater Self, in itself expands the scope of my conatus: my will-to-exist now encompasses the wider systems of Nature.[69]

However, such a position trades upon the ambivalence between whole/part in this style of thinking. Whole and part coincide in the identity of the conative aspects of the cosmic and human self. Here two levels of self-realisation meet. But such a result can be achieved only if my self-realisation makes a contribution to the realisation of the cosmic self – a position which Mathews explicitly endorses.[70]

Which means that the whole of the cosmic self is determined by my conative will: a curious understanding of the whole! That is, for her position to be successful, Mathews must allow for the 'wholes' of self-realising systemic selves to qualify the cosmic self. Needless to say, this lapses into logical nonsense. The only other way to go is to insist on the primacy of the cosmic whole. But this places us in a determinism which Mathews wishes to avoid. Mathews is right to propose some account of a cosmic 'law of being'. But the result is to fall into a naturalism which she is trying, I think, to avoid. If there is a common conatus, then self-realisation takes place within an enclosed deterministic system; if there is to be freedom and genuine self-realisation, Mathews's account of the cosmic self requires revision.

I claimed above that deep ecology operates with the totality or whole of the expansive self. We have seen some of the theoretical commitments that such a view entails. But we can see also that this privileging of a 'natural self' issues in an ideology of the natural. Given that the self has the capacity to engage in expansive identification – although this capacity may need to be recovered and then educated – the basic goodness of the self is affirmed. In that commonality turns upon the incorporation of the goodness of other natural entities, the affirmation of a general goodness in nature is affirmed. Mathews is explicit on this point: all of the cosmos

---

69. Ibid., p. 155.   70. Ibid.

enjoys a basic level of value.[71] Yet how that relates to evil in nature (which includes evil in human nature of course) remains unclear. Furthermore, although deep ecology might consider itself to be in opposition to the moral extensionism of, say, the utilitarian ethicist Peter Singer, there is a form of extensionism operative here. Instead of moral extensionism we have idealist extensionism. The 'whole' posited is that of the expansive self which incorporates all other entities.

Is this not, however, a *shallow*, that is, anthropocentric, position? Value is here located in the self and is bestowed through incorporation of others. At least the intrinsic value approaches are able to rely upon a theory of value in common (which does not mean or imply 'equally in common'). What is truly in common in Fox's position of the inflationary, self-aggrandising self? Mathews can respond to this complaint by arguing that for her the cosmos has intrinsic value. However she insists that each aspect of the cosmos has the same, background, value. But is this true, given her view – reported above – of the nature of selves?

Fox claims that deep ecology is thoroughly 'this-worldly'. In fact, the notion of the expansive self has sustained difficulties engaging with the world. In that it seems to propose a substantive view of selves-in-commonality which does not relate well to the actual structures and processes of contemporary global, capitalist, urban life, deep ecology seems strangely *other*-worldly. It fails the 'this-worldly' test in a further sense: its lack of a democratic–ecological political theory, its reduction of the world to a single quality (which includes an affirmation of the quantitative diversity of the single quality: 'may all life forms flourish!') and its monological voice all suggest authoritarian tendencies.

The cosmic heights of deep ecology

Despite all these difficulties, deep ecology remains an important force in green politics. Why? Where lies the attraction of deep ecology? At the end of *The Cosmological Self*, Freya Mathews offers an important clue: deep ecology is also concerned with meaning. That is, in this formulation deep ecology has profound 'religious' commitments. For the correct interpretation of the human self as related to the cosmic self bestows meaning. In one sense, Mathews's position permits the theoretical identification of our

71. So not a gnosticism; or, if this is gnostic, it is without the presence of evil in materiality; we may indeed be god-in-the-process-of-becoming which suggests optimism, perfectibility, modernity.

place in the universe: like every other being, I am 'one' with the universe, the acknowledgment of which may engender feelings of awe and wonder. Here I learn that I am not at all alienated from nature but in fact find my home in it.[72] Yet a more significant account of meaning can be traced from a consideration of the human self in its relation to the cosmic self. As self-realising, my self makes a contribution to the development of the selves in which I am placed. I quote Mathews at some length:

> It is through my conatus that I mirror, and am mirrored in, the wider systems of Nature. It is through my conatus that I, and other selves, achieve oneness with the ecocosm. Recognition of the fact that my conatus unites me with the ecocosm, which is thus seen to be my greater Self, in itself expands the scope of my conatus: my will-to-exist now encompasses the wider systems of Nature . . . Since I am ontologically at one with nature, my conatus actually feeds the cosmic conatus, actually helps to maintain the ecocosm in existence![73]

So the matter is clear at last: we are co-creators with the cosmos. And Mathews proceeds to make a further, even bolder, claim. When we act in support of the cosmos, that is, we practise what Naess and Fox have described as self-realisation, are we connected to the universe in anything more than a voluntaristic sense? Is our joy at seeking to affirm and preserve the conatus of the universe merely accidental or am I in tune with the deepest commitments of the universe itself? Here she suggests that, in our feelings of joyful affirmation of the cosmic conatus, the cosmos is indeed expressed in and through us. Thus the affirmation of the universe is not merely a kind of shadow which falls across an unheeding universe nor is it the invention of those with a rare ecological sensibility. Instead, 'what we call love is perhaps the faint psychological shadow in us of that inner spiritual impulse of which our universe is the external manifestation'.[74] Thus our 'inward' affirmation – love – is the expression of the cosmic will-to-affirmation; by our interiority we are connected to the interiority of the cosmos; by this route my acts of self-realisation – my attempts to identify with other selves, including the cosmos – contribute to cosmic self-realisation. Thus we learn that, despite our concerns about our excessive power as the source of environmental degradation, we are makers of the cosmos after all.

Here Mathews provides the metaphysics missing from the psychology of Fox and Naess. For a central difficulty, as we saw, was how the

72. Mathews, *The Ecological Self*, pp. 149–50.   73. Ibid., p. 155.   74. Ibid., p. 159.

process of self-realisation genuinely related to other selves and whether self-realisation was anything more than a psychological expression of ecological awareness. Yet here we see two contemporary prejudices combine: inward spirituality and psychotherapy. Mathews argues that the real ecological work may in fact be such self-cultivation: the development in ourselves of 'the spirit of pure self affirmation, the well spring of "love", that creates and perpetuates the universe'. Thus the point of access of the human self to the cosmic self is, finally, psychological (although the range of identification is cosmic) and the aim of the individual is psychotherapeutic establishment of meaning (and for the cosmos the maintenance of its own conatus). What began in cosmology turns upon the spirituality of inwardness. And the universe is defined as self-enclosed cosmos. Indeed, its unity is given by reference to the 'interiority' of the cosmic conatus with which the human individual achieves meaning.

In summary, the common realm of God, nature and humanity is displaced by the realm of Nature–cosmic self, neighbourliness is replaced by interior cultivation, otherness is collapsed into the interior will-to-maintenance of the cosmic self, the social life of humanity receives no clear articulation and the place of human beings is not decentred but rather by the route of inwardness is placed at the centre of the cosmos. Here deep ecology appears as decisively modern: centred on the interior life of the individual who creates and preserves the cosmos. I am proposing a different view: by contrast to self-realisation, I suggest friendship; to interconnectedness, I suggest social relationality; to cosmic conatus, I propose the world as gift. In sum, a relational account that accounts for the proximity and difference of nature and which – *contra* this deep stoicism – 'shifts'. Thus the crucial dynamic is not 'from one self to another', but friendship; the crucial ontology is not that of a cosmic conatus, but a common realm.

And yet. Despite my misgivings, Naess's commitment to elaborate on his early view of a 'relational, total-field image' towards an holistic, relational ontology is warmly to be welcomed. Accompanying this ontology is an affirmation of the diversity, complexity and symbiosis of nature. Central to this ontology is a focus on concrete particulars as a way of affirming that our sensuous interaction with nature is not merely subjective but rather may be relied upon as an adequate guide as to what nature is. In other words, the secondary and tertiary qualities that comprise our 'felt' experience of nature are not to be dismissed. Such experience emerges from an understanding of epistemology as relational. Naess speaks approvingly of a dictum of Heraclitus: 'everything flows'.[75] A theological account of the world as becoming, as proposed in part I, converges with such a view. However, Naess's phenomenological epistemology privileges human description of nature. The theme of the otherness of nature is not central to his position.

Despite the oft-repeated claim that the basic problem identified by deep ecology is the severance of humanity from nature, the movement that governs Naess's position seems to be from the human towards nature. A truly relational epistemology might foreground more strongly the otherness of nature as epistemic rupture. In sum, Naess's position, as Eric Katz argues forcefully, is anthropocentric.[76] And part of that anthropocentrism is an undeveloped political theory with an authoritarian logic. A political theology of nature will wish to develop an ontology as radical in intention as the one proposed by deep ecology. However, it will wish to do so in ways that are less indebted to naturalism and which are politically more robust.

75. Naess, *Ecology, Community and Lifestyle*, p. 50.
76. Katz, 'Against the Inevitability of Anthropocentrism', pp. 17–42.

4

Ecofeminism: the reproduction of nature

Women–nature?

Ecofeminist theory makes a highly important contribution to this study. The common realm is not a patriarchal construct nor is it sex/gender blind. The healing of the relations between 'humanity' and nature does not turn upon the fracturing of women's lives nor does the production of nature exclude its reproduction. I have already noted that the requirement to rethink the relations between nature, humanity and God has been proposed in ecofeminist religious thinking. Further, ecofeminist commitments have already been presented: in chapter 2, the model of production was expanded to include vital issues concerning the *re*production of the human. In this chapter certain aspects of ecofeminist philosophy will be considered. Ecofeminism merits treatment at this point in the argument because the theoretical development of ecofeminism has been secured partly by way of the critique of deep ecology.[1]

Important though these considerations are, the crucial contribution that this political theology of nature learns from ecofeminism is the theme of the 'agency of nature'. As Donna Haraway notes: 'Ecofeminists have perhaps been most insistent on some version of the world as active subject.'[2] Of course, such a view of the agency of nature is deeply consonant with the common realm of nature, humanity and God: the tendencies and movements of nature in a mutual yet asymmetrical dynamic indicate *activities* with which un/natural humanity interacts. Humanity indwells nature;

---

1. See further pp. 96–98.
2. Donna J. Haraway, 'Situated Knowledges: The Science Question in Feminism and the Privilege of Partial Perspective', in *Simians, Cyborgs and Women: The Reinvention of Nature* (London: Free Association Books, 1991), pp. 183–201 (p. 199).

nature indwells humanity. However, this account of the co-constitution of nature and humanity – of humanity and nature as co-emergents in a realm sourced to the activity, ground and force of God – is not well presented in standard ecotheology. In political–ideological interpretation, by contrast, the radicality of the co-sociality of humanity and nature privileges the theme of the encounter of nature and humanity. Nature inhabits humanity, humanity inhabits nature: ecofeminism enables political theology of nature to relearn the insight of the agency of nature.[3]

Moreover, there are important affinities between the theological concept of the common realm and the philosophical commitments of some ecofeminisms. In what way? In a memorable formulation, Ariel Salleh proposes an ecofeminist analytic thus: M[en]/W[omen] = N[ature].[4] And this schema has the following valuation: 1/0, in which M has the value of 1 and W and N the value of 0. The strength of ecofeminist analysis is here depicted: there can be no crossing by women over the patriarchal forward-slash to join men, for after such a journey Nature would still be awarded the value, nil. Yet, on account of the forced association of 'Women' with 'Nature', certain epistemic benefit may accrue to those women who act as mediators of nature to men.[5]

To move onward, the relations between Women, Nature and Men must be transformatively reshaped. Therein lies the connection with the common realm of God, nature and humanity: as we have seen, implicit in this concept is the rethinking of the relations between humanity and nature on account of their mutual orientation towards the triune God who is also their author. The significant conceptual advance secured by the common realm is to make problematic the relations between humanity and nature; to suggest that because both are orientated towards God a political theology of nature is free to reconsider the relations between humanity and nature; to present humanity and nature according to their mutual interdependencies as well as modes of transcendence.

Ecofeminist thought is here especially interesting on account of a certain homology between its commitments and the political theology of nature being presented here: the former proposes a double move which seeks the affirmation of nature but not the re-emphasis of the association

---

3. It is instructive that in his *Redeeming the Time: A Political Theology of the Environment* (New York: Continuum, 1997), ch. 5, Stephen Bede Scharper overlooks this point.

4. Ariel Salleh, *Ecofeminism as Politics: Nature, Marx and the Postmodern* (London: Zed Books, 1997), pp. 35–49.

5. See Salleh, *Ecofeminism as Politics*; Vandana Shiva, *Staying Alive*; Mary Mellor, *Feminism and Ecology* (New York University Press, 1997).

of women with nature which devalues both,[6] the latter encourages and supports a view of nature's agency and *telos* in God in a linked, but not identical, manner to humanity's agency and end. A certain parallel is operative here: the common realm seeks to locate human society within natural society, but sees both as authored by and oriented towards God; ecofeminism seeks to affirm the place of humanity in nature, but notes the gendered way this has commonly been done, to the devaluation and domination of both women and nature.

Materially, ecofeminism requires the expansion of the theme of production to include reproduction. The identity of the human in the common realm includes reproductive activities: procreation, and the fulfilment of basic needs (food, water, shelter). To ignore these reproductive activities is to ignore the ways in which, as Ariel Salleh puts it, women mediate nature to men. As I hope to make clear shortly, I reject those attempts to secure mystical or intuitive connections between women and nature.[7] Instead, the case made here draws on the social/ist side of ecofeminism: Salleh writes of the labour of women as a bridge between men and nature as part of the '*women–nature–labour nexus*'; Mary Mellor argues for a 'material relation' between women and nature. That there is a deep and persistent set of connections between the domination of nature and the subjugation of women is the basic claim of ecofeminism. What follows is a brief excursus on how I shall understand this claim towards the sexing/gendering of the common realm.[8]

Sexed/gendered relations, un/natural identities

As a mode of inquiry, ecofeminism is beset by two difficulties: first, to persuade feminists that their position requires them to embrace *eco*feminism; and, second, to persuade ecologists, especially deep ecologists, that gender-blind analyses are insufficiently radical.

In philosophical ecofeminism, several essays by Karen J. Warren are treated as of central importance. With these I shall begin. Although Warren notes that there is little agreement on the 'important connections

---

6. In making this point, I am indicating a preference for social ecofeminism over against affinity or cultural ecofeminism. I shall return to this point in the next section.
7. Stephan Elkins, 'The Politics of Mystical Ecology', *Telos* 82 (1989–90), 52–70.
8. In what follows I shall continue to use the term, ecofeminism. However, I share the reservations of both Janet Biehl and Mary Mellor that this term has come to be associated with affinity or cultural ecofeminism. Biehl, *Finding our Way*, refuses the term; Mellor, *Feminism and Ecology*, prefers 'green feminism'.

between the oppression of women and the oppression of nature', she argues that ecofeminism unites around the following four claims:

> (i) there are important connections between the oppression of women and the oppression of nature; (ii) understanding the nature of these connections is necessary to any adequate understanding of the oppression of women and the oppression of nature; (iii) feminist theory and practice must include an ecological perspective; and (iv) solutions to ecological problems must include a feminist perspective.[9]

How are the connections between these double oppressions to be understood? The key insight is the 'logic of domination' that ecofeminism exposes: such a logic ascribes value to the 'upper' part of dualisms and denies value to the 'lower' part. Thus it is not the division between 'upper' and 'lower' to which ecofeminism objects: distinctions of this kind could be an affirmation of diversity. Instead, that those on the lower side are understood to be inferior and subordinate is the outcome of the logic of domination. In a later essay, Warren reproduces this analysis: the logic of domination is 'explanatorily basic', for it is by such logic that the hierarchies and dualisms are employed as the basis for subordination and domination.[10] Warren's argument, although schematic, is valuable in two ways: first, hierarchies themselves are not dismissed but only those hierarchies incorporated within a logic of domination; second, her account leaves open the significance of the patriarchal identification of women with nature and men with the 'human', culture and reason.[11]

For, as already intimated, there is no agreement in ecofeminism as to the status of the relation between women and nature.[12] There is agreement that the connection between women and nature has been used to place women on the 'down' or inferior side. However, there is less agreement on the way forward: is the connection between women and nature true but instead in need of a positive valuation? Is it then correct to say that women

9. Karen J. Warren, 'Feminism and Ecology: Making Connections,' *Environmental Ethics* 9:1 (1987), 3–20 (4–5).

10. Karen J. Warren, 'The Power and Promise of Ecological Feminism', *Environmental Ethics* 12:2 (1990), 125–46 (126–32).

11. Already answered therefore is Scharper's question to dualisms in ecofeminist theory, see *Redeeming the Time*, pp. 163–4.

12. Roughly speaking, the types of ecofeminism correspond to the types of feminism: liberal, socialist, cultural affinity. That, anyhow, is the way that ecofeminism is usually presented: see Merchant, *Radical Ecology* pp. 183–97, who also discusses a fourth type, dubbed social ecofeminism; Karen J. Warren, 'Introduction' to section on Ecofeminism, in Michael E. Zimmerman (ed.), *Environmental Philosophy: From Animal Rights to Radical Ecology* (Englewood Cliffs, NJ: Prentice-Hall, 1993), pp. 253–67.

are 'closer' to nature and thereby have access to important knowledge towards the healing of ecological relations? Or should ecofeminists be concerned to emancipate women from the association with nature. (Such a move has been common in the politics of nature: as part of a sustained attempt to affirm their full humanity, note Keith Thomas and Ynestra King, emancipation movements have often been concerned to accentuate the difference between themselves and non-human animals.[13]) Or, is the matter, as Val Plumwood suggests, not to be treated merely in terms of either straight reversal or denial?[14]

Finally, as must be clear by now, I think the ecofeminist case is best supported within the theological context offered by the common realm of nature, humanity and God; more on this point in the final section. For the moment, however, I want to note that the style of ecofeminist theory being attended to here is supported by the interpretative interests of the work of women under present patriarchal conditions rather than any 'natural affinity' women may have with 'nature'. Until now, the cultural or affinity tendency has perhaps been the dominant voice in ecofeminism.[15] Characterising affinity or cultural ecofeminism, Mary Mellor writes that such ecofeminism: 'tends to combine a celebration of women-centred values (mothering, nurturing, caring) with a celebration of women's bodies' and understands the difference between women and men in either biological or cosmological terms.[16]

Such a location of difference is not accepted throughout ecofeminism. Mellor characterises responses by radical or social/ist types of ecofeminism to spiritual ecofeminism in the following way: 'Divisions between men and women are not seen either as biologically based or accidents of historical development, but as representing distinct material interests.

---

13. Thomas, *Man and the Natural World*, pp. 48f.; Ynestra King, 'The Ecology of Feminism and the Feminism of Ecology,' in J. Plant (ed.), *Healing the Wounds: The Promise of Ecofeminism* (Philadelphia: New Society Publishers, 1989), pp. 18–28 (pp. 22–3).

14. Plumwood, *Feminism and the Mastery of Nature*, pp. 31f.

15. Two important anthologies – Plant (ed.), *Healing the Wounds*, and Irene Diamond and Gloria Feman Orenstein (eds.), *Reweaving the World: the Emergence of Ecofeminism* (San Francisco: Sierra Club Books, 1990) – feature the cultural voice strongly.

16. Mellor, *Feminism and Ecology*, p. 56. Mellor distinguishes between strong and weak tendencies in cultural ecofeminism: 'Affinity ecofeminism offers a strong and a weak version of the relationship between women and nature, affinity and difference. The first is to assert a strong version of both affinity and difference. This would claim a fundamental difference between men and women based on biology and/or cosmological forces that are irreconcilable (immanent goddess versus patriarchal god) and a direct biological or cosmological link between women and nature. A weaker emphasis on both affinity and difference would see differences between men and women as based on biological and/or cosmological differences that are complementary, and therefore reconcilable, as in the Taoist concept of yin and yang' (p. 57).

Social change will not come from spiritual rebirth, the weaving of dreams or spells or the re-emergence of the "female" as body or spirit, but from active political struggle against the structures and institutions of current society.'[17] I share these objections to affinity ecofeminism and what follows will draw on the social/ist forms of ecofeminism.[18]

Un/natural relations

Ariel Salleh writes: 'What ecofeminism demands is a fully amplified critique of capital's degradation of the "conditions of production", based on a recognition of the *nature–women–labor nexus* as a fundamental contradiction.'[19] We may note, first, that such a nexus is not the only contradiction. But central to the ecofeminist case I am drawing on here is the insistence that attention must be paid to the interrelation between social relations of production and material relations of production. That is, ecofeminism seeks to hold together the intimate relations between human production and human *re*production. As 'women's work', the latter has tended to be rendered invisible in main/malestream ecological thought. Attention is focused on actions in the formal economy with attention paid to processes of extraction and exchange. Of course, attention to the interactions between ecology and production is vital. But the relation between production and reproduction – the capacity of human beings to renew themselves both biologically and socially – remains crucially important. In short, true engagement with the theme of sustainability must

17. Mellor, *Feminism and Ecology*, p. 57. Incidentally, I think that Mellor is incorrect (see ibid., p. 45) in making a connection between theological ecofeminisms and spiritual ecofeminisms. She notes that some ecofeminist theologians owe more to socialist traditions than to the traditions of spirituality. But that judgment is rooted in a lack of awareness of the rather different roots of Christian and spiritual feminism.

18. In coming to this judgment, I have been strongly influenced by Val Plumwood's critique of 'cosmic anthropocentrism'. As will have been evident from my comments on deep ecology in the previous chapter, I detect in some ecotheories precisely an account of anthropocentric cosmology. See Val Plumwood, 'Androcentrism and Anthropocentrism: Parallels and Politics', in Karen J. Warren (ed.), *Ecofeminism: Women, Culture, Nature* (Bloomington and Indianapolis: Indiana University Press, 1997), pp. 327–55. I should add that I am not here making any comment on the charge of 'essentialism' which has been levelled at cultural ecofeminism. My question to cultural ecofeminism is not concerned with its alleged attempt to construct women's identity in too ideal a fashion but instead with its confidence in women's experience as the point of epistemic access to true, oppositional, knowledge under capitalism and the devaluing of political agency which follows, in my view, from such a position.

19. Ariel Salleh, 'Nature, Women, Labor, Capital: Living the Deepest Contradiction', in Martin O'Connor (ed.), *Is Capitalism Sustainable? Political Economy and the Politics of Ecology* (New York and London: Guilford Press, 1994), pp. 106–24 (p. 117).

be extended to cover this area. Too often the excessive use of resources is the focus of inquiries in sustainable development. Yet, in truth, if there is no concern for biological reproduction and adequate social reproduction – the decline of fertility through hazards in the environment, for example, or systemic failures in processes of socialisation on account of the collapse of education systems in urban areas – then what sustainability comprises has been arbitrarily restricted.[20]

Social/ist ecofeminism is thereby concerned to affirm the embodiment of women and women's embeddedness in nature, but in liberatory rather than restrictive ways. For human dependence on embodiment and embeddedness cannot be overcome. Yet the ways in which, as Mellor puts it, 'The needs of human embodiment are shared by all humanity but are disproportionately borne in the bodies and lives of women', requires corrective action.[21] We are referred back to Warren's 'logic of domination'. Human reproduction is not a 'problem'. Instead, the ways in which reproductive labour is regarded as inferior and of little account in ways similar to the objectification, manipulation and abuse of non-human nature needs to be resisted. Nor is the growth in population to be understood as the cause of poverty which in turn – in an instrumentalist, coercive programme – justifies and requires interventions such as sterilisations.[22] It is the association of women with nature – the basic claim of ecofeminism together with the denigration of nature and the domination of nature on account of this association – which is at issue here. Or, as Salleh puts it: 'By proposing that the nature–women–labour nexus be treated as a fundamental contradiction of capitalist patriarchal relations, ecofeminism affirms the primacy of our exploitative gender-based division of labour, and simultaneously shifts the economic analysis towards an ecological problematic.'[23]

Ecofeminism is thereby dedicated to overcoming the destructive capitalist and patriarchal ontology which 'divides History from Nature'.[24] How does ecofeminism do this? By tackling the relationship between socially constructed relationships and the physical realities of embeddedness and embodiment, especially the latter.[25] This is the crucial point: the tension between social production and embeddedness and embodiment, between production and reproduction is the vital theme of ecofeminism.

20. See Merchant, *Radical Ecology*, pp. 8–14.   21. Mellor, *Feminism and Ecology*, p. 183.
22. Maria Mies and Vandana Shiva, *Ecofeminism* (London and New Jersey: Zed Books, 1993), pp. 277–96.
23. Salleh, *Ecofeminism as Politics*, pp. 90–1.   24. Ibid., p. 133.
25. See Mellor, *Feminism and Ecology*, p. 7.

In chapter 2, I noted that the re-relating of humanity and nature could not be achieved except by reference to the concept of God. We are now in a position to note that the un/natural relations of the common realm need to be understood in the perspective of sex/gender; the common realm is a site of gendered conflict. So un/natural identities in the common realm are reproductive: embeddedness in nature and human embodiment are thereby identified as central themes. Whether or not human beings are natural (embedded) or transcendent of nature is not the issue. Rather, a social materialism cannot lose sight of the issue of reproduction: the insight of ecofeminism identifies and counters the mechanics of the domination of women as this relates to the domination/manipulation/control of nature.

That is, in that women are the bridge between men and nature, nature is consistently devalued along with women's labour as the mediator of that nature. Paradoxically, the directness of relations between women and nature may provide a useful indicator of how human–nature relations are to be understood. Not least, un/natural relations are always reproductive: the long-term survivability of the human race turns upon the capacities of human beings to reproduce, biologically and socially. Ecofeminism searches for ways to show how human beings are both natural yet social, reproductive and productive, dependent on physical realities yet transformative of human habitat. This will be a recurrent theme in part III.

Common totality: sexed/gendered relations

Ecofeminist thought in North America and Australia has engaged in an extensive critique of deep ecology.[26] Reprising some themes in that debate provides a useful starting point for grasping the account of totality operative in some ecofeminist theory. Although criticisms of deep ecology are directed towards its politics and strategy, some ecofeminist misgivings focus on the ontology maintained or required by deep ecology. For example,

---

26. Here I am drawing on the following: Plumwood, 'The Ecopolitics Debate and the Politics of Nature', pp. 64–87; Plumwood, 'Nature, Self, and Gender', pp. 155–64; Plumwood, *Feminism and the Mastery of Nature*, ch. 7; Jim Cheney, 'Eco-feminism and Deep Ecology', *Environmental Ethics* 9:2 (1987), 115–45; Jim Cheney, 'The Neo-Stoicism of Radical Environmentalism', *Environmental Ethics* 11 (1989), 293–325; Jim Cheney, 'Nature, Theory, Difference', pp. 158–78; Ariel Salleh, 'Deeper than Deep Ecology: The Eco-feminist Connection', *Environmental Ethics* 6 (1984), 339–45; Ariel Salleh, 'The Ecofeminism/Deep Ecology Debate: A Reply to Patriarchal Reason', *Environmental Ethics* 14:3 (1992), 195–216. For a more extensive bibliography, see Ariel Salleh, 'In Defense of Deep Ecology', in Eric Katz, Andrew Light and David Rothenberg (eds.), *Beneath the Surface* (Cambridge, MA and London: MIT Press, 2000), p. 122.

ecofeminists question whether deep ecology's ontology can in fact articulate notions of difference, especially as these relate to the difference of otherness. Despite the reference to relationality, there is a strong concern that the account of identification required by deep ecology overcomes the dualism of nature opposed to humanity by lapsing into an undifferentiated monism (Plumwood, Cheney). How is such *fusion* also the affirmation of *relations*? Deep ecology opposes the domestication of nature but then seems to lapse into the elimination of nature. With this monism comes an affirmation of the expansive self, as we saw in the last chapter. But how, some ecofeminists ask, does such an account overcome the stress on the autonomy of the individual and the centrality of the ethics of nature construed as rights that deep ecology proclaims that it wishes to overcome (Cheney)? Moreover, how can the discussion of the relations between humanity and nature proceed when the generic term, 'humanity', goes unexamined and its patriarchal assumptions remain buried (Salleh)?

If the totality posited by deep ecology is that of an ever-expanding self, co-creative with the cosmos, what notion of totality is operative within social/ist ecofeminism? Nature–humanity is here understood to be a broken totality: contrary to much current practice, 'the human metabolism with nature can be based on a logic of reciprocity and nurture rather than exploitation or control. This dialectical logic is contained in the sensuous practice of women workers.'[27] Thus women's work – agricultural, procreative, socialising – is concerned with reproduction and the relation of reproductive to productive (as in agriculture) work. The roots of social/ist ecofeminism are to be found in the historically constituted 'women's objective relation to social reproduction'. Further: 'The shared materiality of this structural position persists globally despite differences of region, class, religion and language.'[28] Thus the work of women provides access to a totality fractured by practices of domination and subjugation in which both women and nature are conceived as externalities to production.

Yet in and through these processes of domination and subjugation may be discerned the reality and otherness of nature. So ecofeminists often affirm the agency, but not the subjectivity, of nature. In turn, ecofeminists are dismissive of postmodern attempts to affirm strongly the cultural construction and discursivity of nature. Plumwood considers this position as merely the determined opposite of the affirmation of nature as a unified

27. Salleh, *Ecofeminism as Politics*, p. 82. Cf. Salleh's claim, following Carolyn Merchant, that the interpretation of nature as dialectical fits with a 'sociology of conflict and change', p. 57.
28. Salleh, *Ecofeminism as Politics*, p. 109.

structure. Both positions are to be rejected.[29] Although there is some debate as to the relations between ecological–scientific descriptions of nature and those proposed by ecofeminism,[30] on account of actual practices – especially the procreative and the agricultural – ecofeminism maintains that women have a particular material relation to nature. However, here I reject the claim – a rejection maintained by some ecofeminists of course – that women are 'closer' to nature. In short, a number of ecofeminist writers are sensitive to the charge of essentialism which works out as an epistemology of direct, seemingly unmediated, experience of nature on account of some reified notion of women's embodiment on which the claim to being 'closer to nature' depends.

Consider the following comment by Karen Warren: 'Because there are no "monolithic experiences" that all women share, feminism must be a "solidarity movement" based on shared beliefs and interests rather than a "unity in sameness" movement based on shared experiences and shared victimization.'[31] In fact, I think that the 'standpoint epistemology' promoted by a number of ecofeminists is preferable even to Warren's account: what is vital here is the social location of women as point of epistemic access to true, that is liberative, knowledge of nature. To be preferred, then, is an understanding of the standpoint of women as a set of overlapping positions which have something in common. Nancy Hartsock provides a good example of such overlapping: the centrality of women's work in the care of children is almost universal (has a place in every culture) yet is varied in cultural practice.[32]

Knowledge from the underside[33]

The issue of standpoint epistemologies emerges in debates in feminist theories of science. As Sandra Harding explains, such standpoint theorising 'originates in Hegel's thinking about the relationship between the

29. Plumwood, 'The Ecopolitics Debate and the Politics of Nature', p. 79.
30. See Salleh, *Ecofeminism as Politics*, ch. 10; Karen J. Warren and Jim Cheney, 'Ecological Feminism and Ecosystem Ecology', *Hypatia* 6:1 (1991), 179–97. For a critique of Warren and Cheney, see Catherine Zabinski, 'Scientific Ecology and Ecological Feminism: The Potential for Dialogue', in Warren (ed.), *Ecofeminism*, pp. 314–24.
31. Warren, 'The Power and the Promise of Ecofeminism', p. 131.
32. Reported in Mellor, *Feminism and Ecology*, p. 107.
33. The next few paragraphs may also be found in my ' "Return to the Vomit of Legitimation"? Scriptural Interpretation and the Authority of the Poor', in Craig Bartholomew, Jonathan Chaplin, Robert Song and Al Wolters (eds.), *A Royal Priesthood: The Use of the Bible Ethically and Politically* (Exeter: Paternoster, and Grand Rapids: Zondervan, 2002).

master and slave and in the elaboration of this analysis in the writings of Marx, Engels, and the Hungarian Marxist theorist, G. Lukács'. How does standpoint epistemology operate? Harding again: 'Feminism and the women's movement provide the theory and motivation for inquiry and political struggle that can transform the perspective of women into a "standpoint" – a morally and scientifically preferable grounding for our interpretations and explanations of nature and social life.'[34] Some ecofeminists have appropriated this standpoint, arguing that the ecofeminist women's movement identifies the ways in which women reproduce nature for men and thereby occupy an oppositional location which is vital in the production of oppositional knowledges. In this connection Vandana Shiva (*Staying Alive*) has stressed the agricultural labour of Third World women; the same point is generalised by Ariel Salleh (*Ecofeminism as Politics*).

Such an epistemological privilege being granted to a group in a particular social location has been fiercely criticised within feminism. In 'A Cyborg Manifesto', Donna J. Haraway argues that such epistemologies require the presumption of a stable identity which is simply not available. We should, she maintains, be 'freed of the need to ground politics in "our" privileged position of the oppression that incorporates all other dominations, the innocence of the merely violated, the ground of those closer to nature'. In the desire 'to construct a revolutionary subject from the perspective of a hierarchy of oppressions and/or a latent position of moral superiority, innocence, and greater closeness to nature', we may detect the Western self present through philosophical epistemologies. Appealing to a certain type of postmodernism, Haraway rejects the notions of identity and self which, in her judgment, such epistemologies require and entail.[35]

Yet, as Sandra Harding has pointed out, there are aspects of a standpoint epistemology in Haraway's essay: that knowledge should be oppositional and political are common themes in both standpoint epistemologies and Haraway's work. Furthermore, Harding is not convinced

---

34. Sandra Harding, *The Science Question in Feminism* (Ithaca and London: Cornell University Press), p. 26.
35. Donna J. Haraway, 'A Cyborg Manifesto: Science, Technology, and Socialist-Feminism in the Late Twentieth Century', in *Simians, Cyborgs and Women*, pp. 149–81 (p. 176). Although in a strong critique Hewitt objects to Haraway's notion of a 'cyborg', in my judgment her criticism fails to grasp the radicality of Haraway's proposal. For, if Haraway is right, what it means to be(come) human is being transformed through technology. Therefore, to appeal to the need to humanise our circumstance, as Hewitt contends, is now strangely without content. See Marsha Hewitt, 'Cyborgs, Drag Queens, and Goddesses: Emancipatory–regressive Paths in Feminist Theory', *Method and Theory in the Study of Religion* 5:2 (1993), 135–54 (138–41).

that Haraway has, in her tendency to offer a narrative of the development of political economy, in fact escaped Marxist–modernist epistemological assumptions.[36]

In a subsequent and highly significant response to Harding, Haraway moves closer to the standpoint epistemologies which she had previously questioned. Interestingly, as I noted at the opening, she claims that: 'Ecofeminists have perhaps been most insistent on some version of the world as active subject, not as resource to be appropriated in bourgeois, Marxist or masculinist projects.'[37] In making this case, Haraway seeks to qualify her earlier view which has been read as the most severe social constructionism, but also, of course, to avoid a claim to the impartiality of 'objective knowing'.[38] Identifying the problem in epistemology as follows: 'how to have *simultaneously* an account of radical historical contingency for all knowledge claims and knowing subjects . . . *and* a no-nonsense commitment to faithful accounts of a "real" world', she proposes 'politics and epistemologies of location, positioning, and situating, where partiality and not universality is the condition of being heard to make rational knowledge claims. These are claims on people's lives; the view from a body, always a complex, contradictory, structuring and structured body, versus the view from above, from nowhere, from simplicity.'[39] Given such commitments, standpoint epistemologies have a certain attractiveness in that they represent the views of agents from below. These Haraway calls 'subjugated knowledges'.

Shortly I shall briefly rehearse some helpful cautionary notes offered by Haraway on the limitations of standpoint epistemologies. However, I return now to ecofeminism proper to sketch the employment of such an

---

36. Harding, *The Science Question in Feminism*, p. 194. The point Harding seeks to make against Haraway is not, I consider, accurately presented in a critical commentary by William Grassie ['Donna Haraway's Metatheory of Science and Religion: Cyborgs, Trickster, and Hermes', *Zygon* 31:2 (1996), 285–304 (294)] who states that Harding is seeking to argue for 'grand theorizing' and maintaining 'a discourse of objectivity'. On a different reading, which the selective quoting by Grassie disguises, Harding is attracted by Haraway's postmodernism but is not altogether sure that the 'successor science' of standpoint epistemologies is persuasive. Thus Harding does not reject Haraway's postmodern epistemology in favour of modernist epistemological strategies, as Grassie indicates. Rather, she rejects modernism but remains unsure whether or not the rejection of such modernist strategies also requires the rejection of standpoint epistemologies.

37. Haraway, 'Situated Knowledges', p. 199.

38. This point is well made in a very helpful commentary on Haraway's work by Jill Marsden, 'Virtual Sexes and Feminist Futures: The Philosophy of "Cyberfeminism"', *Radical Philosophy* 78 (1996), 6–16 (11). Which means, in turn, that the judgment on Haraway's work by David Demeritt ['Science, Social Construction and Nature', pp. 173–93 (p. 176)] as 'artefactual constructivism' requires qualification.

39. Haraway, 'Situated Knowledges', pp. 187, 195.

epistemological strategy within social/ist ecofeminism. Contrary to those who maintain that standpoint epistemologies require essentialism and the erasure of difference (essentialism, in that there appears to be something inherent 'in' women for this position to be maintained; erasure, in that cultural differences and power differentials between actual women – between, say, a white, middle-class European academic and a fieldworker in India – appear to be obliterated), the argument depends on an account of the social location of women. What is privileged is not 'the position of women' but rather the range of practices which are – under present patriarchal conditions – the preserve (but not the reserve) of women. As Salleh notes: '[T]o say this is not to say that women are any "closer" to nature than men in some ontological sense. Rather, it is to recall Marx's teaching that human consciousness develops in a dialectical way through sensuous bodily interaction with the material environment.'[40] Thereby the attempt is made to recover the centrality of women's reproductive working for ecofeminist theory and politics. For Salleh, such an affirmation is the rejection of a positivist essentialism in favour of 'a complex socially elaborated sex and gender difference, privileging women temporarily as historical agents par excellence'.[41]

Such an epistemology must be attentive to the *subjugated* or *disadvantaged* actions of women: its source lies not in some reified notion of women's bodies but the position of women in a sexed/gendered division of classist, racist labour. Or, as Mary Mellor puts it: 'For ecofeminists, women, because of their structural disadvantage, can see the dynamics of the relationship between humanity and nature more clearly than can (relatively) privileged men.'[42] What is this position of structural disadvantage? Sometimes this position, as articulated by Salleh, for example, can appear

---

40. Salleh, 'Nature, Woman, Labor, Capital', p. 116. In articulating her position in such fashion, Salleh has, I think, moved away from a more 'essentialist' position in her earliest papers on ecofeminism and deep ecology.

41. Salleh, 'Nature, Woman, Labor, Capital', p. 120. Celice Jackson's complaints about ecofeminist epistemology, 'Radical Environmental Myths: A Gender Perspective', *New Left Review* 210 (1995), 124–40 (133–4) are unpersuasive – see the reply by Mary Mellor, 'Myths and Realities: A Reply to Cecile Jackson', *New Left Review* 217 (1996), 132–7.

42. Mellor, *Feminism and Ecology*, pp. 105–6. The objections raised to this position by Deborah Slicer, 'Wrongs of Passage: Three Passages to the Maturing of Ecofeminism', in Warren (ed.), *Ecological Feminism*, pp. 29–41 (p. 35) fail to make a clear distinction between affinity and social/ist ecofeminism. Slicer rehearses four objections to such epistemic privilege: (1) Is it women or feminist women who are accorded such privilege? (2) Is it only women who have this privilege? (3) Are totalising claims about a single feminist position evident here? (4) Does this epistemic privilege issue in an account of general truths which, as general, is too indebted to the Enlightenment? These objections may be answered thus: (1) in that such knowledge is oppositional and is born in struggle, it is acquired by women undertaking ecofeminist actions; (2) the second question cannot be known in advance and, as this is a

somewhat misty-eyed (the woman–nature–labour nexus described as a co-evolution of 'reciprocal practices over centuries'), but at its core is a critical claim: the cognitive capacities founded in a standpoint epistemology are located in reproductive labours 'embedded in a matrix of social relations which in turn are sustained by subsistence activities embedded in cycles of biological time'.[43] This is the 'vantage point of *critical otherness*' of which Ynestra King writes.[44]

All romanticism, as Haraway advises, must be rejected here: the *social location* of women does not provide some automatic or innocent access to liberative knowledge; subjugated knowledges are not naturalised knowledge 'mysteriously' available if you inhabit the 'correct' body and position. If such knowledge is to be critical, it must be learned: 'To see from below is neither easily learned nor unproblematic', writes Haraway. '[H]ow to see from below is a problem requiring at least as much skill with bodies and language, with the mediations of vision, as the "highest" techno-scientific visualizations.'[45]

A good example of a standpoint epistemology in practice, so to speak, is the account given by Vandana Shiva of the damaging ways in which development – or *maldevelopment*, as Shiva calls it – affects women in the 'Third World', especially Indian women. Explicitly questioning the identification of nature and women, she affirms a 'feminine principle' which identifies the religious-cum-philosophical support for an 'ecological struggle' aimed at both the emancipation of nature and the overcoming of the marginalisation of Indian women, the principal actors in survival in rural India. What in a hasty reading might be interpreted as an essentialist

historically constituted claim for privilege, women are the privileged, but not the only, bearers of such epistemic access; (3) the material relations of women's labour are here privileged, which is not, of course, a single standpoint; (4) universal claims are made here but from a particular location – such universality is not the same as generality. However, a question by Slicer on whether knowledge produced from the privilege of partiality is also liberatory knowledge – the issue of criteria for liberative knowing – is well taken; part III of this book is an attempt to frame an answer to this question, to be tested by Christian pedagogy.

43. Salleh, *Ecofeminism as Politics*, p. 146. The argument by Lori Gruen, 'Toward an Ecofeminist Moral Epistemology', in Warren (ed.), *Ecological Feminism*, pp. 120–38 (pp. 131–4), that knowledge of nature should be direct is thereby denied: knowledge of nature is always socially mediated; what is at issue here is not the bare acknowledgement of the 'facticity' of nature but rather epistemological attitudes which seek to discern our indebtedness to nature.

44. Ynestra King, 'Feminism and the Revolt of Nature', *Heresies* 13 (1983), 12–16 (14).

45. Haraway, 'Situated Knowledges', p. 191. It should be clear also that the themes of the sacredness and re-enchantment of nature, which are so prevalent in the eco-literature, are not supported by the type of social/ist ecofeminism presented here. The re-enchantment of nature is an important theme in chapter 9.

position in fact presents the centrality of women's work as the mediators of nature in production and reproduction to society and thereby as the primary agents in practices of sustainability: 'Women produce and reproduce life not merely biologically, but also through their social role in providing sustenance.'[46] Thus she argues that 'the feminine' is not 'biologically determined' but is instead to be understood as 'socially and culturally constructed'.[47]

The policies of maldevelopment issue, in Shiva's view, in poverty. 'This poverty crisis', she writes, 'touches women most severely, first because they are the poorest among the poor, and then because, with nature, they are the primary sustainers of society'.[48] Opposed to this maldevelopment is the traditional work of women which 'has been based on contributions *to* the land, not just exploitation and benefit from it'.[49] She presents the various ways in which women have in agriculture, forestry and conservation of water engaged in active cooperation with nature in order to meet fundamental human needs for food, warmth and shelter.

This, in turn, suggests that the 'feminine principle' is not a state of being in which women participate but is rather to be understood as 'the principle of activity and creativity in nature, women and men'.[50] Further, Shiva notes the epistemic privilege given by living within and from the 'feminine principle': drawing on the work of Ashis Nandy, she writes, 'one must choose the slave's standpoint not only because the slave is oppressed but also because he [*sic*] represents a higher-order cognition which perforce includes the master as a human, whereas the master's cognition has to exclude the slave as a "thing"'.[51] Which, we may gloss, is to say that the partial standpoint is one of love.

Sexing/gendering the common realm

The common realm is not sex or gender blind. To argue that the relations between humanity and nature are best understood only in mutual co-explication with the triunity of God is not thereby to obscure the different relations and associated power differentials between women and men,

---

46. Shiva, *Staying Alive*, p. 42. Cf. Shiva, 'Development as a New Project of Western Patriarchy', pp. 189–200; Shiva, 'The Greening of the Global Reach', in Wolfgang Sachs (ed.), *Global Ecology: A New Arena of Political Conflict* (London: Zed Books, 1993), pp. 149–56.
47. Shiva, *Staying Alive*, p. 48.   48. Ibid., p. 5.   49. Ibid., p. 107.
50. Ibid., p. 52.   51. Ibid., p. 53.

on the one hand, and between men, women and nature on the other. (Nor, as I hope to have indicated, does it propose a monochrome account of the domination of women.)

Yet there remains the suspicion that theology seeks to *simplify* relations by generalisation and abstraction. Salleh captures this suspicion nicely: 'in an attempt to bridge its experiential fracture from the life process and 'natural time', the alienative consciousness of men has invented compensatory 'principles of continuity' such as God, the State, History, now Science and Technology'.[52] To the contrary, my argument, which reaches its full complexity only in part III, is that the *theological* principles of an ecosocial ontology are not compensatory obfuscations but instead reflective attempts to deny such continuity. By way of a Trinitarian interrogation and reconstruction, I am arguing, the concrete detail and intimate relations – the fine dependencies and modalities of transcendence – of humanity in nature are revealed.

Such detail turns upon an account of human reproductions in nature. Space, time and society, the central themes of the ecosocial ontology proposed throughout this book, are the basic ontological commitments governing the reproductions of human interaction with nature. The spatial, social and temporal dynamics of theological anthropology are always reproductions: in short, the common totality of human–nature relations notes the centrality of reproductive activities and their non-liberative implications for women, and, arguably, for men also. Put positively, the concept of un/natural relations proposes the non-identity of women and nature against pressures to see women and nature as identical and external. Un/natural relations include *re*production.

In its theoretical commitments, such a theological position is not so far from some social/ist ecofeminisms. For example, Mary Mellor writes:

> I do not think that for humanity there is an original harmony that has been lost or a teleological harmony to come. If anything, humanity is *essentially* in conflict with non-human nature in using human consciousness and reflexivity to create a special and privileged niche. In doing this humanity is neither natural nor unnatural.[53]

In my terms, she rejects 'natural' and 'antinatural'/'non-natural' relations. But in denying a common *telos* for humanity and nature (which is

---

52. Salleh, *Ecofeminism as Politics*, p. 40.   53. Mellor, *Feminism and Ecology*, pp. 187–8.

not in my view best described by the phrase 'teleological harmony'[54]), she
is obliged to discount the descriptions of 'natural' and 'antinatural'/'non-
natural' of the human situation in nature. What is required is a third
term – un/natural relations in a common realm – which seeks to deny and
affirm naturalism and deny and affirm the transcendence of personalism.
That is, we require a Trinitarian materialism.

Indeed, as Val Plumwood points out, what is at stake here is a new conception of the human.[55] But, against Plumwood, we must add that a new
conception of the human cannot be constructed without attention to the
un/natural identity of humanity in relation to nature. That is, we need a
new conception of nature. To be included in this new anthropology would
be, as Plumwood indicates, 'a *different* concept of closeness to nature'.[56]

Or, rather, the notion of the common realm surpasses notions of 'closeness to nature' and, further, 'distance from nature'. One lesson to be
learned from social/ist ecofeminism is that the common realm cannot
be constructed upon domination. A second lesson is that there are insights into human–nature relations which ecofeminism furnishes from
the perspective of women's practices of reproduction and production.
There can be no falling behind the insight that un/natural relations include *re*production; the common realm is not sex or gender blind. But we
need to find some way beyond the antitheses of 'closeness to nature' and
'distance from nature' towards a richer, active, more dynamic account of
un/natural relations.

At the back of a more dynamic account of un/natural relations is a re-
construal of nature. Ynestra King argues along these lines: to overcome
the dualisms that in her view undermine all types of feminism to date,
what is needed is a non-dualistic or dialectical theory in order to 'reconcile
humanity with nature'. However, the ontology that she proposes for this
speaks merely of the requirement to see the human as emergent from nature, the organic as emerging out of the inorganic. This she calls a project
of 'rational reenchantment': the attempt in practice to bridge the dualism of spirit and matter.[57] The concept of nature operative here is not at

---

54. For a different account of eschatological *telos*, see my 'The Future of Creation: Ecology
and Eschatology', in David S. Fergusson and Marcel Sarot (eds.), *The Future as God's Gift*
(Edinburgh: T. & T. Clark, 2000), pp. 89–144.

55. Val Plumwood, 'Women, Humanity and Nature', *Radical Philosophy* 48 (1998), 16–24.

56. Plumwood, 'Women, Humanity and Nature', p. 23.

57. Ynestra King, 'Healing the Wounds: Feminism, Ecology and the Nature/Culture
Dualism', in Diamond and Orenstein (eds.), *Reweaving the World*, pp. 106–21 (pp. 116, 120–1).

all clear and seems to presuppose a kind of dualism. Certainly, it is not a dualism that requires an account of nature as objectified, contained and domesticated; nor is nature to be understood as some kind of naturalistic web to which humanity conforms. However, neither is nature construed as some kind of dialectical other: as subject or agent. The dialectic with which King operates is surprisingly inert, related in turn to the lack of liveliness in her account of nature.

The religiously charged language of 're-enchantment of the world' is also employed by Mies and Shiva. Previously, Shiva had spoken of 'Nature as a living force' and had identified nature, together with women, as 'active subjects'. Indeed, in an excellent example of nature construed as *natura naturans*, the Hindu notion of prakriti is defined as 'the living force that supports life'.[58] Using the phrase 'the sacredness of life', Mies and Shiva later insist that spirituality is to be construed actively as immanence: 'There is only immanence, but this immanence is not inert, passive matter devoid of subjectivity, life and spirit.'[59] Their qualifying phrase is important, but none the less it is not easy to see how an account of the immanence of nature in which human beings participate supports a notion of its liveliness, of nature as an active subject. Shiva will speak of the importance of acknowledging and respecting nature's capacity for self-renewal. Nevertheless, how her account of immanence supports this commitment is unclear.

My reading suggests a more radical account of the otherness of nature than Mies and Shiva propose. The notion of difference with which they operate is benign, as if the otherness of nature only identifies a space in which human beings and nature cooperate. The sometimes raw indifference of nature to human projects suggests a different, more dialectical, notion of the otherness of nature. Such an account of otherness is assured by considering the transcendence of nature: the destiny of the natural parts of the common realm in their author, God. Yet precisely such an account of transcendence is not presented by Mies and Shiva.[60] In a strenuous attempt to avoid the tendencies of personalism and naturalism, the fundamental matter of the *telos* of nature is occluded. Therefore it remains unclear whether or not nature is anything other than oriented towards humanity. Put differently, the theme of the spatiality of nature is not foregrounded in their account. This occlusion is in its turn obscured because

---

58. Shiva, *Staying Alive*, pp. xix, 46, xvii.   59. Mies and Shiva, *Ecofeminism*, p. 17.
60. Ibid., p. 18.

the structure of engagement with nature in their account focuses on the carefully controlled zones of the agricultural and the medical.

A more dynamic account of nature is also present in the ecofeminist literature. Subscribing to the view of 'the world's active agency', Jim Cheney resists the containment of nature and insists on nature's encounter with us and therefore, in turn, its difference from humanity. Drawing on Haraway's work, Cheney denies that the anthropomorphising of the world is the result, although he is not above such formulations as 'the land must *speak* to us'.[61] What is required then is an ontology of difference. Indeed, Cheney agrees with Tom Birch that what is required is a 'principle of *universal* considerability' by which 'universal attentiveness to otherness, to difference, promotes the kind of experiential encounters which lead to the discovery of our moral obligations'. Despite a welcome emphasis on the agency of nature manifest in encounter, Cheney offers no ontology. Indeed, we should note that the common realm of God, nature and humanity secures such universal considerability: the source and end of nature and humanity is God. Moral considerability can thereby be ascribed – not merely imputed or extended – to nature on account of its eschatological destiny. In a gross caricature of 'salvational movements', which he claims 'desire to create a safe place outside time and circumstance', Cheney denies himself these resources.

Furthermore, salvation does not *negate* time according to the Christian schema, as he seems to think. Indeed, his affirmation that 'truth and justice be negotiated'[62] is only intelligible from the theological view I am promoting here. For the affirmation of negotiating with non-human nature is defensible only if nature's destiny is not identical or equivalent to humanity's. Such a destiny bestows on nature its true otherness: the social, spatial and temporal movement of nature is oriented towards God and thereby towards humanity. The differentiations and distinctions are secured as wholes and parts, as we have seen, by their reference to God. Cheney's nature is merely alien, not other.

The account of Trinitarian totality that I am developing in this political theology of nature is deeply indebted to ecofeminism's account of nature as active subject in the dynamic of encounter. This is a vital lesson, hopefully well learned. However, I am unconvinced that ecofeminist theory can supply the ontological commitments required to support its insight. In

61. Cheney, 'Nature/Theory/Difference', pp. 158–78 (p. 175).
62. Ibid., p. 166.

turn, the account of un/natural relations proposed by ecofeminist theory is caught between personalism and naturalism, between temporality and spatiality and thereby remains insufficiently dialectical. Differently from deep ecology, ecofeminism none the less emerges as a very important resource for the conceptual articulation of the common realm of God, nature and humanity. As such, ecofeminism as critique will be found through most of the remaining chapters of this book.

5

Social ecology: the dialectical emergence of nature and society

Introduction

In this chapter, political theology of nature interacts with the political theory of *social ecology*. To begin the discussion, I offer three interpretative principles by which any ecological inquiry must be oriented today. These three principles are:

First, the issue of the scaling of the human in relation to the non-human: can such scaling be achieved in non-reductive ways, both for the human creature and the *mundus*? In what ways are we to think of such a scale, of such proportioning? Can human–nature relations be thought of, and practised, as both rich and satisfying and yet as working within certain constraints? The interpretative issue is no longer the dependence of the human on the non-human. Instead, what is at stake is how to *interpret* that dependence.

Second, the matter of scaling cannot be addressed without attention to how it is that the human emerges from the non-human. What is the relation between what Bookchin calls 'first nature' and 'second nature'? Bookchin defines 'first nature' like this: 'Biological nature is above all the cumulative evolution of ever-differentiating and increasingly complex life-forms with a vibrant and interactive inorganic world.' Bookchin defines 'second nature' as a 'cultural, social and political "nature" that today has all but absorbed first nature'.[1] What is the relation between these two? That the human is an emergent creature is not contested; the *interpretation* of that emergence is.

1. Murray Bookchin, *The Philosophy of Social Ecology: Essays on Dialectical Naturalism* (Montreal, New York and London: Black Rose Books, 2nd edn 1996), pp. 29, 31.

Third, because the notion of nature is dangerous, and has been used to reinforce nationalisms and fascisms, the political outworking of nature is here important: how is the human creature a participant in nature? How is non-human nature a participant in the human sphere? How is the *zoon politikon* also a citizen of nature, and how is nature also a 'political agent'?

How these issues impinge upon a Christian, political theology of nature is the central concern of this chapter. Is social ecology helpful in addressing these principles theologically? Christianity, of course, is not without its own resources: it needs no help with the grammar, but the vocabulary and the syntax . . . these are different matters. Or, to put the issue in terms I used in chapter 1, Christianity knows of the relations which govern the world of creatures in its contingency and dependence on God. The matter, however, is to develop further this rich Trinitarian ontology: social creatures in a common realm, oriented towards the triune God.

Socialising ecology

Although it has other adherents in, for example, John Clark and Janet Biehl, social ecology is associated primarily with the work of Murray Bookchin. Suspicious of the academy, none the less Bookchin's œuvre includes at least ten books; neither holding nor seeking an academic position, he co-founded in 1974 the Institute of Social Ecology in Rochester, Vermont. With a history of political activism going back to the late 30s, Bookchin has moved through several phases: communist, Trotskyite and now anarchist. Bookchin has been involved in a well-known spat (beginning in 1987) with deep ecology: in a sustained polemic, he has accused it of being a form of nature mysticism.[2] In this he is, as we saw in chapter 3, partly right. However, he has made the mistake of claiming that deep ecology is fundamentally misanthropic. It has been easy for deep ecology to reject this charge. Yet the disagreements between deep ecologists and social ecologists continue to reverberate through the environmental movement in North America. More recently, Bookchin has fiercely refuted criticisms of his position made by fellow social ecologist and one-time collaborator, John Clark.[3]

2. See, *inter alia*, Murray Bookchin, 'Social Ecology versus Deep Ecology', *Socialist Review* 88:3 (1988), 11–29.
3. Murray Bookchin, 'Comments on the International Social Ecology Network Gathering and the "Deep Social Ecology" of John Clark', *Democracy and Nature* 3:3 (1997), 154–97. A

Social ecology departs from one of the principal commitments of socialist ecology (the topic of chapter 6). For socialist ecology (at least, in the Marxist tradition) has stressed the centrality of human relations to nature; alienation follows on from the division of labour; and labour is concerned with human interaction with non-human nature.

Bookchin argues differently: the *idea* of the domination of nature by humanity, he contends, follows on from the domination of humanity by humanity. Bookchin can state this position very baldly: 'the notion that man must dominate nature emerges directly from the domination of man by man'.[4] Or, 'the idea of dominating nature stems from human domination, initially in hierarchical forms as feminists so clearly understand, and later in class and statist forms'.[5] At other times, a caution is introduced: 'nearly all our ecological problems arise from deep seated social problems'.[6] It is important to note the precise formulation: in and through intrahuman domination emerges the *idea* of the domination of nature. The notion precedes the performance, we might say. Of course, such a reading allows Bookchin to accept that human beings may have, in pre-hierarchical times, dominated nature. However, such domination was not reflective and thereby not purposive. Such an affirmation of the 'centrality' of human hierarchy runs through Bookchin's writings of the last 30 years.

What is primary, then, is hierarchy and domination, and the suppression of spontaneity, within and between human groups. From this denial of freedom, the exploitation of the planet follows. For Bookchin claims that our central problem is hierarchy. Moreover, the proper response to hierarchy is freedom. The emancipation of nature must thus wait on the emancipation of humanity. What then is required is 'a coherent view of the social sources of our ecological crisis'.[7] These social sources are to be traced to the fact that an ever-expanding capitalist economy seems unaware of the ecological limits to expansion. Bookchin is suspicious of

revised version of the essay that is the subject of Bookchin's critique is now published: see John Clark, 'Municipal Dreams: A Social Ecological Critique of Bookchin's Politics', in Andrew Light (ed.), *Social Ecology after Bookchin* (New York: Guilford Press, 1998), pp. 137–91. On the disagreement between Clark and Bookchin, see further Andrew Light, 'Introduction', in Light (ed.), *Social Ecology after Bookchin*, pp. 1–23 (pp. 8–12).

4. Murray Bookchin, *Post-Scarcity Anarchism* (Montreal and New York: Black Rose Books, 1986), p. 85.

5. Murray Bookchin, *The Modern Crisis* (Philadelphia: New Society Publishers, 1986), p. 71.

6. Murray Bookchin, 'What is Social Ecology?', in Michael Zimmerman (ed.), *Environmental Philosophy: From Animal Rights to Radical Ecology* (Englewood Cliffs, NJ: Prentice-Hall, 1993), pp. 354–73 (p. 354).

7. Bookchin, *The Ecology of Freedom: The Emergence and Dissolution of Hierarchy* (Montreal and New York: Black Rose Books, revised edn 1991), p. xvii.

attempts to trace the core of the environmental crisis to the relation between first nature and second nature. For the projection of human ills onto first nature can lend an immutability to human ills; these ills suddenly become 'natural'. Throughout Bookchin's work there is the sustained rejection of the ascription of hierarchy to nature. He remains deeply impatient with those discourses that call lions the 'king of beasts', etc. These are, for Bookchin, restrictive anthropomorphisms. Such anthropomorphisms abound in popular culture. For example, much of the commentary that accompanies BBC "wildlife" programmes – saturated as they are by reference to hierarchical patterns of organisation – would be rejected by Bookchin. A few years ago, one of these multipart series – on the lives of insects – was titled *Alien Nation*. For Bookchin both words of this title are senseless: insects cannot form a nation and cannot, as products of evolutionary nature, be dubbed alien. (Neither, for the same reason, could human beings be called alien.)

Why social? Why ecology? As for ecology, Bookchin wishes to speak of the complex and dynamic interaction and interdependence of living and non-living things. Ecology is thus the way of speaking of the balance of nature. And human beings are included in nature. So there is a sense in which Bookchin wishes to speak of a natural ecology. But he also regards human beings as emphatically social. (Bookchin reserves the use of the word social for human organisation; and he recommends the use of the word 'community' for natural forms of organisation. So ants are communal, not social, creatures.) It is in the social phase of their development – that is, the *institutional* phase – that human beings have become misaligned from nature. Thus Bookchin calls for a 'social ecology': an inquiry into the balance of nature which human beings currently have a tendency to interfere with or disrupt. As Bookchin writes: 'The time has come to integrate our ecological natural philosophy with an ecological social philosophy based on freedom and consciousness.'[8]

Thus it is the themes of freedom and consciousness in the human, that is, social, sphere to which Bookchin directs our attention: 'that humanity must dominate and exploit nature stems from the domination and exploitation of man by man'.[9] Thereby Bookchin insists that in an ecological theory no form of hierarchy can be appealed to in nature or society. The only way forward is thus the criticism and overturning of hierarchies

8. Bookchin, *Toward an Ecological Society* (Montreal: Black Rose Books, 1980), p. 27.
9. Ibid., p. 40.

in human society. A constant sub-theme is the rejection of any hierarchy in nature. In other words, if intrahuman domination is the source of eco-cide, then any amelioration in our circumstance must attend to that same domination. Diagnosis and cure mirror one another. What Bookchin pro-poses therefore is 'a reharmonization of nature and humanity through a reharmonization of human with human'.[10] Bookchin's thinking culmi-nates in an anarchist political prescription which in his latest writings is called 'confederal municipalism'.

So far, so good. Yet Bookchin's position involves more even than this. By way of an appeal to a dialectical naturalism, he argues for the emer-gence of human second nature from first nature. This emergence is both dialectical and naturalistic. Dialectical naturalism is to be understood as the philosophy of social ecology, and also as an ethics which, in turn, is derived in part from a tradition of anarchist thinking, especially the work of Peter Kropotkin. Here Bookchin uses the language of 'free nature': by rethinking the relations between first and second nature, social ecology affirms free nature. In this sense, Bookchin may be understood as invok-ing 'natural aid'.

There is no space here to discuss all of Bookchin's social ecology, so my approach is restricted to certain key themes: some of the core concepts and the movement of his thinking; the evolutionary ontology that he invokes in support of his anarchist position; the political outworking of this anar-chist position; and, finally, the ways in which the common realm of God, nature and humanity may be pressed in an anarchist direction. These con-clusions will be taken forward in the discussions of an ecological Christol-ogy in chapter 7 and an ecological pneumatology in chapter 8.

From domination and hierarchy to freedom and participation

I have used the term 'anarchist' in my initial description of Bookchin's position. In what senses is Bookchin's position anarchist? Five aspects of ecoanarchist thought have been identified by Robyn Eckersley: a rejec-tion of the nation-state; the mutual and interactive compatibility of ecol-ogy and anarchism; a rejection of hierarchy in both human and natural worlds; an emphasis on local, extra-parliamentary political (direct) action; and, finally, 'the importance of maintaining consistency between ends

10. Bookchin, *The Ecology of Freedom*, p. 11.

and means in Green political praxis'.[11] All these aspects may be found in Bookchin's work.

Further, Bookchin develops the central theme of anarchism: the importance of community. Socialism, we might say, emerges out of one of the constructions of capitalism: the bifurcation of society into classes. Anarchism, by contrast, emerges out of the (earlier?) deracination and displacement of communities by capitalist forces of production. Bookchin will therefore criticise capitalism for its effects upon the human spirit and not from the standard socialist (that is, productivist and economistic) perspective of class. His criticisms of Marxism and ecosocialism are made from this perspective: for class, Bookchin has hierarchy; for exploitation, domination; for the abolition of the state, liberatory institutions; for justice, freedom; for happiness, pleasure.[12]

Such commitments inform Bookchin's criticism of the mysticism of deep ecology: that is, its anti-rationalism and, especially, its failure to develop an account of the current hierarchical political organisation of human beings. It follows, in turn, that Bookchin's politics are resolutely anti-statist: he denies the importance of 'politics as statecraft' in favour of politics as direct democracy – a municipalism. One feature of Bookchin's style of arguing is the way that he robustly presses his case. This can lead to some surprisingly non-dialectical conclusions coming from this self-professed dialectical thinker.[13] For example, in maintaining the anarchist perspective from community, Bookchin notes that one strand within anarchism – the anarcho-syndicalist – has privileged labour as the principal agent of emancipatory politics, but does not develop this point dialectically.[14] Narrowing the anarchist tradition, Bookchin *opposes* community to class. Indeed, the failure to maintain an account of reason as dialectical will be my chief criticism of Bookchin's view.

Domination is the key word in Bookchin's writing, argues Alan P. Rudy.[15] Domination, exercised through hierarchies, is a social phenomenon. That is, such domination applies only to the human realm, to

11. Robyn Eckersley, *Environmentalism and Political Theory: Toward an Ecocentric Approach* (London: University College London Press, 1995), p. 145.

12. Bookchin, *The Ecology of Freedom*, p. 1.

13. For a reading of this tendency to non-dialectical interpretation, see Joel Kovel, 'Negating Bookchin', *Capitalism, Nature, Socialism* 8:1 (1997), 3–35.

14. See John Clark, 'Reply', *Capitalism, Nature, Socialism* 9:1 (1998), 37–45 (38).

15. Alan P. Rudy, 'Ecology and Anthropology in the Work of Murray Bookchin', *Capitalism, Nature, Socialism* 9:1 (1998), 57–90 (57).

'second nature' and not to 'first nature'. Through his *magnum opus*, *The Ecology of Freedom*, Bookchin gives an account of the emergence of hierarchy and offers social ecology as the theory and praxis for its overcoming. Domination and hierarchy are, Bookchin concedes, separable: a hierarchical society might not dominate nature; there is no guarantee that a non-hierarchical society will not dominate nature. However, he argues that the idea of dominating nature emerges only after the calcification of hierarchy. Bookchin describes hierarchy in this fashion:

> By hierarchy, I mean the cultural, traditional and psychological systems of obedience and command, not merely the economic and political systems to which the terms class and State most appropriately refer . . . I refer to the domination of the young by the old, of women by men, of one ethnic group by another, of 'masses' by bureaucrats who profess to speak in their 'higher social interests', of countryside by town, and in a more subtle psychological sense, of body by mind, of spirit by a shallow instrumental rationality, and of nature by society and technology.[16]

The aim of social ecology is to explain the emergence of such hierarchy, account for the economy of command and obedience that it supports, and propose a political path towards the overcoming of such hierarchy. The aim is therefore the achievement of what Bookchin terms 'free nature' when 'human beings intervene in natural evolution with their best capacities – their moral sense, their unprecedented degree of conceptual thought, and their remarkable powers of communication'.[17] Throughout, Bookchin rejects a dominant view of nature, in his view maintained by both socialist and liberal thinking, that nature is to be seen as '"blind", "mute", "cruel", "competitive", and "stingy", a seemingly demonic "realm of necessity" that opposes "man's" striving for freedom and self-realization'.[18] Instead, the attribution of stinginess to nature is to be related to hierarchy and domination: 'The myth of a "stingy" nature has always been used to justify the "stinginess" of exploiters in their harsh treatment of the exploited.'[19] In other words, Bookchin holds true to his method: such a false – and ideologically biased – characterisation of nature as blind, etc. is always the projection of intrahuman domination through hierarchy.

16. Bookchin, *The Ecology of Freedom*, p. 4.   17. Bookchin, 'What is Social Ecology?', p. 370.
18. Bookchin, *The Modern Crisis*, p. 50; cf. p. 11.
19. Murray Bookchin, *Remaking Society: Pathways to a Green Future* (Boston, MA: South End Press, 1990), p. 32.

From where does Bookchin's confidence come that free nature is a po-litical objective, both actual and possible? This is another form of the ques-tion: is not Bookchin overly optimistic about human nature? A superficial answer would appeal to Bookchin's account of the organic society which existed 'before hierarchy'. Much of *The Ecology of Freedom* is taken up with an account of the emergence of hierarchy out of organic society. However, Bookchin never proposes a movement *ad fontes*: this is no philosophy of Eden in which return to a former state is recommended. The development of technology alone, Bookchin argues, makes such a return impossible. In-stead, Bookchin argues that his account of organic society makes the case – in fact, a point common to all types of anarchism – that human beings are *naturally* social and that hierarchy is a contingent, not a natural, fact. In other words, the central point that Bookchin makes is ontological: if hierarchy and domination are not necessary, then how is the world to be interpreted 'in favour of' the actuality of participation and freedom?

Bookchin's response comes in two parts, deeply intertwined: first, a reading of the anarcho-communist tradition in which he participates;[20] and, second, an account of nature as evolutionary. Restating the concept of social ecology, Bookchin argues that his views amount to a *holism*: that is, the aim of social ecology is not merely to note the domination of na-ture by humanity but to overcome this domination; not merely to identify the damaged and damaging relations between nature and society but to contribute to their healing. Holism is never monism: 'In conceiving them holistically, that is to say, in terms of their mutual interdependence, so-cial ecology seeks to unravel the forms and patterns of interrelationships that give intelligibility to a community, be it natural or social.'[21] It is there-fore proper to speak of the unity of nature and society, but never of their oneness.[22]

Bookchin is thereby proposing a holism that is best described as 'unity in diversity' or 'unity in difference'. Nor is this unity static. A key word here is development: Bookchin proposes a 'logic of differentiation' in which the diversity and fecundity of nature phases into human development. The point is not to look for false analogies between the human and the animal world – queen bees, colonies of ants, etc. – but to grasp the ways

20. According to David Macauley, 'Evolution and Revolution: The Ecological Anarchism of Kropotkin and Bookchin', in Andrew Light (ed.), *Social Ecology after Bookchin*, pp. 298–342 (p. 314), there are six strands of anarchism: communist, individualist, syndicalist, mutualist, pacifist and collectivist.

21. Bookchin, *The Ecology of Freedom*, p. 23. Cf. Bookchin, *The Modern Crisis*, p. 60; Bookchin, *Post-Scarcity Anarchism*, pp. 99f.

22. Bookchin charges deep ecology with the employment of the language of oneness.

in which human societies must be understood as phasing out of nature. In this regard, Bookchin argues that nature must always be understood as the condition of human society. Clearly, this is a rather different view from dominant liberal and socialist schemes which identify part of the human project as dominating nature in order to overcome its stinginess. Instead, Bookchin argues that we cannot separate ourselves out from nature to perform such domination. Indeed, we are part of nature's diversity – an evolutionary outcome – and we may either further contribute to that diversity or inhibit and finally reduce such diversity. Bookchin makes this point in an early essay:

> To sum up the critical message of ecology: if we diminish variety in the natural world, we debase its unity and wholeness; we destroy the forces making for a natural harmony and for a lasting equilibrium; and, what is more significant, we introduce an absolute regression in the development of the natural world which may eventually render the environment unfit for advanced [sc. including human] forms of life. To sum up the reconstructive message of ecology: if we wish to advance the unity and stability of the world, if we wish to harmonize it, we must conserve and promote variety.[23]

Bookchin's argument comes full circle: the key ways in which social humanity reduces the variety and diversity of evolutionary nature is through the practices of a hierarchical society. Humanity seeks to *simplify* its relations with nature on account of its attempt to dominate nature. This *libido dominandi* is to be sourced to intrahuman hierarchy. In that human nature phases out of non-human nature in the developmental process of differentiation, any reduction in diversity will also affect human beings. A free and spontaneous life of pleasure can only be attended to by the surpassing of the hierarchical forms of political domination which will then release the potential of human beings in their relations to one another and to the crucial condition of human life, nature. Of course the notion of the logic of differentiation, which in turn supports the distinction between community and society, means that nature cannot function as the basis of 'natural laws': Bookchin is scathing about approaches that propose that 'Nature knows best'. Although advocating a naturalism, Bookchin stresses the importance of dialectic: nature and society form a unity in diversity linked through a logic of differentiation. Nature does not provide a naturalistic template to which humanity must conform.

23. Bookchin, *Post-Scarcity Anarchism*, p. 98.

Furthermore, of vital importance are the ways in which Bookchin stresses the subjectivity and agency of nature. As we shall see in the next section, Bookchin regards the striving of nature as reaching a culmination in humans beings. This is the theme of 'stewardship' in Bookchin's writings.[24] Those aspects that make humanity different from nature – self-consciousness, reason, freedom – have important precursors in that same nature. Thus nature is the permanent companion of human society: 'not only does humanity place its imprint on the natural world and transform it, but also nature places its imprint on the human world and transforms it'.[25] Nature thereby has a certain 'subjectivity' which persists in interaction with human society. Nature is not only the precondition for the emergence of human society, but also the condition for its *development*. 'Labor's metabolism with nature cuts both ways', writes Bookchin, 'so that nature interacts *with* humanity to yield the actualisation of their common potentialities in the natural and social worlds'.[26] The invitation is therefore to think of nature in distinctly non-modern ways.

That is, Bookchin is arguing that the affirmation and development of diversity, fecundity and stability in nature requires certain sorts of political organisation that foster such diversity. Diverse, spontaneous, interactive, purposive, rational polities will be required to support and match the diversity of nature. To simplify human relations in hierarchical ways is to simplify our relation with non-human nature, to the detriment of both. From this vantage point, it is easy to see why Bookchin's position confuses: he seems to be proposing an anthropocentrism. After all, is not the domination of nature rooted in domination of humanity? However, the overcoming of such domination, Bookchin proposes, requires human societies to acknowledge their interdependence with non-human nature. 'A new type of community, carefully tailored to the characteristics and resources of a region, must replace the sprawling urban belts that are emerging today.'[27]

The vision is compelling. Is it convincing, however? One problem is Bookchin's insistence that the domination of humanity is always separable from the domination of nature. On an intuitive level, such a position seems curious on Bookchin's own premises: if 'nature is there all the time',[28] can it be argued that the idea of the domination of nature must

---

24. See Bookchin, *The Philosophy of Social Ecology*, pp. 176, 186; Bookchin, *The Philosophy of Social Ecology*, 2nd edition, p. 131.
25. Bookchin, *The Ecology of Freedom*, p. 32.   26. Ibid., p. 33.
27. Bookchin, *Post-Scarcity Anarchism*, p. 97.   28. Bookchin, *The Ecology of Freedom*, p. 317.

always be preceded by intrahuman domination? Bookchin's position implies that any tendencies away from unity in diversity must always result in simplifying or reductive pressures within human society. But, on the grounds of wholeness that Bookchin proposes, what sense can be made of the claim that, when it comes to the origins of the domination, one reading of that wholeness – the unity of nature and society – can never be cited? It appears that Bookchin has two conceptions of 'whole' running in tandem: from the perspective of development, nature and society; from the perspective of domination, human society only. The relevant question is: on what grounds is the dialectic operative in the first 'whole' denied its operations in the second? Why cannot the logic of differentiation, *dialectically conceived*, require attention to the domination of nature *and* the domination of humanity?

On a conceptual level, it is not certain that Bookchin's claim to the source of the domination of nature is in fact supported by his historical argument concerning the emergence of hierarchy. Bookchin argues that gerontocracy was the first hierarchy to emerge: the old had to find ways of making themselves indispensable to preliterate societies when, in terms of their practical contribution to such a society, they were redundant. In order to maintain the support of the community, the old required that society be organised in ways that acknowledged their wisdom and authority. Bookchin writes: 'their need for social power, and for hierarchical social power at that, is a function of their loss of biological power. The social sphere is the only realm in which this power can be created and, concomitantly, the only sphere that can cushion their vulnerability to natural forces.'[29] Thus, hierarchy results. What makes this argument curious is, as Alan Rudy has pointed out, that the emergence of domination is 'rooted in struggles associated with human biological nature'.[30] It would certainly be odd for a dialectical position in ecological thought to maintain that there is *no* relationship between human biological nature and non-human nature. Given that Bookchin traces the emergence of hierarchy to responses to ageing *bodies*, sourcing the idea of the domination of nature to the domination of human by human lacks credibility.

Bookchin comes close to considering this point when he writes that 'The ambiguity that permeates the outlook of the primordial world

---

29. Ibid., p. 81. In following at this point Bookchin's argument in *The Ecology of Freedom*, I do not wish to imply that Bookchin in all his writings presents gerontocracy as the lead emergent hierarchy. Gerontocracy, always linked by Bookchin to gender-based divisions of labour and expanding populations, is not always given such priority.
30. Rudy, 'Ecology and Anthropology in the work of Murray Bookchin', p. 74.

toward nature . . . is accented among the aged with a measure of
hatred, for in so far as fear is concerned they have more to fear from
nature's vicissitudes than do the young.' A qualification is immediately
offered: we have here 'nature internalised, the nature in humanity itself'.[31]
We are told further that 'the attempt to dominate external nature will
come later, when humanity is conceptually equipped to transfer its social
antagonisms to the natural world outside'. The cogency of the argument
depends, it seems, on whether human embodiment is best interpreted as
nature 'internalised'. Even on Bookchin's own argument, to speak of the
human body in terms of internalised nature cuts against the commitment
to understand the relationship between first and second nature in terms
of a logic of differentiation. Bookchin's position appears to be closer to a
logic of separation.

Such a logic of separation may also be traced in the contrast that
Bookchin everywhere draws between 'community' and 'society'. For
Bookchin, as already noted, groupings of animals may be called communities. However, the institutionalised communities that human beings form
are better described as 'societies'. By this manoeuvre, Bookchin ensures
that social, that is, human, organisation, cannot be read off communal,
that is, animal, organisation. The problem with this view for Bookchin's
overall programme is the privilege that it gives, on account of his commitment to anarchist principles, to the notion of community. Community is,
for Bookchin, the ground of social being. Hence his strong affirmation of
a political programme that privileges the face-to-face direct democracy of
the municipality. In turn, Bookchin affirms that such municipalities will
also be ecocommunities.

Clearly, there is a problem here over terminology: community is contrasted with society when considering the relations between non-human
nature and humanity; yet community is also the ground of human social being.[32] In short, confederal municipalism is about the establishment
of eco*communities*. But ecocommunities, Bookchin tells us, are not ecosocieties. What, then, does his position amount to apart from a sustained
attempt to protect the privilege that he gives to the anarchist notion of
community? Given the relations of interdependency that Bookchin wishes
to identify between nature and society, in my judgment it makes better
sense to bypass the language of community as overly anthropomorphic
and instead to interpret these relations as social.

31. Bookchin, *The Ecology of Freedom*, p. 82.
32. Clark, 'Municipal Dreams: A Social Ecological Critique of Bookchin's Politics', p. 146.

These criticisms do not refute Bookchin's position. Instead, they question the absolute priority that he gives to intrahuman hierarchy as the source of the idea of the domination of non-human nature. (In similar fashion, a mirror-image position that declared that *all* social hierarchy is to be sourced to the domination of nature by the human would also have to be subjected to detailed scrutiny.)

Why Bookchin encounters these difficulties is, I think, beginning to emerge: he wishes to affirm the centrality of the community as the ground of social being. To be precise, Bookchin wishes to affirm the *polis* as the ground of social being: the communitarian municipality in which face-to-face democracy is practised and where the individual is immersed in the strenuous *paideia* of citizenship. This is the anarchist perspective, interpreted by Bookchin in terms of municipality, that insists that humans are naturally social. By this means, Bookchin resists any attempt to retroject hierarchy in society or the state into non-human nature. The distinction between community and society serves this purpose also.

However, Bookchin wishes to give an ontological foundation to this centring of community or *polis*. To argue that human beings are by nature social is no mere rhetorical flourish: this argument must, for Bookchin, have an 'objective' ground in nature. Bookchin is thereby not recounting the origins of organic society and its 'fall' into hierarchical societies to offer some historical warrant for the anarchist position. It sometimes reads as if, by tracing this history of anarchist forms of association, Bookchin is delivering a 'golden thread' type of argument: we can have confidence in the attempt to build an anarchist polity because there have been many attempts to do so in the past. But that 'golden thread' of anarchist events is not, I think, the hard core of Bookchin's position. Rather, confidence in anarchism relates to the emergence of the human out of nature. 'Libertarian' is thereby to be defined by reference to his 'description of the ecosystem: the image of unity in diversity, spontaneity, and complementary relationships, free of all hierarchy and domination'.[33] There is some truth therefore in Eckersley's suggestion that Bookchin denies any movement from society to nature, but permits movement in the other direction, from nature to society.

Why Bookchin affirms this position is, on one level, clear enough: he wishes to avoid the retrojection of hierarchy onto nature by a society and the consequent legitimation of hierarchy in society by means of appeal to

33. Bookchin, *The Ecology of Freedom*, p. 352.

that already 'hierarchialised' nature. However, the issue is probably more complex: seeking an objective basis for his naturalistic ethics, he is obliged to protect 'first nature' from any taint of hierarchy. That is, nature must be fundamentally benign. Hence the affirmation by Bookchin of Kropotkin's appeal to metaphors of mutuality to comprehend evolutionary development. And first nature must be protected from any taint in order to defend the anarchist claims of the centrality of community and that human beings are by nature social. Bookchin is obliged to argue in this way, I think, because he finds the warrants supplied by a 'golden thread' defence of anarchist politics too weak and insufficiently ecological. Nor is he prepared to accept what we might call, broadly, cultural resources – including the religions – as one of his ways of building a case for anarchist politics. To make his case for an objective ethics, Bookchin turns instead to an account of evolutionary nature, which he dubs the 'philosophy of social ecology'. To an assessment of this philosophical position, I now turn.

Dialectical naturalism

'A social ecology, as a holistic vision', writes John Clark, 'seeks to relate all phenomena to the larger direction of evolution and emergence in the universe as a whole.'[34] In his 'dialectical naturalism', Bookchin proposes to think together nature and society. 'Social ecology, in effect, stands at odds with the notion that culture has no roots whatever in natural evolution.'[35] We cannot then be freed from nature; if capitalism seeks to do so, it is false. Bookchin thereby opposes attempts to separate society from nature (which he terms dualism) or collapse society into nature (which he calls monism). Bookchin holds to the term 'dialectical' as a way of indicating that he wishes to hold together natural development and social development.

This development is always evolutionary. At this point, however, Bookchin takes issue with standard treatments of evolution which privilege 'struggle' and 'competition'. He writes: 'Ecologists have yet to come to terms with the notion that symbiosis (not only "struggle") and participation (not only "competition") factor in the evolution of species.'[36] Here we may detect the influence of the work of Peter Kropotkin.[37] This dialectical naturalism is also organic: Bookchin proposes that social evolution

---

34. John Clark, 'A Social Ecology', *Capitalism, Nature, Socialism* 8:3 (1997), 3–33 (10).
35. Bookchin, *The Philosophy of Social Ecology*, 2nd edition, p. 85.
36. Ibid., p. 78   37. Ibid., p. 61.

has its precondition in – indeed, phases out of – natural evolution. In the development of evolution, a continuum of the emergence of the human from nature may be discerned.

Bookchin's naturalism makes a strong claim concerning the emergence of the human from natural conditions. 'The power of social ecology lies in the association it establishes between society and ecology, in understanding that the social is, potentially at least, a fulfilment of the *latent* dimension of freedom in nature, and that the ecological is a major organising principle of social development. In short, social ecology advances the guidelines for an ecological society.'[38] We should be careful here: Bookchin is not proposing that we should read off from nature blueprints or templates for human, social organisation. Rather, he wants to argue that some of the characteristics of humanity have precursors in natural evolution; human characteristics such as freedom, creativity and rationality are the products of evolution; humanity is evolutionary nature become self-conscious.

The emergence of second nature thus has as its precondition a vibrant and lively first nature. More than this, 'one may claim . . . that there is a natural *tendency* toward greater complexity and subjectivity in first nature, arising from the very interactivity of matter, indeed a *nisus* toward self-consciousness'.[39] We may now appreciate the ontological foundation of the claim that nature is not only the precondition of the emergence of the human but also the precondition of its *development*. As Bookchin confirms, 'the study of nature exhibits a self-evolving *nisus*, so to speak, that is implicitly ethical. Mutualism, freedom, and subjectivity are not solely human values or concerns. They appear, *however germinally*, in larger cosmic or organic processes.' In other words, Bookchin seeks an objective basis for the ethics that he is proposing. 'If social ecology', he continues, 'can provide a coherent focus on the unity of mutualism, freedom, and subjectivity as aspects of a cooperative society that is free from domination and guided by reflection and reason, it will have removed the difficulties that have plagued naturalistic ethics for so long'.[40] In such fashion, Bookchin seeks to break down the epistemological *cordon sanitaire* that has separated mind from matter, the human from non-human nature.

Hence Bookchin can describe his naturalistic ethics as objective. As he puts it, 'we must invert Nietzsche's dictum "All facts are interpretations" and demand that all interpretation is rooted in objectivity'.[41] The

<hr>

38. Ibid., p. 87.   39. Ibid., p. 31.   40. Ibid., pp. 65–6.   41. Ibid., p. 179.

objectivity to which he appeals is set out in this dialectical naturalism, in which nature is seen as lively, active substance, out of which the social evolution of humanity phases. Thus we must see 'nature as a *ground* for ethics' as long as that nature is construed not hierarchically but instead as 'a nascent domain of freedom, selfhood, and consciousness'.[42] Important clues are thereby given in this movement, always dialectical, from first to second nature.

As human beings are by nature social, Bookchin appeals to a concept of nature to ground his anarchist ethics. The anarchist emphasis on freedom, creativity and rationality is not subjective or arbitrary, but instead has an objective basis. Thus we may appreciate that the anarchist politics that Bookchin proposes elsewhere – the self-governance of human communities by citizen's assemblies, and the privileging of citizenship as both a crucial way of understanding the human individual and as offering a training for individuals – has its objective basis in a naturalistic ethics. This anarchist politics emerges out of the tendencies to participation and differentiation that Bookchin has already detected in nature; and hierarchy and domination interrupt such participation and differentiation.

'In what sense does social ecology view nature as a grounding for an ethics of freedom?' asks Bookchin.[43] To avoid the charge that naturalism leads to natural law, or fascist construals of *Blut und Boden*, or Stalinist natural dialectics, Bookchin stresses that his position is dialectical. Dialectical reason is not deductive but, rather, eductive reasoning: 'Dialectic . . . is a logic of evolution from abstraction towards differentiation.'[44] Thus Bookchin will insist on a continuum of the emergence of the human from nature but such a continuum is always dialectical. The natural and the social should not be run together: 'indeterminacy' in nature is not 'autonomy' in humanity; 'openness' in nature is not 'freedom' in humanity. Instead, the integration of second nature with first nature involves 'an abiding ecological sensibility that embodies nature's thrust toward self-reflexivity'.[45] In short, the relationship is always dialectical. As Bookchin summarises the ontological–ethical commitments of social ecology:

> The power of social ecology lies in the association it establishes
> between society and ecology, in understanding that the social is,
> potentially at least, a fulfilment of the *latent* dimension of freedom in
> nature, and that the ecological is a major organizing principle of social

42. Bookchin, *The Modern Crisis*, p. 10.   43. Ibid., p. 72.
44. Bookchin, *The Philosophy of Social Ecology*, 2nd edn, p. 112.
45. Ibid., p. 132.

development. In short, social ecology advances the guidelines for an ecological society. The great divorce between nature and society – or between the 'biological' and the 'cultural' – is overcome by shared developmental concepts such as greater diversity in evolution; the wider and more complete participation of all components in a whole; and the ever more fecund potentialities that expand the horizon of freedom and self-reflexivity. Society, like mind, ceases to be *sui generis*. Like mind, with its natural history, social life emerges from the loosely banded animal community to form the highly institutionalised human community.[46]

A political theology that explicates a common realm of God, nature and humanity will find much to welcome in this dialectical naturalism: a holistic emphasis on the unity of nature and society; a dialectical account of human–nature relations towards the affirmation of diversity and differences; the stress that nature is a companion of society and is always the condition of its development; and the insistence that restrictive or oppressive political organisation cannot be read off this dialectical construal of nature. Before beginning a critique, I want to complete my analysis of the political trajectory of Bookchin's position by reviewing his notion of confederal municipalism.

Confederal municipalism

Social ecologist John Clark writes: 'If social ecology is an attempt to understand the dialectical movement of society within the context of a larger dialectic of society and nature, ecocommunitarianism is the project of creating a way of life consonant with that understanding.'[47] Although 'confederal municipalism' is Bookchin's preferred term for his programme of anarchist politics, Clark's summary captures well the trajectory of Bookchin's political theory. Bookchin proposes a politics, a critique of contemporary urbanisation, and, moreover, suggests a programme for moving towards municipalism.[48]

True to his anarchist commitments, Bookchin argues that, although politics is today ordinarily associated with statecraft, politics should instead be associated with a polity organised by direct democracy. To make

---

46. Ibid., p. 87.   47. Clark, 'Municipal Dreams', p. 137.
48. Through this section, I draw mainly on Bookchin's most recent statement on this topic, *Urbanization without Cities: Towards a New Politics of Citizenship* (London and New York: Cassell, revised edn 1995). A case could be made, I think, that Bookchin's confederal municipalism represents a *narrowing* of his politics; nevertheless, here I concentrate on his most recent, substantial statement.

his point, Bookchin distinguishes between three 'realms': the social, the state and the political.[49] Arguing that 'politics' is usually understood as the operations of the state, Bookchin argues for the recovery of a genuine *polis*. Properly understood, the political is independent of the social and the state. The state he characterises as the 'professional apparatus with a monopoly of violence that is used by ruling classes to control meddlesome lower classes'.[50] Opposed to this are the face-to-face democratic operations of the municipality. Bookchin identifies certain precursors to this municipal politics: the Athenian *polis*, of course, but also the Parisian sections of the French Revolution and the tradition of town-hall meetings in New England. Whether or not these precursors have had an ecological component, Bookchin argues that his confederal municipalism includes the attempt 'to achieve a new harmonization between people, and between humanity and the natural world'. Further, 'any attempt to tailor a human community to a natural "ecosystem" in which it is located cuts completely against the grain of centralized power, be it state or corporate'.[51] We see how the outworking of the critique of domination together with a critique of statism emerge as a political programme. Any hierarchical society – which for Bookchin must include a statist society – will be unable to tailor itself to its natural surroundings but will, rather, dominate them. Hierarchical, statist society is anti-ecological.

Confederal municipalism is thereby dedicated to formulating a political programme that is non-hierarchical, opposes the centralising power of the state and affirms the values of diversity, participation and freedom. Nor is the link between confederal municipalism and dialectical naturalism hard to discern: a statist society – particularly the modern city – secures the 'dissolution of nature and society's evolutionary thrust toward diversity, complexity and community'. And this must be regarded as 'an ecological problem in the sense that diversity, variety, and participation constitute the basis not only for the stability of human consociation but also for the creativity that is imparted to us by diversity, indeed, ultimately, the freedom that alternative forms of development allow for the evolution of new, richer, and well-rounded social forms'.[52] On account of the dialectical relations between nature and society, a municipalist form of politics is thereby also an ecological politics. We are back at Bookchin's point that nature is the precondition for not only the emergence but also the *development*

---

49. Bookchin, 'Comments on the International Social Ecology Network . . .', 158.
50. Bookchin, *From Urbanization to Cities*, p. 3.
51. Ibid., p. 237.   52. Ibid., p. 158.

of society. The development of society is thereby interpreted – in terms of unity in difference – always in relation to the development of nature; both developmental paths are evolutionary. And what is the *telos* of such development? Bookchin's answer privileges an ever-increasing richness, diversity, complexity and, in human society, rationality. For such a state to be achieved, the political programme must be one that secures a non-hierarchical, non-dominating polity in which human freedom and participation towards self-realisation are secured, and in which the variety, diversity and fecundity of nature are protected. Hence, Bookchin's municipality is an ecological municipality: it seeks harmonious relations with non-human nature, which is its dialectical ground.

What Bookchin then attempts – perhaps with too little justification – is to deduce his confederal municipality from these premises. In such fashion, Bookchin renews the anarcho-communist tradition of political organisation founded in neighbourhoods, with its principal forum of decision-making being face-to-face discussion in an assembly (in which all citizens of a neighbourhood would be eligible to participate). The governing principle here is unity in diversity: through such assemblies the good of a community can be established and diverse expression of that good can be respected. The small-scale nature of the polity also permits the natural context in which the neighbourhood is situated to be acknowledged: the assembly dialectically includes in its holistic deliberations the content of its relations with its regional nature. This political programme is confederal as well as municipal: by confederal (earlier anarchist tradition employed the term, federal), Bookchin means 'democratic and truly communitarian forms of interdependence'[53] in which localism is rescued from parochialism and by which neighbourhoods interact with one another (which may include a group of neighbourhoods calling to account a fellow neighbourhood for, say, anti-ecological practices).

In coming to an interim assessment of Bookchin's politics, I focus on two issues: the characterisation of the three realms of the social, the state and the political; and the character of the political relations between nature and the polity.[54]

53. Ibid., p. 252.
54. Plainly, these are not the only criticisms that might be made. Other areas for critique are: the utopian aspects of Bookchin's politics; the concentration on libertarian municipalism as the only form of anarchist politics; the polyvalence of the notion of citizenship; whether confederalism is an adequate response to the range of relations operative between ecocommunities in an age of globalisation.

First, I review the relation between the social, the state and the political. Clearly, the aim of this threefold distinction is to find ways of construing politics as *other than* statecraft. Rather than, say, operate a distinction between civil society and the state, Bookchin tries to open up a third political front, so to speak, as the realm of true citizenship and authentic political *paideia*. Furthermore, it must be true that the state can be undermined only by means of a 'shared communitarian practice' that opposes the state.[55] I fail to see why, however, such shared practice might not emanate from the realm of the social. That is, why should opposition to the state be sourced only to the municipal polity? May not such opposition also emerge by way of shared communitarian practice in the realm of society? (And, to put my theological cards on the table, the church as community may also, I contend, be a guarantor of, as well as a contributor to, that shared practice towards social and ecological unity in the common realm.) A more dialectical reading would see the variety of society and polity in a unity that is in distinction from (although also dialectically related to) the state.

At the root of this effort to privilege the municipality is, I would argue, a determination to protect the centrality of community. The trajectory of his thought therefore begins in community (note the construal of an organic, non-hierarchical past). The community suffers the privations of hierarchy of which the modern city and the modern state are outcomes. To these unhappy developments, municipality as *polis* is opposed. Such a reading renders intelligible the high significance that Bookchin ascribes to the concept of municipality. Consider this statement: 'Conceived in more institutional terms, the municipality is not only the basis for a free society; it is the irreducible ground for genuine individuality as well.'[56] Yet why should the *political* organisation of a society be its basis and ground? We may agree with Bookchin that the elements of a true society are communal but that is not the same as maintaining that these elements are municipal. A true society must be tested by reference to activities undertaken throughout the social realm rather than only in the municipality. Bookchin seems to grant normative status to the *polis* but not also to the *societas*. Thereby he grants prevenient status to the political over the societal. The societal may be described as 'the overall quality of a society which at its best has a supportive and enabling culture, a culture whose root

55. Clark, 'Municipal Dreams', p. 144. Through the next few paragraphs, my thinking is deeply indebted to Clark's essay.
56. Bookchin, *From Urbanization to Cities*, p. 226.

paradigms are intact and capable of comprehending both differentiation into particularities and universals which hold the human together in the ancestral sense of a *religio*, a mutual binding informed by a Gospel of grace and truth'.[57] By proposing the municipality as the ground and basis of society, Bookchin protects his anarchist presuppositions, but at the expense of the societal.

Second, how are the political relations between nature and the municipality to be understood? For Bookchin, the municipality must operate on the basis of face-to-face democratic procedures in which citizens gather to deliberate and decide on matters that affect the whole community. Forms of democracy that are not based on such direct interaction turn upon systems of representation. Such systems are rejected by Bookchin. However, a difficulty arises when one considers the relations between the municipality and non-human nature. Within a dialectical naturalism, such relations must be attended to: after all, the municipality is the context and agent of a political programme where humanity, as nature rendered self-conscious, seeks both the affirmation of diversity, complexity and spontaneity in the human polity and ecologically benign ways of affirming these same tendencies in the natural realm. None the less, how is nature accounted for in the political deliberations of the polity? Bookchin says very little about this in his proposal for a confederal municipality.

One reason for this lack of discussion may be that any attempt to conceive the polity and nature holistically will, of course, require some system of representation. For Bookchin, however, all systems of representation are anathema. In a non-representational politics such as Bookchin's, such representation cannot be thought, much less achieved. None the less, a different conclusion is here inescapable: in the *political* realm (the realm of *human* deliberation) nature must be *represented*. Nor should this matter of representation surprise us: as Clark notes, there are many people and entities that are represented in the democratic process: 'Just as we can relate as moral agents to entities that are not agents, we can exercise duties of citizenship in relations to other beings who are not citizens.'[58] Indeed, we must effect such representation over, say, water supplies and sewage disposal, not least as these affect 'other beings', if such matters are to be attended to at all as part of the political process. So the question returns: in

57. Richard R. Roberts, 'A Postmodern Church? Some Preliminary Reflections on Ecclesiology and Social Theory', in D. F. Ford and D. L. Stamps (eds.), *Essentials of Christian Community* (Edinburgh: T. & T. Clark, 1996), pp. 179–95 (p. 179).
58. Clark, 'Municipal Dreams', p. 146.

a non-representational system, how is the representation of non-human nature to be achieved? (And are not many of our ecological problems to be sourced to the fact that the West has not been able to secure in its democratic deliberations a workable system of representation for nature?)

An anarchist common realm?

One striking aspect of Bookchin's position is that he refuses the notion of hierarchy in nature not by widening but by *reducing* the gap between society and nature.[59] Such a reduction ensures that Bookchin's position addresses effectively the questions posed at the beginning of this chapter. The distance between nature and society is reduced through the commitment to read both in terms of the developmental emergence of diversity, mutuality and spontaneity. Yet the reading is dialectical in order to insist that the narrowing of distance is never the overcoming of difference. Hierarchies cannot be projected onto nature; neither can nature be interpreted as a resource for natural laws (or, worse, fascist notions of blood, race and soil or Stalinist materialist dialectics) to which humanity must conform. Bookchin also offers a sophisticated account of the emergence of the human from the non-human and offers an account of the dependence of the human on the non-human. The diversity of humanity and the diversity of nature are linked in a dialectical relationship.

As such, Bookchin may be understood as a thinker in the movement of Left-Aristotelianism. According to John Ely, whose designation this is,[60] such Left-Aristotelianism offers, first, a civic republicanism theory of democracy, based on the participation of the citizen, which, in turn, involves a criticism of the nation-state and the Weberian construal of 'politics as statecraft'. As Ely notes, citizen is a 'non-ascriptive' notion which thereby undercuts identities based on familial, ethnic or racial characteristics. Second, Left-Aristotelianism provides a philosophy of nature. That is, Bookchin offers an account of nature in relation to an '"objective" or "substantive rationality"' which cannot in turn be disassociated from the 'problem of ontology in general'.[61] Bookchin is a Left-Aristotelian to the extent that a moral pluralism and relativism is to be rejected in favour of an ethics grounded in an ontology of nature.

59. Bookchin, *The Modern Crisis*, p. 64n.
60. John Ely, 'Ernst Bloch, Natural Rights, and the Greens', in David Macauley (ed.), *Minding Nature: The Philosophers of Ecology* (New York: Guilford, 1996), pp. 134–66 (p. 143).
61. Ibid., pp. 137, 139.

How does this discussion inform a political theology of nature? What is remarkable and important about Bookchin's position is the way that he relates nature and society. Bookchin refuses to oppose some abstraction dubbed humanity to an abstraction called nature. Instead, Bookchin specifies the hierarchies of domination that blight contemporary society and explores how these cannot be read off a non-hierarchical nature. Such a conclusion is very important for the concept of the common realm of God, nature and humanity. How so? Because the common realm also proposes a holism in which the unity of the created order – humanity in, with and alongside nature – forms a whole (in asymmetrical relation to the activity of God). However, the construal of such a holism must be alert to differences: nature and society are internally differentiated.

The common realm is also committed to the affirmation of diversity or difference within that unity. Nor does the common realm wish to deny the restrictive 'differences' to be associated with hierarchical structures and patterns of domination but rather wishes to theorise these in oppositional fashion. The construal of the common realm as a theological holism must, in short, be alert to differences. Nature and society are internally differentiated. And the differentiation within society may be hierarchical. Furthermore, the relations between these zones should not be construed in domineering ways in which nature is employed in support of dominating and unjust practices. For Bookchin, the principal errors in this regard are the projections of nature in Stalinism and Nazism, and the view of nature as mean, cruel and stingy.

At the risk of making a crass political judgment, in my view the principal political problem for a politics of nature in the Western democracies is neither a sclerotic Communism nor a restrictive fascism. Rather, contemporary politics of nature situates itself around the problem of the stinginess of nature. This is especially true in the discussion of population growth. In other words, the stinginess of nature is employed to underpin the scarcity of 'natural goods' and hence their unequal distribution. A liberal state will therefore seek to persuade us of three conclusions: that the human story may be told without reference to the story of nature; that difficulties with nature's lack of fecundity will best be addressed by the technical resources of the state; and, finally, that the best arbiter of access to nature's goods is the state. Of all three conclusions, a political–ideological interpretation of nature is suspicious.

Against these conclusions, a political theology of nature affirms the continuities between humanity and nature, insists that the interactions

between nature and society must be the subject of political deliberation, and queries whether the state has a monopoly of insight in these
matters. Furthermore, in denying that these are merely technical matters,
an ecological theology founded on the common realm of God, nature and
humanity will always wish to ask: which hierarchies are served, and dis-
guised, by this construal of access to nature as a technical problem? At the
very least, Murray Bookchin's social ecology invites a political theology of
nature not to construe the whole of humanity and nature in terms of an
harmonious unity or convergent political or social interests. The common
realm is fractured both by gender (as we saw in the previous chapter) and
by the elitism of technical managers who assign nature's goods in some
underspecified yet 'general' interest.

What is vital here is to subject this account of the domination of nature by technique to the scrutiny of the concept of temporality. Two results follow from such an affirmation. First, that nature is not to be zoned
off from human society but is rather always the companion of a society;
nature, as Bookchin reminds us, is the condition of the development, not
merely the emergence, of human society. Second, how nature relates to society is always a matter of temporal emergence: the full range of how nature is incorporated in human society must be attended to. In other words,
such incorporation must not be restricted to the activities of the state. Furthermore, the stress on emergence as temporal indicates that the modalities of emergence are not fixed and can be countered and tested through
forms of agency, both natural and social. Put another way, nature is not
static nor are nature–society relations unalterable. In relation to both
these commitments, the notion of agency – ours and nature's – needs to be
rethought.

A second way in which Bookchin's social ecology contributes to the development of a political theology of nature is more problematic. The way
that Bookchin construes the polity as the ground of social being I have already rejected as too undialectical a formulation. By privileging the community of the municipality in this fashion, Bookchin overlooks the themes
of the sociality and spatiality of nature. Although he maintains a welcome
emphasis on the subjectivity of nature, the teleological–evolutionary
strain in Bookchin's thinking considers human beings as extending and
completing this subjectivity. Hence the lack of detail offered by Bookchin
on the relations between a municipality and nature. Throughout, I have
preferred to stress the sociality of human–nature relations: nature in its
otherness is the companion of humanity across all dimensions of human

society. In such fashion, the *necessary* transformation of nature if there is to be human life at all is properly accounted for. Indeed, as part of its nature, humanity shares this stress on the construction of a habitable 'society' with all other life.

This, in turn, leads to a third issue which a political theology of nature may derive from Bookchin's social ecology: the political representation of nature. Nature is always present, for Bookchin, but not in the political life of the *polis*. Bookchin thereby breaches my rule of sociality, for he cannot specify under the conditions of *direct* democracy how nature is to be construed as present. That is, Bookchin protects his notion of anarchist community construed as polity but at the expense of the political representation of nature. Bookchin is forced to arrive at this conclusion because for him direct democracy is constitutive of his account of the *polis*. And, because it is not a democratic subject in the ordinary sense, non-human nature cannot be present in face-to-face democratic discussion. Here the dialectic between the social and the ecological in Bookchin's social ecology comes to a halt. What is required is the mediation of nature so that it may be present in the political sphere. However, Bookchin's proposal domesticates nature by thrusting it outside of the political realm. (There is a further, ecclesiological, issue here: Bookchin's schema in fact places the church 'beyond' the polity in ways that are theologically unacceptable. For the Church in its identity is witness to the political rule of God and thereby cannot be excluded from the political realm.)

To put the matter somewhat differently, community alone cannot be understood as the ground of social being. Instead, the ground of social being is always in part natural. Immediately, we see that, if community needs to be supplemented by natural conditions, the notion of community is called into question. This is because, although communities are situated in particular regions yet nature cannot be zoned into regions. The spatiality of nature requires that the horizon of nature, as this surpasses all communities, cannot be ignored. (If the city of Bristol, where I am writing these lines, may be called a community, then Bristol makes a contribution through its pollution to the accumulation of greenhouse gases and thereby to *global* warming. In this fashion, Bristol makes a contribution to the melting of the ice caps and the disruption of the lives of polar bears whose habitat – especially access to food – is being altered by shorter, warmer winters. In sum, nature *surpasses* community.) In this context, attempting to understand nature as a local phenomenon makes no sense. The question returns: how is such nature to be represented politically?

Recall that back in chapter 2 I argued that the philosophical theology being proposed in this book interprets God in terms of activity, ground and force. Such differentiation in God is required if the totality of reality, in its determinations and in its wholeness, is to be thought theologically: without privilege either to the whole or to the parts. Thinking through the totality of the world from this perspective requires that both parts and wholes are related to the activity of God: the 'whole' of creation does not compete with God, and God is the ground of all the parts and the force that secures the whole.

These are abstract categories. However, in the light of the discussion of Bookchin, the theologico-political content of these categories may be enriched. We may conclude that nature–society forms both a whole, and a variety of parts. Nature and society comprise a unity, but always a unity of differences. Nature must be understood as both part and whole: it is the context of human living but also a horizon that surpasses all human habitats. Functioning as a whole in relation to humanity, nature does not function as the source of hierarchy. However, the presence of nature through all human endeavours is to be affirmed. There persists between nature and society a dialectic of continuity and difference. (Epistemologically, this is the correct order: the consideration of continuity precedes the identification of difference.) Nevertheless, the continuity is not that secured by some variant of natural laws, and the difference is not one of 'mastery'.

A political theology of nature will thereby be alert to any attempt to construe the unity of nature as a template for humanity, and to construe the unity of humanity in the form of the supremacy of the human. Nor will a political theology of nature invest in accounts of nature as support for hierarchical thinking but will agree that humanity is *by nature* social. The sociality of humanity and nature is thereby confirmed as the principal theme of the common realm, with spatiality of nature affirming the critical otherness of nature, and temporality affirming that both nature and society name processes of becoming.

A political theology of nature will take issue with some aspects of Bookchin's thought: the tendency of social ecology is perhaps towards a personalism in which humanity summarises and completes nature: humanity is nature become self-conscious. There are other tendencies in Bookchin's thought, but this Hegelian stress fits uneasily with the affirmation of nature as always present. The movement of social ecological inquiry tends not to highlight an encounter with the otherness of nature. The whole of nature is thereby somewhat downplayed in this holistic account. And the tendency towards voluntarism and idealism is evident in Bookchin's thought: the structure of Bookchin's inquiry focuses on the tendency to stress the centrality of a certain sort of politics as the way forward, rather than on the material labour by which humanity transforms nature.

None the less, the themes of sociality, spatiality and temporality are acquiring further definition: the whole of the common realm is not to be interpreted as hierarchical, nor should nature be employed as the source of hierarchy. Only by such means are the wholes and parts of the common realm to be construed in liberatory ways.

6

Socialist ecology: the production of nature

Ecological reconstruction of Marxism

'In almost every period since the Renaissance', writes Murray Bookchin, 'the development of revolutionary thought has been heavily influenced by a branch of science, often in conjunction with a school of philosophy'.[1] Can the development of the revolutionary thought of Christianity be advanced by a combination of ecological science and Marxist philosophy of praxis?[2] That is the question for this chapter. In what ways might the task of a political theology of nature be advanced through dynamic yet critical articulation with socialist ecology?

Of vital importance to a political theology of nature is how to think about natural limits, and their relation to scarcity. The notion of natural limits suggests that nature is mean and indifferent, to pick up one of Bookchin's refrains, and offers an explanation of the scarcity of social goods by reference to nature, thereby stabilising present society. However, a straightforward denial of natural scarcity is unpersuasive, not least as such a denial invites an expansionism without limits. Much ecotheology and political theory seems uncertain on this issue of limits. Socialist ecology is highly pertinent to this study, as we shall see, in that it offers a way of exploring the relationships between scarcity, social limits and the finiteness of nature. Further, socialist ecology has paid some attention to the ecological aspects of place which will inform a discussion of eucharistic place at the conclusion of this book (see chapter 9). For these two reasons, then, socialist ecology is relevant to this study.

1. Bookchin, *Post-Scarcity Anarchism*, p. 79.
2. That Marxism has contributed to the development of Christian theology needs little defence: consider only the theologies of Barth, Bonhoeffer and Tillich; Rahner, Moltmann and Metz; Gutiérrez, Sölle and Schüssler Fiorenza.

Socialist ecology neither stresses the ecosphere over the technosphere nor privileges the technosphere to the detriment of the ecosphere.[3] In Castree and Braun's summary, ecoMarxism has 'tempered the unabashed anthropocentrism of Marx's political economy, but without evacuating it altogether' and 'has widened both Marxian notions of political action and challenged the political separatisms of "green politics"'.[4] Over against the anti-capitalistic, yet romantic, strains of deep ecology, with its turn to nature, socialist forms of ecology stress the production of nature and the matter of the just distribution of the results of human labour. Yet environmentalists have, in turn, complained that Marxism, first, is productivist and, second, promotes the mastery of nature.[5]

Are these charges fair? In one sense, it is true to say that Marxism is a form of humanism. Yet the humanism of Marxism is both *pessimistic* and *natural*. In other words, the means of human advancement is by way of struggle, and the measure of the human cannot be taken without reference to the natural conditions of humanity. Thus we should expect to find within ecological Marxism a firm stress on the construction of nature as a human project, coupled with a sense that the reconstruction of humanity's relations with nature turns upon the alteration of human social relations. To these two commitments a third must be added: a stress on the social metabolism between humanity and non-human nature. Ecological Marxism explores ways in which Marxism has been weak in its attentiveness to nature, and offers a reconstruction of human economy and natural economy in ways that are more attentive to the otherness of nature.

Acknowledging important difficulties in the work of Marx and later Marxists, the ecological reconstruction of Marxism has concentrated on the concept of historical materialism. In other words, attention is focused on the theme of human production and the use of nature rather than paying attention to, say, the nature of Nature under discussion or nature as

---

3. For the terminology, see Barry Commoner, *Making Peace with the Planet* (New York: The New Press, 1992), p. 7.

4. Noel Castree and Bruce Braun, 'The Construction of Nature and the Nature of Construction', in Braun and Castree (eds.), *Remaking Reality: Nature at the Millennium* (London and New York: Routledge, 1998), pp. 3–42 (pp. 9–10). Cf. the critique of Marxism in David Harvey, *Justice, Nature and the Geography of Difference* (Oxford: Blackwell, 1996), p. 193.

5. See O'Connor, *Natural Causes*; Kate Soper, 'Greening Prometheus: Marxism and Ecology', in Ted Benton (ed.), *The Greening of Marxism* (New York: Guilford Press, 1996), pp. 81–99. Other grounds for disagreement are the lamentably poor environmental records in the countries of 'actually existing socialism' and social agency being located by Marxism almost exclusively in the working class.

the measure of the human.[6] In one sense, such ecological reconstruction suffers from some of the standard weaknesses for which Marxism is traditionally attacked: lack of attention to the normative bases of the good life; excessive attention to the material interpreted as the economic to the detriment of the material interpreted as cultural. To begin, however, I wish to draw out some themes from the work of Marx and Engels which will set up the analysis of the ecological reconstruction of Marxism.

In their analysis of capitalism, Marx and Engels were concerned in part with the ideologies of Malthus and liberal political economy. Understanding ideology in the strict, negative, sense to indicate a theoretical practice in which the emancipatory potentials of a circumstance are persistently misrecognised and misrepresented, their concern about both these ideologies may be understood in terms of tendencies to de-historicise the workings of capital.[7] To combat such ideology, Marx stresses the social forms, practical and epistemological, of capitalism.[8] For Marx's main target was the tendency of capitalism's apologists to dehistoricise capitalism and thereby to place it outside the realm of human agency. However, as a consequence of emphasising that capitalism is a historical formation, and thereby reformable, Marx tended to understate, undervalue and undertheorise the fact that production is always ecoproduction. That is, human productive activity includes aspects of nature.

If we follow the Marxian emphasis that the fundamental creative/ productive human relation is between humanity and nature,[9] the division of labour that follows is to be interpreted from this basic insight. In ecological perspective, humanity produces its social life yet always in the context of the 'inorganic body' of Nature. What is this 'inorganic body'? This is, Marx claims, both humanity's 'direct means of life' and 'the material object and instrument of humanity's life activity'.[10] It follows from this claim that nature is independent of humanity yet is also the essential condition of human life. Nature, as Marx writes, is not a human product.

6. See Ted Benton, 'Introduction to Part II', in T. Benton (ed.), *The Greening of Marxism* (New York: Guilford Press, 1996), pp. 103–10 (p. 104); Ely, 'Ernst Bloch, Natural Rights and the Greens', pp. 134–66.

7. For a fuller articulation, see my *Theology, Ideology and Liberation*, chapter 1.

8. The questioning of the notion of natural limits in the work of, say, György Lukács may thereby be traced back to one aspect of Marx's work. See György Lukács, *History and Class Consciousness* (London: Merlin Press, 1972); cf. John Ely, 'Lukács's Construction of Nature,' *Capitalism, Nature, Socialism* 1 (1998), 107–16.

9. Such a position contrasts with Bookchin's argument that the idea of the domination of nature is to be sourced to intrahuman domination.

10. Karl Marx and Friedrich Engels, 'Marx and Engels on Ecology', in Merchant (ed.), *Ecology* pp. 28–43 (pp. 30, 36).

Is this a naturalism? Not quite, because Marx argues – on the basis of a distinction that human beings produce nature yet animals collect from it – that it is not possible to transfer laws of nature to human social life. Indeed, he states quite specifically that there are no 'eternal natural laws of society'.[11] What is truly human is not attributable to natural laws transferred to the social sphere but rather to the mastery by humanity of its social life. And, as is well known, he saw in the capitalism of his day not mastery but rather irrationalities of a punitive kind.

Our mastery of nature is incomplete yet need not be so: Marx links the theme of freedom as the mastery of our social circumstance with the theme of the mastery of nature.[12] A significant weakness may now be discerned in Marx's thinking. The mastery of social life is to be thought together with the theme of the mastery of nature; social irrationalities involve irrationalities in our productive relations with nature also. Scarcity is here theorised not as a basic limit in the forces of production but as restrictions, located in capitalist relations of production, to be overcome. It remains true that Marx noted that capitalism denudes natural wealth: 'Capitalist production, therefore, develops technology, and the combination together of various processes into a social whole, only by sapping the original sources of all wealth – the soil and the labourer.'[13] However, it is not clear, according to Marxist commentators, that Marx in emphasising the overcoming of 'natural irrationalities' developed an adequate theoretical account of such exploitation.

From historical materialism to environmental ecomaterialism

From such a reading, it is not hard to see why James O'Connor might characterise historical materialism as neither sufficiently historical nor material.[14] To overcome this lack, two moves are required. First, environmental history must be grasped as the culmination of historical inquiry: the history of nature is now to be included alongside the history of humanity. Second, ecology (not restricted to the discipline of the life sciences) must be understood as the *telos* of materialism in which the relation between the materialities of human ecology and nature's economy is theorised. How, then, is historical materialism to be rethought to incorporate

---

11. Ibid., p. 33.   12. Ibid., pp. 41–2.   13. Ibid., p. 36.
14. O'Connor, *Natural Causes*, pp. 48–70.

such a double amendment? Here I survey briefly the work of O'Connor and Ted Benton.

O'Connor and Benton respond in similar fashion to the demand for the ecological reconstruction of Marxism by attending to the way in which Marxism theorises the production of nature. According to standard interpretations of Marx, an important distinction is drawn between the forces and relations of production. Productive forces refer, broadly, to the resources used in production – people, plant, sometimes land – understood as a mode of cooperation. Relations refer to the social/economic relations in which these productive forces are operated: capitalist relations of production are always class relations. This is the classical *first contradiction of capitalism* identified by Marx: the *social* nature of the productive processes of capitalist accumulation is disclosed as capital goes through crises of overproduction, produces enormous wealth and yet leaves some in poverty.

Yet O'Connor notes, with some caveats, that Marx offers the beginnings of an account of a second contradiction: here the tension resides not between the forces and relations of production but instead between the forces and relations of production on the one side and conditions of production on the other. What are these *conditions of production*? According to O'Connor, Marx proposed three conditions of capitalist production: physical conditions; personal conditions of labour power; communal or general conditions of social production. Hidden behind this technical armature are, O'Connor suggests, three basic ecological conditions of capitalist production which may be described as follows:

> Today, 'external physical conditions' are discussed in terms of the viability of ecosystems; the adequacy of atmospheric ozone levels; the stability of coast-lines and watersheds; soil, air, and water quality; and the like. 'Laborpower' is discussed in terms of the physical and mental well-being of workers; the kind and degree of worker socialisation; toxicity of work relations and the workers' ability to cope; and human beings as social productive forces and biological organisms generally. 'Communal conditions' are discussed in terms of 'social capital,' 'infrastructure,' and so on.[15]

In such fashion, O'Connor retheorises Marx to offer an account of the basic environmental conditions of the interaction of human economy and nature's economy. Against the overly abstract commitments of the second

15. Ibid., pp. 160–1.

platform of deep ecology, presented here are not only the crucial ecological conditions of life but also reference to the conditions of the individual worker (the theme of much trade union negotiation) and that which develops and sustains the capacity of labour to labour: education, the urban transport system, the family. The metabolism of the relations between humanity and non-human nature thus has three modalities: physical conditions, environment of the worker and social infrastructure.

O'Connor identifies the tension between the natural conditions of production, and capitalist forces and relations of production, as a *second contradiction of capitalism*. In the increasing struggle over use of non-renewable resources, the toxicity of workers' environments and the increasing traffic congestion in cities (with the attendant health risks) – to give a few examples – the nature of the social arrangements that structure these problems becomes more apparent. Green movements, trade unions and urban justice groups emerge in response to the greater awareness of the social origin and cause of environmental problems. In the same way that the first contradiction of capitalism generated the labour movement, so the second contradiction generates an environmental, if heterogeneous, movement.

Is this merely anthropocentric? Let us note, first, that this question may not be the best one to ask: we saw in chapter 3 that the determined attempt to overcome anthropocentrism in favour of biocentrism generates a series of theoretical difficulties, including the affirmation of a self and the steady retreat of nature. However, O'Connor notes that Marx generally failed to interpret the mode of production with sufficient radicality to grasp that labour has the form of cooperation between nature and culture.[16] Nature is, properly, to be understood as 'an autonomous partner'.[17] Elsewhere, O'Connor indicates the importance of acknowledging, theoretically and practically, that non-human nature has its own dynamics and tendencies:

> Nature's economy, however, is organized (or organizes itself) on very different principles [to that of capital]. As biological and physical systems, hydraulic cycles, heat/energy systems, soil cycles, ecosystem diversity, and so on, at some point on the production curve, nature's productivity is self-limiting – a 'barrier to be overcome' by capital.[18]

O'Connor also introduces the concept of a logic of reciprocity. Such a reciprocating logic complements an understanding of the mode of production as a mode of cooperation. To this theme we shall return.

16. Ibid., p. 39.   17. Ibid., p. 45.   18. O'Connor, *Natural Causes*, p. 181.

Whereas O'Connor appears to regard Marx's work as normative yet underdeveloped, Ted Benton's view is more sceptical. However, Benton also begins his analysis from the conceptual apparatus of historical materialism: the productivity of the labour process. Benton argues that the way in which Marx conceptualises the labour process fails adequately to give an account of the natural conditions of human life and features only one intentional structure (the transformative). According to Marx, in Benton's interpretation, there are three aspects of the labour process: the worker, that which is worked on and the instruments of labour. Furthermore, the instruments of labour refer both to the 'natural' condition of land and the 'produced' condition of social infrastructure.

Two important criticisms of this schema are made by Benton. First, the intentional structure of the labour process is depicted as one of transformation. While the privileging of this account is readily understandable given the context in which Marx and Engels were writing, Benton concedes, yet such a model seems appropriate only for the production of certain types of commodity. The eco-regulatory practices of agriculture which do not transform but instead establish and maintain the conditions for crop growth are not properly described in the model. A second example, which has yet a different structure, is that of mining: here the basic material – coal, for example – is not transformed but rather appropriated or extracted.

What are the consequences of such a valorisation of one model of production, that is, the transformative? These are many: the claim that raw materials and the instruments of production are limited in quantity is occluded; lost to sight is the important point that all raw materials have their origins in collection from nature; the reproduction of labour power – reproduction itself, the home – is undertheorised; the contours of contextual conditions – natural and produced – need greater definition; unforeseen consequences of labour processes are not attended to.[19] The larger conclusion to be drawn here is that Marx persistently overinterprets the transformative capacity of his own productivist – that is, already narrow – account of the labour process. Benton concludes that certain contextual conditions of production need to be theorised separately from instruments of production; how the sustainability of contextual conditions is to be secured needs theoretical articulation; and theoretical

19. Ted Benton, 'Marxism and Natural Limits: an Ecological Critique and Reconstruction', in T. Benton (ed.), *The Greening of Marxism*, pp. 157–83 (pp. 165–6).

purchase is required to explain unintended consequences of labour processes (e.g. pollution).

These commitments apply a fortiori to the type of intentional structure – eco-regulative – which governs the labour process in agriculture. Here the language of transformation is unhelpful, Benton contends. Agricultural labour is not transformative but is instead directed to the maintenance of the natural conditions as good for growth; such a context of natural conditions also suggests a certain rhythm in which crops are grown; nor do humans have complete control over these conditions (for example, climate and weather).[20]

What is the significance for a political theology of nature of such ecological reconstructions of Marxism? First, we must note that we are presented with interpretations of the range of ways in which human ecology relates to nature's economy. We shall have reason to test their strengths and weaknesses shortly, but we can already see an important emphasis which is new to the present study. Whereas deep ecology, for example, tends to focus on the general 'fact' of the placing of humanity in nature in a biocentric account, here the emphasis is on the discernment of relations between humanity and nature. A detailed account of the ways in which humanity *produces* nature – earlier identified as a lacuna in Bookchin's work – is presented. And, furthermore, whereas deep ecology tends to concentrate on people and their capacities for identification with nature, here the matter is social and economic practices in their contextual conditions. We are presented with a tendency towards concretion: the attempt to explore how non-human nature acquires the characteristics of use-value under a determinate set of conditions. This matter of concretion is vital, as we shall see when it is raised in materially theological terms, in chapter 7, under the rubric of Christology. In addition, the ecological reconstruction of Marxism raises interesting questions for a political theology of nature about the meaning of the *mastery of nature*, *natural limits* and the relation of *scarcity and abundance*. To these issues, I now turn.

The 'mastery of nature' and the concept of 'limits'

Raymond Williams has commented on the ideological employment – 'mystique', he calls it – of the concept of the 'mastery of nature'.[21] Developing Williams's argument, in what senses should the mastery of nature be

---

20. Benton, 'Marxism and Natural Limits', p. 161.
21. Raymond Williams, *Resources of Hope* (London: Verso, 1989), p. 214.

regarded as ideological? First, mastery suggests that humanity is not part of nature: in a triumph of alienation, humanity is *against* nature rather than being both *in* and against nature. Second, the impression is given that humanity has knowledge of nature which is conformable and suitable to such mastery: epistemic triumphalism. Third, mastery advocates that humanity has the full capacity to judge errors in its attempts at mastery: a self-reflexive triumphalism. Fourth, it proposes that human beings do have, as practical agents, the capacities – what Marx would call the 'instruments of labour' – to master nature: technological triumphalism. At this point, the gendered aspect of the metaphor comes into focus: for what is required as operative presuppositions of the metaphor, in its ideological capacities to make a meaning stick, is disembodied, self-correcting rationality which can both properly determine the needs of humanity and respond to new circumstances: the abstract and triumphalist rationality of liberal capitalism.[22]

The social aspect of this metaphor of the mastery of nature is manifest. The social project of a certain sort of society, the political project of a certain type of polity, and the economic project of a certain way of producing nature is summarised – accurately yet untruthfully – under the rubric of the 'mastery of nature'. However, to offer a critique of the metaphor is not to attend properly to the difficult matter that the metaphor conceals: the *limits of nature*.

Much of the ecological literature, including ecotheology, trades upon a somewhat diffuse account of limits. There is a limit to the number of people the earth can support; a limit to the amount of pollution and waste that natural ecosystems can absorb; a limit to the destruction of natural habitats; a limit to the reduction in species diversity beyond which the complexity of ecosystems, and thereby their fragile capacity to support life, is threatened. (This reading of limit is concerned with the *preservation* of species, etc.) In other areas, a different concept of limits is operative: with regard to the extraction of resources for the supply of energy, the finitude of oil and gas supplies is noted – hence limit in the sense of a finite amount. The term 'non-renewable' has, as part of its meaning, precisely such a sense of limit. (Here limit is concerned with the *conservation* of resources.)

What is less clear in the literature is precisely how these limits are constituted and, furthermore, how such limits apply to knowledge of nature.

22. We should here, in advance of a full discussion in chapter 8, note the analogies between the mastery of nature and the reinterpretation of dominion as stewardship.

What is striking in the deep ecological literature reviewed in chapter 3 is – not least given the range of disciplines on which such arguments draw – the sheer *confidence* by which claims are made.[23] If ecological thought provides us with such sophisticated yet general knowledge regarding the relations of humanity with nature, why does the notion of limits lack specification? Is there not a strange mismatch between, on the one hand, the wide-ranging prescriptions on the greening of the world and, on the other, the vagueness regarding the discussion of limits?

On account of such vagueness, the appeal to the mastery of nature is at least intelligible, if not persuasive. The appeal to mastery, in other words, raises questions against the positing of limits. Defending such mastery, Reiner Grundmann argues that Marx maintains the modern attitude to nature: human beings seek, and should seek, to dominate nature; human beings are both in and against nature and enact their domination of nature through the construction of a 'second nature'.[24] From such a position Grundmann argues that if a society encounters ecological problems, this is clear evidence of a *failure* in the mastery of nature. Ecological difficulties are social irrationalities which require practical resolution. In a sense, then, such problems require more domination, not less.

This affirmation connects directly to the consideration of limits. For Grundmann, failure to attend to the domination of nature is thereby to admit to naturalism. To go with biocentrism and ascribe value to nature in the attempt to reduce its exploitation is to engage in naturalistic 'mysticism'. In good Marxist fashion, he connects such mysticism to religion: 'But, unless one adopts a mystical or religious standpoint, there is always a human interest behind the attitude that nature should be left out there "for itself".'[25] To travel this way is to posit natural laws to which human beings are asked to conform, and so to naturalise scarcity. To take this 'mystical' way, Grundmann argues, is to fall back behind the modern treatment of nature to which the theme of mastery is central. The outcome of such 'scarcity' is an alienated projection of the fixity of laws on to nature so as to protect the interests of the rich and powerful – after all, is it not the West that would benefit most if, in accordance with 'nature's laws', the target of zero economic growth was adopted? How do we guard against an

23. Cf. Hans Magnus Enzensberger, 'A Critique of Political Ecology', in Benton (ed.), *The Greening of Marxism*, pp. 17–49 (p. 18).
24. Reiner Grundmann, 'The Ecological Challenge to Marxism', *New Left Review* 187 (1991), 103–20.
25. Ibid., 114.

overreaching naturalism which lays out a set of laws – nature knows best, to use Barry Commoner's formulation – to which human beings must conform?

The matter of the limits of nature is complex. It is possible, as in some forms of naturalism, to set out the limits of nature yet in abstraction from the ways in which nature is produced in a capitalist economy. Alternatively, it is tempting to try to avoid the issue by reference to the mastery of nature. Neither approach is theologically congenial: one construes the common realm in favour of nature, the other in favour of humanity.

Limits and scarcity

For Marx and Engels, the issue of scarcity was always associated with the 'Malthusian problem': the attempt to trace scarcity back to some abstract account of the relation between food production and the 'human population' rather than the dynamics of a particular society. Hence reference to natural limits tends to be rejected in their thinking. Benton takes a different view: as we have already seen, the attempt to theorise the matter of the natural conditions of the process of production indicates limits. Benton readily acknowledges that such limits must be understood as relative; limits may be overcome but it is likely that other limits will subsequently take their place.[26] Are there, then, limits in our knowledge of nature?

Benton argues in favour of what he calls 'epistemic conservatism': limits in our knowledge of nature. He acknowledges that Marxism has tended to be triumphalist in its interrogation of nature: nature is a social project, as Lukács once noted; there is no such thing as nature 'in itself'. On this view, there is no sense to the claim that nature might, in however attenuated fashion, be the measure of humanity. However, Benton argues that there is a realist path between social constructionism and naturalism.[27] It is not the case that, epistemologically speaking, nature knows best. However, neither is it the case that humanity knows best: if everything must go somewhere, to take another of Commoner's ecological rules, it is not clear that humanity knows where that 'somewhere' is.

Tim Hayward has also pressed this theme of epistemic conservatism in his critique of unsubtle views of ecological and Enlightenment rationality. Hayward draws on the theme of Enlightenment rationality as critique

---

26. Ted Benton, 'Ecology, Socialism and the Mastery of Nature: A Reply to Reiner Grundmann', *New Left Review* 194 (1992), 55–74 (62).
27. Benton, 'Marxism and Natural Limits', pp. 56–8.

rather than domination as a way of stressing the importance of limit in our thinking on nature: 'Thus although enlightenment thinking is sometimes criticized for arrogance, in its best and most critical form it also emphasizes the *limits* to possible knowledge.'[28] Of course, there are real difficulties, as Hayward readily acknowledges: does the appeal to reason, for example, validate the superiority of the human or only its epistemic primacy? Yet Hayward holds to the view that central to Enlightenment rationality is the *omnicompetence of criticism* rather than the omnicompetence of reason. Rationality as critique, Hayward suggests, should be rethought in relation to ecological values.

However, the discussion of limits in Marxist circles is not restricted to epistemology. Benton argues that Marx and Engels, reacting strongly against the connection drawn by Malthus between human population and food production, tend instead to stress human productivity. Beyond noting the theme, Marx and Engels do not offer an adequate theoretical account of natural limits. We have already seen that, in Benton's view, Marx offers only one account of the production process: the transformative. Such a restriction is unhelpful, according to Benton, in that the focus of Marxist inquiry is not on the intentional structures governing other processes of production, the eco-regulative and the extractive.

Furthermore, Benton sharpens his critique by adding that even Marx's account of the labour process as featured in the modality of transformation is too narrow. For the tendency of Marxist discussion has been to concentrate on the antagonisms generated between labour and capital in the process of production. Thus, what has received less attention – even in the discussion of the transformative intentional structure – is the interaction between labour and nature. According to Benton, there are at least five aspects of the engagement with nature (human and non-human) left out of account or insufficiently attended to in Marxist theory.

These are: first, both the instruments and the objects of labour are material. As such, they enjoy certain resistances to human intentionality. Second, all processes have their origin – at whatever remove – in collection from nature. Third, Marx pays insufficient attention to the conditions of production, including the conditions of reproduction, of workers. Persistently undertheorised in Marx's account is, then, the 'domestic' sphere – birth and care of children – which has eco-regulative aspects but also its own independent structure. Fourth, natural conditions are not

---

28. Tim Hayward, *Ecological Thought: an Introduction* (Cambridge: Polity, 1995), p. 11.

manipulable, especially when we are speaking of geographical or climatic conditions. Fifth, Marx pays too little attention to the unintended consequences – pollution, accidents – of human actions in production.[29]

From this perspective, Benton concludes that the ecological reconstruction of Marxism must include the following amendments: (1) contextual conditions of production are not instruments of labour and should be considered separately; (2) how these contextual conditions are to be maintained so as to permit the sustainability of productive processes is a vitally important issue; (3) some account of unintended consequences must be given: the use of fertiliser may have the unintended consequence of desertification; the generation of electricity by means of nuclear fission may have the unwelcome consequence of creating nuclear waste which is difficult to dispose of safely.

Although it is not clear from the argument, I take it that Benton intends these three points to be developed in relation to all intentional structures: transformative, eco-regulative and extractive. What account of natural limits emerges here? First, Benton insists that the natural conditions of production need to be theorised separately. Thus, in steel production processes (car manufacture, for instance), the source of iron would need to be noted; or, in paper production, the source of the wood pulp needs to be acknowledged; with regard to human work, the care and raising of children is an important theme. Second, what is required is more than just bringing these conditions to mind, it is also attending to the conditions of their long-term maintenance. Different considerations will apply in connection to the sustainability of different conditions. Third, unintended consequences which flow directly from processes of production and which may, for a variety of different reasons, react back on the production processes, need to be treated. What emerges as significant is the ways in which various natural conditions are drawn into production processes, how these conditions are used and how renewed, and whether or not polluting outcomes threaten the integrity of the production process itself.

The work of James O'Connor is less concerned with the issue of natural limits considered abstractly from the processes of capitalist accumulation. O'Connor readily concedes that nature has its own laws to which Marx and Marxists have not always paid sufficient attention. The 'active, autonomous role of nature' was too often ignored in Marx's work. Furthermore, 'no account of production conditions can ignore the fact

29. Benton, 'Marxism and Natural Limits,' pp. 165–6.

that external nature has its own autonomous "laws" or developmental principles'.[30]

However, the central issue, as O'Connor presents it, is not limits – strictly, capitalist expansion has no limits[31] – but rather how capitalist accumulation engages the conditions of production. Recall that the conditions of production refer to the external, physical conditions (ecosystems and like) as these enter into productive processes, the reproduction of labour power (including the 'domestic sphere') and the matter of social infrastructure (transport systems, education). The key issue is: if there are no limits to capitalist expansion, then *the matter of ecological limit will be encountered only in the form of economic crisis*. If there are genuine limits to the conditions of production, under capitalism these will only take the form of crisis. How then does capitalist accumulation employ external conditions through periods both of accumulation and crisis? If there are two basic modalities of capitalist accumulation – expansion and crisis – how do these relate to the production of pollution and waste, the treatment of nature as a free good, etc.?

It is likely, O'Connor contends, that through periods of expansion capitals will use up natural resources more quickly than at other times: resource depletion and pollution can be expected to increase through 'good times'. It may also be the case, of course, that capital seeks to improve its profitability by reducing the costs of the reproduction of labour power and the costs of sustaining the infrastructure.[32] There is an important opportunity here for environmental groups in that, through periods of high profitability, capital firms do at least have resources to invest in more efficient ways of using materials and undertake the clean-up of the environment. However, capital may also accumulate through crisis: here capitals seek the cheapest raw materials, whatever their ecological cost, and wish to avoid the costs of clearing up pollution, etc. In summary: capital always accumulates, sometimes through expansion, sometimes through crisis. (In fact, O'Connor argues, most of the time capital accumulates through both crisis and expansion at one and the same time.[33])

Hence, O'Connor insists, there are two dynamics of ecological degradation operative in capitalism; there are two ways in which capitalism depletes resources; there are two ways in which it generates pollution. In general, these dynamic tendencies are operative simultaneously. The

---

30. O'Connor, *Natural Causes*, p. 147.   31. Ibid., p. 181.
32. Cf. Harvey, *Justice, Nature and the Geography of Difference*, pp. 195–6.
33. O'Connor *Natural Causes*, pp. 180–6.

analytical task is therefore to ascertain which sectors of capitalist production are accumulating through expansion and which through crisis and, of course, to take into account a set of further circumstances concerning the reproduction of workers, infrastructure and what have you. We should not be surprised that through these processes, combined and uneven as they are, that capitals degrade, and sometimes destroy, their conditions of production.

Scarcity, sustainability and 'marginality'

There are important differences between the views, presented above, of natural limits by two contemporary Marxists. O'Connor concentrates on the theme of political economy and seeks to introduce the matter of political ecology only and always in relation to economic accumulation: hence a second contradiction of capitalism is proposed in a tension between the development of the forces and relations of production *and* the conditions of production. Thus the basic shape of historical materialism is here *extended*. Benton is bolder in his attempt to reconstruct, rather than extend, historical materialism. Although he does note that Marx theorises the theme of the conditions of production, he argues that the standard Marxist account of the labour process is too narrow. Furthermore, the matter of cultural resources for engaging with ecological crisis, a factor largely omitted in O'Connor's account, is stressed by Benton. Hence Benton proposes the *reconstruction* of historical materialism.

Of what use is this discussion for a political theology of nature? We are able now, I think, to reconsider the matter of scarcity. One reason why most of us are environmentalists now has to do with the sense that crucial resources – non-renewable sources of energy, clean air and water, safe working conditions, good schools – are felt to be in short supply. This despite the fact that our culture is very creative and has already secured the potential for providing the basic levels of subsistence many times over.[34] One way a sense of environmental unease presents itself in the North is, objectively, through the anxiety regarding overpopulation and, subjectively, in potential parents' anxieties as to whether they should have more than one, or any, children. And this matter is present in political ecology: for instance, population reduction is part of the deep ecology platform.[35]

---

34. William Leiss, 'The Domination of Nature', in Merchant (ed.), *Ecology*, pp. 55–64 (p. 60).
35. We saw in chapter 3 that population reduction is one of the eight points of the 1984 platform of deep ecology. As northern populations are already reducing, this position may

Marx and Engels confronted the problem of scarcity in the theory of Malthus; contemporary Marxists, as David Harvey has noted, also confront the contemporary resurgence of the theory in neo-Malthusianism. Indeed, it is a long-running show: although it emerges with full force in the nineteenth century, there were important precursors to Malthusianism in the eighteenth century.[36] What, then, is the 'Malthusian problem'? Harvey presents it this way: 'Passion between the sexes (a self-realization argument) produced population growth beyond the natural capacities of the earth's larder and emancipation from poverty, war and disease was necessarily frustrated as a result. The drive for self-realization automatically thwarted any hopes for emancipation from material want.'[37] Clearly here is presented the theme of natural limits. I want now briefly to present Harvey's reading of Malthus and his rather brief commentary on the work of Benton and O'Connor.[38]

It is important to note, says Harvey, that Malthus himself derives his argument from two basic deductive principles: 'food is necessary to the existence of man and the passion between the sexes is necessary and constant'.[39] The more recent neo-Malthusian argument operates from the same principles yet within a technological context. Thus, the relation between population and ecoscarcity is noted, but also the fact that technological productivity can mitigate but not overcome the connection. Harvey helpfully notes that Malthus' argument is class-based, part of which is well known: support for the poorest bucks the natural law that food is scarce and cannot support a steadily increasing population. Yet Malthus also argues that the wealthy are charged with the task of consumption. For, if the wealthy do not consume, then there is a threat to capital accumulation: the economy requires a steady demand for goods.

The same argument is employed today: in order to ensure the smooth working of the international economy, the wealthier nations should be encouraged to consume as much as possible, preferably in an international zone of free trade, in order to ensure that a demand for goods from other parts of the world is maintained. In the background may also be detected

---

function as code for the reduction of southern populations. For a sustained critique of the 'population problem', see Commoner, *Making Peace with the Planet*, ch. 7.

36. Clarence Glacken, *Traces on the Rhodian Shore: Nature and Culture in Western Thought from Ancient Times to the End of the Eighteenth Century* (Berkeley, Los Angeles and London: University of California Press, 1967), pp. 623f.

37. Harvey, *Justice, Nature and the Geography of Difference*, p. 139.

38. Note here that I am not concerned to treat Malthus directly but rather to consider the treatment by socialist ecology of Malthusianism and neo-Malthusianism.

39. Harvey, *Justice, Nature and the Geography of Difference*, p. 141.

the – finally, racist – view that the South is required to produce some
of the goods which support the consumption of the North but that the
South's own internal economic difficulties – including the pressure on environmental goods – is the result of overpopulation, economic misman-
agement, 'innate' propensity to violence, etc.

That such a position – both in its Malthusian and neo-Malthusian
forms – is illogical needs to be noted. What, we may ask, is the relation between population growth and ecoscarcity amongst the working classes/the South and the consumption among the upper classes/the
North? Would not one obvious way forward be to invite consumption by
the working classes/the South? Malthus, in Harvey's view, has a double
response to this question. First, in fact the upper classes have a way –
through frugality – of avoiding the imperatives of population growth and
ecoscarcity. Second, capitalists will not wish to sell goods to their workers: in other words, workers are the source of exploited worker power, not
consumption.

In a sense, too, the same position is articulated today: the North, in its
reduction in the growth of population, has shown itself able to emancipate
itself from Malthus's law: it accumulates rather than procreates! In addition, only the wealthy can truly accumulate: capitalism turns upon *high-
value* consumption which only the North can engage in. The self-serving
character of such an argument is all too apparent. In rejecting such arguments, Harvey appeals to Marx. We should note that included in the
appeal is the aside that 'Marx . . . had a profound respect for the qualities of nature and the relational–dialectical possibilities within it.'[40] Yet
Harvey explicitly rejects the ecoMarxist turn as a sad capitulation to capi-
talistic arguments. Even for Marxists, Harvey reports, 'the universality of
"natural limits" and the deeper appeal to "natural law" as inherently
limiting to the capacity to meet human desires, is now increasingly
treated as an axiomatic limiting condition of human existence'.[41] Harvey's
constructive proposal, however, falls behind his earlier commitment to the
independence of nature. It is worth quoting his conclusion against the
notion of ecoscarcity at length:

> To declare a state of ecoscarcity is in effect to say that we have not the
> will, wit or capacity to change our state of knowledge, our social goals,
> cultural modes, and technological mixes, or our form of economy, and
> that we are powerless to modify either our material practices or

40. Ibid., p. 145.   41. Ibid., p. 146.

'nature' according to human requirements. To say that scarcity resides in nature and that natural limits exist is to ignore how scarcity is socially produced and how 'limits' are a social relation within nature (including human society) rather than some externally imposed necessity.[42]

Of course, the warning is salutary: scarcity must be construed socio-historically and not simply as a natural fact. Limits are a social relation and society may be reshaped according to human requirements. Yet the crucial issue remains unattended: do not human requirements need to be informed by a dialectical interpretation of humanity–nature which ensures that human requirements incorporate nature's requirements?

The problem needs to be stated differently from Harvey's formulation. The issue is neither agency nor social production but rather whether the measure of human advance is only the human or whether it is the human in dialectical relation to nature. Thus Harvey is correct when he writes: '. . . all debate about ecoscarcity, natural limits, overpopulation, and sustainability is a debate about the preservation of a particular order rather than a debate about the preservation of nature *per se*'.[43] However, the issue which Harvey fails to tackle is whether or not the overcoming of this current capitalist order involves the construction of a social order founded on a society–nature dialectic. 'Nature' becomes a mere cipher in Harvey's account rather than a material presence. And the movement of the dialectic is discovered to be conservationist rather than preservationist: in the dialectic, the human is privileged.

What more can be said from within the resources of socialist ecology on this matter of scarcity? As already noted, Harvey dismisses the work of Benton and O'Connor as capitulating to the current discussion on scarcity and limits. Yet, given the above presentation of their views, this seems a hasty judgment. Indeed, their work provides, in my view, important resources on which Harvey could draw.

First of all, we should note that Ted Benton's work offers a way of making more complex the dialectical process. To the productive process construed as transformative, Benton adds two further ways of construing production processes: eco-regulative and extractive. The premise of such an enlargement is that Marxist theory needs to be reframed to allow for the logic of cooperation and interchange between humanity and non-human nature to be recognised more clearly. The second point made by

42. Ibid., p. 147.   43. Ibid., p. 148.

Benton points towards the ecological reconstruction of Marxism elaborated in O'Connor's work. Benton recommends that each mode of production should be analysed for its 'contextual sustaining conditions and
liability to generate naturally mediated unintended consequences'.[44] This
is to attribute the problem of the unequal distribution of social goods
to neither industrialisation nor the effects of increasing population.
Benton's contribution is to remind us that the fecundity of nature resides
in part in its own tendencies, regulative processes and systemic feedback
loops. Nature is always capitalised nature; and capitalised nature is always
second nature. However, that does not mean such capitalised nature does
not relate to a first nature, as yet not capitalised, with its deep structures,
tendencies and processes.

Further, one way of interpreting O'Connor's work would be to acknowledge that he has indeed found a way of thinking in a Marxist – and
anti-Malthusian – fashion about 'scarcity' which supports directly some of
the emphases of Harvey's work. Recall that O'Connor identifies three conditions of production: external, physical conditions; personal conditions
of production; and the communal, general conditions of production. By
means of such conceptuality, can we discern ways in which the operations
of capitals destroy their own conditions of production and thereby harm
potential for profitable accumulation? According to O'Connor, the answer
is an emphatic, 'yes!'

> The warming of the atmosphere will inevitably destroy people, places
> and profits, not to speak of other species life. Acid rain destroys forests
> and lakes and buildings and profits alike. Salinization of water tables,
> toxic wastes, and soil erosion impair nature and profitability. The
> pesticide treadmill destroys profits as well as nature . . . This line of
> thinking thus also applies to the 'personal conditions of
> production . . . laborpower' in connection with capital's destruction of
> established community and family life as well as the introduction of
> work relations that impair coping skills and create a toxic social
> environment generally.[45]

In my view, O'Connor here presents the root of the social production of
scarcity of which Harvey writes. Furthermore, there is here a sense of the
ways in which external physical operations have their own proper spheres
of regulative action.

44. Benton, 'Marxism and Natural Limits', p. 175.
45. O'Connor, *Natural Causes*, p. 166.

We have, then, the introduction of 'scarcity' into the theory of economic crises in a Marxist, not a neo-Malthusian, way. At issue is not the relation between food production and population, nor a technologically mediated version of the same relation, but instead a reading of how capitalism relies upon nature to secure its profits and how, furthermore, in the process of accumulation, it degrades its own conditions. Here O'Connor proposes that capitalism *under*produces: the failure to maintain the conditions of production is precisely a feature of capitalist underdevelopment. Given that development is uneven, any socialist transformation of capitalist economic forces and relations will also have to attend to the ways in which environmental clean-up, supportive family life and good education, and the costs of traffic congestion and urban degradation – to give a few examples – all require urgent attention.

The theme of this section is scarcity. In affirming the Marxist rejection of the relation between population and the availability of food, we have noted that too Promethean a stress should not be placed on the correct judgment that scarcity is a social limit. If capitals do indeed destroy the conditions of their own production, then these conditions may be impaired to such a degree as to create significant resistance to any liberatory, socialist, project. In order to theorise the *social construction of limits* – the capitalist production of nature – together with an account of the reality of natural processes, we may conclude that scarcity should be understood as 'marginality'.

To what does the concept of marginality refer? A compressed answer is: the placing of nature – here referring to the conditions of production – to the margins. It is not natural scarcity with which we have to deal but rather natural marginality. Such conditions are to be considered not as scarce but marginal: nature is treated both as free tap and sink, and the conditions of the reproduction of labour power are overlooked as the environmental infrastructure is degraded in an attempt to increase the profitability of capitalism. In this manner, capitalism displaces its problems to the social and natural margins. This conclusion is of some importance both for Christology, in which the marginality of nature is connected with the marginality – that is, the cross – of Christ and for the marginality of the place called Church. There will be explicit discussion of both points in chapter 9. More generally, the theme of marginality runs through part III: facing central Christian themes of the abundance of God and the goodness of creation, a political theology of nature resists the construal of scarcity in apolitical ways, such as by reference to a stingy or mean nature. Scarcity as marginality contains two truths: that the scarcity of goods is a social phenomenon and that such scarcity forces the use of nature's resources in exploitative ways. Which is to say that natural limits are always social limits, and vice versa. Any redirective and restitutive effort against marginality must reckon with both themes, as will be demonstrated through the Christology and pneumatology of part III.

Space, place and environment

Marginality, in turn, requires a further step towards concretion. For marginality, the practical interpretation of scarcity and natural limits, occurs only within concrete processes of space and time. 'Implied in the concepts of "external physical conditions", "laborpower", and "communal conditions"', writes O'Connor, 'are the concepts of space and "social environment".'[46] Only through temporal–spatial practices are problems of scarcity and limit to be grasped. The theme of scarcity cannot be divorced from the place of scarcity which is the *locus* of the social force of circumstance. So, for example, communities may endure in a particular place through extreme scarcity.

To attend to the concept of place is an acknowledgement by historical materialism that the relations of humanity with nature cannot be engaged without attention to the cultural desires of those who occupy – sometimes marginal – places. (Indeed, communities may defend their place from attempts to 'improve' it.) What emerges at this point is a recognition of the need to subjectivise and historicise the interpretation of the conditions of production. David Harvey has written at some length on the theme of space and its relation to place and environment; to his account I now turn.[47]

There are three points, central to Harvey's account, that I wish to present: (1) That spatio-temporalities are always configured in and through social practices: in a specific and restricted sense, space and time are socially constructed; as such, these practices are open to amendment. (2) A relational account of space and time can be employed to explore the relation between space and place. (3) Considerable practical and theoretical difficulties exist in the construal of a liberatory relation between

---

46. Ibid., p. 161.
47. I should add that Harvey's account in his *Justice, Nature and the Geography of Difference* is both wide-ranging and diffuse; what follows may make Harvey's account more systematic and coherent than in fact it is.

space and place: the connection is sometimes oppressive, at other times oppositional.

What does it mean to say, first, that space and time are always configured by social practices? We must note, according to Harvey, that to say that space and time are social constructions is not to say that these are subjective. 'Social constructions of space and time operate with the full force of objective facts to which all individuals and institutions necessarily respond. To say that something is socially constructed is not to say it is personally subjective.'[48] A sense of the objective, yet amendable, aspect of space–time may be won by attention to the ways in which new practices, together with new accounts of space–time, can be imposed on a society (from within and without). Hence, Harvey argues, following the work of William Cronon, that the clash between the first English settlers and the American Indians can be traced to different accounts of space–time; furthermore, the imperatives of Fordist-type working conditions means strict adherence to time set by a clock (an imposition that was itself resisted).

At this point Harvey rehearses the well-known argument from his earlier *The Condition of Postmodernity*[49] on the compression of space–time: after the oil crisis of 1973, 'Time-horizons for decision making (now a matter of minutes in international financial markets) shortened and lifestyle fashions changed rapidly. And all of this has been coupled with a radical reorganisation of space relations, the further reduction of spatial barriers, and the emergence of a new geography of capitalist development. These events have generated a powerful sense of space–time compression affecting all aspects of cultural and political life.'[50] Nor should we say that there are two dimensions of space–time in capitalist society. Harvey rejects a duality posited between the operation of the market economy – and the spatio-temporalities which comprise such a market – and the different, multilayered and variegated spatio-temporalities embedded in the practices of the household to which most turn for relationships governed by the imperatives of affectivity rather than the imperatives of 'efficiency gains'. In rejecting this duality, he notes the 'crossover' between the market and household: fashions changed by the shortening timescales of capitalist accumulation; previous spatial conditions in collapse, as indicated by the fruit and vegetable display in any supermarket (in Britain, you can

48. Harvey, *Justice, Nature and the Geography of Difference*, pp. 211–12.
49. David Harvey, *The Condition of Postmodernity* (Oxford: Blackwell, 1989), esp. part III.
50. Harvey, *Justice, Nature and the Geography of Difference*, p. 245.

buy blueberries cultivated in the USA, potatoes produced in Egypt and corn grown in Thailand).

Second, what are the details of this relational account of space–time? Harvey's argument moves by way of a loose combination of the views of Leibniz with those of Whitehead. Here Leibniz seems to have the priority. Yet this is a Leibniz whose philosophy is secularised and later 'materialised' by reference by Whitehead. From Leibniz, Harvey suggests that space and time are not to be privileged one over the other; space is to be understood as comprised of distinct spaces rather than a single over-arching space with its sub-divisions; space and time inhere in particular practices. Harvey rejects Leibniz's metaphysical judgment that our world is the best of all possible worlds. Although Leibniz holds to this view based on an account of God's providential ordering of the world, Harvey notes its deeply conservative implications. By contrast, the present ordering of the world is not to be traced to God's will, Harvey recommends, but rather to a determinate *social* ordering.

For my purposes, this is an important point: we have already seen the relation between the metaphysical judgment as to the 'balance of nature' and the matters of scarcity and sustainability. Here Harvey makes a similar point: the dynamics of space–time are not given; instead, these inhere in specific practices – political, economic, social, personal. To revise the dynamics of space–time thereby requires the alteration of such practices. The metaphysical presumption in force is thus *against* harmony, in a double sense: there is no presumption as to harmony either in intrahuman relations or relations between humanity and nature.

What follows from this is less clear. Harvey certainly seeks to respond to the epistemological question: how can resistances to such processes be thought? Before that, Harvey applies his reading of the dialectical inter-relating of spatio-temporalities to the concepts of place and environment. He summarises his conclusions thus:

> Entities achieve relative stability in their bounding and their internal ordering of processes creating space, for a time. Such permanencies come to occupy a piece of a space in an exclusive way (for a time) and thereby define a place – their place – (for a time). The process of place formation is a process of carving out permanencies from the flow of processes creating spaces. But the 'permanencies' – no matter how solid they seem – are not eternal: they are always subject to time as 'perpetual perishing'. They are contingent on the processes that create, sustain and dissolve them.[51]

51. Ibid., p. 261.

We have here Harvey's attempt to relate together the processes of time and production of space. Such a perspective may be applied in straightforward ways to what Harvey dubs environment or nature. On such a view it is no longer possible to separate out the spatio-temporal processes governing nature from those governing society. Academic disciplines which operate on the basis of some such distinction are thereby to be rejected. Yet, when applied to place, as Harvey notes, the matter is not so simple: for place is more than a temporary permanence in the churning of spaces. Instead, place is often associated with the affections and memory. How is this to be thought?

So we come, third, to the consideration of the liberatory and oppressive aspects of place. Harvey proposes two ways of considering the construction of place. Of course, place is always constructed through social processes. One sort of analysis might then concentrate on the ecological processes which are included in the spatio-temporal processes of the production of space as place. A different approach is to attend to the ways in which the international movement of money over the last twenty-five years has produced space. Harvey notes the threats to place (through de-industrialisation, for example), and that capitals have become more sophisticated in detecting the differences between particular places which are advantageous to accumulation. The competition between places for capital investment and the steady overinvestment in land in the last decade or two are clear evidence of this development.[52] But, as Harvey notes, that hardly accounts for the continued attachment to place. Why will people dedicate themselves to defend a particular place? Why do some people not wish to leave an impoverished housing estate even when offered alternative, 'superior' accommodation? Why is a people's sense of identification with landscapes so strong that they persistently fail to see that the landscape is everywhere worked over by human labour?[53]

The importance of place as a privileged location where people seek to connect with the environment as the *locus* of community is noted by Harvey. Useful objections to both these commitments are discussed. As regards identification with a particular landscape, Harvey notes that the knowledge that governs such areas is necessarily small scale and thereby tends not to be concerned with the ways in which such spaces are produced by larger processes (the recoding of landscape by the heritage

---

52. Ibid., pp. 297–8.
53. '[T]here was a perfectly well-balanced eco-system in place before man began trespassing on it', letter in Princeton *Town Topics* (23 September 1998), p. 25, in connection with a proposed deer cull.

industry, for instance). Nor is Harvey persuaded by the claim implicit in some of these positions of direct, largely unmediated relationships with nature. Instead, he considers that such notions might be constructed in ways which are anti-capitalist in a romantic sense, but hardly opposi-tional. With regard to place as community, the usual objections concern-ing tendencies to sectarianism, hierarchicalism and suppression of dissent are noted.[54]

Yet the constructive position advanced – a response to the question: how is the relation between the construction of space and place to be thought? – is brief and unpersuasive. Harvey makes the valuable point that 'cultural politics in general (and the search for affective community in par-ticular) and political–economic power intertwine in the social processes of place construction'.[55] And, although some examples of the contradictory processes of place construction are given, what is crucially missing from the argument is a presentation of how to detect the difference between positive and negative construals of place.

So the question remains: what are the tendencies and dynamics of lib-eratory, rather than merely alternative, places? Harvey's argument is es-pecially valuable in its insistence that the cultural representations of a particular place are as material as the other outcomes of social processes. Thereby rejected is a common perception in Marxism that ideas are to be denigrated as not being the causal motors of history. However, despite this welcome emphasis on the materiality of representation, no account is given of the relation between the construal of place and conceptions of nature. More especially, which representations of nature might be consid-ered liberatory?

In sum, Harvey is right when he suggests that spatio-temporal pro-cesses are social constructions which are material and objective. But the vital issue occluded in this formulation is how does humanity relate to an abundant nature? And the question which must be answered first here is: what is this nature to which humanity both refers and is the mea-sure of? Answering this question would enable Harvey to explore how the construal of nature in a particular place does not necessarily yield a local, 'unmediated' knowledge. I return to this theme in chapter 9 in a discus-sion of eucharistic place.

---

54. Harvey, *Justice, Nature and the Geography of Difference*, pp. 303–4.
55. Ibid., p. 320.

A materialist theology of nature?

Whereas deep ecology did not yield many insights into the relations between humanity and nature, ecoMarxism – by its attention to the conditions of production – offers a conceptuality for consideration of these matters. Further, the issues of the 'mastery of nature', natural limits and scarcity are also considered by Marxism. We noted also the stress in the work of James O'Connor on the importance of the state as the mediator between capitals and nature's economy. That is, under contemporary conditions, it is the agency of the state which regulates access to nature: to give some examples, permissions for strip mining and new roads, and the setting of permissible levels of pollution, all fall within the provenance of the state. The theme of resistance to capitalist processes of accumulation was also discussed by reference to the construction of space and place: are some places cultural sites of resistance to expansionist capital?

From the vantage point of a social or practical materialism, ecosocialism inquires how matter is produced in a particular social context. That the matter of nature is being degraded is not disputed. What requires elucidation is the social and economic processes in and through which such degradation occurs. Should we then say that natural limits are merely some externally imposed 'necessity' that mask an economic process? Are these limits therefore only social limits? Or should we say, by contrast, that there are important natural conditions (the otherness of nature) to economic processes that capitalist development will respond to by developing through crises? For a political theology of nature, this issue must be faced in order to avoid the air of unreality that characterises much ecotheological discussion. Consider the following programmatic statement by Larry Rasmussen on the task of ecotheology: 'Substantively, *conversion to the Earth* means measuring all Christian impulses by one stringent criterion: their contribution to Earth's well-being.'[56] In the context of this chapter, any contribution by theology to the well-being of the Earth must indicate the ways in which the well-being is being threatened if any conversion to the Earth is not to be merely voluntaristic and abstract. Such voluntarism and abstraction are evident, so I shall argue in chapter 8, in the popular affirmations in ecotheology of stewardship and the value of nature.

56. Larry Rasmussen, 'Eco-Justice: Church and Community Together', in D. Hessel and L. Rasmussen (eds.), *Earth Habitat: Eco-Injustice and the Church's Response* (Philadelphia: Fortress Press, 2001), pp. 1–19 (p. 7).

The matter is made yet more complex by the fact that Christianity will wish to affirm the abundance of a creation whose source is the loving purposes of a good God. Does reference to abundance invite sustained scepticism towards notions of scarcity and natural limits? Or can the issue of abundance be adhered to theologically while at the same time accepting that social limits are always natural limits? To give an indication of the difficulties here, what are the relations between Harvey's denial of natural scarcity and the Christian commitment to abundance, and how should these relations be determined theologically? If, on account of its independence – real yet circumscribed – from God, the theologian wishes to stress the finiteness of creation, how should such an emphasis be related to O'Connor's claim that capitalism accumulates through processes of *under*development, as well as development? If the overriding criterion is well-being of the Earth, can the well-being of nature be affirmed at the expense of humanity without detailed consideration of the ways in which nature's well-being is being denied? A materialist theology of nature will need to develop responses to these questions.

Which is not to say that the socialist ecologies presented in this chapter are beyond criticism. First, there remains a sustained reluctance in these Marxist theories to specify the otherness or independence of non-human nature. Of course, there are legitimate concerns here: does the positing of nature as independent play into the hands of neo-Malthusians? Yet materialism of a social and practical sort requires such an account of the material interactions between humanity and nature in order fully to theorise the relations between humanity and non-human nature. When speaking of human–non-human relations, a comprehensive materialism will wish to speak not merely of a first nature and its relations to a second nature. Instead, the schema is tripartite: (1) nature independent of humanity; (2) the natural conditions of human life; (3) the cultural or social sphere of human life.[57] The ecosocialist positions reviewed so far have focused on the second and the third areas. As we have seen from the discussion of ecofeminism, however, a political account of the liveliness and subjectivity of nature is vital for a full consideration of nature.

A liberatory materialism will thereby analyse the structures of human–nature interaction by way of this tripartite schema. Suddenly, Grundmann's sniffy point about naturalism appears unpersuasive. Recall his claim that to hold to nature as 'for itself' is to maintain a

---

57. I am drawing on John Clark, 'The Dialectical Social Geography of Elisée Reclus', *Philosophy and Geography* 1 (1997), 117–42 (123), as well as the ecosocial ontology presented in chapter 2.

religious – that is, false – viewpoint. However, the issue now is: can a materialism be developed that supports and develops the tripartite schema set out in the previous paragraph? That is the vital question: the proof of a liberative materialism is its capacious ability to encompass the tripartite schema. In my view, such a materialism can be developed by theology: I offer the outlines of such a theological materialism in the next chapter. In other words, the relevant test is the 'materiality' of one's materialism, rather than whether or not a materialism is religious.

Such materiality may follow Benton's proposal to understand human interaction with nature in three ways: the transformative, the eco-regulative and the extractive require and shape different modalities of interaction. These modalities each require different structures of interrelation, different sorts of technologies and thereby different types of human action, and are supported by different construals of the movement of nature.[58] Our most difficult issue resurfaces: what is the conception of nature operative here? And what might a political theology of nature have to offer such a discussion? To this question I turn in the next chapter.

Connected with the first point is, second, the matter of a philosophy of nature as a proper basis for a normative theory of human social life.[59] An important strength of Marxism is its power to explain the emergence and persistence (in contradiction) of capitalism. However, it is less persuasive in its account of the normative political life of humanity. In a commentary on the political theory of Marx, David McLellan has noted important contributions in the area of agency, relation of the state to civil society and the analytic power of the concept of class.[60] However, this is not to make a contribution to the area of political theory which seeks to articulate the political structures which might be both liberatory and sustainable in relation to non-human nature. To discern social and economic movements and structures is necessary but not sufficient. What is also required is an account of the tendencies, liberatory and oppressive, of the political life of humanity. And the determination of liberatory and oppressive must be made in relation to some account of non-human nature.

Involved here are normative claims on the relation between humanity and nature towards the construction and inhabiting of good space and time: that is, towards liberatory accounts of place. Cultural resources are

58. We may note that Shiva's account of the mediation of nature by women, discussed in chapter 4, draws almost exclusively on the eco-regulative modality.
59. Ely, 'Ernst Bloch, Natural Rights, and the Greens', p. 138.
60. David McLellan, 'Politics', in D. McLellan (ed.), *Marx: The First 100 Years* (London: Fontana, 1983), pp. 143–87.

required which might be brought to bear on the attempt to overcome the alienation of capitalist society from non-human nature in the form of its natural conditions of production. In the work of O'Connor and Harvey, we saw that the emphasis is placed on how to think of the operations of the political economy of capitalism. Yet, even if O'Connor is correct in his insistence that the interests of workers need to be foregrounded, the important matter of the cultural resources which might be brought to bear in support of the pursuit of these interests needs development. It may be true that, through the second contradiction of capitalism, a path to a socialist society may be discerned. However, the cultural resources which remind us of the importance of sociality, often sustained through the qualities and pleasures associated with place, need specification. In addition to liberative political and economic analyses, anti-capitalist movements need oppositional cultures to sustain the analyses and undertake practices which support and anticipate an anti-capitalist end-state. In sum, in which directions should communities of hope develop cultures of place in memory and sensibility? I return to this matter in a discussion of eucharistic place in chapter 9.

Third, the difficult problem of the political representation of nature emerges in consideration of O'Connor's view that the state functions as the contemporary mediator between capital, civil society and nature. Such a position contrasts strongly with Bookchin's stress on the community as municipality as the central political *locus*. Without doubt, the contemporary state functions in the way described by O'Connor. Does the contemporary state function democratically, however? Should the contemporary political task be to control the state and thereby control the ways in which the state grants access to nature? Or should the political task be to drain the state of its power in favour of different arrangements in political authority? The political representation of nature is thereby raised. As we have seen in the consideration of Bookchin's confederal municipalism, the representation of nature is indirect. However, nature should be granted a democratic standing and democratic participation encouraged. Both are needed if the processes that develop well-being are to be participatory and inclusive, and if the notion of the political is to include the non-human. How should this be thought? I address this matter further in chapter 8.

Ecosocialist insights are informed by an understanding of nature as temporal and social: the holism proposed in these views stresses the interactive relations between humanity and nature through time. Such interaction is understood materially: by an analysis of the practical ways in which humanity transforms or regulates or extracts nature. The matter of the independence of nature is less well theorised. How might a political theology of nature take forward such readings in political ecology and yet also hold true to its own concerns? Part III of this book, 'The triune God and un/natural humanity', offers a response to this question.

Part III

The triune God and un/natural humanity

7

The worldly Christ: common nature

Reconstructing a political theology of nature: theological holism

In this part, we come to the last movement in the dialectical passage of this study: the dynamic yet critical articulation of Christian theology and political ecology culminates in a Trinitarian reading of un/natural humanity oriented towards the triune God. This chapter offers a theological grounding of the key concepts of sociality, temporality and spatiality: that is, a Christological ecosocial ontology. In chapter 8, the discussion moves into pneumatology. As the operation of the Word is always with the Spirit, I develop the transcendental of openness by seeking to explore how the ecological relations given determinate content in this chapter are to be construed as dynamically drawn towards and oriented towards fellowship. An ecosocial ontology, in other words, is always directed either towards the greater richness or intensity of community or towards patterns of alienation, fragmentation and breakdown. Lastly, I hold to the view that Christianity is not best understood as a set of beliefs but instead as a way of life, and thereby as participation in the community of disciples. Thus, in chapter 9, I discuss, as one way of completing a political theology of nature, participation in the eucharist as the principal political resource that Christianity offers in and for an ecological age. Throughout, I shall indicate how the adventure in political ecology of the previous four chapters clarifies the theological eco-anthropology proposed in this part and assists in the development of a political theology of nature.

The theological orientation of this inquiry has been secured from the outset by the concept of the common realm of God, nature and humanity. Presenting a theological holism, the common realm has as its central premise a dialectical unity in which all three actors are oriented towards each other, yet asymmetrically. As I sought to make clear in chapter 1, my position affirms the creator/creature difference but regards that very difference as the source of differences in the creaturely realm. Moreover, the concept of the common realm also indicates that nature and humanity are best understood in mutual co-explication with the concept of God. The difference between creatures and the creator is the difference that enables the identification of wholes and parts, unities and differences in the creaturely realm. In this connection, I am intrigued by Michael Welker's argument that the standard 'model of production and dependence' should not, on biblical grounds (that is, by reference to Genesis), be understood as an adequate doctrine of creation. Welker argues that the doctrine of creation has been colonised by this understanding of God's creative activity in which God's activity and the theological understanding of creation have been unduly simplified. In my view, however, Welker's highly important conclusion, which I discuss below, can be supported only by *creatio ex nihilo*. Or, to put the matter more weakly, I do not think that the notion of God's creative activity as the tradition has construed it points towards a monistic interpretation of the creaturely realm, as Welker seems to think.[1]

A preliminary attempt to make good such a bold claim was offered in chapter 2: I argued that a philosophical theology must, in order to do justice to the world and to God, think in terms of unity and difference in understanding both God and world. As a unity or unifying force, God secures the unity of the world: nature (including humanity) has its source in the activity of God. God is present as its ground to all parts (humanity *and* nature) of the unity of the world. To think otherwise on either point would be for the whole or the parts to compete with God. Such a competition would, of course, breach the rule of God's freedom secured by *creatio ex nihilo*. I argued from these theological grounds that fixing the zones of nature and humanity, and their interactions, is a task made *more* difficult by reference to the God who is activity, ground and force. Although unity in difference of the world is secured by reference to the differentiated unity of God, a detailed programme of the demarcation of the world into nature and humanity does *not* follow from this theological judgment.

However, such epistemological reticence on the relations between humanity and nature is, finally, unhelpful. In such indeterminacy, neither

---

1. Michael Welker, *Creation and Reality* (Minneapolis: Fortress Press, 1999), pp. 6–20 (quotation from p. 12).

political nor practical agency are well or truly founded. If we are to act differently, or desist from acting, in this manifold of unity and differences, some further specification is required. After all, the four inquiries of part II report efforts to persuade us to think about unity and differences in very precise ways. In support of this aim of further specification, I proposed the four transcendentals of becoming, unity, sociality and openness. Thinking about the common realm, I argued, was properly secured by understanding reality as unitive, social, open and in the trajectory of becoming. And the theological warrant for such a view is the resurrection of Jesus Christ. In a further move, I argued that the transcendental of sociality is best ascribed metaphorically to the Word in creation, liberation and fulfilment.

What does it mean to maintain that the frame and ground of the created order is *social*? I offered a very brief answer in chapter 2: affirmed are continuities between humanity and nature. In developing the terminology of whole and part, one such whole comprises the relations of humanity and nature. Analytic to the notion of sociality are spatiality and temporality: the otherness of nature in temporal becoming. These three notions – sociality, temporality and spatiality – are my attempt to present afresh the material commitments of Colossians 1.16–17: ' – all things have been created through him and for him. He himself is before all things, and in him all things hold together' (NRSV). The creating of the creaturely through Christ, in whom the creaturely has its unity, is to be understood in terms of sociality, temporality and spatiality within a differentiated whole. In a terminology developed for an ecological age, the wisdom of Christ may be restated: all parts and wholes participate, as social, in a unity which disassembles and recomposes into wholes and parts through the temporal and spatial dynamics of creatureliness. This activity is the agency of Jesus Christ. Furthermore, according to the interpretative principles which I am calling transcendentals, set out in chapter 2, it is important to note that order, relations and temporality are capable of transformation. The order is already dynamic, but not unstable; disorderly, but not disordered. Such ordering is, finally, to be traced to the life of God.

These are the theological commitments that have informed the critique of political ecologies undertaken in part II. They will be developed further in Trinitarian fashion through this part. To begin, we may note that, in recent Trinitarian theology, two tendencies are evident: on the one hand, a stress on the importance of a Trinitarian account of the economy of salvation; on the other, an emphasis on the importance of the inner-Trinitarian relations of the immanent Godhead for true knowledge of and right action in the world.[2] I affirm both these tendencies but wish to develop them in a particular way.

On the first tendency, the four transcendentals do indeed emphasise God's presence in the economy of creation: the form of the presence of God lies in the unity, sociality, openness and becoming of the parts and whole(s) of the world. Furthermore, these transcendentals can be 'drawn forward' in theological interpretation to present creaturely reality as social, temporal and spatial. And I have noted that the transcendentals may be appropriated to the persons of the Trinity: unity to the creator, sociality to the Word/*Logos* and openness to the Spirit. Such an account, I have argued, denies a naturalism in which the world is regarded as self-sufficient, thereby excluding God; and a solipsism in which humanity never truly encounters nature and so regards itself as *sicut Deus*. Yet there is truth in both these aspects: for naturalism insists rightly that humanity is in nature; and a certain type of idealism affirms rightly that nature exceeds our knowledge and control. The theological transcendentals and the ecosocial ontology are attempts to honour the truths of naturalism and idealism yet overcome these towards the common realm of God, nature and humanity. The triune economy of grace in creation has thereby been the subject of this adventure in philosophical theology.

On the second tendency – that is, the significance of the inner-relations of the triune God – my position is ontologically bold yet epistemologically cautious. In chapter 2, I argued for the importance of differentiation in God. Yet I stressed there also that such differentiation is not the same as the differentiation in the world. Furthermore, I emphasised the importance of ascribing unity, sociality and openness to the Trinitarian persons. Yet I also stressed that such an attribution is *metaphorical*: for we cannot know what we mean when we say this. However, the becoming of God is genuinely social: the attempt to imitate the sociality of God is both gift and responsibility in the economy and is pleasing to God in God's own life.

Thus the world is not to be deduced from the inner-Trinitarian relations of the Godhead. Instead the approach adopted here is to draw in anthropological and natural matters yet correct them theologically. The task of theological criticism is to show how God is present despite the attempts

---

2. See Catherine Mowry LaCugna, *God For Us: The Trinity and the Christian Life* (San Francisco: Harpers, 1991); Hodgson, *Winds of the Spirit*; Jürgen Moltmann, *The Trinity and the Kingdom of God* (London: SCM Press, 1980); Colin E. Gunton, *The Promise of Trinitarian Theology* (Edinburgh: T. & T. Clark, 1991); John D. Zizioulas, *Being as Communion: Studies in Personhood and the Church* (Crestwood, NY: St. Vladimir's Seminary Press, 1985).

in human knowledge and practice to obscure that presence. For the identity of God revealed in Jesus Christ is a Trinitarian identity. As Trinitarian, God invites consideration of God's Trinitarian, that is, non-identical, presentation. Thus the creaturely identity bestowed by God upon the world follows after this non-identical God: human identity is not to be found in nature but then neither is it not to be found there. The end of nature is not to be found in humanity but neither is it not to be found there. God's identity is not to be traced to the world but neither is it not to be traced there. In sum, the implications of the resurrection of Christ-in-nature are radical: in Christ, we have the reordering of humanity–nature out of the Trinitarian life of God. How is this to be thought?

Creation and incarnation

How is the creaturely to be understood Trinitarianly – that is, by reference to Jesus Christ – to include both ecological society and ecological nature? At issue here, I shall argue, is the matter of creaturely difference and the origin of that difference in the creative act of the triune God in incarnation. From the matter of creaturely difference, the issues of both the common origin and destiny of ecological society and ecological nature and the contingency of creation come into theological focus.

Incarnation
The theme of incarnation suggests that distinction from God is both part of what it is to be a creature and that, as the perfect 'summary' of creatureliness, Jesus of Nazareth, in his perfect practice of obedient self-distinction, is the Word enfleshed of the creator God.[3] As the concrete embodiment of the *Logos* of God, Jesus of Nazareth thereby points to God's intention to create an independent creation and, in Trinitarian perspective, recommends the interpretation that the origin of creation, the source of the creative act, is the differentiation of the *Logos* from the creator God. Incarnation is not thereby some 'emergency measure' of the creator God (who suddenly appears 'down here' because things cannot be managed properly from 'up there'), nor an action externally related to creation, nor some general process whereby God is reconciled to God,[4] but is rather the

---

3. Pannenberg, *Systematic Theology*, II, p. 34.
4. For such a view, see Hodgson, *Winds of the Spirit* in which the world is presented as the mode of God's self-differentiation, and Christ as the gestalt moment in that process of differentiation and reconciliation. A similar difficulty may be detected in the work of Jürgen Moltmann in relation to the suffering of Jesus of Nazareth: see Douglas B. Farrow, 'In the

most concentrated expression of God's intentions in creation. Creation is thereby intended by God to be independent in and through its origin in the self-distinction of the second person of the Trinity from the first. Creation is then not merely 'other' than God; nor is creation the principle of difference by which the fullness of God is somehow secured. Rather, if incarnation is to be properly acknowledged, creation, of which incarnation is the summary, has its source and ground in the relation of the *Logos* to the creator.

Both Wolfhart Pannenberg and Karl Rahner have argued along these lines for a Trinitarian account of creation that understands the *Logos* to be the mediator of creation and the ground of creaturely life. Rightly, in my view, Pannenberg sees the second person of the Trinity as the origin of the difference, the independence of creation. In turn, he traces the differences of creaturely totality to the presence of the *Logos* in creation. '[T]he Logos of creation', Pannenberg writes, 'gathers the creatures into the order that is posited by their distinctions and relations and brings them together through himself (Eph. 1.10) for participation in his fellowship with the Father'.[5] Although his argument is differently organised, in formal terms Rahner makes the same point: 'If God wills to become non-God, man comes to be, that and nothing else.'[6] Rahner relates the otherness of the creation to God by reference to a primal difference in God: 'The immanent self-utterance of God in his eternal fullness is the condition of the self-utterance of God outside himself, and the latter continues the former.'[7] Although Rahner is here materially discussing the doctrine of the incarnation in relation to the assumption of human nature and 'change' in God, the usefulness of his position for my argument is readily apparent: here the incarnation 'qualifies' creation in the sense of being its inner rationale, origin and destiny. Creation is 'authored' in the distinction of creator and *Logos*, made known in the incarnate, Jesus of Nazareth.[8]

End is the Beginning: A Review of Jürgen Moltmann's Systematic Contributions', *Modern Theology* 14:3 (1998), 425–47. See also Pannenberg's discussion of Hegel in *Systematic Theology*, II, pp. 27–8, 31.

5. Ibid., p. 32. Again, comparison with the work of Peter Hodgson is instructive: see the final chapter of *Winds of the Spirit*.

6. Karl Rahner, 'On the Theology of the Incarnation', *Theological Investigations* (New York: Crossroad 1982), IV, pp. 105–20 (p. 116). Cf. Karl Rahner, *Foundations of Christian Faith: An Introduction to the Idea of Christianity* (New York: Seabury Press, 1978), pp. 212–28 (p. 225).

7. Rahner, 'On the Theology of the Incarnation', p. 115.

8. In stating the matter thus, I seek to do no more than represent the commitments of John 1.1–18.

Interpreting creatureliness theologically

We need now to develop further a vocabulary with which to consider the theme of ecology: the creaturely contours, movements and interactions of ecological society and ecological nature. Rahner's concern lies in the origins of creation in relation to incarnation rather than the creaturely outworkings of God's creative activity. When Rahner does engage in a discussion of anthropology, he reiterates his well-known view of the transcendental openness of the human creature to the mystery of God. Such a resolutely anthropological interpretation of transcendentality is ill suited to the determination of ecological relations.

Difficulties with Pannenberg's position from the perspective of our theme also emerge: the conceptuality proposed is insufficiently detailed to offer an account of the relation between humanity and its habitat. The evidence for such a judgment emerges most forcefully on the occasion of Pannenberg's defence of dominion as a function of the *imago Dei*. He is careful to make clear that dominion must be understood absolutely as restricted. Yet what dominion presupposes – the transcendence of humanity over its natural conditions – is neither elucidated nor defended. Thus the radicality of Pannenberg's conceptuality is blunted.[9] Noting the level of generality with which Pannenberg is content to operate in the domain of ecology is also to make a judgment on the *politics* of Pannenberg's theological position.[10] A different way is required to set out the relations between humanity and nature in order to speak, for theology, of their common origin and destiny. I return to this task in the following sections.

Contingency of creation

We must note that, if the foregoing discussion of the relation of incarnation to creation approximates to the truth, creation must be understood

---

9. Pannenberg, *Systematic Theology*, II, pp. 116, 131–2, 137. In contrast, Moltmann, rightly, notes the importance of the interaction between concepts of *polis* and *eschaton*: see *The Coming of God: Christian Eschatology* (London: SCM Press, 1996), p. 133.

10. It is the merit of Jürgen Moltmann's position that he sees this issue clearly. Yet his attempts to engage the matter are, in my judgment, unsatisfactory. For Moltmann links incarnation to creation in resolutely soteriological terms. We may agree with Moltmann on the importance of the social character of the career of Jesus of Nazareth: see Moltmann, *The Way of Jesus Christ*, pp. 145–50, esp. p. 149. Yet it remains unclear how the 'whole' of the career of Jesus of Nazareth qualifies the totality of that which we call nature. Further, although Moltmann seeks to link history and nature in a second Christological sense, yet the result in *The Way of Jesus Christ* appears to be two Christologies: the suffering God and the cosmic Christ. What, crucially, needs elucidation – which Moltmann does not provide – is the relation between these two. Lately, in *The Coming of God*, Moltmann places ecological issues in the discussion of cosmic eschatology when, it could be argued, such issues are transgressive of the conventional divisions of eschatology into personal, historical and cosmic.

as having its contingent origin in the loving act of God. Creation emerges, so to speak, not out of an abstract determination to create, but out of the primacy of God's own life as love. If the resurrection of Jesus Christ is the election of social nature, such election points forward to the completion of nature, human and non-human, in eschatological glory. As contingent, then, the created order lives out of the future of God. To speak of ecological nature as contingent is to say that the creation is not a necessary emanation of God but is rather rooted in God's primary determination, as a loving God, to love. It is also, by holding to the unity of God's acts in creation and fulfilment, to maintain the openness of creation: its orientation to the future and its living 'out of' that future.

A highly significant point may be derived from such an eschatological clue: to affirm, as part of the interpretation of the common realm, the eschatological destiny of humanity and nature in God is to press the matter of the eschatological destiny of nature. Against a tendency in some sections of Christianity to deny this point, the eschatological fulfilment of nature cannot be denied, in my view, without severely distorting the basic Christian schema. To argue for an eschatological consummation is not, of course, to argue that the consummation for nature and humanity will be identical. As Bonhoeffer notes, whereas humanity will be reconciled, nature will be set free from its enslavement.[11] None the less, in the theme of consummation lies the theological rationale for speaking of the otherness and spatiality of nature.

Incarnation as pedagogy

The further reconstruction of a political theology of nature will need to consider the implications of the inquiry in philosophical theology undertaken in part II. Given the theological critique of the previous chapters, which ways forward are to be affirmed? And which denied?

In the theologico-political analyses presented through chapters 3 to 6, the problem of nature as 'whole' was raised. We have found ecocentric approaches to be, at the least, problematic. The ascription of good, worth and value to nature trades upon either an account of nature as totality or an account of an expansive self. There is a totalitarian logic at work here: the aggrandisement of the self or the suppression of differences and determinations. Either way, we move quickly to an account of identity thinking.

11. Bonhoeffer, *Christology*, p. 64.

However, the importance of the development must be noted: although it may be Romantic, it is anti-capitalist. Of course, we must be suspicious of such general anti-capitalism: short on analysis, anti-capitalism fails to grasp the ways in which capitalism degrades the environment. Yet a movement that is anti-capitalist cannot be all wrong.

The welcome stress on the agency of nature was one of the important lessons learned from an engagement with social/ist ecofeminism. The second important lesson was the affirmation of the *re*production of nature: the centrality of such work needs to be foregrounded, together with women's role in that labour. Women are not to be *identified* with non-human nature; neither are women and nature external to the human project. Instead, such ecofeminism points towards the demand for a new conception of nature in which the continuities of humanity with nature, and the differences of humanity and nature, are construed in fresh ways. Similarly to the positions of social and socialist ecologies, such a development of a human–nature materialism cannot be founded upon domination. Domination affirms differences and continuities but in the wrong sequence and in restrictive ways. What, however, was identified as missing in the ecofeminist literature was a persuasive account of how the otherness of nature is to be thought.

Of special importance for a political theology of nature was social ecology's attempt to relate more closely nature and humanity in ways that opposed hierarchy and domination: to secure an objective yet dialectical basis, as Bookchin understands it, for social ethics. That human society cannot be thought except by reference to nature is an important conclusion, although I am not convinced that Bookchin always adheres to this insight. However, Bookchin does press the matter of an ecological holism: nature and society must always be understood as a whole. For a political theology of nature, a vital amendment follows: in a theological holism, such a whole is to be understood as reformed as part within a common realm of God, nature and humanity.

It is the strength of socialist ecology that it seeks to identify the ways in which nature should be interpreted as being degraded. The presentation of natural conditions of production – together with a stress that such a production might be transformative, eco-regulative or extractive – is clearly valuable in advancing some differentiating categories. Furthermore, ecosocialism notes that there are difficulties concerning neo-Malthusian tendencies, underproduction and the issues of scarcity and limits of nature. What emerges less clearly in these accounts is whether or not, and if yes, in which fashion, nature is to be considered as other. What tends to be less developed, we might say, is a philosophy of nature. Furthermore, the relation between culture and nature is not carefully presented. On the one side, the relation between natural conditions and nature is undertheorised; on the other, the relation between such conditions and culture is underdeveloped.

It is not difficult to trace these political valuations of nature back to the distorted social performance of humanity. The expression of the deep need to seek ontological wholeness and security in nature can, of course, be traced in Romanticism. If humanity is not to be its own measure, then to appeal to nature seems a useful option. Yet it is also easy to see why the appeal to a naturalism invokes a humanist response: humanity may not be the measure of all things but it is the measure of its own difficulties with nature. Such a humanist response discloses its own deep anxieties, for we have abundant evidence that we are not even a good measure of our difficulties with nature. As Bonhoeffer notes, to go this route is to acknowledge that in the end all is thrown back on humanity.[12] In that there is a deeply felt concern that we need new resources, we now have an explanation as to why, throughout the various ecologies studied in part II, there is reference to 'spirituality'. Such reference to spirit tries in a variety of ways to indicate the openness of humanity to nature as a way either of reducing the immersion of humanity in nature ('we are spiritual beings!') or of softening the opposition between humanity and nature (spirituality as affective relationship with nature).

The political issues are not hard to see: on naturalist principles, the theorising of abundance is difficult. Quickly, we arrive at the point at which the health of nature is to be judged by the integrity of its systems – to which humanity is a threat. It is, as we have seen, a short step from the affirmation of such integrity to the affirmation of neo-Malthusian principles. Yet the humanistic reaction seems partial also: for now the relations, active and variable, between humanity and nature – how a humanism relates to a philosophy of nature – are less than clear.

The theological issues are easily identified: Christian theology does not support a hard naturalism. To go that way is to accept that the common realm is constituted by humanity and nature (or only by nature?) – to the exclusion of God. Nor is a stress on humanity as the measure of its own relations with nature acceptable, as this position connects humanity to God

---

12. Bonhoeffer, *Letters and Papers from Prison*, p. 380.

in ways which, as we have already seen in the critique by Gordon Kaufman (chapter 2 above), use the terminology of moral personalism to describe the humanity–God relationship – to the exclusion of all that is not-human and not-God. Instead, if the commitments of chapter 2 are well founded, the common realm of God, nature and humanity has a Christological foundation.

In the literature in ecological theology or the theology of nature one finds the affirmation of certain descriptions of nature but too little attempt to relate such descriptions in the doctrine of creation to Christ. (We have already seen as much in the discussion in chapter 2 of the avoidance of explicit consideration of transcendentals in the work of Sallie McFague and James Nash.) However, if truly theological transcendentals must be derived from, and related to, the economic actions of God in the career of Jesus of Nazareth, how nature (and humanity) are to be thought from such a perspective is raised. In other words, we are engaging here with God *for us*. The content of that *for us* requires elucidation. As Welker puts it, '"The relation" between creator and creatures cannot be illuminated in abstraction from the fundamental "relations" between complex structural associations of creaturely existence.'[13] If creation emerges *ex nihilo* in a moment of difference between triune persons, and is presented and recapitulated in the resurrection of Jesus Christ, in evidence is the *pro nobis* structure of creation and incarnation. *Creatio ex nihilo* also points towards this *pro nobis* structure. *Ex nihilo* secures the claim that there is no compulsion or arbitrariness in God's creating; creation is *God's free act*. As Rowan Williams argues:

> [T]he absolute difference between God and the world presupposed by the doctrine of creation from nothing becomes also a way of asserting the *continuity* between the being of God and the act of creation as the utterance and 'overflow' of the divine life. Belief in creation from nothing is one reflective path towards understanding God as trinity; and belief in God as trinity, *intrinsic* self-love and self-gift, establishes that creation, while not 'needed' by God, is wholly in accord with the divine being as being-for-another . . . For God to act for God's sake is for God to act for our sake.[14]

Creation, as an act of God's triune life, is God being for God which is for us. God is divine being-for-one-another; the world is God in divine being-for-us. And the content of that being-for-us is best discerned by reference to the incarnation of the *Logos* in Christ. Incarnation emerges as a

---

13. Welker, *Creation and Reality*, p. 2.   14. Williams, *On Christian Theology*, p. 74.

pedagogical category in which the *for us* structure and dynamic of the world is affirmed and reordered. What do we learn, then, of non-human nature, and human relations to that nature, if we say that the incarnation of the Word/*Logos* in Christ is the origin, rationale and destiny of creation? The remainder of this chapter essays an answer to this question: what do we learn of this common realm?

'For us' : the sociality of nature and humanity

In chapter 2, I proposed the concept of sociality as the principal transcendental for the interpretation of the resurrection of Jesus Christ. The resurrection of Christ requires, I argued, the interpretation that in the return of Christ to the world by God the creator, which is praise of Jesus by the Father in the Spirit, we have a Godly judgment on sociality. That is, the breach in sociality – the solidarity of human beings to be for one another – does *not* concretely in and for Jesus of Nazareth end in death. God, nature and humanity are thereby *social* concepts which are fully intelligible only if their social intention is drawn out: in sociality are the concepts of self, society and God properly explicated. I also argued that humanity and nature share in the transcendentality of sociality. Thus the promise of the continuation of solidarity even through death pertains also to nature. The promise of God the creator in Jesus Christ grants a future to that which is social. Hence if the act of election by God the creator in the resurrection of Jesus Christ is the election of *social* humanity then that same act of God is the election of *social* nature.

The scriptural witness is the source of this position. As David Tracy points out, 'The "appearance narratives" of the resurrection intensify those relationships [to earth and cosmos] by their relationship to both resurrected "body" and cosmic reality'.[15] The point is made explicitly when the commission to evangelise given by the risen Jesus is prefaced by the claim that all authority both in heaven and earth has been given to him (Matt. 28.18) and in the pre-Passion prayer in which Jesus asks his Father to glorify him in the manner of the glorification that he enjoyed with the Father before the creation of the world (John 17.5). The theme is also explicit in the accounts of the ascension of Jesus (Mark 16.19; Luke 24.51) and is anticipated by the event of the transfiguration (Matt. 17.1–8;

---

15. David Tracy, '*Models of God*: Three Observations', in R. Gill (ed.), *Readings in Modern Theology* (London: SPCK, 1995), pp. 82–6 (p. 85).

Mark 9.2–8; Luke 9.28–36). The theme of the relationship between the resurrected body and creation continues in the Christological debates of the early Church until it is established that the creativity associated with the return of Jesus from death is to be connected with the transcendence of God who creates *ex nihilo*: 'So Jesus shares the creativity of God . . . he is God *as* dependent – for whom the metaphors of Word, Image, Son are appropriate.'[16]

What is established by reference to the resurrection of Jesus *in* sociality and thereby the renewal *of* sociality is a sacrificial dynamic: the sociality of nature and humanity is part of the ordering of creation and its liberation is secured through the passion of Jesus Christ. The 'for us' character of the creaturely realm is reaffirmed in the actions of Jesus Christ.[17] The relation between resurrected body and the world both affirms and redirects the world according to the logic of sacrifice. As Colin Gunton notes, 'Jesus' sacrificial recapitulation of human life is achieved for the human purpose of a completing of the creation, of a setting free for the living out of creaturely being.'[18] Sociality insists that such living out of creaturely being refers both to nature and humanity and, especially, to their social interaction. In sum, the appearance narratives in the Gospels are the basis for the Church's connection of the sacrifice of Jesus to the 'sacrifice' of creation: 'it is not a mistake', argues Gunton, 'to conceive creation, too as a function of the self-giving of God, in which out of the free, overflowing goodness of his life he gives reality and form to something that is other than he'.[19] The connection between Christ and creation is being explored here by way of the notion of sociality.

Sociality proposes, then, the presentation and development of a sacrificial ontology of relations that encompasses humanity and nature. If we conceive of humanity and nature as interacting in a series of overlapping 'societies', how are these societies to be thought? How are such 'societies' subject to change through time (i.e., how are these societies temporal)? How does alteration in one area affect the rest?

To affirm both humanity and nature as social is to make a first, and vitally important, point: humanity is 'in' nature. If we must think in spatial images, we have not a humanity alongside nature but rather a humanity placed, in its societies, in the societies of nature. This point is nicely caught

16. Williams, *On Christian Theology*, p. 140.
17. Scott, *Theology, Ideology and Liberation*, pp. 195–203.
18. Gunton, *The One, the Three and the Many*, p. 226.
19. Colin Gunton, *The Actuality of Atonement* (Edinburgh: T. & T. Clark, 1988), p. 149.

by David Harvey when he, provocatively, describes New York City as an ecosystem. Michael Welker comes close to this view of interlocking societies when he argues that '[C]reation is the construction and maintenance of associations of different, interdependent creaturely realms.'[20] Later, Welker will stress that the centrality of such interdependence should be construed in relational terms. Welker's account helpfully points away from any tendency in a doctrine of creation to construe the creaturely in terms of a single *quality*. Instead, Welker performs a (perichoretic?) decentring: the emphasis is on a multitude of interacting realms rather than a single theme or quality.[21] However, the character of the associations Welker proposes, and an account of the interdependencies he identifies, lack detailed specification.[22]

Sociality in a political theology of nature is, I have argued, to be sourced to the resurrection of Jesus Christ, which, in turn, indicates that the orientation of human beings towards each other, and orientation of nature towards humanity, have eschatological significance. To think through the sociality of humanity and nature is thereby to begin from the actuality of relations between human and natural societies. That is, it is with continuities between humanity and nature that theological analysis must begin. The common realm of God, nature and humanity agrees thus far with Murray Bookchin's dialectical naturalism: the distance between humanity and nature operative in Western sensibility must be challenged. However, the common realm represents a materialism in which the dominant ways humanity works over nature cannot be disregarded. Although commitment to the continuities between humanity and nature functions here as a default theological position, yet the dominant modes of interaction of Western humanity with nature presuppose the separation and domestication of nature. Nature is regarded in Western society not as a co-participant in the common realm but either as domestic servant or wild animal (requiring to be tamed). A theology of nature must face such political circumstance.

Jesus' table-fellowship suggests such political 'realism' and recommends a standpoint from which to analyse the fractures and distortions in

---

20. Harvey, *Justice, Nature and the Geography of Difference*, p. 186; Welker, *Creation and Reality*, p. 13.
21. Welker's proposal also helpfully stresses the interaction between creaturely realms that may involve no human participation at all. However, it must now be doubted whether there are realms on this earth in which human beings do not participate in some fashion.
22. There is an exception: Welker's defence of human dominion over nature, which I shall briefly discuss in chapter 8.

the performance of Western humanity of its continuities with nature (see Luke 5.29–32; Matt. 9.10–13; Mark 2.15–17). As David Tracy notes: '"The table fellowship with outcasts" suggests not only a prophetic liberationist strand but also, by the very choice of eating and food, our intrinsic relationship to earth as well.'[23] In other words, the matter of interaction with nature towards the fulfilment of basic needs is not alien to Jesus' ministry, and indicates that the 'fruits of the earth' occupy a place within the economy of God's liberating *basileia* project. It is true that the emphasis has been on the prophetic aspect: 'The central symbol of the new vision of life, the Kingdom of God', writes Sallie McFague, 'is a community joined together in a festive meal where the bread that sustains life and the joy that sustains the spirit are shared with all'.[24] In this commitment, an important feature of the life of Israel, as in the feeding of the people of Israel with manna in the wilderness (Exod. 16), is continued.

However, what is 'recentred' in such an account as requiring theological attention is not only the 'radical inclusiveness of this vision' but also the modes of access to nature's goods which groups enjoy (or not). Agency is always linked in the Gospels to responsibility: consider only the parable of the widow's mite or the rich man and Lazarus. The range of modalities of interaction with non-human nature is opened up by this commitment. McFague hints at this conclusion: 'Without enough bread, some cannot be invited.'[25] We must address the range of labouring practices that engage non-human nature, but also attend to the ways that the needs and interests of the disadvantaged are engaged in this dispensation. To draw on a distinction made by James O'Connor: we must attend to that contradiction of capital through which goods are produced, distributed and exchanged *and* to the ways in which such production processes interact with the natural conditions of human life. Do such production processes serve the interests of others, when such others must also include non-human nature itself? The issue is: who benefits from these arrangements? Are these arrangements generous to the needy, and generous to the purveyor, nature itself? It cannot be denied: nature is *in nobis*. However, such a commitment cannot be read abstractly: is the *for us* dynamic employed restrictively or generously?

Although it is vitally necessary to see humanity as placed in the middle of nature through a series of interlocking societies which relate to

---

23. Tracy, '*Models of God*: Three Observations', p. 85.
24. McFague, *Models of God*, p. 52.   25. Ibid.

other – natural – societies, we must note, further, that such nature is oriented towards humanity. We have already seen that temporality is a crucial way of thinking of the orientation of nature towards humanity. If nature were not temporal, it would be spatially fixed. As spatially fixed, it would thereby not be amenable to transformation by humanity. However, as temporal, a social nature is oriented towards a social humanity through a range of interactions and relations. Nature persists in and through its temporality thereby providing stable conditions for the development of human life. We are already, by our embodiment, co-participants in nature's economy. Nature, we might say, is oriented towards humanity in the mode of preservation. This theme is clear in the Gospel of Mark, in the narratives of Jesus' power over natural forces (Mark 4.35–41 (and parallels at Matt. 8.23–7 and Luke 8.22–5), Mark 6.45–52 (and parallels at Matt. 14.22–33 and John 6.16–21)). As Robert Faricy summarises: 'Jesus' divine power to rescue his followers from nature-as-hostile represents his lordship over all creation.'[26] Interpreted sacrificially, nature is *pro nobis*.

Understood in such fashion, we may appreciate that human actions are bound to alter natural societies. In fact, this is too abstract a way of putting the matter: for all human actions, as embodied, already presuppose interactions with air, food and water. The pursuance of basic human conditions thereby demands alterations. Yet, on the view proposed here, such alteration is not in itself the issue. As Richard Lewontin has argued, 'Organisms . . . do not *adapt* to environments; they *construct* them. They are not simply *objects* of the laws of nature, altering themselves to the inevitable, but active *subjects* transforming nature according to its laws.'[27] The sheer facticity of change is not the issue; life requires processes of alteration; life requires reproduction and ecoproduction. Life, above all, requires through ecological transformation the shifting of the boundaries in the relations between what we call 'humanity' and 'nature'.

Consider some of the advanced techniques now available to ensure the safe delivery of a human baby. One could not say that such human reproduction is *not* a natural process (with, as we shall see, natural conditions). Yet, due to various sorts of medical interventions, the capacity for life has been changed: medical practices have altered the capacity for life (although not the conditions of life itself). Hence there is deep mutual interaction between two tendencies: the first, the natural process

26. Faricy, *Wind and Sea Obey Him*, p. 44.
27. Richard Lewontin, 'Organism and Environment', cited in Harvey, *Justice, Nature and the Geography of Difference*, p. 185.

of reproduction, the second, the dis/enabling techniques of modern medicine. Here natural processes have the qualities of *pro nobis* materiality; medical techniques have the quality of interventions in the otherness of nature. That is why, despite the paraphernalia of medical technology, the birth of a child remains so extraordinary: for the child is the gift of processes largely outside of our control yet clearly oriented towards us (in the manner of the reproduction of humanity). To intervene, medically or surgically, is thereby to engage the otherness of nature, that aspect which we do not truly understand, and which has been glossed as the sublime, the monstrous, the unruly. Yet, of course, the child remains the gift of the economies of nature oriented towards us: the reproductive potential, now realised, of parents; the sustenance of the mother and thereby the sustenance of the child; the process of childbirth itself. Nature is *pro nobis*.

The final aspect of the relations between the economies of the human and natural is the otherness of nature. Although such otherness can be interfered with (for example, as in the present-day increase in the incidence of human infertility), otherness is the very condition of its creativity and points to a dialectical relation in the mode of nature's preservation. For part of nature's capacity to preserve human beings is its otherness. Consider a simple oil slick: the spillage threatens landscapes and animals, animals on which people may rely for food or exchange. On occasion, despite predictions, the sea is able to absorb such a spillage . . . inexplicably. The otherness of nature is one way of speaking of this capacity of nature for self-renewal. Which is to acknowledge that nature does not have its ends only in humanity. This point is made clear by the concept of the common realm of God, nature and humanity: the fulfilment of nature lies in God. Nature is *extra nos*.

Of course, to speak of the otherness of nature is also to speak of the demand which nature places on humanity. We tend to see this expressed more in literature and art than in theology or philosophy. Yet its recovery in theology and philosophy is vitally important. According to Tim Hayward, philosopher Jürgen Habermas notes that we might enjoy very different practical or aesthetic relations with nature.[28] Yet Habermas contends that, on account of our particular interests in the production of knowledge, such considerations of the otherness of nature do not apply in epistemology. In other words, there can be no knowledge that is not governed by human interests. And there can be no knowledge of nature

---

28. See the discussion in Tim Hayward, *Ecological Thought*, ch. 1.

that is not governed by the human interest in the control of nature towards the support of human life.[29] However, the position advanced here is
that knowledge of nature invokes the principle of its otherness: we need, as
Haraway notes, to combine the view from subjugated bodies with a stress
on a realist account of knowledge of the world. Part of the demand – epistemological and practical – placed on humanity is the sense of the unknowa-
bility of nature which includes its knowability, and a sense of caution
in engaging nature in that many of the consequences of human–nature
interactions cannot be foreseen. Nature is *extra nos*.

So far, I have argued for the interactions of humanity and nature together with a sense of nature as both other to and oriented towards humanity. However, how are the differences between humanity and nature
to be thought? There is no denying that the incarnation of the *Logos* in
human form privileges the human in a certain way: for the human person
is the greatest concentration of the capacity to be social.[30] Thus the claim of
creaturely reality to be social also notes that the human is different, in specific ways, from the social dynamics of non-human nature. In other words,
what is proposed here is not a theological naturalism but rather a theological materialism.

What is the difference between naturalism and materialism? The incarnation of the *Logos*, and the theme of the common realm of God, nature
and humanity, require that humanity and nature cannot be separated,
yet neither can humanity be folded into nature. On the one hand, what
matters are the ecological relations between humanity and nature. On the
other hand, these relations are not to be secured by reference to a naturalism to which human beings must conform. For the claim that 'nature
teaches', is always selective and generally ideological: what nature imposes
'by necessity' trades upon a non-dynamic reading of nature (the balance of
nature) and is usually reductionist.[31] If critiques of deep ecology find their
mark, the dangers of naturalism are not always avoided in contemporary

---

29. For more detail, see my 'Imaging God: Creatureliness and Technology', *New Blackfriars*
79:928 (1998), 260–74 (here 265).
30. Here I am formally repeating the point made by Pannenberg and Rahner regarding the
rationale for the incarnation of the *Logos* in humanity. The justification for such incarnation
must, in some way, relate to the human as universal. For Pannenberg, only the human is both
universal and concrete (*Systematic Theology*, 11, p. 64) and thereby 'matches' the creating
concrete principle of the *Logos*; for Rahner, the human universal resides in the claim that
'Man is . . . mystery in his essence, his nature' ('On the Theology of the Incarnation', p. 108).
My position is different: both concretion and universality reside in the human capacity to be
social.
31. See Harvey, *Justice, Nature and the Geography of Difference*, p. 163; O'Connor, *Natural Causes*,
p. 121; Grundmann, 'The Ecological Challenge to Marxism', pp, 114–15.

ecological theory.[32] Such an ecological perspective, we might say, is insufficiently *generative*.

The generative, Christological, principle of sociality proposed here requires a theory of a dynamic, concrete order that brings into focus the determinations – the permanencies and alterations – of ecological relations. In a highly interesting passage, Ernst Bloch moves towards a materialism consonant with this view.[33] Building on the philosophical traditions of German idealism, yet crossed by the commitments of the early Marx to see the interchange between humanity and non-human nature through the metaphor of metabolic exchange, Bloch proposes an account of humanity as building its home on its 'nature-subject', arguing along the way that the steady failure of Western humanity to grasp the 'subject of nature' may be traced to our alienated conditions of living. Indeed, Bloch astutely notes that progress in human mastery over nature can readily coexist with the greatest social retrogression. Bloch does not develop the implications of his view with reference to either an account of ecological relations or a political theory. Yet, he is working towards an account of properly proportioned human living in its natural habitat or homeland in a way that takes seriously the openness of nature and history (including the present social and economic arrangements).

Christological shaping: sociality

In chapter 2, I stressed the importance of sociality by noting that, metaphorically, it is to be ascribed to the second person of the Trinity. Through this chapter, the implications of this claim are being explored. We have seen through the last section – in the exploration of nature as *extra nos* and *pro nobis* – that spatiality and temporality are analytic to sociality. How could there be social interactions, which the concept of sociality as transcendental indicates, without space and time? The condition of society thereby requires the conditions of space and time. However, given its importance in the argument, I propose, through this section, to offer more detail on the concept of sociality.[34]

---

32. See Plumwood, *Feminism and the Mastery of Difference*, ch. 7; Plumwood, 'Nature, Self and Gender', pp. 162–4; Northcott, *The Environment and Christian Ethics*, pp. 116–18.
33. Ernst Bloch, *The Principle of Hope* (Cambridge, MA: MIT Press, 1995), II, 658–98. For an attempt to contextualise Bloch's work for ecology, see Ely, 'Ernst Bloch, Natural Rights and the Greens', pp. 134–66.
34. Through this section I am indebted, in ways that I cannot now discern, to the writings of Dietrich Bonhoeffer. For an attempt to acknowledge the debt, see Peter Scott, 'Christ,

To speak of sociality as transcendental is to argue that society is not produced by human beings. Instead, social relations always pre-exist human beings. Human beings thus enter into social relations (of work, of culture, of embodiment, including reproduction). All these social relations have natural conditions. Sociality points towards a materialism: human beings engage in social activities which have the unintended outcome of reproducing society. This we might call a transformational account of society: there is no society without human agency, and yet social outcomes are not identical with the intentions of social agents. We should also add: there is no society without natural agency, and yet social outcomes may not be identical with the intentions of natural agents. To speak of a society is thereby to speak of the reproduction of society, and the utilisation of already established social products: to speak is to participate in a culture (with its natural condition of a voice); to make is to work with already established social products (including relations with non-human nature); to act is to participate in a situation governed by social rules (which have their own reference to nature).

To speak of a society from the perspective of the social transcendental is thereby always to maintain nature as co-participant: through all projects, non-human nature is active. Such a view is working with the grain of Daniel Hardy's insight into the situated character of human society: 'The conditions for human society are, loosely speaking, situational: sociality is formed and constrained by ecological conditions, such as location on a delimited land area and the natural resources that are available there.'[35] This circumstance must be presented in its full radicality: however society is organised, every transformative activity has nature as co-participant; all practices are co-constituted by nature. We should therefore speak of the mutual, shaping and irreducible interrelationality of all things in sociality. Indeed, we might say: nature lies between people.[36] On this view, ecological nature is the 'in-between', the middle of life. In the interstices, the joints of human living, nature is always already present. Nature is not then in the middle of life but is that middle. What happens between selves is never not nature; as 'in-between', nature insinuates itself everywhere. Thus, in any human project, we must assume the in-between of nature: in

Nature, Sociality: Dietrich Bonhoeffer for an Ecological Age', *Scottish Journal of Theology*, 53:4 (2000), 413–30.

35. Hardy, 'Created and Redeemed Sociality', p. 44.

36. Here I am adapting some remarks by Hannah Arendt, as reported by Douglas John Hall, *The Steward: A Biblical Symbol Comes of Age* (Grand Rapids: Eerdmans and New York: Friendship Press 1990), p. 230.

farming, however mechanised; in production, the transformation of nature; in extraction, the drawing out of nature; in urban living; in the health and safety of workers and others; in education; in aesthetic enjoyment. The metaphor also works in terms of human embodiment: what I am in-between my sense of myself and myself is, precisely, nature. Thus, medical therapies and disciplines are performed on my body, as nature; to alter the genetic constituents of human, or other, life, is always an intervention in nature. In theological theorising we need to understand nature as that which is in-between.[37] Nature, we may affirm, is a dialectical concept: it demands an account of humanity in nature, yet as differentiated from nature. Yet such differentiation is not the distance of domination but the difference of otherness which both preserves and exceeds us: nature is in-between.[38]

Keywords that emerge in this analysis of sociality are: self, nature and relation. Through participation in and enactment of social relations, the self reproduces society, and him or herself, in relations with nature. Furthermore, as present to social relations, nature is an essential partner in the reproduction of self and society. Indeed, on account of the concept of sociality, it would be theoretically proper to begin not from the concept of self but from the concepts of nature or relation. From either of these concepts, an inquiry into the transcendental character of the transformation and production of society may be pursued dialectically. Such a dynamic of social interaction, in which the whole is to be grasped dialectically by reference to sociality, is the *natura in nobis* structure of human ecology.

We have here a conceptuality – which does, of course, need to be augmented by reference to temporality and spatiality – that permits the specification of a number of interactions with non-human nature (and human embodiment) across a variety of dimensions. On this view, we are not merely placed in non-human nature. Rather, nothing can humanly be done without nature as co-participant; nature is in-between all human projects. We must, finally, stress the important interactive dynamic of social relations. By being placed in nature, humanity is able to respond to nature as directed to humanity and as the otherness of demand. Responding

37. We encounter here the problem of abstraction: we learn that nature is an abstract concept. The dimensions of its conceptuality emerge as vitally important: nature functions as a Kantian regulative idea by interpreting that which cannot be grasped in its entirety by theory. A certain modesty of reason is required here; nature cannot be 'mastered' in an epistemology.

38. Joel Kovel, 'Commentary on Herbert Marcuse's "Ecology and the Critique of Modern Society"', *Capitalism, Nature, Socialism* 3:3 (1992), 40–2 (42).

to the other as creative, and responding to the proximate as preservative, involves changes in relationships. Such is the logic of sacrifice, a 'setting free for the living out of creaturely being'.[39]

Christological relating: temporality

I have already said that temporality is analytic to sociality. Through this section, I explore what it means to speak of the temporality of nature. Such temporality can be ascribed, I think, to the inner dynamics of the triune life, specifically to the relation between creator and *Logos*. What follows is an attempt to explore the notion of difference in God in terms of a divine boundary or limit which informs our notion of temporality. Although what follows is too brief to do more than indicate a path, if the notion of difference in God as this relates to temporality could be defended, we would have a theological way of engaging with nature as various. In short, I shall argue through this section that differences in the interpretation of nature are to be sourced theologically to difference in God. In a further sense, the sociality of nature and humanity is thereby to be understood as sacrificial.

I am making a double claim: temporality provides a key for ordering and relating the senses of nature; temporality has its prefiguration and condition in a difference of the triune life. To sketch the case for this claim all too briefly, I quote from Donald MacKinnon:

> Yet within the context of totally uninhibited, but triadic aseity, we have to reckon with the actuality of limit, of *peras* or boundary. It is through this actuality that, for instance, the *idiotes* of the Son as eternal receptivity is constituted, a receptivity that in the manner of the Incarnate life is expressed in his dependence . . . and also in the role of the Spirit. If we suppose that in the theology of the Trinity an *analogia personarum* can be complemented by an analogy of *limits* . . . it may go some way towards grounding within the eternal, the essentially human element of temporality, the sense of inescapable limitation. For this element of temporality (clearly dependent, as it is, upon awareness of temporal direction as a cosmological ultimate) belongs to the substance of Jesus' comings and goings.[40]

39. Gunton, *The One, the Three and the Many*, p. 226.
40. Donald MacKinnon, 'The Relation of the Doctrines of the Incarnation and Trinity', in Richard W. A. McKinney (ed.), *Creation, Christ and Culture: Studies in Honour of T. F. Torrance* (Edinburgh: T. & T. Clark, 1976), pp. 92–107 (p. 104).

Dependence in the form of receptivity is a mark of the life of the Incarnate and is grounded in the boundary of God's triune life. Constitutive of the dynamics of the inner Trinitarian life of God is the notion of boundary, not in the sense of limitation but in the sense of the nature of divine relationality. That is, in the Godhead, in a moment between creator and *Logos*, there is that which prefigures the sending forth of the Son in Jesus Christ (see pp. 173–4). Such dependence in the form of openness can be understood in terms of the life of Jesus as the transcription of the immanence of God. God's boundary is the condition of *Christus pro me*; the 'who' of Jesus Christ is constituted by triune limit. (Nor would it be difficult to show that some notion of ethical limit is characteristic of our thinking on personhood. As Bonhoeffer has suggested, personal otherness requires holding to a view of the other as a genuine ethical limit.)

The notion of limit in the Godhead has a pleasing Christological derivation. The unity-in-difference of God constitutes the openness-in-dependence of Jesus Christ, the temporal struggle in finitude to be obedient to the Father. Such a triune limit thus enables that which is not God, but formed by God, to become itself. Precisely, to become itself not through independence alone but through openness. The presence of God, we must say, is given yet contingent. The *peras* of God confers dependence-in-openness on Jesus; yet the actuality of such conferment is through the freedom of Jesus. Obedience in action is given by the difference in God and enacted by Jesus in the blessing of the second difference of the Spirit.

What are the basic conditions of the temporality which marks the openness-in-dependence of the life of Jesus? These are two: the temporal irreversibility of the universe and the temporality of sociality. To explore these conditions directs our attention towards a theology of creation which makes the incarnation intelligible. What now becomes clear is that Jesus does not emerge out of a culture which is separate from nature. Instead, if the motifs of temporality, obedience, openness and freedom are to be treated with theological seriousness, these aspects must be understood as the transcription in creaturely structures, by analogy, of the limit of God revealed in the career of Jesus Christ.

In other words, the theme of temporality must be explored anthropologically and cosmologically and not simply as a contingent feature of the life of Jesus Christ. Temporality is a basic feature of the universe which renders a context for the temporality of Jesus Christ, which, in turn, reinterprets what temporality is (it is from God). Indeed, we must say that temporality is directed towards creatures. Interpreting temporality this

way – not as a Kantian intuition but as a universal, unconditional category – enables a reconfiguration of the relations between humanity and
nature. Indeed, such phraseology itself is called into question. We would
do better to speak not of nature and culture, but of 'fields of difference'
(Haraway). These fields, overlapping and not separable, are mapped by
the concept of temporality. Anthropologically, the *pro nobis* form of temporality is sociality, part of which comprises the histories of socio-ethical
encounters.

Yet such sociality is also *extra nos*, founded in the proper freedom of
others and is thus contingent. We might, following Roy Bhaskar, describe
this in terms of the distinction between condition and outcome. Sociality is the given condition of the freedom of human beings, yet it is also the
contingent outcome of the freedom-in-action of social persons. Embodied
human personhood must be seen as emerging through a series of socio-
ethical relations; humanity is the temporal emergence of embodied selves-
in-relation. Such a notion of sociality – truly given (that is, temporal) and
yet contingent on the actions of persons (that is, temporal again) – can be
ascribed to difference in God. The 'openness' of human social life, which is
a condition for Jesus Christ, is to be ascribed to the difference between the
actions of the creator and *Logos* in creation. The location of social freedom,
receptivity and openness is prefigured in the actions of the triune God in
creation. The *pro nobis* form of God's presence in creation is the blessing of
the temporality of sociality: the basic human solidarity to be for one another. Yet, of course, such sociality has natural conditions; sociality and its
natural conditions are separable only as fields of difference in temporality.
Thus sociality has a contingent, *extra nos* character.

Such a view is secured if we also consider the theme of temporality in cosmological, rather than anthropological, perspective. Wolfhart
Pannenberg has stressed the irreversibility of time and the temporality of
the universe, according to the 'Big Bang' model.[41] The totality of natural
structures is to be understood as enjoying its own form of openness, of receptivity, to the actions of God. Nature, in the sense of totality, thus has its
own form of dependence on God, its own openness and directedness towards God. Nature is thus both contingent and yet has its ground in God;
it, too, has God as *extra ipsam* and *pro ipsa*. We have seen already that such
dependence in openness is to be ascribed to the difference in God's life as

41. Pannenberg, *Toward a Theology of Nature*.

this is transcribed in creation. Temporality is part of God's blessing to the orders and life of natural being. The finite totality of the world may be cursed, as Bonhoeffer suggests in his interpretation of Genesis, but it is not without hope. That is, God has a future for nature. Neither fixed by a static metaphysics nor caught up in cycles of endless return, the temporality of nature invites attention to its own future.[42]

Temporality, grounded in the immanence of God, and transcribed in the dynamics of creation, liberation and fulfilment, is thereby a theological way of engaging with concepts of nature. Yet temporality – the form of God's condescension – has a range of reference: from the temporality of the life of Jesus Christ to the natural history of sociality to the temporal irreversibility of the universe. Nature can thus refer to human embodiment, the natural conditions which allow the emergence of the social life of humanity and the totality of processes and structures of the universe. Responsibility, respect for a common habitat and wonder are all proper human attitudes to nature. All these references refer to the contingency as well as the condescension of God's action. Condescension refers to the development of nature – nature's freedom – that is permitted in this interpretation; yet such openness in dependence is contingent upon the actions of God.

In this theological perspective, nature can be read Christologically, anthropologically and cosmologically: humanity can be understood as other than nature, in continuity with nature and part of the totality of nature. That is, the field of human actions can be related to the field of natural actions in a number of ways. These fields are never separate, although the relations can be construed differently. Yet such a construal is not possible apart from reference to difference in God. The presence of God is thus not to be understood in terms of a single extended incarnation (Sallie McFague). Instead, the condescension of God is to be understood in terms of temporality, an action known on account of the revelation of God in Jesus Christ. Temporality is God's *pro nobis* way with God's world.

'Human social activity . . . is therefore capable of reconstituting its own ways', writes Daniel Hardy.[43] The theme of temporality denies that

42. This paragraph, and the previous, are reworked from my 'The Technological Factor: Redemption, Nature and the Image of God', *Zygon: Journal of Religion and Science* 35:2 (June 2000), 371–84.
43. Hardy, 'Created and Redeemed Sociality', p. 45.

a theological concept of nature is to be framed in a static manner such that human beings, facing a static cosmology, are unable to reconstitute their own ways. To the contrary, the theological account of temporality presented here operates within the logic of sacrifice: the gift of time by God is an enabling gift. A theological account of temporality does not simplify human–nature relations through time. Instead, it makes these relations more differentiated and complex: three different conceptions of nature (human embodiment, natural conditions of society, totality of all processes) are invoked by the notion of temporality.

Christological placing: spatiality

The enlisting of Simon of Cyrene to carry the cross of Jesus, as reported in the Synoptic Gospels (Matt. 37.32; Mark 15.21; Luke 23.26), is an interesting literary device: this carrying of the killing instrument by a passer-by functions to delay Jesus' encounter with its unyielding wood. However, it is against this worked-over tree that the body of Jesus is eventually smashed. Nor is this Jesus' only encounter with non-human nature: during his post-baptismal testing, Jesus lives with the wild animals (Mark 1.13). Moreover, there is his celebrated encounter with the fig tree (Matt. 21.18–22; Mark 11.12–14) which, in its Markan version, is perplexing: despite the fact that it is not the season for figs, Jesus curses the tree and as a result it withers. I cite these episodes to emphasise that the encounters of Jesus with what we might broadly call natural space and its inhabitants are a theme in the Gospels. Too often, theological attention is focused on the healing miracles and the occasions in which Jesus demonstrates his power over natural forces. In fact, Jesus' comings and goings include not only missionary journeys but also encounter with natural circumstance. Jesus is placed in a natural context which includes other agents in their own ecological space. How should this ecological space be understood?

The claim of the emergence of the world in the difference of *Logos* from creator recommends, as I have argued, the interpretation of creatureliness by way of the concept of sociality. Thus, we are referred to the doctrines of creation and incarnation, guided by the commitment to see the world as dependent on God, yet contingent. Yet I have also argued that the theme of space is analytic to the notion of sociality. Temporality, the theme of the previous section, invokes a conception of space (and vice versa). By reference to spatiality, we are referred to the notion of the critical otherness of nature that we have encountered at various points already.

Transcendentals, as metaphysical concepts, are ways of construing difference.[44] How, then, shall the otherness or difference of nature be construed?

In a relevant analysis, Jürgen Moltmann argues for an ecological concept of space which is, he argues, acceptable to and compatible with an account of creation as kenotic.[45] That is, it is through the restriction of God's omnipresence (and eternity) that creation comes to be.[46] Moltmann's argument moves by way of the presentation of general anthropological accounts of ecological space. A summary of this reading of space, which, he argues, approaches the understanding of space in biblical traditions, is as follows: 'every living thing has its own world in which to live, a world to which it is adapted and which suits it'.[47] Moltmann argues that such an ecological conception of space as 'living space' resists reduction to a geometrical conception of space.

Moltmann's position presents a series of difficulties. It is not clear, as critics point out,[48] that Moltmann manages to avoid a container view of space. This problem is associated with a second: drawing on the anthropological findings of Max Scheler, Moltmann seeks a way of moving beyond the ecological concept of space to take on some of the quantitative aspects of the geometrical account of space. Why he might want to do this is not hard to discern: for in the construal of space as ecological, the universal aspect of space is lost. We cannot merely talk of space associated with objects, for in that case the relation of God to the whole of the created order is imperilled. However, neither can we affirm a geometrical account which, posing as infinite and absolute space, in fact substitutes for God.

The notion of ecological space is, of course, vital for the argument of this book. For agents and ecosystems to have their living space is also to speak of their otherness. I do not mean such otherness simply in terms of geometric space: for example, that the space of an ecosystem is not the space of another system. I mean rather that natural agents and systems have their own world. In that world, these agents and ecosystems develop

44. For the claim that a concern for difference is finally a metaphysical undertaking, see Rowan Williams, 'Between Politics and Metaphysics: Reflections in the Light of Gillian Rose', in L. Gregory Jones and Stephen Fowl (eds.), *Rethinking Metaphysics* (Oxford: Blackwell, 1995), pp. 3–22 (p. 5).
45. See Moltmann, *God in Creation*, pp. 140–57; cf. Moltmann, *The Coming of God*, pp. 296–308.
46. See Moltmann, *God in Creation*, pp. 79–98.
47. Ibid., p. 147.
48. Alan J. Torrance, '*Creatio ex Nihilo* and the Spatio-temporal Dimensions, with special reference to Jürgen Moltmann and D. C. Williams', in Colin Gunton (ed.), *The Doctrine of Creation* (Edinburgh: T. & T. Clark, 1997), pp. 83–103 (pp. 84–93).

their own life: seeking 'to maintain themselves by metabolizing materials from their environment and reproduce their like'.[49] Such processes, which require their own room, have a developmental trajectory. Such a position is the basis for speaking of the otherness of nature and, finally, of nature as subject.

Geometric and ecological space: can these two be harmonised? Moltmann's own proposal centres on a kenotic doctrine of creation. The idea seems right: God wills to be not God through a restriction or letting-be which has creation as its consequence. Here, however, I plan to follow Robert Jenson, who writes of the 'roominess' of God: 'for God to create is for him to open a place in his triune life for others than the three whose mutual life he is . . . In that place, he *makes room*, and that act is the event of creation.'[50] How then should we think theologically about space? Jenson argues that we must interpret space in terms of time: 'Space is the distention within which things can be now there for us.'[51] Space is thereby unintelligible without reference to time: the spatial extension of things through time is their *pro nobis* structure. In fact, this movement of spatio-temporalities Jenson calls 'histories', which returns us, of course, to the matter of sociality. Furthermore, interpreting Kant, Jenson points towards an ecological account of space: 'Space . . . is the a priori of otherness.' That is, space is the transcendental (in a Kantian sense) condition of the interpretation of the other as other. The first problem with such transcendentality, as Jenson notes, is that it remains unclear how it relates to geometric space in which the spatial otherness of things is maintained. If space is understood restrictively as a condition of experience (as in Kant), how does it also inhere in objects?

Jenson's response to this dilemma is elegant: by developing the doctrine of creation, he argues that God grants space. 'God opens otherness between himself and us', he writes, 'and so there is present room for us'.[52] And such room is to be understood in a double sense: 'space can be at once an *a priori* of our consciousness and a structure within which we locate ourselves, because it is an aspect of God's enveloping conscious life'.[53] In other words, the God who creates *ex nihilo* establishes an independent spatial

49. Robert Jenson, *Systematic Theology*, vol. 2, *The Works of God* (Oxford and New York: Oxford University Press, 1999), p. 15.
50. Jenson, 'Aspects of a Doctrine of Creation', pp. 17–28 (p. 24). Cf. Jenson, *Systematic Theology*, II, p. 25.
51. Jenson, *Systematic Theology*, II, p. 46.   52. Ibid., p. 47.   53. Ibid.

reality that has its own structure and dynamic. As independent, space – the way that things are ordered for agents – may be understood as the condition of otherness and of the relations that pertain between others.

Here Jenson draws explicitly on the type of Trinitarian doctrine of creation discussed earlier in this chapter. The *extensio* (my term) of space must be referred to the agency of the Word as the mediator of creation. The difference of creation from creator may be sourced to the difference between creator and *Logos*. As Jenson writes earlier, the creative agency of the Son may be understood 'to *hold open* the creatures' space in being'. Jenson develops the theme thus:

> The relation of the creature to the Creator, by which the creature is, holds in the present tense of created time without thereby being a timeless relation, in that one of the three, the Son, has his own individual identity *within* created time, in that he is himself one of those among whom and upon whom the creatures' participation in God's story is being 'worked out'.[54]

Thereby we are returned to the beginning of this section with its portrait of some of the comings and goings of Jesus. There we noted in the Gospels some encounters in what we might call ecological space. The ecosocial ontology of spatiality points, we may conclude, to a *principle of encounter*. The dynamism of human–human, human–nature and nature–nature relations may be referred to the active relations of spatial encounter. For in the differences and commonalities of human and non-human nature, in their range of interactions, we have a series of encounters: of humanity by nature; of nature by humanity. This is perhaps a difficult principle to grasp. Why so? Because it contradicts a dominant Western view that humanity is self-sustaining. On this dominant view, the Western attitude to nature concentrates on the ways that (non-)human nature is a problem for us: diseased bodies, animals in the 'wrong place', 'inadequate' crop yields, etc. Nature is part threat, part challenge.

By contrast, the principle of encounter in social interaction suggests a sense of the demands placed on humanity by a lively nature. Humanity is truly placed in nature: we must speak of the reality of humanity in nature. This is, to borrow some formulations from Jim Cheney, the core of the theological attempt to affirm the otherness, the difference of nature: against strategies of containment which seek – either through negation or

54. Ibid., p. 27.

immersion – to organise nature, the emphasis here is on 'genuine recognition, acknowledgement, and embracing of the other'.[55] Indeed, the otherness of nature – precisely, its spatiality – indicates its capacities for renewal (including the renewal of the habitat for human living). We should not be sentimental here: sometimes nature's embrace is unkind. This is one aspect of its otherness.

Such a dynamic of encounter is to be sourced to a theological reading of spatiality: the otherness to be found in the spatial relations between things is given in the space God grants for the creaturely realm. Jenson's position needs development thereby: space as the condition of otherness needs to be construed dynamically. The trajectory of nature is through modalities of social interaction. Through spatial movements things are there for us and for each other in ecological space. Nature is *extra nos*.

That nature has its space is the source of the claim of nature as active subject. Arguing along such lines, Donna Haraway proposes to speak of nature as actor or agent.[56] Indeed, perhaps it is now time to affirm the independence of nature but to do so without reference to subjectivity, language and consciousness that 'nature as subject' suggests. So the position that we saw first in ecofeminism here receives theological warrant. From such a warrant a theological correction follows. The correction is this: I remain unconvinced that any quick move should be made to code nature as, say, coyote or trickster.[57] Of course, the metaphors are intended to destabilise our views of nature. However, I am not persuaded that nature should be quickly coded, and the notion of trickster carries furthermore the suggestion that nature is capricious and deceitful. Neither fits easily with the perspective of *creatio ex nihilo*. Which is not to deny, of course, that nature is sometimes not benign.

The independence of nature, secured by reference to spatiality, functions in a political theology of nature as a delegitimating strategy. Politically restrictive uses are here denied. Such restrictive uses tend to domesticate nature by reference to God for certain political purposes: political arrangements are 'naturalised'. Nature as heterogeneous agent – as proposed here – denies such naturalisation.

55. Cheney, 'Nature, Theory, Difference', pp. 158–78 (p. 164). As a consequence, democratic 'negotiation' will emerge as a key theme in chapter 8.

56. Constance Penley and Andrew Ross, 'Cyborgs at Large: Interview with Donna Haraway', in Penley and Ross (eds.), *Technoculture* (Minnesota and London: University of Minnesota Press, 1991), pp. 1–20 (p. 3).

57. Of course, I have taken the metaphors from Haraway: see Donna Haraway, 'The Actors are Cyborg, Nature is Coyote, and the Geography is Elsewhere', in Penley and Ross (eds.), *Technoculture*, pp. 21–6. I thank Elaine Graham for this point.

Word made fleshly: the realm of nature–society

To invoke the name of Jesus Christ is, in my account, to propose a differentiated and complex holism. Interpreted by reference to sociality, the ecological situatedness of un/natural humanity must be grasped dialectically: by reference to human societies, natural societies and their relations in the *pro nobis*, sacrificial structure of creation. The description of humanity as un/natural is dialectical: humanity cannot be grasped by reference to itself (anti-natural) nor can it be subsumed in nature (natural). Humanity, as located in a common realm of God, nature and humanity, is thereby best understood as un/natural: oriented towards the triune God as both social and natural. In turn, non-human nature may be understood as oriented towards the triune God as both natural and social. Ecological identities must therefore be understood as given yet not static: human identities are to be interpreted relationally with reference to God and nature; natural identities are to be interpreted relationally with reference to God and humanity; the divine identity is to be interpreted relationally (that is, as triune) by reference to the act of God in incarnation as fleshly: social and natural.

A rich Trinitarian ontology emerges which affirms the organisation of the world as social, permits an account of the proper otherness of nature and recommends three different modalities of human interaction with nature. Can theology engage with the complexity of the concept of nature and yet reform such complexity in relation to the idea of God? The answer is in the affirmative: difference in the interpretation of nature in political theology is required by *creatio ex nihilo*. Differences of nature in the common realm are founded in the idea of God as triune creator. That is, the implication of the claim that Christ transcribes the intrinsic character of God is considered from the perspective of creation.

> What is realised in the mission of Jesus and perfected in the Father's raising Him from the dead is the very unity of God, the consistency of God with himself in relation to his creation. We have to do with a privileged human action that is grounded in God, that in fact provides the very rationale of creation itself.[58]

In this compressed passage, Donald MacKinnon reprises the Christology of the theology of the common realm of God, nature and humanity presented in this chapter. Such theology is 'revealed', related to the incarnation of God in Christ. The unity that is founded in the economic actions

---

58. MacKinnon, 'The Relation of the Doctrines of the Incarnation and Trinity', p. 99.

of the narrative of the creator and Son has to do with the triune unity of the immanent God. The immanent unity of God precedes the economic unity of God: the career of Jesus, especially the cross and the resurrection, is the 'repetition-in-difference' (Catherine Pickstock) of the immanent Godhead. That is not to say, as MacKinnon may perhaps be read as suggesting, that creation is *for* the incarnation. Rather, both may be regarded as sacrificial actions of God: acts of condescension which grant a future to creatures. Yet, of course, we know of creation only in the perspective of the narrative of suffering and dereliction which is the conclusion of the career of Jesus Christ. Creation and incarnation are related: the *Logos* of God is the Incarnate, Jesus Christ; the *Logos* as the shaper of creation emerges in the very texture of shaped, material, sociality which is the life of Jesus Christ. If the incarnation provides the 'rationale of creation', this should be read in the sense not of 'justification', but rather of the continuity between God's commitment to redeem and God's initial and continuing action to create.

The practical significance of this multiconstrual of human–nature relations can easily be seen. In theological perspective, humanity is other than nature, nature is mediated only through social contexts and humanity has natural conditions which escape its control. Further, there is no requirement to opt for naturalistic interpretations of the relation between humanity and nature nor to propose Stoic attitudes in the face of nature. The blessing of natural life is to be understood in a number of ways but always interpreted as mediated by God (in Christ). Christian wisdom here resists any hasty divisions and determinations in the 'worldly' interpretation of human–nature relations.

Throughout this chapter, although I have tried to learn from them, I have not sought to correct the positions in political ecology presented in part II. Instead, I have sought to highlight the contours of an emerging theological ecomaterialism which stresses both the actual, material relations operative in ecosocieties, and the theme of cooperation between the human and the non-human. Thinking theologically with the transcendental of sociality we have learned of the mutual relations of nature and society, maintained in a Christological thought. None the less, the picture is incomplete. In that Christ is never Christ without the Spirit, we must consider once more the theme of un/natural humanity situated in a common realm but this time from the different perspective of pneumatology.

8

Life in the Spirit: un/natural fellowship

A dynamic common realm

The theology of the common realm of God, nature and humanity considers God's action towards non-human nature and un/natural humanity, and specifies the difference in God which such action presupposes. To this end, in the previous chapter a Christological reading of human–nature relations was offered. That is, if any account of nature's economy is to be persuasive for theology, it must be interpreted in relation to the *Logos* as agent of creation. In such fashion is both the dependence on the creator and the contingency of the created order to be understood. In engagement with a number of disciplines in political ecology, I have stressed the otherness of nature to humanity together with an emphasis on encounter in human–nature relations best understood in the dynamic interaction – demand and response – of natural–human societies in processes of becoming in time and space. In exploring this theme of a worldly Christology, I stressed the dynamic, interactive shifts in boundaries which such a relational view of the ecology of humanity and nature requires. Through this chapter, I explore the logic of fellowship – that is, the pneumatology – which is indicated by the Christology of the previous chapter to answer the question: how shall we learn to act in the common realm? In other words, what are the tendencies of the practices which are both the gift of the Spirit and to which the Spirit provides the mode of participation? Such practices will be 'excentric': the economy of that which is social, spatial and temporal surpasses itself towards new forms of organisation.[1] How might this be thought?

---

1. Cf. Hardy, *God's Ways with the World*, p. 83: 'The right use of our freedom is excentric.'

I begin to answer this question by setting out some of the contours of a pneumatology of fellowship. An accent on the Spirit stresses non-human nature, the human nature of Jesus and the eschatological perfection of all creation of which the resurrection of Jesus Christ is proleptic anticipation. As will become clear, however, attention to the theme of fellowship is not the most common way of approaching the matter of Christian responsibility in an ecological age. Hence, I criticise and reject the popular themes of stewardship and valuing nature. The chapter closes with a constructive theologico-political proposal: a 'democracy of the commons' as a concrete political way of considering the fellowship in sociality of humanity and nature as the gift of the Spirit.

In sum, the wisdom of Christianity is reframed towards the discernment of God's particular and universal presence in the world, to which human action should reorientate itself in order to recover the fullness of God's blessing of creatureliness in fellowship. The actions of the Spirit, co-working with the Word, relate the movements of encounter through the spatio-temporal field of sociality. Through practices towards fellowship, which are the gift of the Spirit, and the enjoyment of fellowship, which is the life of the Spirit, the presence of the Spirit is to be understood. By attention to losses of fellowship, to deformations in the realm of spatio-temporal sociality, we glimpse the counter-evidential actions of the Spirit who seeks the reprising and redoubling of fellowship and provides the means to fellowship. What is this 'reprising and redoubling of fellowship'? What are these 'means to fellowship'?

By the Word yet in the Spirit, creatures are placed in a material order which is premised upon fellowship and oriented towards fellowship. Through the practices of the common realm, including the practices of human–nature relations, fellowship is both given and practised. In other words, the relations of the social realm are real and yet dynamic. And, of course, the quality of fellowship of these relations depends on how the agents of the social realm interact with one another – that is, towards fellowship, difference and peace or enmity and violence. The means to fellowship is provided through those practices which enhance the mutual orientation of the agents of the common realm towards one another (although, of course, the orientation is not symmetrical). I shall suggest that there are enough structural similarities between an eschatological orientation towards newness and democracy, such that the practice of ecological democracy may be seen as one such 'means to fellowship'.

An ecological pneumatology

A much-cited and early Christian benediction interprets the Holy Spirit in terms of fellowship: 'and the fellowship of the Holy Spirit be with you all' (2 Cor. 13.13 New Jerusalem Bible; NRSV has 'communion'. Cf. 1 Cor. 12.13). In the Nicene Creed, the Spirit is described as 'the Lord, the giver of Life'. How shall these commitments be understood to develop the theology of the common realm of God, nature and humanity?

The first point is to note that fellowship is not to be restricted only to human agents: 'To experience the fellowship of the Spirit inevitably carries Christianity beyond itself into the greater fellowship of all God's creatures. For *the community of creation*, in which all created things exist with one another, for one another, and in one another, is also the *fellowship of the Spirit*.'[2] Against a tendency to associate the actions of the Spirit with the benefits of Christ and thereby to restrict arbitrarily the sphere of the efficacy of the Spirit to the Church,[3] the third person of God's Trinity[4] is here understood as *Creator Spiritus*. The theological warrant for such an affirmation is easily discerned: '*God's* spiritual transcendence of matter, and of all other spirits than himself', writes Geoffrey Wainwright, 'is the unique transcendence of their *Creator*'. Out of this logic, Wainwright concludes: 'In Christian tradition, therefore, the Holy Spirit may be invoked as *Creator Spiritus*.'[5]

We may then concur with Michael Welker that the benefits of the Spirit are not for humans only but are also for 'spatial and temporal, proximate and distant environments'.[6] In what ways is the notion of fellowship for a common realm to be further specified? What is ecological fellowship? Moltmann argues that 'Fellowship means opening ourselves for one another, giving one another a share in ourselves'.[7] Although referring here only to human persons, Moltmann argues that fellowship enables and permits sharing amongst those who are different. To speak of fellowship

2. Jürgen Moltmann, *The Spirit of Life: A Universal Affirmation* (London: SCM Press, 1992), p. 10. Cf. p. 219: '*The creation of community* is evidently the goal of God's life-giving Spirit in the world of nature and human beings.'

3. Identified by Colin E. Gunton, *Theology through the Theologians* (Edinburgh: T. & T. Clark, 1996), pp. 105–6.

4. This formulation from Nicholas Lash, *The Beginning and the End of 'Religion'* (Cambridge University Press, 1996), p. 64.

5. Geoffrey Wainwright, 'The Holy Spirit', in C. E. Gunton (ed.), *The Cambridge Companion to Christian Doctrine* (Cambridge University Press, 1997), pp. 273–96 (p. 281).

6. Michael Welker, *God the Spirit* (Minneapolis: Fortress Press, 1994), p. 338.

7. Moltmann, *The Spirit of Life*, p. 217.

in the Spirit across the common realm is, of course, to speak of communion between creator and creatures: difference indeed! Which means, of course, that, if fellowship is granted by the gift of the Spirit between God's Trinity and *human* creatures, the difference between creatures and creator cannot be used to exclude the non-human from participation in fellowship. The fellowship bestowed by *Creator Spiritus* knows no such arbitrary restriction.

Moltmann associates the gift of fellowship with the giving of life. There is only life through fellowship: 'There is no life without its specific social relationships.'[8] As the giver of fellowship, God the Spirit is also the giver of life: 'In fellowship with himself and through his creative energies, God the Spirit creates a network of social relationships in which life comes into being, blossoms and becomes fruitful.'[9] Diversity is thereby not alien to the project of creation. Instead, diversity is to be sourced to the giving of the Spirit. In *God in Creation*, Moltmann makes the same point: 'Creation is also the differentiated presence of God the Spirit, the presence of the One *in* the many', in which the relationality of the world subsists in the presence of the Spirit of the triune God.[10] To interpret this 'differentiated presence' requires a further range of distinctions: creating subject, renewing energy and consummating potentiality form the acts and efficacy of the Spirit. It makes no sense to restrict such differentiated presence to human community alone: 'for all human communities are embedded in the ecosystems of the natural communities, and live from the exchange of energy with them'. Acknowledging this point is 'not the least important element in a full understanding of the fellowship of the Spirit'.[11]

What more may be said of the fellowship of the common realm? In chapter 2, I proposed that the transcendental of *openness* should be ascribed to the work of the Holy Spirit. The sociality of nature–humanity is to be construed in terms of a dynamic of openness. Elsewhere, I have argued that 'The presence of the Spirit is the opening up, the raising up, the freeing up of social forms of social organisation . . . social life is from the Creator (whose "mark" is creative liberty) in the ordering and reordering work of the Word (in creation and redemption) and is to be brought to its eschatological futures in the action of the Spirit.'[12] This view needs expanding for a political theology of nature. If, as proposed, the Spirit's actions are eschatological actions, and the resurrection of Jesus Christ – and

---

8. Ibid., p. 219.   9. Ibid.   10. Moltmann, *God in Creation*, p. 14.
11. Moltmann, *The Spirit of Life*, p. 225.   12. Scott, *Theology, Ideology and Liberation*, p. 228.

thereby the reinstantiation of sociality – is the model for considering eschatological destiny, then among other things the Spirit's actions renew the varied and variable social relations between humanity and nature and enable their fuller openness. The Spirit energises the dynamics of sociality eschatologically. As Elizabeth Johnson recommends, the Spirit may therefore be understood as eschatological movement in and towards the openness of creaturely reality: 'the Spirit characteristically sets up bonds of kinship among all creatures, human and non-human alike, all of whom are energized by this one Source'.[13]

A second point emerges: the actions of the Spirit are *eschatological* actions. John Zizioulas has forcefully made this point: contrary to some emphases in theological tradition, if we must ascribe the categories of immanence and transcendence to God's Trinity, we should say that the *Logos* becomes history, whereas 'the Spirit is the *beyond* history, and when he acts in history he does so in order to bring into history the last days, the *eschaton*'.[14] Such a theological position is in conformity with, and develops, the Trinitarian doctrine of creation proposed in the previous chapter. There I argued that creation is to be understood as authored in the movement of God's triune life *ad extra* in the difference of the creator from the *Logos*. Creation is intended by God to be independent in and through its origin in the self-distinction of the second person of the Trinity from the first. Further, if incarnation is properly acknowledged, creation, of which incarnation is the summary, has its source and ground in the relation of the *Logos* to the creator. It is theologically appropriate, therefore, to refer to the incarnation of the *Logos* in Jesus Christ as the principle of immanence, for want of a better term, in Christianity. Immanence is a Christological 'function': creation, the realm of immanence, is to be sourced to the difference between *Logos* and creator; the *Logos* becomes history.

Transcendence is thereby to be ascribed to the Spirit, as Colin Gunton – consistently amplifying Zizioulas's insight – has long argued: 'The Son is the mode of God's immanence in the world . . . The Spirit is God's eschatological transcendence, his futurity, as it is sometimes expressed. He is God present to the world as its liberating other.'[15] Such a view requires that a certain tendency to regard the Spirit as unrestricted divine

13. Elizabeth A. Johnson, *Women, Earth and Creator Spirit* (New York/Mahwah: Paulist Press, 1993), p. 44.

14. Zizioulas, *Being as Communion*, p. 130.

15. Gunton, *Theology through the Theologians*, p. 122; also p. 108. Cf. Gunton, *The One, the Three and the Many*, pp. 180ff.

presence is checked.[16] The turn to the Spirit in some ecological theologies exhibits this tendency. For example, Mark I. Wallace at one level helpfully argues that 'hope for a renewed earth is best founded on belief in the Spirit as the divine force within the cosmos who continually works to sustain all forms of life . . . [T]he Holy Spirit [is] God's invigorating presence within the global society of all living beings.'[17] While there is much to be welcomed in Wallace's essay, a tendency to stress the immanent presence of the Spirit is evident.[18] Thus, in a paradigmatic statement, Wallace contends that the Spirit is best understood 'as a living, embodied being who works for healthy communion within our shared planet home . . . nature in all its variety will be construed as the primary mode of being for the Spirit's work in the world'.[19] Such an argument is open to Gunton's objection that the Spirit is identified with 'cultural and historical developments', here construed broadly as the historical development of natural forms.[20] As a consequence of such identification, the actions of the Spirit are construed as internal to creation in such fashion that the actions of the Spirit as the opening up and turning outwards of the social ordering of creation are obscured.

A more serious objection concerns the way in which the unity and diversity of creation is handled theologically. Wallace correctly argues that this matter of unity and diversity can be stated adequately only by reference to the immanent Trinity, the triune God in God's own life. In an unclear formulation, he writes: 'As the Spirit exists perichoretically in the Godhead to foster communion between the divine persons, my proposal is that the Spirit also performs the role of the *vinculum caritatis* within nature in order to promote the well-being and fecundity of creation.'[21] The unity of creation is grounded theologically thereby; the essay is replete with phrases that reinforce the sense of the unity of creation. What of the diversity of creation, however? Following the logic of Wallace's argument, the basis for

---

16. The stress on the presence of the Spirit also diverts attention from the important matter of the Spirit's *hypostasis*: more on this below.

17. Mark I. Wallace, 'The Wounded Spirit as the Basis for Hope in an Age of Radical Ecology', in Dieter T. Hessel and Rosemary Radford Ruether (eds.), *Christianity and Ecology: Seeking the Well-being of Earth and Humans* (Cambridge, MA: Harvard/CSWR, 2000), pp. 51–72 (p. 52). In an earlier work, *Fragments of the Spirit: Nature, Violence and the Renewal of Creation* (New York: Continuum, 1997), pp. 133ff., Wallace offers a pneumatology that can barely be distinguished from pantheism. As 'The Wounded Spirit' essay avoids such pantheism, a charitable reading requires a concentration on this later statement.

18. It may be that both tendencies are to be sourced to what appears to be a breach in the traditional view of *creatio ex nihilo*: see Wallace, 'The Wounded Spirit', pp. 60–1.

19. Ibid., p. 55.   20. Gunton, *Theology through the Theologians*, p. 108.

21. Wallace, 'The Wounded Spirit', p. 56.

diversity must also be found in the role of the Spirit in the being in communion who is the triune God. The closest that Wallace comes to making such an affirmation is the following comment: 'It is the move to embodiment – the procession of Godself into the biotic community that sustains life [in three ways: creator Spirit; embodiment of divine life in Jesus; union of Jesus with the Spirit] – that is the basis for unity within the Godhead.'[22] This is baffling: how can the actions of Jesus and the Spirit in the economy be the *basis* of the unity of God in God's immanence? Not only does the direction of the argument have the trajectory of projection, but the unity of God is not understood in Trinitarian fashion. The result is a rather forbidding divine unity. How can the diversity of creation be secured if a monolithic God is the author of creation? Wallace's is a bold and welcome attempt to recover the theological theme of *Creator Spiritus*. However, the resources of a Trinitarian theology need to be deployed more fully.

A third point becomes clear: for there to be true theological interpretation of the common realm (which, as we shall see, involves political judgments), the matter of the *hypostasis* of the Spirit cannot be avoided. The Spirit's work, argues Wolfhart Pannenberg, is 'creative activity in the bringing forth of life and movement'. However, no immanent process is named thereby. Instead, as Pannenberg suggests: 'By the Spirit creatures will be made capable of independence in their relation to God and at the same time integrated into the unity of God's Kingdom.'[23] How is such independence and unity to be thought? In an important essay, Colin Gunton argues that the recovery of an account of the Spirit's action in the economy cannot be fully and properly secured without an account of the personal being of the Spirit in God's own life. The impersonal descriptions of the Spirit as – for example – force, energy and power are not entirely wrong. That is, the actions of the Spirit are directed towards the renewal of *matter* which invites an identification of the Spirit in impersonal terms.[24] However, personal metaphors cannot be avoided if the freeing and opening out of the Spirit's personal and particular acts are to be established conceptually.

Differently from Wallace, Gunton argues that the recovery of the Spirit as personal being cannot rely on the Augustinian understanding of the Spirit as *vinculum caritatis* or *vinculum Trinitatis*. To take such an

22. Ibid., p. 58.
23. Wolfhart Pannenberg, *Systematic Theology* (Edinburgh: T. & T. Clark, 1998), III, pp. 7, 12.
24. In *The Spirit of Life*, pp. 274ff., Moltmann identifies three sets of impersonal metaphors: formative, of movement and mystical.

Augustinian path, Gunton argues, is to see the immanent actions of the Spirit as the 'closing of an eternal circle' in which the Spirit functions as a link between Father and Son, A better option, Gunton maintains, and one more in conformity with the biblical witness, is to see the work of the Spirit as the agent of 'the unity of the Godhead, but also of the diversity of the persons'.[25] The Spirit frees the becoming-in-communion who is God's Trinity to become 'itself' but not in the sense of undifferentiated unity but rather as a community of free persons. The Spirit perfects the Godhead but not towards a unity but rather towards excentric community. Such excentric community is 'not a closed circle, but a self-sufficient community of love freely opened outwards to embrace the other'.[26] From this position, Gunton draws the following conclusion: 'if the Son is the basis of God's movement out into creation to bring that which is not God into covenant relation with him, the Spirit is the dynamic of that movement, the one who perfects creation by realising the communities of persons and the transformation of matter'.[27] Secured thereby is an affirmation of diversity: the opening-out actions of the Spirit are directed not towards unity but instead to the perfection of human and non-human societies, for which 'the resurrection of Jesus Christ from the dead serves as a model for the possibilities for the transfiguration of matter in general'.[28] Interestingly, Moltmann makes a nearly identical point, sourcing true fellowship to the inner, yet personal, triune life: '[Fellowship] issues from the essential inward community of the triune God, in all the richness of its relationships; and it throws this community open for human beings in such a way that it gathers into itself these men and women and all created things, so that they find eternal life.'[29] What, however, is the significance of this conclusion for the development of a pneumatology for a common realm?

The reference to the resurrection of Jesus Christ gives a clue: the perfecting of creation cannot be thought except by the renewal of sociality secured by the resurrection of Jesus Christ. The 'bringing forth of life and movement', as Pannenberg puts the matter, directs theological attention to particular liberations in which relations between humanity and non-human nature are renewed. The *vinculum* of creation is in fact secured by the *Logos*; the opening-out of this *vinculum* is to be sourced to the actions of the Spirit who affirms the diversity of creation. That is, the Spirit does not obscure diversity, but instead is a theological discourse that *demands*

---

25. Gunton, *Theology through the Theologians*, p. 126.   26. Ibid., p. 128.
27. Ibid., p. 127.   28. Ibid., p. 120.   29. Moltmann, *The Spirit of Life*, p. 219.

it. More precisely, the discourse on the Spirit affirms and requires libera-tory affirmations of diversity: a diversity, in other words, that can be under-stood only in terms of the renewal of sociality, only by way of the renewal of the human (although not only human) practices of sociality, temporal-ity and spatiality in a common realm. (Which means in turn that I am not convinced by Gunton's argument that the actions of the Spirit must be re-lated to praise: 'whenever the created order, in any of its levels or aspects, is able to praise its maker, there is the agency of the Spirit'.[30] Praise is, to be sure, a category of agency and interaction, but it is also a cognitive and affective notion. Therefore I remain unsure what it can mean to say that, for example, inorganic nature praises God.)

The task of un/natural humanity is thereby understood by considera-tion of the form, energy and direction of the Holy Spirit of God's Trinity in the world. 'Being in the truth of God', as Bonhoeffer might have put it, is core to my position. The issue is not possibility – the possibility of human action, etc. – but instead the identification of the actuality of God's presence-in-difference to which human praxis must reorientate it-self. This presence is always eschatological. The wisdom of Christianity is reframed towards the discernment of traces of God's presence in the world, to which human action should reorientate itself in order to recover the fullness of God's blessing of creatureliness.

We arrive at a fourth point: in turn, the *vinculum caritatis ad extra* needs to be rethought in order to indicate some of the detail of the Spirit's life in creaturely life. Obliquely, Pannenberg makes this point:

> The Spirit's work is always in some measure linked to an imparting of his dynamic even though he is not in the full sense always imparted and received as gift. We are to find the Trinitarian basis for this in the fact that in the Trinitarian life of God the Son is in eternity the recipient of the Spirit who proceeds from the Father. But only to the degree that the Son is manifested in creaturely life does the work of the Spirit in creation take on the form of gift. This is definitively so only in relation to the incarnation of the Son.[31]

Much of the discussion of this section is recapitulated in these few sentences. In my discussion of incarnation, I have linked the ecosocial ontology of sociality, temporality and spatiality to the life, death and res-urrection of Jesus Christ. How is such an ontology – an ontology of the resurrection – to be understood as gift, and as made dynamic in the agency

30. Gunton, *Theology through the Theologians*, p. 120.
31. Pannenberg, *Systematic Theology*, III, p. 9.

of the Spirit? How is the social openness in God's life that is secured by the Spirit to be thought in terms of the social openness in God's world, in this common realm? How is the *vinculum caritatis/Trinitatis, ad extra* to be given further specification?

In a highly interesting essay, Daniel Hardy has argued for the importance of understanding the Spirit's interweaving in the interweaving of our contextuality. Defining contextuality as 'the interweaving of human subjects with their cultures and the natural world, and of cultures with each other and the natural world', Hardy argues that one of the tasks for a pneumatology is 'discovering the way in which God is present through the interweaving of human beings, cultures and nature'.[32] If, in my terms, un/natural humanity must grasp in theory and in practice that nature is the in-between of all human projects, how is the agency of the Spirit of God to be understood in such circumstance? How is our contextuality to be understood in terms of unity and diversity, as the dynamic towards the building up of the social through the spatio-temporal realm?

Hardy conceives of the activity of the triune God economically and immanently in terms of energy. In the economy, Hardy argues that God 'is himself in maintaining the consistency of his life in an ordered but energetic congruence [sc. by the Son] with his world; he is capable of self-restructuring in a controlled response to the perturbations (constructive or destructive) which occur in that interaction and in those with whom he interacts'. Openness is here construed in terms of order and freedom, stability and alteration in and through which God's orderly life is reordered but always with consistency. Such consistency is sourced immanently to an understanding of God in God's own life which comprises 'a dynamic consistency, not inert but energetic in the consistency of his self-structuring in self-sameness ... God is a dynamic structured relationality in whom there is an infinite possibility of life.'[33] What is remarkable about this theological position is that it permits the identification of the dynamic of movement in God's life and in God's life with the world: the open contingencies yet orderly structures of our contextuality are God's ways with us in which the gift of the fellowship of the Holy Spirit is imparted. The triune God is not isolated from contextuality; rather, by the Spirit, God seeks to bring

---

32. Hardy, *God's Ways with the World*, p. 70.
33. Ibid., p. 81. Cf. Daniel W. Hardy, *Finding the Church: The Dynamic Truth of Anglicanism* (London: SCM Press, 2001), p. 16: 'That is, the Trinity immanent in God is his consistent performance of holiness, but this is maintained – as the Trinitarian economy in the world – through God's energetic congruence with the world.'

such contextual fellowship to its fullness. The 'outpouring of energy' that Hardy employs as a trope for the interpretation of the dynamic life of God also occurs through (and throughout) God's creation in the consistency of God's own being. The triune God constitutes and sustains contextuality but not from a position of some unity posited behind the forms. Instead, the consistency of God's triune being is transcribed into the creaturely realm in forms of diversity: such 'active unity' arises in the 'diversity of all things'.[34]

How does such energy manifest itself in creation in the reconciling works of the Spirit? The infinite possibility of life in the Godhead arises in creation as 'excentric': 'the right use of our freedom is excentric, outward turning, conferring the benefits of our particularity upon those with whom we are interwoven. Our freedom confers freedom through our love'. Again, 'The sign of the blessing which God confers is in our conferral of such blessing on others, with all the natural and social modifications that may require, and even the creativity to fashion new and more humane contextual interweavings.'[35] This is a remarkable conclusion: reconciliation occurs in and through our contextuality as agents seek to practise more humane – perhaps we should add, more just, freer, more peaceful and truer – life in the in-between of nature.

Nor is this idealist: Hardy acknowledges that mostly we live in a 'contextuality of falsehoods' in which the energies of God conferred on us in our contextuality are diminished or dissipated. In turn, this leads to a lack of order, presumably to be understood in terms of either licence or simplification.[36] Hardy also operates a version of the 'preferential option for the poor': 'the principal means by which God reconciles is to be interwoven in the lives of those most "decontextualized", those most diminished in their contextuality, providing new life for them in their abandonment.'[37] The *vinculum caritatis ad extra* thereby exhibits a tendency: towards the rescue of those who are impoverished in and by their contextuality.

Where Hardy's position is less secure is in facing the theme of the otherness of nature. To speak of the conferral of blessing by the human to the human in freedom and by love is to restrict the reconciling work of the Spirit to the interhuman. What lacks attention is the ways in which nature may confer blessing on human beings through its own agential

34. Hardy, *God's Ways with the World*, p. 81.   35. Ibid., pp. 83, 84.   36. Ibid., p. 70.
37. Ibid., p. 87.

processes. That is, as *extra nos*, nature has its own agency in the common realm, both in relation to God and to humanity. In my judgment, Hardy needs some account of the otherness of nature in its spatiality to ground more convincingly his argument – with which I agree – that the 'fuller dynamic order from which the ecosystem operates, by which it is energized for its unity and reconciliation' cannot be framed only by reference to the energy within the ecosystem. However, to speak in theological idiom of a 'higher quality of relationality' does not exclude the possibility that God's energetic recovery of just and peaceful contextuality is by way of the 'natural order'. Although it is proper to speak of the restoration of the full contextuality of human beings with the natural world, we must also note – if the actions of the Spirit are eschatological and are thereby directed in and towards matter – that nature requires its full contextuality restored to it. This is not to say that nature can become itself without the human. However, it is to say that the redoubling of the blessing of contextuality is not directed only towards the human. Part of the problem may lie with Hardy's basic metaphor, energy. To speak of the exchange of energy arguably requires more detailed specification than given by Hardy: for example, the exchanges of energy operative in extractive, eco-regulative, and transformative interactions of the human with non-human nature are different. To be convincing, Hardy's metaphor of energy would need to demonstrate some structural similarities with such descriptions (while, of course, bearing a theological supplement of meaning).

I have argued that the notion of fellowship encompasses the non-human. This may be described as the theme of *Creator Spiritus*; that the actions of the Spirit are eschatological: the turning outwards and the intensification of the social nature of creatureliness are to be sourced to the Spirit; that the diversity of creaturely life can only be fully accounted for by insisting on the personal becoming of the Spirit whose actions in the Godhead secure the diversity as well as the unity of divine life – put a little too simply, only if there is personal fellowship of the Godhead, can there be a creaturely diversity in fellowship; and that human–nature relations are part of contextuality and, although contingent, are highly ordered and are to be traced to the actions of the triune God. The Spirit is to be understood as the movement that seeks to re-establish peaceable social relations between humanity and nature after the model of the overcoming of the interruption of sociality in the resurrection of Jesus Christ. These are aspects of an ecological pneumatology.

Standard theological options: stewardship; valuing nature

This section has the character of a hiatus, because now the shout goes up: 'But what about stewardship?' In my view, the task of glorifying God given to un/natural humanity *cannot* be achieved through stewardship: that is, the attempt at the administration by the human of God's realm according to the will of the creator. In putting the matter thus, I am rejecting the two standard ways of construing Christian responsibility in the face of non-human nature. Stewardship I have already mentioned; the other option found wanting is that of valuing nature. Why are these options to be rejected?

Stewardship

There are, of course, a number of non-theological objections to the notion of stewardship.[38] These are, I consider, largely persuasive. However, here I wish to attend to the theology which supports the notion of stewardship. What are the theological commitments which the notion of stewardship requires?[39] And what are its weaknesses?

The notion of the steward is an attempt to reinterpret the presentation of the role of the human in the first chapter of Genesis: 'Then God said, Let us make humankind in our image, according to our likeness; and let them have dominion over the fish of the sea, and over the birds of the heaven, and over the cattle, and over all the wild animals of the earth, and over every creeping thing that creeps upon the earth ... God blessed them, and God said to them, "Be fruitful and multiply, and fill the earth and subdue it; and have dominion over the fish of the sea and over the birds of the air and over every living thing that moves upon the earth"' (Gen. 1.26, 28 NRSV). As Douglas John Hall has pointed out, the metaphor of the steward is the attempt to reconstrue this theme of the lordship of the human or the dominion of the human. Indeed, the sub-title of one of Hall's books is: *Dominion as Stewardship*. The notion of stewardship is then an exercise in contextual theology for an ecological age: humanity is not lord of nature, but steward; humanity does not have rights of dominion but the responsibilities of a steward. As such, stewardship, in my judgment, enjoys a

38. See Clare Palmer, 'Stewardship', in Ian Ball, Margaret Goodall, Clare Palmer and John Reader (eds.), *The Earth Beneath: A Critical Guide to Green Theology* (London: SPCK, 1992), pp. 67–86; Kathryn Tanner, 'Creation, Environmental Crisis, and Ecological Justice', in Rebecca S. Chopp and Mark L. Taylor (eds.), *Reconstructing Christian Theology* (Minneapolis: Fortress, 1992), pp. 99–123; Rasmussen, *Earth Community, Earth Ethics*, pp. 233–6.
39. I thank Dee Carter for conversation that has helped me to clarify my thinking on stewardship.

Christological basis and rationale. For example, the themes of incarnation, sacraments and stewardship are to be found in the stress on the primacy of humanity over nature in the work of Thomas Sieger Derr and the interpretation of dominion as stewardship by Douglas John Hall.

The incarnation of God in Christ and the sacraments are noted by Derr as constitutive of the Christian view of the goodness and reality of nature.[40] Yet Derr does not hesitate to hold to the view that God's self-revelation occurs in history; nature shares only derivatively in this revelation. Hence, in theological perspective the drama of human history is primary; the development of natural processes has only secondary status. Human beings are thereby placed by God in a special position: in that nature is for humanity, the latter has a special responsibility to care for the former.[41] Derr vigorously rejects attempts to downgrade this stress on the responsibility of humanity for the non-human order. True dominion thereby requires the subjugation of nature. What the current ecological crisis teaches is that humanity has failed to exercise dominion fully and responsibly; the ideal must be the 'full human dominion' portrayed, it is claimed, in chapter 1 of Genesis. This view is closer to that of stewardship than the strong sense of dominion (humanity is in relation to nature as God is to the world and thereby imitates God's rule[42]). The purposes of humanity in relation to nature are in correspondence with God's purposes for nature. Dominion, to stick with Derr's term, is always 'for God'. Derr thereby qualifies his stance regarding the superiority of the human by understanding human agency in terms of stewardship.

In his book on stewardship, *Imaging God: Dominion as Stewardship*, Hall resists the term 'theology of nature' as a description of his work. Instead, he suggests that the view humanity has of itself in relation to nature needs altering. Here, theological reflection on the *imago Dei* is the principal Christian resource for considering the difference between humanity and nature. Indeed, Hall holds to the view that the biblical ontology presupposed and required by the *imago Dei* rejects the views that humanity is over against nature or that humanity is subsumed under nature. Instead, biblical ontology suggests that humanity is *alongside* nature.[43] Although Hall

40. Derr, *Ecology and Human Need*, p. 20.
41. Ibid., p. 87. In a reading of Aquinas, van den Brom, 'The Art of a Theo-ecological Interpretation', 299, argues that dominion requires an account of an order of being, hierarchically organised, in which 'the world is made exclusively for the benefit of humanity'. Cf. Rasmussen, *Earth Community, Earth Ethics*, p. 229.
42. Tanner, 'Creation, Environmental Crisis, and Ecological Justice', pp. 104–6.
43. Hall, *Imaging God*, p. 162.

concentrates on the idea of *imago Dei*, the root of his position is Christological. The movement of God towards the world, together with the 'worldliness' of the Hebrew scriptures and the love ethic, are the principal, if ambiguous, clues to the Christian affirmation of the world. In the final chapter, Hall connects the tradition of *theologia crucis* with the theme of stewardship in order to stress the sacrificial – in the sense of self-sacrificing – aspect of human responsibility towards nature.

In a later book, *The Steward: A Biblical Symbol Come of Age*, the Christological and ecclesial basis of stewardship is clearer still. Consider this programmatic statement by Hall:

> The Steward is a particularly apt metaphor for humanity because it encapsulates the two sides of human relatedness, the relation to God on the one hand and to non-human creatures on the other. The human being is, as God's steward, accountable to God and responsible for its fellow creatures.[44]

Notice how the claim to relatedness slides easily into an affirmation of responsibility; the claim about human situatedness slips into a moral claim. Hall thereby often refers to the physical interrelatedness of the world, but without development.[45] It is true that Hall seeks to identify humanity with nature in terms of a dialectic of difference and participation: we are creaturely but not reducible to non-human nature. Yet large consequences are drawn from this view: 'We can represent them [other creatures] because we participate in the same creatureliness as they.'[46] The resonances of incarnational language are unmistakable. However, no account is offered of how we participate in nature. For example, do 'we' all participate in nature in the same way? Does not this language of 'participation' thereby both level and simplify? And why should nature not present itself before God? May God not have purposes for non-human nature directly which do not require mediation by human beings? How are we helped in then thinking through the relations between humanity and non-human nature if such reconciling mediation is worked through by humanity? If I am right about nature being in-between human projects, the language of mediation denies this intimacy. It suggests two abstractions – humanity and nature – one of which is mediated by the other.

Why, we may ask, should such language of participation and representation be privileged? Because, I consider, Hall is working with a Christological basis within the dynamic of reconciliation. '[T]he symbol

44. Hall, *The Steward*, p. 20.   45. See ibid., p. 131.   46. Ibid., p. 212.

of the steward is at bottom a symbol of representation . . . the steward is a vicar, deputy, *Stellvertreter.*'[47] Resonances with key concepts in the articulation of the logic of atonement are evident here. Such representation turns upon the substitutionary, participatory and representative understanding of Christ's death: in that death God is reconciling all things to God (2 Cor. 5.18).

Stewardship remains a popular option in the ecotheology literature. We can now discern part of the reason for that popularity: stewardship operates as an atonement metaphor, albeit an atonement metaphor on vacation.[48] One of the central difficulties in theological interpretation of the atonement is to avoid subjectivist and exemplarist tendencies. That is, to focus overmuch on the response of believers following the example of Christ downplays, as Donald MacKinnon has pointed out, the identification of God in Christ and the depth of moral evil.[49] But is that not exactly what stewardship proposes?

Stewardship, it seems to me, displays the weaknesses of subjectivist and exemplarist models of atonement. First, it fails to notice how the construal of stewardship in voluntaristic ways is eminently *suitable* for our present culture of bureaucratic managerialism. Second, it does not attend to the sheer wickedness evident in our relations with non-human nature: how access to natural goods is entwined with access to social goods (access to medical care and a safe environment are good examples of this). Nor, third, does it attend to the ways that nature itself may be a source of evil.

This may seem strange. Is not stewardship derived somehow from the Genesis narratives? That is, should not stewardship be considered from the perspective of the doctrine of creation?[50] Indeed, the eco-theological literature pushes this line. However, in my view, stewardship remains

---

47. Ibid., p. 240; cf. p. 241.
48. In a double sense: it turns up where you do not expect it; and it does not do much work! Additionally, I note that stewardship is not an atonement model but 'only' a metaphor. It is largely exemplarist in tendency and, as John McIntyre points out, *The Shape of Soteriology* (Edinburgh: T. & T. Clark, 1992), 49, exemplarist models of atonement rely on other models: for the promotion of Christ as an example requires an account of the nature of the death that 'ends' the exemplary performance. But which model is operative – McIntyre lists 12 others: ransom; redemption; salvation; sacrifice; propitiation; expiation; atonement; reconciliation; victory; punishment/penalty; satisfaction; liberation – remains unclear.
49. Donald MacKinnon, 'Objective and Subjective Conceptions of Atonement', in F. G. Healey (ed.), *Prospect for Theology* (Welwyn: James Nisbet, 1966), pp. 167–82.
50. In *Creation and Reality* pp. 70–3, Welker does hold to the doctrine of creation in proposing that caretaking and dominion be linked in tension in an account of the primacy of the human in the created order. What this position does not explain is how a hierarchy of power – as he concedes that the mandate of dominion must be interpreted – can preserve 'complex structures of interdependence'. How does the simplifying power of hierarchy relate to diversity?

deeply entrenched in the ecclesial imaginary of Christians because it functions as an atonement metaphor; it draws its life as a concept from a partial reading of a Christological dynamic of reconciliation.

A second difficulty now emerges: atonement theory operates with cultic metaphors.[51] But how does such discourse connect to worldly vocation? Hall is convinced that there is a connection. But the connection is asserted rather than explicated. Thus Hall can claim that stewardship has 'apologetic potential for communicating the essential meaning of Christian (and human) representation'.[52] In so doing, he is clearly alert to the problem: if stewardship is to serve apologetic purposes, there must be a relationship between Christian and human representation. But what is that relationship between ecclesial and general representation? How does the concept of stewardship, founded in the dynamic of reconciliation and funded by cultic metaphors, engage the public realm? Hall's position suggests that the human representation of nature to God is intelligible in a post-Christian society. Is that so?

Furthermore, an important weakness of the concept of stewardship is that the content of human–nature relations is left unattended. I acknowledge that Hall proposes that humanity is *with* nature, not *over* or *in* nature. Such a perspective is to be welcomed and is a useful start, but smacks too much of what Arne Naess calls 'the man-in-environment image'.[53] This criticism is reinforced by the fact that Hall appeals to the language of 'vision' in defence of stewardship:

> When we speak about stewardship as the key to the relation between humanity and nature, we are speaking about a vision. Under the conditions of history, this vision is never fully realised. It is an eschatological vision, the vision of a state of final reconciliation, in which the enmity between creature and creator, creature and creature, and creature and creation will have given way to true mutuality and unconditional love: 'being-with'.[54]

However, we must ask, is not one of the rules for thinking eschatologically that there is some connection between the vision and this world? It seems to me that we are left with the impression that stewardship proposes a concept of nature *un*integrated with the practice and experience of present,

---

51. See McIntyre, *The Shape of Soteriology*, pp. 103ff. The primary source of cultic metaphors is the identification of God in Jesus Christ which supports such notions as Jesus as priest, sacrifice, victim.
52. Hall, *The Steward*, p. 241.
53. Naess, 'The Shallow and the Deep, Long-Range Ecology Movement: A Summary', p. 151.
54. Hall, *The Steward*, p. 214.

late capitalist, human society. Or, should we rather say that stewardship is very well integrated into the ideology of present society: the eclipse in human practice of the 'in-between' of nature.

In stewardship, we may conclude, the operative metaphysical schema remains traditionally Christian: God and humanity 'provide the basic framework within which the Christian drama is worked out'.[55] Such a view of human responsibility for nature stresses the 'administrative' role of human beings for the care of nature, a task which is, in turn, bestowed by God: 'As the primary administrators of God's will, human beings are charged with special responsibilities by God, delegated crucial functions in the fulfilment of God's plans, deputized as God's agents.'[56] Thus God's presence to nature is mediated by humanity. 'Human beings', Hall writes, 'are different in certain respects from other creatures because they are, so to speak, "assigned" a particular role in relation to others in the scheme of things'.[57]

What is correct in the emphasis on stewardship is the reference to Christ. In Christian tradition, the human creature is also *imago Christi*. However, by the time some attempt is made to expand the concept of stewardship to indicate that the stewards are also *imago mundi*, a prior *exemplarist* narrowing is usually determining. Thus Hall seeks to connect dominion as stewardship to the *Dominus*. However, the proposals that emerge are disconnected from any consideration of how it is that the human creature is itself creaturely and is situated in its own ecological relations. In fact, a conventional theological picture emerges: Christ, Church, World, in which stewardship operates as the core concept for articulating Christian responsibility in and towards the world. How the Church is located in a specific society which employs nature in particular kinds of ways emerges only at the end of the inquiry, as theology moves into theological ethics. In an ideological moment of unknowing, the Christian churches offer a moral strategy almost entirely isolated from the concerns that animated the beginnings of the inquiry. In a delicious irony, the final theological terminus may be a treatment of the sacraments. Yet such a treatment presupposes the distribution of grace by a universal church – and such universality is precisely not available in this strange post-Christian world in which we live. Thus the churches contribute to the moralising of Christianity. We can be sure that if such moralising gains ground then the functionalising of Christianity is not far behind.

55. Kaufman, 'A Problem for Theology', p. 349.
56. Tanner, 'Creation, Environmental Crisis, and Ecological Justice', p. 110.
57. Hall, *Imaging God*, p. 181.

Valuing nature

A different way of construing the fellowship of humanity and non-human nature is to place all consideration within the sphere of environmental ethics. The crucial matter now becomes not dynamic relations and shifting boundaries but rather the determination and assignment of the value of nature. In Christian theology, such a view – which can be articulated in more than one way – tends to be associated with the attempt to downplay the significance of the relation between the incarnation of God and the particular person, Jesus of Nazareth.

Two examples of this approach I have already mentioned: the work of Max Oelschlaeger and Sallie McFague. Although rather different, the tendency of their views is to converge on a single affirmation: an increase in the value of nature leads to a greater likelihood of its care. I shall concentrate here on the theological commitments operative in support of such a claim.

In a summary of the programme of his book, Oelschlaeger writes, '[the] new metaphor – caring for creation – can engender a psychologically satisfying (emotionally evocative, powerful), religiously distinctive, and scientifically plausible ethic for our time'.[58] Shortly, I shall set out how the metaphor emerges. However, we should first note the aim of the metaphor: to develop an ecologically sensitive ethic. Thus the programme of this civil theology is dedicated to, and oriented towards, the development of an environmental ethics. The way in which Oelschlaeger makes his case is clever: he argues that America (his argument is restricted, he makes clear, to the USA) needs to overcome its narrative of utilitarian individualism in favour of its biblical and republican traditions. In that he argues for a cultural–linguistic construal of Christianity, Oelschlaeger is less concerned about the variety and truth claims of religious traditions. In other words, by appeal to George Lindbeck, in the process giving a strongly pragmatist reading of *The Nature of Doctrine*, the matter of the truth claims of various types of Christianity, and the accounts of appearance and reality required, are all placed to one side in Oelschlaeger's argument. For Christian religion, in all its forms, provides a legitimating narrative within which American society operates.

The basic premise, then, seems to be: 'the modern world devalues nature'.[59] To this commitment is opposed the 'Great Code' of the biblical traditions. It is not quite clear to what these biblical traditions refer:

---

58. Oelschlaeger, *Caring for Creation*, pp. 37–8 (italics removed from original).
59. Ibid., p. 94.

sometimes it seems that what is central is the 'transcendent, creator God-as-person',[60] especially in relation to the critique of idolatry; on other occasions, the 'fundamental inspiration' of Christianity seems to be 'exemplary texts', particularly the creation narratives.[61] The second wins out over the first, I consider. That is, in order 'to expand a cultural conversation about ecology beyond the language of utilitarian individualism', appeal is made to the metaphor of caring for creation which 'might serve to unite all traditions of faith in setting an environmental agenda'. After all, Oelschlaeger informs us, 'A creation story is primordial, carrying both obligations with it and injunctions for human behavior toward all aspects of the world.'[62] Thus we get another glimpse of the ethical nature of the argument being made here: 'environmental questions are not primarily economic questions: they are first ethical and then political'.[63] Of course, this is not all of the argument. Nevertheless, perhaps this bald summary may suffice to disclose the ecumenical method operative here.

Nor is there any doubting the persuasiveness of this argument. Oelschlaeger succeeds in presenting, with some force, the outline of a publicly responsible, ecologically aware and environmentally supportive theology. Indeed, he manages to show – conclusively, in my view – the strength and relevance of mainstream Christian commitments to ecological concerns. Yet, if we ask what theological decisions are operative in the argument, we must note a restriction: the important matter, we may discern, is public, ethical action in protection of the environment. Theology is thus drawn into the conversation by way of providing ethical norms taken from the consideration of the Great Code of the Jewish–Christian creation narratives. Even if Oelschlaeger is right to stress the commonality between various interpretations of the creation narratives (Oelschlaeger operates with a fourfold typology: conservative, moderate, liberal, and radical interpretation of the Genesis narratives), the primary 'result' of these narratives is to stress the origin of the world in God and the problems of trying to map the world into distinct spheres. The concretion of Christ, the actions of God and the ends of creation are subsumed under general ethical principles. However, what if the primary matter is not environmental ethics but concrete interpretation of the actuality of human–nature relations in their dependence on God?

In *The Body of God*, Sallie McFague proposes what at first sight seems to be a different approach: she seeks rather to persuade us of the humanising potential to be derived from her construal of the metaphor of the world as the body of God. Rather than present in summary form the argument, let us attend in some detail to her Christology. Here McFague is a modern: we are told that the scandal of particularity is indeed scandalous. However, as the central message of Christianity is not to do with the individual figure, Jesus Christ, but rather that God became flesh in human form, the high claims of the incarnation of God are here transferred from Jesus to the immanent presence of God in the world, which is then interpreted – for Christianity – by reference (but not sole reference) to Jesus Christ and his disciples.[64] Or, as McFague puts it, what is required is the making of two moves: 'the first is to relativize the incarnation in relation to Jesus of Nazareth and the second is to maximize it in relation to the cosmos'.[65]

Noting that the clue given to us from the incarnation regarding embodiment is that 'the shape of God's body includes all, especially the needy and the outcast', McFague makes a direct connection with the notion of value. For if God's body includes all, and all is related to, and loved by, God, then the intrinsic, as opposed to the instrumental, value of nature is secured. From a 'cosmological and theocentric perspective', we have the overturning in hierarchies of *value*: such a perspective is the criticism of the traditional hierarchical valuation in which instrumental (that is, anthropocentric) ascriptions of value take precedence over the intrinsic value of creaturely life.

From the perspective of the commitments presented here, such a view fails to specify with sufficient clarity the detail of the interactions between humanity and nature. (I have elsewhere criticised what I regard as the inadequate Christology operative here.[66]) The problem is not, it seems to me, immediately the matter of value but rather how we are to think of the relation of humanity and nature in ways which are both theological and political. At issue here, then, is the matter of how to bring in under theological theory the deeply problematic matters of theorising the theme of abundance in relation to scarcity, the technological mediation of nature, the development of ways of negotiating alternative uses of non-human nature. At the back of this is the problem of construing the otherness of nature, and the character of the demand which this otherness places on us.

With this emphasis on value, comes a tendency towards deism. Perhaps this is not surprising: a cosmos or world conceived abstractly in terms of

---

64. McFague, *The Body of God*, pp. 159–60.   65. Ibid., p. 162.
66. Peter Scott, 'Nature in a "World come of Age"', *New Blackfriars* 78:919 (1997), 356–68.

value invokes an abstract, yet still personal, God. As I have been suggesting, the way proposed through this political theology of nature is somewhat different: in the actions of the triune God, the concretion of the world is given; the theological task is then to explicate the dynamics of this concretion.

Fellowship with nature: democracy of the commons[67]

How is the openness of the Holy Spirit as gift and presence to be understood in a political theology? If stewardship and valuing nature are not theologically well-supported ways of speaking of fellowship in the common realm, which way is preferable? Attending to the logic of fellowship, how might the sociality of creaturely life in its dependence and contingency be grasped in the dynamic of movement towards fellowship? In the matter of human–nature relations, how shall fellowship be thought?

I have already argued that the actions of the Spirit are eschatological. If, in eschatological perspective, we are directed towards the quality of eco-habitation (fellowship, by the Spirit), how might such fellowship be practised ahead of the full establishment of the rule of God? An appropriate pedagogy is the vital matter here. For what needs to be learnt by humanity are ways of participating in the common realm towards fellowship. Of especial importance is the matter of the practice of spatiality towards the otherness of nature: humanity learning how to act in friendly ways in ecological space.

One way of approaching the common participation of humanity and nature in a spatio-social field is by *democratising* human relations with non-human nature. As Vandana Shiva notes: 'In the final analysis, the ecological crisis is rooted in the mistaken belief that human beings are not part of the democracy of nature's life, that they stand *apart* from and *above* nature.'[68] In short, what the theological position sketched in this chapter points towards is the extension of democratic, rather than moral, considerability to non-human nature.[69] How so? Extending the franchise to nature is one way of acknowledging that nature–human relations are marked by the dynamics of encounter: a democratic exchange encompasses a number of agents taking different initiatives. Furthermore,

---

67. Of course, the theme of democracy was present in part II, especially in the discussions of deep and social ecologies.

68. Shiva, 'Decolonizing the North', in Mies and Shiva, *Ecofeminism*, p. 265.

69. Cf. Kenneth E. Goodpaster, 'On Being Morally Considerable', *Journal of Philosophy* (1978), 308–25.

democracies function best when all parties are committed to democratic procedures and see themselves as oriented towards one another. Democracy is also concerned with the negotiation of difference and the attempt to explore and negotiate differences in ways that are non-violent and do not lead to violence. Thus democracy is also concerned with fellowship. Analogous to programmes of economic democratisation,[70] such a process of 'natural' democratisation would seek to make nature present in and to the political sphere. Such a recovery of the political dimensions of the common realm I shall call a 'common democracy'.

Thus the recommendation of a 'common democracy' is rooted firmly in the preceding theology of the common sociality of nature–humanity.[71] What, then, is the content of such a 'common democracy'? According to one commentator, a 'consolidated democracy' is 'a system in which the politically relevant forces subject their values and interests to the uncertain interplay of democratic institutions'.[72] The significant challenge in the theorising of a 'common democracy' is how to speak of *non-human* nature as among the politically relevant forces. How might this be thought? It is important to note here that a *theological* claim is being made: non-human nature is rendered concrete within the common realm by democratic practices founded in, and proportioned by, mediations of the *Logos* in creation; democratic practices are founded in the life of the Spirit who is both the agent and harbinger of fellowship. Such practices may be said to be oriented towards the eschatological rule of the triune God in that they relate to creatures, human and non-human, and yet leave the political realm open to new, surprising interactions between humanity and nature: interactions that are unlooked for and which cannot be anticipated.

Hence, the award of democratic status to nature is not thereby a convenient fiction, a conceit by which to bring nature into the human, political realm. It is rather an acknowledgment that humanity is always already placed in the common realm by God with nature. The present-ness of nature to humanity, the crucial condition of its democratic participation, is, as I argued in the previous chapter, to be sourced to the action of the *Logos* in creation. The attempt by humanity to acknowledge such present-ness as part of God's blessing is the practice of eschatological fellowship in

---

70. See Gary Dorrien, *Reconstructing the Common Good* (New York: Orbis, 1990).
71. As such, as I hope to show through this section, there are structural similarities between the fellowship of excentric relations between humanity and nature and the practice of democracy.
72. Adam Przeworski, *Democracy and the Market*, cited in Markoff, 'Really Existing Democracy', p. 59.

the Spirit. Here I am suggesting that the form of such acknowledgement should be the extension of processes of political negotiation to a 'common democracy'. Such a 'common democracy' – sourced to the eschatological actions of the Spirit – is oriented towards God's eschatological rule, and prefigures it, in that it acknowledges that through the interaction of political forces, alterations of relationships between humanity and nature will result. Such alterations are, after all, the point of democratic negotiation (although, of course, not the point of democracy itself).

However, it remains true that the form of a common democracy will be settled by human beings. The scale of any such democracy is anthropological. It is therefore unlikely that a 'common democracy' might be practised without the most radical democracy being secured. If nature is one of God's ways to us – as the common realm invites us to think – such a democracy would emerge in many zones of human social life. To misappropriate Bruno Latour somewhat, we have here the dissolution of boundaries and the redistribution of agents.[73] Human responsibility is thus properly to organise human affairs – here a 'common democracy' – founded in the actuality of the presence of nature to humanity in the common realm. Raymond Williams captures part of this in a discussion of the environment of coal mining in South Wales:

> It is no use simply saying to South Wales miners that all around them is an ecological disaster. They already know. They live in it. They have lived in it for generations. They carry it with them in their lungs ... But you cannot just say to people who have committed their lives and their communities to certain kinds of production that this has all got to be changed. You can't just say: come out of the harmful industries, let us do something better. Everything will have to be done by negotiation, by equitable negotiation, and it will have to be taken steadily along the way.[74]

Commonality with nature cannot be secured without the achievement of commonality among those sharing a human nature. Such an extended democracy will be the crucial way in which human beings may learn to live with the political effects of the tension between ecologically harmful practices and the material well-being of human beings.[75] This we might call the negotiation of the intersection of political and ecological

73. Bruno Latour, 'To Modernise or Ecologise?' in B. Braun and N. Castree (eds.), *Remaking Reality: Nature at the Millennium* (London and New York: Routledge, 1998), pp. 221–42 (p. 229).
74. Williams, *Resources of Hope*, p. 220.
75. See Harvey, *Justice, Nature and the Geography of Difference*, p. 200. Of course, in this instance, the material well-being of the many turns upon the potential ill health of the few.

contingencies, in an anthropological scale but including the otherness of nature. Such a pedagogy of 'living out of the future', sourced to the eschatological actions of the Spirit, will thereby involve all the present complexities of interhuman democratic negotiation together with its extension to the commons.

Democracy and difference

Earlier I argued that the themes of stewardship and valuing nature simplify human–nature relations and, arguably, our notion of God. The concept of common democracy is a theological attempt to develop an ecological pneumatology for a political theology of nature. The eschatological actions of the Spirit engage us in and through our contextuality, towards the renewal of sociality and affirm both unity and diversity. The 'democracy of the commons' is a theologico-political attempt to develop a pneumatology towards such fellowship in a common realm. Vandana Shiva writes: 'An earth democracy cannot be realised as long as global domination is in the hands of undemocratic structures. Neither can it be realised on an anthropocentric basis – the rights of non-human nature cannot be ignored.'[76] Shiva presents a truism, and the reference to rights is to be regretted. However, a common democracy attempts to do justice to the insight that the political representation of nature is the key to the renewal of relations between humanity and nature and the affirmation of diversity. The openness-in-fellowship that arises through the actions of the Spirit in democratic representation prefigures the eschatological renewal of the common realm. In the common realm of creation, the interactions of nature and humanity are best understood by way of the political discourse of democracy.

Why is this so? The intimacy of our relations with nature may be attended to in democratic discourse – what I am calling a 'democracy of the commons'. Democratic practice seeks to secure two aims: the representation of political agents; and peaceful negotiation. The aim of a democracy of the commons is thereby to include the presence of natural agents towards peace.

This is difficult to grasp. Let me make two sets of comments as a way of amplifying this notion of a 'democracy of the commons'. In his account of the historical relations between Christianity and democracy, John

---

76. Shiva, 'The Greening of the Global Reach', pp. 155–6.

de Gruchy suggests that democracy may be thought of as a 'vision' or a 'system'.[77] That is, democracy points either towards a goal of greater representation or peaceful negotiation; or it indicates the operative political structures of a political system. I prefer to think of democracy as a way of life – precisely, as a pedagogy. What is involved in this educative practice of a democracy of the commons is an acknowledgement that nature cannot be contained, managed, or organised; nature is, to borrow a thought from Dietrich Bonhoeffer, disorderly.[78] The way we acknowledge the importance of the negotiation of agency in our political life is democracy. That is, if, on theological grounds, we wish to maintain an account of the world as the common realm of God, nature and humanity, the agency of nature in encounter with us needs articulation and practice. Such articulation and practice is the democracy of the commons.

This reinforces a claim made throughout this book: nature *is* a political concept. In his *Justice, Nature and the Geography of Difference*, David Harvey notes eight different political tendencies – ranging from 'authoritarianism' to 'decentralized communitarianism' – that each construe nature in their different ways.[79] As always a political concept, nature is subject to ideological strategies of containment.[80] In other words, given the culture in which we live, we should expect that the disorderliness of nature is everywhere suppressed, domesticated or negated. Are we to regard ourselves as split off from nature or instead differentiated from it? If we regard ourselves as split off from nature, we may then, of course, grant it the status of the hostile Other: to be tamed, controlled and mastered. However, if we understand ourselves as differentiated from nature, then nature encounters us in a dialectic in which both humanity and nature are changed: nature is the us that is not us; as un/natural, humanity is the nature that is not nature.[81] The notion of the democracy of the commons seeks to represent politically such a commitment.

---

77. John de Gruchy, *Christianity and Democracy* (Cambridge University Press, 1995), pp. 7f.
78. Bonhoeffer, *Ethics*, pp. 123–4. In a similar vein, David Macauley has suggested that what should concern us most is overcoming not the domination of nature but the domestication of nature: see Macauley, 'On Critical Theory and Nature', *Capitalism, Nature, Socialism* 9:3 (1998), 32–4 (34). Cf. David Macauley, 'Be-wildering Order: On Finding a Home for Domestication and the Domesticated Other', in R. S. Gottlieb (ed.), *The Ecological Community* (London and New York: Routledge, 1997), pp. 104–35.
79. Harvey, *Justice, Nature and the Geography of Difference*, pp. 177–81. The remaining six are corporate and State managerialism; pluralistic liberalism; conservatism; moral community; ecosocialism; and ecofeminism.
80. This phrase is from Fredric Jameson, *The Political Unconscious: Narrative as a Socially Symbolic Act* (London: Routledge, 1981), *passim*.
81. Here I am drawing on Kovel, 'Commentary on Herbert Marcuse's "Ecology and the Critique of Modern Society"', 40–2.

Nor, in theological tradition, is such a position of a democracy of the commons so strange.[82] The notion of commonwealth, with its resonance of political participation, has been used in theologies of creation to indicate the status of non-human nature in Christian thought. Commenting on Francis of Assisi, Roderick Nash writes: 'Francis . . . lived long before the age of democratic revolutions, and he did not speak of the "rights" of birds, worms, wolves, and rocks. But he did remove them from the category of "things" by including them with humans in a single spiritual fellowship.'[83] In a sequel to his much-remarked, 'The Historical Roots of our Ecologic Crisis', Lynn White also presses this theme: 'Scattered through the Bible, but especially the Old Testament', he writes, 'there are passages that can be read as sustaining the notion of a *spiritual democracy* of all creatures'.[84] And, finally, Leonardo Boff argues that 'an ecological-social democracy . . . accepts not only human beings as its components but every part of nature, especially living species'.[85]

Nor is this democracy of the commons alien to philosophical tradition: arguing that oppositional moral knowledge is formed in community, Lori Gruen claims that there is no obvious reason why empathetic loving should not include nature. And she claims that one obvious way of including nature in the moral community is to give a place to those 'who are in community with nature'.[86] Val Plumwood also suggests that it is possible within a moral community to speak for those who cannot speak for themselves in ways which are liberatory and not oppressive.[87] We are back to the point made by Daniel Hardy: the conferral of true contextuality by the Spirit is directed to those whose contextuality is most diminished or impoverished, whose *quality* of habitation is degraded. Those to whom society is *least* hospitable – and failures, distortions and interruptions with regard to hospitality will also be structured by race, class and gender – are

---

82. I am here agreeing with van den Brom's judgment, 'The Art of a Theo-ecological Interpretation', 303, that the democratic model has important strengths. However, his preferred account of humanity as servant (310–13) does not, in my view, adequately develop these strengths.

83. Roderick Frazier Nash, *The Rights of Nature: A History of Environmental Ethics* (Madison: The University of Wisconsin Press, 1989), p. 93.

84. Lynn White, 'Continuing the Conversation', in Ian Barbour (ed.), *Western Man and Environmental Ethics: Attitudes toward Nature and Technology* (Reading, MA: Addison-Wesley (1973), pp. 55–64 (p. 61, italics mine).

85. Boff, *Ecology and Liberation*, p. 89. Although Boff sets out various types of democracy, he does not develop his ecological–social democracy in relation to any of these.

86. Gruen, 'Toward an Ecofeminist Moral Epistemology', pp. 120–38 (p. 129). Cf. Lori Gruen, 'Revaluing Nature', in Warren (ed.), *Ecofeminism: Women, Culture, Nature*, pp. 356–74 (pp. 362f.).

87. Plumwood, 'Androcentrism and Anthropocentrism', pp. 327–55 (pp. 348f.).

likely to be those either most in community with nature[88] or those denied sustained and sustainable access to natural goods. These are the voices that need to be heard in a democracy of the commons.

In making this point, I do not think an account of nature's strong subjectivity is required in defence of the notion of a democracy of the commons. Certainly, neither Gruen nor Plumwood would support the view of nature as a knowing, speaking subject. Nor does the concept of common democracy require such a view. An account of the agency of nature, as proposed in the previous chapter, is sufficient, as is suggested by the following comment by Jim Cheney: 'This sort of expansion of moral community... is simply (or complexly) a matter of trying to come to an understanding of what it might mean to care, to respond to something in the nonhuman environment as a member of one's moral community.'[89]

The democracy of the commons is a theological as well as a political concept. That is, why Christians take the positions that they do in the debate on ecology is for theological reasons.[90] The theological account of the difference of nature in a common realm being proposed here suggests it is neither possible nor required to separate nature and humanity. A common democracy thereby seeks to *extend* – in a pneumatological thought – the commitments of the perspective of the common realm of God, nature and humanity. If the intimate relations between humanity and nature require specification in a rich, Trinitarian ontology, common democracy is one way of giving an account of such interrelationality. It is, of course, a position in which a 'mastering' humanity is called into question. For democracy requires the redistribution of agency and the reconfiguration of power in negotiation. Such redistribution and reconfiguration are, I suggest, the gifts of the Spirit of God in redemption. And such gifts invite an appropriate pedagogy in response. By this means, that human beings are 'the subjects, not the objects, of history'[91] may be honoured. The redistribution of agency and the reconfiguration of power are ways of securing the subjectivities and histories of those who have been placed on the underside of history and thereby had their cultures subjugated or denigrated.

88. In making this point, I seek to maintain the dialectical stance of social/ist forms of ecofeminism: in a historicising move, the patriarchal identification of women with nature may be interpreted as ontologically false yet epistemologically liberative.
89. Cheney, 'Eco-feminism and Deep Ecology', p. 140.
90. In other words, to discern: 'What is really at stake in any political dispute, the real life questions involved, and why different people take the positions that they do' (Bertell Ollman, *Dialectical Investigations* (London: Routledge, 1993), p. 104).
91. Rasmussen, *Earth Community, Earth Ethics*, p. 233.

What the proposal of a 'common democracy' amounts to is a political and ecological defence of an extended *representative* democracy. We have seen already in chapter 5 the difficulties encountered by the type of *participatory* democracy proposed by Murray Bookchin's social ecology. Such participatory democracy, I argued, must exclude nature, perhaps contrary to Bookchin's intentions in this matter. A democracy of the commons extends democratic community to include non-human nature by demanding that the representation of such nature is secured by the voices of those 'identified' with nature or denied access to nature's goods. The democratic rationality that emerges will thereby be 'holistic', to borrow a term from Adolf Gundersen.[92] For Gundersen, such rationality is holistic in the sense that it grasps environmental issues as interrelated. The position proposed in this book is bolder, more radical: holistic here refers to the political representation of the agency of nature which is to be understood as the co-constituting ground of the development (not merely the emergence) of human, social life. Present systems of democratic representation will have to be altered, therefore, in two ways.

First, the argument for some form of proportional representation is compelling from this pneumatological perspective: that is, there needs to be greater participation by groups whose social and economic situation requires them to deliberate in holistic ways.[93] A contrast is often drawn, certainly in British political culture, between an apathetic electorate in a system of representative, 'winner-takes-all', governance and the vibrancy of 'single-issue' campaigns, especially environmental campaigns. Perhaps the contrast is overstated: what we have here is, rather, the failure of the present system of representation to enable the representation of nature which, in turn, creates and enforces the division between 'system' and 'enthusiasm'. When traditional politicians complain about apathy, they fail – according to the democratic rationality proposed here – to see the way in which the present system of political representation is the source of that apathy. When environmental activists complain at the indifference of the representative government to their concerns, they fail to see that it is only a specific configuration of democratic representation that funds and requires such indifference. Second, the view of what counts as collective – that is, political – action requires expansion. If, as Gundersen argues, all

---

92. Adolf G. Gundersen, *The Environmental Promise of Democratic Deliberation* (Madison: University of Wisconsin Press, 1995), p. 22; cf. pp. 159 and 170f. For Gundersen, environmental rationality is collective, long-term and self-reflexive/concerned with environmental ends, as well as holistic.

93. Cf. Gundersen, *The Environmental Promise of Democratic Deliberation*, p. 204.

political action is collective action[94] – democratic politics, at least, is the attempt to develop common responses to common problems – then the notion of collectivity needs to be extended to non-human nature, and those groups that claim to represent such nature. These two points are intimately related.

A third point: I have argued that the representation of nature must be understood dialectically by reference to groups (self-)identified with nature or denied in some manner access to nature's goods.[95] However, in connection with the second group, it must be acknowledged that 'the biggest structural barrier to [democratic] deliberation . . . is poverty'.[96] To make a contribution to collective action depends on the enjoyment of economic security by individuals and groups. The proposal of a democracy of the commons thereby has a social and economic component: there will be a continuing failure to represent nature adequately should chronic poverty persist. For such groups in poverty – that is, without sufficient economic security – are the principal mediators of non-human nature in the political realm. The issue of poverty is made more difficult if we note that part of what poverty means is difficulties over access to nature's goods. As the socialist ecologists stress, with poverty goes an impoverished environment. We are therefore in a vicious circle: those most able to witness to an impoverished environment are, on account of the associated poverty, least able to make a democratic contribution. Thus we may now see that the present configuration of representative democracy (at least in Britain) has an *ecological* – strictly, *anti*-ecological – component. I cannot claim any expertise in knowledge of democratic arrangements, but there is clearly an *ecological deficit* in present democratic arrangements, which needs to be addressed. Such a deficit is, on a theological level, an incursion into the fellowship and gift of life of the Holy Spirit. From the perspective of the democracy of the commons, we may conclude that present democracy supports the denial of difference: the difference of nature, and the difference of groups (self-)identified with nature or impoverished in relation to nature.

The Holy Spirit: giver of common life

So far, I have argued that the actions of the Spirit in support of unity and diversity are contextualised with reference to democracy: the political

94. Ibid., pp. 165f.
95. As Boff notes, *Ecology and Liberation*, p. 88, social injustice must be related to ecological injustice.
96. Gundersen, *The Environmental Promise of Democratic Deliberation*, p. 196.

affirmation of peaceable relations between humanity and nature identifies an ecological deficit, human impoverishment and political paths to fellowship. These are the contours of un/natural fellowship. A concrete pneumatology, indeed, for a political theology of nature! By this means the openness of God's Trinity and of the common realm is best understood. Such openness is, to borrow again from Pannenberg, 'creative activity in the bringing forth of life and movement'. This life is fellowship in a democracy of the commons. Such movement is to be understood as democratic negotiation in an extended system of representative democracy. How then – to return to the question I put at the beginning of this chapter – shall we learn to act in the common realm of God, nature and humanity? Not, I have maintained, as stewards or as valuers of nature, but as democrats-in-common, committed to the political representation of nature by reference to groups who are (self-)identified with nature or who experience difficulties in accessing nature's goods. This is my recommendation of a theological account of contextuality – a political way of acknowledging the in-betweenness of nature – for a political theology of nature.

Such democratic practices are sourced to the eschatological actions of the Spirit. Such actions are liberatory affirmations of diversity towards fellowship through the personal work of the Holy Spirit. In this account, the Spirit is not some general divine presence through the world but is rather the force and movement of democratic extension, negotiation and renewal through the common realm. Such force and movement is not to be understood as levelling or simplifying. (This tendency can be safely left for the bankrupt options of stewardship and valuing nature.) Instead, pneumatological force and movement turn outwards and intensify the social relations that bind together nature and humanity. These relations are rendered concrete and energised by the actions of the Spirit who liberates diversely into diversity. Such liberative diversity is the direction of a common democracy, enlivened by the Holy Spirit, towards fellowship.

Democratic practice, we may conclude, diversifies but always in the unity of collective action. Here the terminology of movement, structure and tendency, first broached in chapter 2, may be grasped in its full significance: as categories of historico-natural emergence to be related to the openness of the Holy Spirit. In the account of the Spirit's actions given here, through the open structure of a representative democracy, the movement is towards the intensification of the rich ontology of human–nature relations in a tendency that affirms both humanity and nature, yet differently. Democratic negotiation in a common democracy is the impress of, and towards, the fellowship of God: of God with God, of God with creatures. Such a pedagogy of fellowship presents the practice of the common realm towards richer forms of association. Such associations in turn enliven, energise and empower the social, temporal and spatial dynamics of the common realm by the conferral of the blessings of the Spirit. Hence, in the movement towards fellowship sourced to the diversifying actions of the Spirit – who opens up and turns outwards – humanity and nature in their social relations practise the redoubling of the blessing of creatureliness, in eschatological expectation and preparation.

9

God–body: un/natural relations, un/natural community in Jesus Christ

From distorted sociality to the common realm: God–body

The subject of a political theology of nature is the distortions of social relations of un/natural humanity with nature, in relation to God's Trinity. At the conclusion of this theological inquiry, the contours of such a political theology are now evident: a theological social anthropology in a doctrine of creation has emerged, constructed out of an intensive engagement with political ecology, which is both Trinitarian and founded in the resurrection of Jesus Christ, the God–body. Some of the central concepts and commitments of Christianity have therefore been deployed in a dynamic, yet critical, articulation with political construals of nature. Important political issues – for example, the otherness of nature; democratic negotiation – have emerged during the inquiry. Yet these political issues have emerged always within a theological argument. The Christology of chapter 7 stresses the placing of human society in its wider environment: the situatedness of un/natural relations. The pneumatology of chapter 8 stresses fellowship towards overcoming distorted social relations of humanity with non-human nature and the overcoming of distorted social relations of nature with human habitats.

The concepts of common realm and pedagogy of the commons have emerged through consideration of the identity of the creator God and the identity bestowed by God on creation. The identity of God revealed in Jesus Christ is Trinitarian. As Trinitarian, God invites consideration of God's non-identical presentation in the economy of the world. God's identity is not to be traced to the world, but neither is such identity not to be traced there. The creaturely identity bestowed by God upon the world is also dialectical: human identity is not to be found in nature, but then neither is such identity not to be found there. The end of nature is not to be found in humanity, but neither is that end not to be found there. The ecosocial conceptuality of the Christological relating of temporality, the Christological shaping of sociality and the Christological placing of spatiality are, of course, dedicated to the elucidation of this claim.

This Trinitarian theology of nature stresses the *sufficiency* of the liberation of nature in Christ. For, in the perspective of the sufficiency of the salvation which inheres in Christ, there is no Christian imperative to 'save the world'.[1] To make such an attempt would be to deny the actuality of the common realm of God, nature and humanity. Furthermore, if we are not to fall into Pelagian traps, we must stress also the *necessity* of the liberation of Christ. Attempts by human beings to reorient their practices must be worked through by re-entering the blessing of common fellowship: a redoubling of the blessing of the ecological relations of the common realm.

These commitments are central to the argument of this book. However, we may discern an omission in the discussion so far: how are we to think of the life, death and resurrection of Christ in the context of a political theology of nature? How are they internal to a pedagogy of fellowship and friendship? Of course, as I stressed in chapter 2, the theological, transcendental inquiry practised here begins from the career of Jesus of Nazareth. Yet I have pressed the insights drawn from such a beginning towards the consideration of a Trinitarian doctrine of creation. What happens if we now return from such a theology of creatureliness – a Trinitarian theology of ecological nature (human and non-human) – to consider explicitly how the God–body, crucified and resurrected, may inform and support the theology of creaturely relations proposed here?

God–body: the subject of this chapter is how attention to the 'career' of the Christ of God may be grasped as internal to un/natural relations and un/natural fellowship and may guide and test such practice. I understand such a pedagogy of the commons, to which the cross and resurrection of the God–body are internal, as open to two persistent temptations: ignoring or evading the non-identical relations between humanity and non-human nature, and substituting discourses and practices of identity – that is, respectively, personalism and naturalism.

Against such temptations, praise of the God–body resituates human beings in the un/natural relations of the common realm. Praise of,

---

1. The obverse side of claims to save the world are those which maintain that we can with impunity ruin the earth and deny its capacities to support humanity. See Harvey, *Justice, Nature and the Geography of Difference*, pp. 194–5.

participation in, the God–body occurs in actual gathered congregations: 'Christ existing as community', as Bonhoeffer put it in *Sanctorum Communio*.[2] Participation in the life of the God–body invites anew the affirmation of the creaturely blessing of life in its un/natural fellowship with non-human nature, in the orientation of the common realm towards the eschatological fellowship of the triune life of God.

In this final chapter, I explore the matter of the cross and resurrection as internal guides to un/natural relations and the criticism of humanised and natural relations. In a discussion of the eucharist, I consider more directly the church as the principal 'location' in and from which Christians construe place. I briefly reconsider the gift of the Spirit and the God–body: participation in Christian community is to participate in and practise un/natural fellowship and friendship. Here is the nerve of a political theology of nature: against a dominant order which carelessly treats nature as backdrop, and which permits a few alternative protests, oppositional ecclesial practices undermine the false, unsatisfying and ecologically destructive antithesis of 'either us or nature'.

The crucifixion of nature and the realism of the cross

The political theology proposed here addresses the matter of the shape of creatureliness in the perspective of the cross and resurrection of Jesus Christ. Attempts to reconfigure un/natural humanity will always encounter the cross of Christ: all utopian attempts are, indeed, 'crossed'. Put differently, Christian hope is founded upon a cross; thereby, it is intensely realistic. For a political theology of nature, what does this mean? According to Peter Hodgson, the cross has a certain *meaning*: the *basileia* vision of Jesus Christ ends in death, thereby indicating that world-historical projects of liberation are bound to fail. This is not quietism: the significance of the cross for God indicates God's involvement with and against suffering. The cross thereby indicates the presence of God through suffering and God's work against negation. 'The meaning of the cross', summarises Hodgson, 'is the victory of life over death, the resurrection of the dead'.[3]

Despite this welcome affirmation, Hodgson's account fails to underscore that on the cross the God–*body* is crucified. Contrary to Hodgson's tendency to treat the cross as a cipher in the interaction of God and world,

---

2. Bonhoeffer, *Sanctorum Communio*, *passim*.   3. Hodgson, *Winds of the Spirit*, pp. 263–4.

I wish to emphasise that part of the 'meaning' of the cross is dead (human) nature. If we are to accept the point that in the cross all attempts to save the world are indeed crossed, such wisdom and judgment can only be maintained if we follow in the steps of the God–body: the crucifixion is a political death *in nature*. How then might the cross of the God–body be construed and practised as *internal* to the Christocentric practice of friendship towards fellowship in the Spirit?

This is a paradoxical matter: the cross of Christ is both an event of the margins and the place of the redemption of the world. For a political theology of nature, the cross is the liberation of nature; the *telos* of nature is to be discerned by way of the cross of the God–body. However, in this connection 'emancipation' is commonly practised by humanity, as we have seen, either as mastery over nature or the demand for immersion in nature: as anti-natural or natural. Thus the cross of Christ as the centre of nature is construed by humanity as a boundary to be overcome, as curse rather than blessing;[4] or the cross of Christ is marginalised in order to stress the self-sufficiency and purity of nature. In other words, personalism denies the sufficiency of Christ's liberatory work and understands the cross as a boundary in the middle to be overcome: the world must be saved by human effort through technological artifice. In contrast, naturalism minimises the boundary as middle, denies the necessity of salvation and thereby regards nature as self-sufficient: human beings should then in some fashion seek immersion in or mimicry of that nature.

In contrast to these positions, I am arguing that, as mediated by the cross, nature features both as centre and as boundary: as affirmation and judgment, blessing and curse. Where does this get us? In chapters 2 and 7, I stressed the election of nature as social: in the resurrection of Jesus Christ, all that is social is resurrected. If nature is social, as I have argued, then such social nature is also resurrected. Yet, of course, there is no resurrection without crucifixion; that which is resurrected is previously crucified. Thus we may speak of the crucifixion of non-human nature. If the commitments of social nature and resurrection are right, then nature is crucified also. Yet, in that nature is a created unity, such nature is crucified as both middle and boundary; in the God–body, nature is also crucified as middle and boundary. If the Spirit returns the social Christ to the world, the cross of Christ is the representation of nature as middle and boundary. Thus, the cross of Christ stands with marginalised nature and with nature as the

---

4. Here I am drawing freely on Dietrich Bonhoeffer, *Christology*, pp. 59–65.

centre. To explore further the realism which the cross of Jesus Christ invites in our construal, practical and theoretical, of nature, we must return to the interpretation of nature as social, spatial and temporal.

To speak of the cross as middle and boundary in connection with nature as *social* is to stress the distorted sociality which sinful humanity seeks to overcome yet cannot. As we have seen, nature does not have its ends in humanity. Yet neither are its ends to be understood as not in relation to humanity. As a way forward, humanity is not obliged to reanimate a humanism which sees humanity as the end of nature. For nature has its end, and does not have its end, in humanity. From this perspective, perhaps some of the commitments of the recent renewal of wisdom theology might be reinterpreted. Of the crucifixion of Jesus, Denis Edwards has written: 'in his death the Wisdom of God is revealed in an even more shocking way as radical compassion which knows no limits . . . The foolish excess of the cross reveals what is at the heart of the processes of the universe.'[5] In a more restricted way, perhaps we might say – by reference one more time to the theme of sacrifice – that the cross indicates that God does not abandon God's creation. Indeed, God re-employs nature as a way to us.

To speak of the cross as middle and boundary in connection with nature as *spatial* is to note the ways in which humanity is placed in the life of nature. Nor does the God–body, the *Logos* incarnate, escape the natural destiny of creatures.[6] Attempts by human beings to act *sicut deus* are countered by the cross of Christ. Nature therefore cannot be overcome, except in fantasy. Of course, as Bonhoeffer notes, un/natural humanity may prefer to understand itself as *anti*-natural: 'This means that for his knowledge of God man renounces the Word of God which constantly descends upon him out of the un-enterable middle and limit of life. Man renounces life from this Word and snatches it for himself. He is himself in the middle.'[7] By contrast, true theory and practice must be oriented towards the cruciform reminder of bodiliness. Here the blessing which the cross invites is recognition and acknowledgement of, together with discernment and response to, the ecological situatedness of creatureliness. If here we are warranted to speak of wisdom's 'radical compassion,' to borrow a phrase from Denis Edwards, the death of the God–body refers to not so much a compassion 'without limits' nor to the vulnerability of God in the world,[8]

5. Denis Edwards, *Jesus the Wisdom of God: An Ecological Theology* (New York: Orbis, 1995), pp. 75, 76.
6. Moltmann, *The Way of Jesus Christ*, pp. 169–70.
7. Bonhoeffer, *Creation and Fall*, p. 74.   8. Edwards, *Jesus the Wisdom of God*, p. 75.

but a recommendation that God's actions cannot be understood apart from creatureliness. Or, as Bonhoeffer liked to put it: 'The bodily is the end of God's ways.'[9]

To speak of the cross as middle and boundary in connection with nature as *temporal* is to stress the ways in which our relation with nature as oriented towards us is always mediated by the cross. In cruciform interpretation, all attempts by humanity to 'save the world' are ruled out. Although oriented towards us, nature cannot be incorporated comprehensively within humanity's schemes. The simplification of human–nature relations in favour of a single metaphor (for example, master or steward) is thereby to be rejected also. At issue here is the vulnerability of nature as it is brought under human administration and the foolishness of the humanity that attempts such administration. Failure to attend to the cruciform – that is, realistic – interpretation of nature is to miss the vulnerability of nature and the foolishness of humanity.

Through this section, I have been sketching an answer to the following questions: in what ways may the cross of Jesus Christ be construed as a guiding protocol for Christian practice? How might the cross of the God-body – as an un/natural event – be construed and practised as *internal* to the Christocentric practice of friendship towards fellowship in the Spirit? As befits the complexity of the concept of nature itself, the response offered is itself complex. The crucifixion of nature invites, supports and reinforces practices which acknowledge the un/natural relations between humanity and non-human nature, affirm the un/natural shape of creatureliness and yet deny attempts to 'master' or organise such creatureliness.

Against the 're-enchantment of nature'

A stress on nature as space persistently invites the Romantic interpretation of the re-enchantment or resacralisation of nature. That is, natural relations are persistently preferred over un/natural relations: human ends are to be found in nature. The attraction of the re-enchantment of nature lies in its rejection of the theme of the 'salvation' of nature by humanity. 'Saving nature' describes a hubristic and unsustainable programme that denies the *extra nos* of nature.[10] Given that, at first sight, re-enchantment

---

9. Cited by Rasmussen, *Earth Community, Earth Ethics*, p. 273. The phrase is originally by F. C. Oetinger.
10. Of course, we are also invited, by the blandishments of the Nature Company and the Body Shop, to contribute in a rather different way to the salvation of nature: through consumption.

appears opposed to saving nature, why, from the perspective of the resurrection of the God–body, is hope in the re-enchantment of nature to be rejected as false?

To answer this question, and before addressing the issue of the resurrection of the God–body as internal guide to un/natural relations, we must first establish what is meant by the phrase, 'the re-enchantment of nature'. In one sense, we have already attended to this theme: deep ecology and one strain of ecofeminism are attempts to re-enchant nature. The tendency here is to invoke nature, within a specific conceptuality, for the interpretation of human–nature relations. The weaknesses of these approaches I have already rehearsed: the naturalism of deep ecology deconstructs into an anthropocentrism within an authoritarian logic (chapter 3); cultural ecofeminism problematically proposes 'direct connections with nature'[11] (chapter 4).

However, an important strength of the theme of the re-enchantment of nature is its promotion of 'deep feelings of connectedness' with nature.[12] Such sensibilities do, indeed, function in criticism of the rhetoric of 'saving nature'. In a discussion of Martin Heidegger, David Harvey forcefully makes this point: the stress on 'dwelling' in Heidegger's later writing, together with the importance of 'dwelling' in the construction of 'place', indicates the priority of home, and associations of home and place, in thinking on the human predicament.[13] Indeed, Heidegger employs his argument in criticism especially of Cartesian notions of geometric space, thereby questioning the preoccupation with the mathematical denotation of space. Furthermore, in giving priority to dwelling, Heidegger questions the primacy given to material satisfactions to be wrought out of nature in advance of attention to 'aesthetic' matters of place.[14] To amend a *dictum* of Brecht's, Heidegger rejects the commitments captured in the phrase, 'Eats first, aesthetics later'.

Nevertheless, Harvey acknowledges that Heidegger's position cannot be accepted as it stands. Indeed, in line with the commitments of his earlier work,[15] Harvey interprets the works of Marx and Heidegger on nature

---

11. See Charlene Spretnak, 'Ecofeminism: Our Roots and Flowering', in Diamond and Orenstein (eds.), *Reweaving the World*, pp. 3–14 (p. 13).
12. Neil Smith, 'Nature at the Millennium: Production and Re-enchantment', in B. Braun and N. Castree (eds.), *Remaking Reality: Nature at the Millennium* (London and New York: Routledge, 1998), pp. 271–85 (p. 280).
13. Harvey, *Justice, Nature and the Geography of Difference*, pp. 299–302.
14. Martin Heidegger, 'Modern Science, Metaphysics, and Mathematics', in D. F. Krell (ed.), *Basic Writings: Martin Heidegger* (London: Routledge, 1993), pp. 271–305; Martin Heidegger, *Being and Time* (Oxford: Blackwell, 1962), pp. 122–48.
15. Harvey, *The Condition of Postmodernity*.

as dialectical oppositions in the struggle between modernism and post-modernism. Although Marxism, as he acknowledges, has stressed capitalism as totality to the detriment of the adequate theorisation of locality, yet the Heideggerian affirmation of the re-enchantment of nature also requires criticism. Marx and Heidegger are names which stand for traditions of inquiry which need to be related to each other if the complexities of space and place under capitalism are to be adequately understood.

Doyen of left theoreticians of nature, Neil Smith, also struggles with the tension between space and place. Here the tension is explored in the relation between the social production of nature – which includes the debunking of the natural – and the otherness of nature. For, as Smith notes, a stress on discursive nature plays into the hands of an environmental managerialism. As constructed by social interests, nature here is already shaped for administration by human beings: amenable, that is, to appropriation by the accelerating demands of capitalist accumulation. The otherness of nature is the contrast position: Smith writes of 'the emotional appeal . . . from experiences of nature', citing along the way the claim made by Donna Haraway that, in short, we cannot not desire nature.[16] But how, Smith asks, can this desiring be thought which leads to neither 'save the world' managerial environmentalism nor Romantic escapism? Here Smith finds himself unable to answer his own question: it may well be that the ideology of nature is too strong to permit a re-enchantment which avoids political terrors. Yet, if the energies which support the idolatry of nature could be refashioned, he concludes, would that not make for the beginnings of a liberative re-enchantment of nature?

Regrettably, no such reservations about the re-enchantment of nature mark the work of theologian Sallie McFague. In recent writing on spirituality, she coins the term, 'super, natural Christians', which clearly indicates the direction of her thinking: the end of humanity lies in care of nature.[17] The two levels which we have been investigating – the production of nature under capitalism and the connection to place – are not present in McFague's argument. Indeed, as we might suspect, her argument is stronger on the theme of connection with place, especially the

16. Smith, 'Nature at the Millennium', p. 280. Smith cites Haraway's *Simians, Cyborgs and Women* as the textual reference; however, a more likely source is Donna Haraway, 'The Actors are Cyborg, Nature is Coyote, and the Geography is Elsewhere', in Constance Penley and Andrew Ross (eds.), *Technoculture* (Minnesota and London: University of Minnesota Press, 1991), pp. 21–6 (p. 25). In turn, Haraway cites Gayatri Spivak as the source of the remark!
17. Sallie McFague, *Super, Natural Christians: How we should Love Nature* (London: SCM Press, 1997).

relation of humans to animals. Nevertheless, little indication is given on how this relates to the wider uses of nature. At the point of moving beyond the local, McFague offers a form of sacramentalism which seeks to understand the diversity of natural forms in God. However welcome such a development is, its theological cogency is not obvious: ecological thought seems to provide all the resources. There is no sense in which the forms of nature need to be redescribed in theological perspective. Indeed, Christianity's main function seems to be to relieve the human self of its anxieties and direct the human eye to the poor and the outcast, including nature.

Yet such a view repeats the errors of the 'Enlightenment Christianity' which McFague criticises elsewhere in the book. In McFague's interpretation, Christianity is presented as an 'enlightened' moralism: we really should pay attention to nature; we are implicated as part of nature; we should mend our ways. To make such a statement, however, you do not need a concept of God. Furthermore, the matter of the relation between the local and the global is effectively occluded in McFague's account. The reason for this is, I think, that McFague adopts the ethical stance, also to be found in deep ecology, of 'moral extensionism'. Yet the weaknesses of deep ecology are evident in McFague's work also: Christianity buttresses and promotes a form of transpersonal identification as we come to understand ourselves as part of nature. The anthropocentrism which underpins this view is all too obvious: consider only the claim to unmediated access by the human to nature which such an argument presupposes.[18] What is more, it is precisely the wrong sort of anthropocentrism: for the theme of the social production of nature is left out of the discussion.

At issue is not, then, the re-enchantment of nature. The natural world is not to be regarded as sacred or as disclosing some numinous presence of God. The reference is too wide: nature, in Christian tradition, should not be seen as sacramental; instead, sacraments refer to particular signs, such as the eucharistic bread and wine. 'The fallen creation is no longer the creation of the first creative Word', argues Bonhoeffer. Therefore: 'The creation is not sacrament.'[19] Yet the reference should not be construed too narrowly: for the capacity of the bread and wine to mediate the presence of God turns upon the orientation of all creaturely order towards God, in the unity of God's acts in creation, liberation and redemption.[20]

---

18. I have tried to indicate the anthropocentrism in McFague's account in my 'Nature in a World come of Age', 356–68. A reading of McFague's other books – *Models of God* and *The Body of God* – would, I think, support such an interpretation.
19. Bonhoeffer, *Christology*, p. 53.
20. Pannenberg, *Systematic Theology*, II, pp. 137–8. The term 'liberation' is mine.

In line with the commitments of this book, what is required instead is an emphasis on the *socialising* of nature. For the common realm of God, nature and humanity needs to be addressed from the perspective of the resurrection of Jesus Christ: God's commitment to 'the commons' persists even through death. The resurrection is concerned with the reordering of that which is social, and the disclosure of such society. Indeed, Christian tradition invites us not to construe the matter in terms of body and presence, but in terms of the actions of the God–body in sociality.

How does this perspective permit us to think of the connections between humanity and nature so that we may speak theologically, and thereby politically, of the production of nature and the connection to place? We return to the central point of this book: the Gospel does not re-enchant; neither does it only secularise. Rather, the Gospel *socialises*. To participate in the dynamics of creatureliness – which is the blessing of God – we are required not to re-enchant or resacralise relations between humanity and non-human nature, but rather to *socialise* these relations. What does this mean?

Ecological degradation cannot be addressed only from the perspective of the local. The ecological relations between humanity and non-human nature require analysis to disclose the global production of nature under capitalism. None the less, how place is socially constructed yet engages sensibilities is also vitally important: the particularism of social struggle over uses of nature, and the social energy which such particularisms provide, cannot be denied. Indeed, such energy needs to be shaped in the direction of the global. Put differently, to stress the production of nature is to move in the direction of explanation by reference to anti-natural relations. To move in the direction of place is to stress the matter of natural relations. Yet, throughout this book, I am proposing a theological alternative: un/natural relations in a common realm.

Such a perspective is helpful in thinking through the relation between the production of nature and locality, the relation of space and place within a political theology. For the construal of place must be referred to the fellowship of the common realm. And consideration of the social production of nature under capitalism cannot be separated from the histories and cultural memories of peoples. The resurrection of the God–body invites the socialising of ecological relations: to refer *place* to fellowship; to refer *space* to active subjects living in friendship in the common realm.

The same point may also be put paradoxically. The true understanding of ecological relations is not to be found in the construal of place, but neither is it not to be found there. The true understanding of ecological relations is not to be found in the interpretation of the totality of space, but neither is it not to be found there. Thus un/natural relations refer us both to the natural associations given with place and the non-natural relations given with space. In the perspective of the resurrection developed here, both sets of relations are denied yet reaffirmed in a new dispensation: oriented towards one another because joined and clarified in the reordering of sociality which is the resurrection of Jesus Christ.

The re-enchantment of nature thereby raises an important point: how are the relations between the global and the local, space and places to be thought in a political theology? I have argued that the re-enchantment of nature contributes inadequately to a theological understanding of fellowship. The blessing of fellowship is conferred through the true practice of sociality. Un/natural relations, as energised by the Spirit, are the 'mechanism' of the conferral of such blessing in which these relations are understood as orderly, preservative and excentric. One way of reconsidering these issues theologically is to attend to the ways in which the eucharist construes place.

Eucharist: ecclesial 'place'

Christianity is best understood as a way of life before and from God, and thereby as participation in the community of disciples. Through this section, therefore, I argue that central to the identity of Christian practice is a social act which relates space to place and globality to locality. That act is the 'time-laden and social'[21] eucharist. How is the community of the eucharist to be interpreted for the common realm? If to participate in the eucharist is to participate in the cross and resurrection of the God–body, how might such participation be understood?

I begin by noting my agreement with Dietrich Bonhoeffer that 'Christ existing as community' called Church has a threefold form: community, word and sacrament.[22] Furthermore, Bonhoeffer makes the valuable point that the sacraments address the natural human being in his or her embodiment: 'The sacrament is the form in which the Logos reaches man in his nature.' '[I]n the sacrament he [sc. Christ] makes use of our body and is present in the sphere of tangible nature. In the sacrament, Christ is by our side as creature, among us, brother with brother.'[23] We are thus reminded

21. Hardy, *Finding the Church*, p. 21.   22. Bonhoeffer, *Christology*, pp. 49–59.
23. Ibid., pp. 53, 57. The restrictively gendered language requires correction.

that the eucharist has – as the basis of its sacramental sign – material elements. Later, explicating the mediation of Christ as the centre between God and nature, Bonhoeffer writes:

> [I]n the sacraments . . . elements of the old creation are become elements of the new. In the sacraments they are set free from their dumbness and proclaim directly to the believer the new creative Word of God . . . Enslaved nature does not speak the Word of God to us directly. But the sacraments do. In the sacrament, Christ is the mediator between nature and God and stands for all creation before God.[24]

Although a theology of the eucharist is more than can be attempted here, for a political theology of nature the material elements of the eucharist are sacramental by their reference to Jesus Christ. That is, neither the material nor the Christological reference can be lost if the sacramentality of the eucharist is to be explicated. Both the bread and wine and their orientation towards Christ are thereby required. How is their relation to be understood?

To begin, we must note the abiding relation between the eucharist, the passion and the table-fellowship of Jesus Christ. Although I do not wish to be drawn into a discussion as to whether the Last Supper was a Passover meal or not, that the eucharist has a central anamnestic aspect is not to be doubted. Indeed, such an aspect of remembrance may, as Wolfhart Pannenberg suggests, be construed broadly: 'We have to evaluate the tradition of Jesus' last supper with his disciples before his crucifixion in the context of the meals that he had with them in the preceding period of his earthly ministry.'[25] By such reference, our attention is directed a second time to the theme of nature in Jesus' ministry. Recall that in chapter 7 I argued that the table-fellowship of the God–body presents a dynamic of generosity in which the hungry are fed and sinners made welcome. Such remembering must, of course, be understood theologically: the recollection of the memory of the crucified One is always to be associated with the presence of Christ by the Spirit. 'But it is of decisive significance', notes Pannenberg, 'if we are to understand eucharistic anamnesis that we do not see here merely an act of human remembering of which we are still the subjects but the self-representing of Jesus Christ by his Spirit.'[26]

---

24. Bonhoeffer, *Christology*, p. 64.
25. Pannenberg, *Systematic Theology* (Edinburgh: T. and T. Clark, 1998), III, p. 284.
26. Ibid., p. 306.

Certainly, if we follow and develop the work of Oliver O'Donovan,[27] the eucharist is to be understood in relation to the passion of Jesus Christ. For O'Donovan, the passion is recollected in the eucharist and invokes the Church as a suffering community. Although O'Donovan stresses the connection between eucharist and suffering – '*The eucharist* is the sign that marks the suffering community . . . It determines the identity of this society by reference to the passion: it is the community of those who have not only gathered to God's Christ, but have died with him.'[28] – the link between eucharist and *place* is less clearly set forth. That is, the passion is not, in my view, merely a report of a death, but is an account of a particular death, at a particular place, Golgotha. Thus, in Christian eucharistic construal, place is associated, first, with suffering.

The resurrection, in O'Donovan's interpretation, is enacted in the observance of the Sabbath and calls forth joy by the community, not least in the acknowledgement of the 'recovery of creation order'. Here O'Donovan's account is especially interesting: 'Gladness belongs to the creature, as glory belongs to the creator . . . If the church's gladness is the gladness of creation, that means it is the gladness of Jesus himself; for the renewed order of creation is present in him.'[29] We may add further: if the renewed order of creation is present in the God–body, then the eucharist is a sacramental means of participation in this new order, in which humanity and nature are understood together in a social conceptuality. As we have already seen, in Jesus Christ is the election of nature as social. Eucharistic theology cannot fall behind this insight. Thus the eucharist, a celebration of and participation in the resurrected life of the God–body, joins again humanity with nature. The God–body who is other in the eucharist is the source and destiny of the sociality of nature and humanity, and provides a sacramental mode of participation in that destiny. And, to be sure, important practical consequences follow from such participation. In a few wonderful sentences, O'Donovan makes this point: '[B]ecause we ourselves are God's work, not mere observers of it, our pleasure is part of that good order of things that God has made; so that by delighting in the created order, we participate in it. Our very joy places us within that order, and by our gladness the ordered creation of God is made complete.'[30] What is suggested by the eucharist is the character

27. Oliver O'Donovan, *The Desire of the Nations: Rediscovering the Roots of Political Theology* (Cambridge University Press, 1996), pp. 174–92.
28. Ibid., p. 180.   29. Ibid., p. 181.   30. Ibid., pp. 181–2.

of our place in the world and the ways in which we share in a common creatureliness.

This line of thought may be developed a little further if we note that, from the perspective of the ascension of Christ, the passion and resurrection may be drawn more closely together than maintained by O'Donovan. We have already seen that the resurrection *socialises*. The eucharist remains the core activity by which the identity of the Church is maintained and its community built up. In fact, for a political theology such a formulation is too anaemic: as William Cavanaugh notes: 'The eucharist is the [church's] true 'politics' . . . because it is the public performance of the true eschatological City of God in the midst of another city that is passing away.'[31] Such a community is committed through its participation as social in a social act to witness publicly to the social character of creaturely reality. Thus, as a political act, the eucharist embodies the goodness of the created order as liberated by the God–body from futility and sin, and invites the recovery of the acknowledgement of the goodness of the created order, precisely as social.[32]

Of course, the association of the eucharist with the place of Golgotha and suffering is never absent. However, the eucharist is also the sacrament which, in its acknowledgement of the resurrection of Jesus Christ and the defeat of evil powers and the surpassment of death by sacrifice, *clarifies* the un/natural circumstance of humanity. It is correct, as O'Donovan suggests, to associate the resurrection with joy and the recovery of creation order. Yet the eucharist, as re-enactment of the table-fellowship/Last Supper of Jesus Christ from the perspective of the community of the resurrection, also indicates the relations of eucharistic community to the wider society. In the eucharist, eucharistic community is bound in sociality to the wider ecological society, and interprets and clarifies it. If, as Rowan Williams argues, the eucharist is God's 'guarantee of hospitality',[33] such hospitality has no ecclesiastical restrictions, and encompasses the non-human.

31. William T. Cavanaugh, *Torture and Eucharist: Theology, Politics and The Body of Christ* (Oxford: Blackwell, 1998), p. 14.
32. Part of what is meant here by social is captured by John Howard Yoder's remark, in 'Sacrament as Social Process', *Theology Today* 48 (1991), 33–44 (here 37), that 'What the New Testament is talking about in "breaking bread" is believers' actually sharing with one another their ordinary day-to-day material substance [*sic*]'. The reference to the materiality of the elements is not, however, developed; indeed, Yoder rejects a 'sacramentalistic' account of the eucharist (38) that might have enabled him to make the connection.
33. Williams, *On Christian Theology*, p. 217.

The eating of bread and the drinking of wine constitute community: material elements are central to the eucharist. As Pannenberg notes: 'Basic here is the fact that the fellowship with Jesus Christ that each Christian receives in the form of bread and wine unites all Christians for fellowship with one another in the unity of the body of Christ.'[34] Yet such unity cannot be had except by the presence of the material elements, bread and wine, that is, by reference to the Last Supper and the earlier table-fellowship which the bread and wine summarise. Thus, in the eucharist, 'sacramental nature' is not only God's way to human embodiment, but is also taken up into the action of the remembrance of cross and resurrection of the God–body. That is, the un/natural event of eucharistic practice draws in non-human nature and re-establishes the un/natural fellowship of the Church.

Here may lie the truth in the following comment by Terry Eagleton on the significance of the eucharist for nature: 'of man's eucharistic relation to nature, the material world: in the symbolism of bread and wine, man's products cease to be alien to his life and become instead, the pliable medium of his expressive communication with others.'[35] What is right about this comment by Eagleton is the stress on the deep relation between nature and the eucharist as a sacramental indicator of the preservation of humanity by nature. What is wrong is that nature does not become plastic in the sense of being at human disposal, but rather the reality of humanity's natural conditions are underscored in eucharistic fellowship as having their own, proper, eschatological orientation. As un/natural, therefore, the eucharist is an eschatological event, indicating the destiny of human and non-human nature.[36] In such fashion, the false construal of space is criticised 'sacramentally'. For example, in a discussion of baptism and eucharist, Barry Harvey argues that, 'The church's existence as other thus signals to a world come of age the ultimate (i.e. eschatological) triumph of time (in the sense of the perfecting of creation) over colonized space, thus interrupting the processes of supervision that mark the modern world.'[37] This is not, as Cavanaugh reminds us, to give up on the

---

34. Pannenberg, *Systematic Theology*, III, p. 292.
35. Terry Eagleton, *The Body as Language: Outline of a 'New Left' Theology* (London: Sheed and Ward, 1970), pp. 46–7.
36. As Cavanaugh notes, *Torture and Eucharist*, p. 226, the *parousia* is central to correct interpretation of the Eucharist.
37. Barry Harvey, 'The Body Politic of Christ: Theology, Social Analysis and Bonhoeffer's Arcane Discipline', *Modern Theology* 13:3 (1997), 319–46 (342).

metaphor of space but rather to construe it eschatologically.[38] Eucharistic criticism thereby informs a liberative pedagogy and directs attention to the spaces of 'decontextualised' others who, in this sacramental perspective, the God of the God–body has not abandoned.

Nor is the eucharist to be supplanted by different forms of practice, as Michael Northcott has suggested. Discussion of local issues – although valuable on other grounds – should not be added to the rite nor should the liturgy be displaced by other activities (such as environmental clean-up). Northcott correctly notes that: 'The Eucharist affirms not just place as building or land but place as community, for in the Eucharist, wherever it is celebrated, the people of God are reconstituted as a community of believers whose meeting creates a sacred place.' Yet the question here is: how do the material elements of the eucharist in fact construe place? If it is true, as Northcott notes, that: 'The Eucharistic transformation of the elements of human sustenance perhaps loses some of its resonance in urban cultures', what needs investigation is how the materiality of the eucharist might function as the criticism of such a sensibility.[39]

Of primary importance in this regard is the eschatological interpretation of the eucharist from the ascension of the God–body. O'Donovan discusses the significance of the Exaltation of Christ, yet he is cautious about the connection between Exaltation and eucharist on the grounds that connecting the ascended Christ to the eucharistic meal undercuts the 'corporeal language of body and blood'. Thus O'Donovan prefers, as we have seen, to relate eucharist to the passion. However, he does acknowledge the importance of an eschatological reference in that we see 'through the meal of Christ's betrayal and suffering the great banquet which was the symbol of God's promised reign'.[40]

What is wrong with this? First, the relation between creation and incarnation is closer than O'Donovan acknowledges. Only a Christological order, as I argued in chapter 7, is material and concrete. Thus, referring the eucharistic meal to the risen Christ is not to be construed as the denial of such concretion. Indeed, a case can be made for saying that the presence of the resurrected Christ, in his ubiquity in the Spirit, is precisely 'dense' and concrete.[41] As David Ford suggests, interpreting the eucharist from

38. Cavanaugh, *Torture and Eucharist*, pp. 269–70.
39. See Michael Northcott, 'A Place of Our Own', in Peter Sedgwick (ed.), *God in the City* (London: Mowbray, 1995), pp. 119–38 (p. 135).
40. O'Donovan, *The Desire of the Nations*, p. 181.
41. Cf. Daniel W. Hardy and David F. Ford, *Jubilate: Theology in Praise* (London: Darton, Longman and Todd, 1984), p. 129.

the ascension protects the 'continuing particularity of his [sc. Christ's] humanity' and maintains 'the eschatological tension of presence and absence in the eucharist'.[42] The importance of the particularity of the *social* body of the God–body, in whose death and resurrection both nature and humanity are elected, is maintained in such an eschatological perspective, and the dangers of a general sacramentality (see the previous section) resisted.

Second, as was also suggested in the previous section, to be intelligible the notion of sacrament requires a double reference: to the material sign (water, bread, wine) and the eschatological destiny of creation by which we are able to understand that creation has a significance, and will enjoy a state, beyond its current condition. Only in this double reference is the notion of sacrament intelligible. *Contra* O'Donovan, we must say that the eschatological reference of the eucharist is rooted in the actuality of part of creaturely reality operating as a sacrament. In other words, the eschatological orientation of creation is a condition of the possibility of sacrament and thereby of the eucharist itself. From a sacramental perspective, we again see how humanity and nature are bound together in the common realm in terms of a common but not identical destiny.

So far in this section, I have sought to construct some aspects of an ecological theology of the eucharist. Throughout, I have tried to hold fast to the eucharist as material and transformative: 'The materiality of the sacraments', writes Colin Gunton, 'reminds us that the transformation of matter is at the heart of the Church's being'.[43] Holding to the commitments adumbrated through this book, I have interpreted the eucharist from the ascension of Christ, thereby protecting the actuality of the bread and wine as a sacramental sign and, further, indicating the common destiny of the human and non-human: participation in the judgment of Christ by the Spirit. The eucharist is, second, to be interpreted from the perspective of the resurrection: creaturely reality is social and joy breaks out in the acknowledgement of the goodness implied by this claim in which the Church participates by the eucharist. And, third, the eucharist has an important anamnestic aspect: the remembrance of the cross at a place called Golgotha, understood as the 'culmination' of the provocative character of Jesus' table-fellowship.

These three interpretative moments require the material signs of bread and wine: the natural elements are those of the Last Supper and,

42. David F. Ford, *Self and Salvation: Being Transformed* (Cambridge University Press, 1999), p. 157, n. 41.
43. Gunton, *Theology through the Theologians*, p. 121.

by extension, stand for Jesus' table-fellowship and thereby recall the 'outcome' of that fellowship, the death of the God–body at the place of the skull; as natural – the result of eco-regulative agricultural processes and subsequent refining transformations – it is these elements, when consumed, which constitute the body of Christ; and, finally, the possibility of the bread and wine being sacramental signs is secured by the participation of nature, as social and elected, in the eschatological event of Christ's sacrificial death.

Similar to ecological pneumatology with its pedagogy oriented towards fellowship (discussed in chapter 8), the eucharist invokes and invests in a pedagogy of human–nature relations. What is the shape of such a eucharistic pedagogy of the commons to which the Church is called? To answer this question, we need to attend to the nature of the non-human nature which is central to the eucharist. What is the commons in eucharistic perspective? What is the theological concept of nature operative here? We might call it a concept of un/natural nature: although eucharistic practice is founded on material elements which are social productions, yet the theological point is the transformation of these elements. In the emphasis on the plasticity of nature as sacramental sign, the theological point is that the eucharist represents the resurrection and crucifixion and thereby the sociality and openness of nature. This non-technological, un/natural, nature is at the centre of Christian practice. Yet sacramental nature stands in here – so to speak – for the creaturely nature. In the sacrament of the eucharist, as Bonhoeffer says, Christ mediates between nature and the creator in a Trinitarian action oriented towards fellowship by the Spirit. Once more, immersion in nature – some naturalistic fantasy – is ruled out.

Furthermore, and of vital importance, the alteration of nature is non-technological. We are not presented with the manipulation of nature by technique. For the nature presented here as creaturely precedes technique: as a creature of God, such nature emerges prior to the modern division of nature and humanity, and the domestication of the former by the latter through technique. As Simon Oliver argues: 'the Eucharist reconfigure[s] nature and culture into a participative relationship in the divine life . . . by viewing them . . . as fundamentally *creaturely*'.[44] There is therefore no mysticism here, such as that invoked by O'Donovan: 'When we make artefacts

---

44. Simon Oliver, 'The Eucharist before Nature and Culture', *Modern Theology* 15:3 (1999), 331–53 (here p. 349, italics in original).

and machines to exploit the forces of nature, it is because we delight in nature, both in its raw givenness and in its possibilities for cooperation, and
that we are glad that God has restored it to fulfil his purposes for it.'[45] It
is not the aesthetics of delight which are our concern, but rather our grati-
tude and thankfulness for a nature both *pro nobis* and *extra nos*. The matter
is not only our reaction to nature, but also nature's claim, as a fellow *creature* in the common realm, on us.

Why do I stress the importance of the eucharistic concept of nature
as non-technological? Such a commitment is vital if we are to avoid the
temptation to opt for a form of asceticism in response to an ecological
crisis.[46] I certainly do not wish to deny that restraint is important in our
relationship with nature. Yet the importance of the affirmation of nature
as non-technological is to insist that we should not play off the technological transformation of nature against ascetic practices. Such a way forward
is reductive and does not fit well with the recovery of the goodness of creation reported earlier. Furthermore, it makes such a eucharistic pedagogy
appear dull and restrictive. There is a sort of wildness to contemporary
capitalist culture, as Arne Naess has noted.[47] I do not think that the attractiveness of eucharistic practice can be founded on a direct opposition to
such wildness.

Here we must be guided by the bread and wine as material elements of
the eucharist: there can be no escape from the facticity of such elements.
Indeed, bread and wine are not raw nature; these are already transformations, the products of human labour. So human society and human technology are invoked by the bread and wine. Indeed, I do not see that the
fact that bread comes in plastic bags and wine in cartons in Western societies, as Northcott laments, is a bar to grasping the un/natural significance
of the eucharist. For eucharistic practice is bound to the bread and wine
produced by a particular society in a particular place.

Perhaps, therefore, one should draw on Bonhoeffer's suggestion as
to the recovery of an 'arcane discipline': eucharistic practice is predicated upon the alteration of nature towards God and thereby towards
humanity. Christian discipleship is a reminder of the destiny of all flesh

45. O'Donovan, *The Desire of the Nations*, p. 183.
46. For example, Albert Borgmann speaks of ascetic practices in the face of ecological
degradation: see Albert Borgmann, 'Prospects for the Theology of Technology', in Carl
Mitcham and Jim Grote (eds.), *Theology and Technology* (Lanham, MD: University Press of
America, 1984), pp. 305–22 (pp. 320–1).
47. Arne Naess, 'Deep Ecology for the Twenty-second Century', in Sessions (ed.), *Deep Ecology
for the 21st Century*, pp. 463–7 (p. 467).

in Jesus Christ. Fellowship between humanity and nature as suggested by eucharistic practice is to be understood in the form of an ecclesial common realm. Here eucharistic sacrament does not suggest, as Larry Rasmussen proposes, that 'God is pegged to earth'.[48] Instead, the fellowship of the eucharist indicates the contingent suffering of creatures, joy in creatureliness and the orientation of all creatures towards God in the Spirit by the judgment of Christ.

Common Spirit: un/natural fellowship

What account of 'place' is suggested by eucharistic pedagogy? How does the Christian community practise 'place'? Place is the *locus* of community, as Harvey observes, where militant particularism originates.[49] Yet a non-dialectical identification with place can fall into the trap of missing the ways in which places are constructed, not least through the flows of international capital. Only by keeping place in relation to space, the local in tension with the global, can we develop a liberative account of place. If the eucharist is the Christological mediation between the 'militant particularism' of the Church and the peaceable Kingdom, what account of place is thereby suggested?

'The survival of religion as a major institution within secular societies', argues David Harvey, 'has been in part won through the successful creation, protection, and nurturing of symbolic places'.[50] Whatever the sociological truth of such a claim, the Church does not seek to create, protect or nurture ecclesial place. Rather, it responds and witnesses to an eschatological event: '[The church] has a place, but that place has its center of gravity in the church's home towards which it remains on pilgrimage.'[51] We have seen three modalities of such a response and witness: eucharistic place can never be disassociated from suffering; place is always to be connected to wider social relations which the eucharist both presents and clarifies; place cannot be separated from the eschatological destiny of all things in God. In the eucharist, the Church remembers, discerns once more its context in the created order and looks forward in expectation to the return of Christ. The Church does not originate a concept of place. Rather, in the eucharist, it receives – by its remembrance and the invocation of the presence of Christ by the Spirit – a notion of place.

---

48. Rasmussen, *Earth Community, Earth Ethics*, p. 273.
49. Harvey, *Justice, Nature and the Geography of Difference*, pp. 310–13.
50. Ibid., p. 322.   51. Cavanaugh, *Torture and Eucharist*, p. 271.

Such a perspective should not be misunderstood or idealised. The eucharist refers us to material elements. So there is a sense that the organisational place of the Church cannot be a matter of indifference. Cavanaugh's *Torture and Eucharist* offers a compelling account of how such indifference led Chile's Catholic bishops under the Pinochet dictatorship to consider the ecclesiality of Chile in terms of an invisible, mystical communion rather than the visible, public performance of the eucharist. Also from an emergency situation, in the Barmen Declaration Karl Barth recommended that the order of the Church must be appropriate for the carrying out of its sacramental operations.[52] Beyond this, however, the Church seeks to neither organise nor dispose of its place.[53]

Here the Church is peculiar. Generally, opposition movements wish to secure their own places and wider spaces. 'Anti-capitalism movements are generally better at organising in and dominating "their" places than at commanding space', notes Harvey.[54] The labour movement is a fine example: only recall the conclusion of *The Communist Manifesto*, which now has an ironic resonance: 'The proletarians have nothing to lose but their chains. They have a world to win. Working men of all countries, unite!'[55] However, a eucharistic pedagogy denies such attempts to dominate place and organise and command space. Instead, place must always be referred to the memory of the crucified and the sufferings of the ecclesial community; to the gladness of the community, not least in its opening out to acknowledge the goodness of creation; and to the expectation of the coming rule of God.

Thus eucharistic pedagogy turns upon the narrowing and broadening of the concept of place. Ecclesial place cannot be understood except by reference to the history of the remembrance of the crucified one, the placing of the Church in creation and hope for the coming rule of God. Harvey argues that work, imagined loyalties and aesthetic representation are present in the construction of place.[56] However, in the ecclesial construal of place set out here, the eucharist presents the material works of bread and wine as the representation of the suffering of the crucified

---

52. Karl Barth, 'The Barmen Declaration', in Clifford Green (ed.), *Karl Barth: Theologian of Freedom* (London: Collins, 1989), pp. 148–51.

53. Citing Balthasar, William T. Cavanaugh, 'The World in a Wafer: A Geography of the Eucharist as Resistance to Globalization', *Modern Theology* 15:2 (1999), 181–96, argues that 'the normal condition of the *Catholica* is . . . diaspora . . . catholicity is not dependent on extension through space' (190).

54. Harvey, *Justice, Nature and the Geography of Difference*, p. 324.

55. Marx and Engels, *The Communist Manifesto*, p. 77.

56. Harvey, *Justice, Nature and the Geography of Difference*, p. 323.

God–body; loyalty refers to praise of the Christ of God as liberator and judge which, in turn, invokes loyalty to the earth; and aesthetic representation may be understood theologically as the expectation of fulfilment which can be understood only in aesthetic and affective categories.[57]

Eucharistic 'place' is therefore the *criticism* of nationalist, sectarian construals of 'place'. How so? Consider this: in a television series on nationalism, *Blood and Belonging*,[58] Michael Ignatieff, observing a funeral in the Ukraine, commented as follows:

> Ukrainian Catholics are reburying the remains of their spiritual leader, Cardinal Slippé, who died in exile in Rome. It's a moment in which modern nationalism taps into its ancient religious roots. Uniate Catholicism is found nowhere else: it's a mixture of Catholicism and Russian Orthodoxy, it's 400 years old and it's the very core of Western Ukraine's distinctiveness. The honour guard at Cardinal Slippé's burial is a sinister crew, white shirted paramilitaries of the Ukrainian right, who claim descent from the guerrillas who fought, sometimes alongside the Nazis, against the Red Army in the Second World War. Nationalism is where religion and authoritarianism sometimes meet: it is the dream of unity, everyone singing the same hymn and moved by the same inspiration.

Does such authoritarianism truly rely on a Christian dream of unity? A sense of the past, and the underpinning of a story, to do with a particular people and a particular place: is this the legitimation that Christianity provides?

In the eucharistic pedagogy outlined here, the sense of the past must always begin from and refer to Golgotha.[59] It is not just 'the past' that is invoked, but the past of the God–body which also encompasses the history of the people of Israel. Further, the construal of land as place cannot be thought except in thankfulness for the goodness of the created order and within an eschatological orientation. It is true that the Christian Old Testament portrays the deliverance of Israel as a deliverance to a land of fecundity and justice but, as H. Paul Santmire argues, that deliverance is accompanied by the blessing of all the earth by the creator.[60] The account of eucharistic nature operative here similarly is related always to creation

---

57. On the importance of affective categories for the interpretation of eschatology, see David H. Kelsey, 'Two Theologies of Death: Anthropological Gleanings', *Modern Theology* 13:3 (1997), 345–70.
58. Programme broadcast on BBC TV, 2 December 1993.
59. Cf. Moltmann, *The Way of Jesus Christ*, p. 204.
60. Cf. H. Paul Santmire, *Nature Reborn: The Ecological and Cosmic Promise of Christian Theology* (Philadelphia: Fortress Press, 2000), pp. 31–5.

and the fulfilment of creation. It thus resists restriction to a particular people and a particular place. As Cavanaugh notes, '[The Church] is a gathering, but it is not therefore marked by a "fascist" binding – a homogeneous exclusion of otherness – precisely because the church must constantly renew itself as a gift of God who is Other in the Eucharist.'[61] Place and land are thereby rendered always excentric on account of such eucharistic otherness: related to others and oriented towards the consummating actions of the triune God. The sacramental vision, to borrow a phrase from Rowan Williams, funded by such an account of the eucharist is radically inclusive and provocative, embodying 'the challenge of how there might be a social order in which the disadvantaged and even the criminal could *trust* that the common resources of a society would work for their good'.[62] True eucharistic place is thereby never sectarian or oppressive.[63]

It remains the case, however, that eucharistic practice is embodied practice: it refers to actual congregations in specific places. Thus it is not possible to counter the nationalism observed by Ignatieff with the *denial* of place. Christian communities are not resident aliens in the sense of being rootless; the eucharist can only be celebrated in places. Thus Christianity denies modern tendencies towards the denial of place, brilliantly presented by Marx: 'The bourgeoisie has, wherever it has got the upper hand . . . left remaining no other nexus between man and man than naked self-interest, than callous "cash payment".'[64] Furthermore, a eucharistic account of place would also deny the tendency under modern capitalist conditions to construe place abstractly, that is, to concentrate on the differences between places not in order to learn of the places themselves but instead to discern which place may yield the highest profit on investment which, in turn, generates a competition between places.[65] For how could the marginalised *trust* such 'discernment' to work for them?

Eucharistic fellowship thereby does, by reference to its material basis, make the spatial, 'platial' and the individual, particular. *This* bread and *this* wine in *this* place represent the God–body. Yet the concept of fellowship operative here refers to the binding of the bread and wine to the crucifixion, the relating of the material elements to creation and the orientation

---

61. Cavanaugh, *Torture and Eucharist*, p. 271.   62. Williams, *On Christian Theology*, p. 220.
63. See further, Peter Scott, 'A Theology of Eucharistic Place: Pilgrimage as Sacramental', in C. Bartholomew and F. Hughes (eds.), *Explorations in a Christian Theology of Pilgrimage* (Aldershot: Ashgate, forthcoming).
64. Marx and Engels, *The Communist Manifesto*, p. 37.
65. See Harvey, *Justice, Nature and the Geography of Difference*, pp. 297–8.

of all space towards eschatological fulfilment. Thus, in the eucharist, fellowship still turns upon the dynamics of temporality, sociality and spatiality. The opposition between nationalist place and deracinated, bourgeois space is denied in favour of eucharistic place: a life of service in the middle of a good creation in a community which endures through suffering and in expectation of the new, by remembrance in the Spirit of the crucified God–body. In such fashion, ecclesial practice construes space in liberatory rather than oppressive ways.

Immanuel! common friendship

This final section proposes friendship between humanity and non-human nature. The eucharist is an ecclesial action which requires a pedagogy; the eucharist is a difference which makes a difference. That difference is a pedagogy of friendship. Friendship implies reciprocity and alteration. It is thus suited as a way of describing a eucharistic pedagogy of human–nonhuman relations in the common realm. It also indicates a way forward out of the distorted sociality of humanity in its relations with nature. The damage of the distortion of sociality cannot be overcome through the naturalistic extrusion of humanity through vitalistic or processive categories. Nor is a resolution to be found in the incorporation of nature into a 'second nature' of humanity. Eucharistic pedagogy takes neither of these routes.

A liberative eucharistic theology of nature holds to the insight that the common realm is to be construed as cruciform and resurrected. Such a political theology of eucharistic nature thereby can never give up on three insights. First, Christian community cannot disassociate itself from suffering. Second, the natural conditions of human life are a matter for joy and thankfulness; being a creature is itself a good. Third, the clue that humanity cannot be understood as separate from nature and God is maintained even in a theology of the eucharist: the bread and wine represent the God–body in whom is the election of social nature and humanity. The community of the common realm of God, nature and humanity is, in Christian witness, that which endures. The Church labours to witness truthfully to this claim: to 'become' eucharistic place, in joy and suffering, and in hope.

Yet we should note that something strange happens here. If my interpretation is right, the unity of the Church as given in the eucharist is then an un/natural community which includes nature. As the representation of Christ, the eucharist invokes the participant members as bodily beings: in its fullest sense, the Church is 'the eternal gathering of all creation by Christ into the Father's Kingdom'.[66] Natural embodiment is not denied in eucharistic community yet neither is it affirmed. Nature is both drawn in and yet reconstituted by reference to the God–body. The eucharistic Church can never regard itself as an alternative 'society' without non-human nature. The elements of the eucharist are material productions of a society: they are nature socially transformed. Indeed, the fact that bread comes in plastic bags and wine in cartons reminds us of the special engagement of the church with its society and as a product of that society. Participants in the eucharist remain creatures, although now creatures 'located' in a new set of relations. This set of relations cannot be fully grasped and practised without attention to the ways in which the host culture construes nature. That is, the Church cannot practice its eucharistic pedagogy fully unless it is attentive to the ways in which its context construes nature.[67]

From this perspective, the judgment that Christianity has no stake in non-theological classifications of the world, as proposed by Stanley Hauerwas and John Berkman, is too hasty.[68] On eucharistic grounds, such an attempt at anti-naturalness in theology should be rejected. If suffering, joy and hope are actions and attitudes in a determinate situation, the practice of common friendship will require precisely the attempt to discern the commonalities and overlaps, as well – of course – as the differences, between Christian and non-Christian readings of nature. Indeed, it is central to the theological integrity of eucharistic practice of friendship that such an engagement be made: at stake is a properly theological construal in which differences are called into question and commonalities affirmed by reference to the purposes of God.[69] These purposes are, of course, 'displayed' in the form of the eucharistic God–body.

If the analysis of this book is right, two temptations are to be avoided in our thinking on nature: the technological and the Romantic. There is an element of truth in both accounts, as we have seen. Humanity is creating a 'second nature' which transforms nature; we remain dependent on the otherness of nature which, as other, is a condition of our continued

---

66. Cavanaugh, *Torture and Eucharist*, p. 224.
67. Cf. Harvey, 'The Body Politic of Christ', 340–1.
68. Stanley Hauerwas and John Berkman, 'A Trinitarian Theology of the Chief End of all Flesh', in Stanley Hauerwas (ed.), *In Good Company: The Church as Polis* (University of Notre Dame Press, 1995), pp. 185–97 (185–94).
69. See Hardy, *Finding the Church*, pp. 38–9.

flourishing. Yet I have offered a theological argument which rejects both understandings as reductionist: we should not see nature's end in humanity nor the end of humanity in nature.

The central way of avoiding these mistakes is to construe these human–nature relations in a social conceptuality, founded in and funded by the resurrection of the Christ of God. In this way, I am suggesting, we may avoid being fooled by the technological model of human beings plugged into machines. Rather, such a world must be analysed and criticised as it contributes to and denies our view of ourselves, and non-human nature, as social. The contrasting temptation to seek the wildness of wilderness, the refreshment of 'pure nature', the solace of the country over against the city will be a recurrent, if minor, theme. Yet such a Romantic modulation must also be tested by reference to the relations of humanity with nature as social.

Jesus Christ, as Dietrich Bonhoeffer noted from prison, engages us in the midst of life. In social interpretation for a political theology of nature, we come to understand ourselves as creatures in the middle of a world of creatures: such creatureliness is the blessing of Christ, and the gift of the Holy Spirit.

Bibliography

Anderson, Perry, *English Questions* (Cambridge: Polity Press, 1992).

Barth, Karl, *Church Dogmatics* 11 / 1 (Edinburgh: T. & T. Clark, 1957).

Church Dogmatics 111 /1 (Edinburgh: T. & T. Clark, 1958).

'The Barmen Declaration', in Clifford Green (ed.), *Karl Barth: Theologian of Freedom* (London: Collins, 1989), pp. 148–51.

Bauman, Zygmunt, *Modernity and the Holocaust* (Cambridge: Polity Press, 1989; 1991 pbk.).

Benton, Ted, 'Ecology, Socialism and the Mastery of Nature: A Reply to Reiner Grundmann', *New Left Review* 194 (1992), 55–74.

'Introduction to Part II ', in T. Benton (ed.), *The Greening of Marxism* (New York: Guilford Press, 1996), pp. 103–10.

'Marxism and Natural Limits: an Ecological Critique and Reconstruction', in T. Benton (ed.), *The Greening of Marxism* (New York: Guilford Press, 1996), pp. 157–83.

Bewes, Timothy, *Cynicism and Postmodernity* (London: Verso, 1997).

Biehl, Janet, *Finding our Way: Rethinking Ecofeminist Politics* (Montreal/New York: Black Rose Books, 1991).

Birch, Thomas, 'The Incarceration of Wildness: Wilderness Areas as Prisons', in George Sessions (ed.), *Deep Ecology for the 21st Century: Readings on the Philosophy and Practice of the New Environmentalism* (Boston and London: Shambhala, 1995), pp. 339–55.

Bloch, Ernst, *The Principle of Hope*, vol. 2 (Cambridge, MA: MIT Press, 1995).

Bloch, Maurice, *Marxism and Anthropology* (Oxford University Press, 1983).

Boff, Leonardo, *Ecology and Liberation: A New Paradigm* (Maryknoll, NY: Orbis, 1995).

Bonhoeffer, Dietrich, *Act and Being* (London: Collins, 1961).

Christology (London: Fount, 1978).

Creation and Fall. A Theological Interpretation of Genesis 1–3 (London: SCM Press, 1959).

Ethics (London: SCM Press, 1955).

Letters and Papers from Prison (London: SCM Press, 1971).

Sanctorum Communio: A Dogmatic Inquiry into the Sociology of the Church (New York and Evanston: Harper and Row, 1960).

'A Theological Basis for the World Alliance', in John de Gruchy (ed.), *Dietrich Bonhoeffer. Witness to Jesus Christ* (London: Collins, 1988), pp. 98–110.

Bookchin, Murray, *The Ecology of Freedom: The Emergence and Dissolution of Hierarchy* (Montreal and New York: Black Rose Books, revised edition 1991).

The Modern Crisis (Philadelphia: New Society Publishers, 1986).

The Philosophy of Social Ecology: Essays on Dialectical Naturalism (Montreal and New York: Black Rose Books, 1990).

The Philosophy of Social Ecology: Essays on Dialectical Naturalism (Montreal, New York and London: Black Rose Books, 2nd edition 1996).

Post-Scarcity Anarchism (Montreal and New York: Black Rose Books, 1986).

Remaking Society: Pathways to a Green Future (Boston, MA: South End Press, 1990).

Toward an Ecological Society (Montreal: Black Rose Books, 1980).

Urbanization without Cities: Towards a New Politics of Citizenship (London and New York: Cassell, revised edition 1995).

'Comments on the International Social Ecology Network Gathering and the "Deep Social Ecology" of John Clark', *Democracy and Nature* 3:3 (1997), 154–97.

'Social Ecology versus Deep Ecology', *Socialist Review* 88:3 (1988), 11–29.

'What is Social Ecology?', in Michael Zimmerman (ed.), *Environmental Philosophy: From Animal Rights to Radical Ecology* (Englewood Cliffs, NJ: Prentice Hall, 1993), pp. 354–73.

Borgmann, Albert, 'Prospects for the Theology of Technology', in Carl Mitcham and Jim Grote (eds.), *Theology and Technology* (Lanham, MD: University Press of America, 1984), pp. 305–22.

van den Brom, Luco, 'The Art of a Theo-ecological Interpretation', *Nederlands Theologisch Tijdschrift* 51:4 (1997), 298–313.

Brooke, John Hedley, *Science and Religion* (Cambridge University Press, 1991).

Buckley, Michael J., *At the Origins of Modern Atheism* (New Haven and London: Yale University Press, 1987).

Castree, Noel and Braun, Bruce, 'The Construction of Nature and the Nature of Construction', in B. Braun and N. Castree (eds.), *Remaking Reality: Nature at the Millennium* (London and New York: Routledge, 1998), pp. 3–42.

Cavanaugh, William T., *Torture and Eucharist: Theology, Politics and the Body of Christ* (Oxford: Blackwell, 1998).

'The World in a Wafer: A Geography of the Eucharist as Resistance to Globalization', *Modern Theology* 15:2 (1999), 181–96.

de Chardin, Teilhard, *The Divine Milieu* (New York: Harper, 1960).

The Phenomenon of Man (New York: Harper, 1959).

Cheney, Jim, 'Eco-feminism and Deep Ecology', *Environmental Ethics* 9:2 (1987), 115–45.

'Nature/Theory/Difference', in Karen J. Warren (ed.), *Ecological Feminism* (London and New York: Routledge, 1994), pp. 158–78.

'The Neo-Stoicism of Radical Environmentalism', *Environmental Ethics* 11 (1989), 293–325.

Christ, Carol P., 'Rethinking Theology and Nature', in Irene Diamond and Gloria Feman Orenstein (eds.), *Reweaving the World: the Emergence of Ecofeminism* (San Francisco: Sierra Club Books, 1990), pp. 58–69.

Clark, John, 'Aujourd'hui l'écologie?', *Terra Nova* 1 (1996), 112–19.

'The Dialectical Social Geography of Elisée Reclus', *Philosophy and Geography* 1 (1997), 117–42.

'Municipal Dreams: A Social Ecological Critique of Bookchin's Politics', in Andrew Light (ed.), *Social Ecology after Bookchin* (New York: Guilford Press, 1998), pp. 137–91.

'Reply', *Capitalism, Nature, Socialism* 9:1 (1998), 37–45.

'A Social Ecology', *Capitalism, Nature, Socialism* 8:3 (1997), 3–33.

Cobb, John B., *A Christian Natural Theology Based on the Thought of Alfred North Whitehead* (London: Lutterworth Press, 1966).

Is it Too Late? A Theology of Ecology (Beverly Hills, CA: Bruce, 1972).

Commoner, Barry, *Making Peace with the Planet* (New York: The New Press, 1992).

Cupitt, Don, 'Nature and Culture', in Neil Spurway (ed.), *Humanity, Environment and God* (Oxford: Blackwell, 1993), pp. 33–45.

Dell, Katherine, 'Green Ideas in the Wisdom Tradition', *Scottish Journal of Theology* 47:4 (1994), 423–51.

Demeritt, David, 'Science, Social Constructivism and Nature', in Bruce Braun and Noel Castree (eds.), *Remaking Reality: Nature at the Millennium* (London and New York: Routledge, 1998), pp. 173–93.

Derr, Thomas Sieger, *Ecology and Human Need* (Philadelphia: Westminster Press, 1975).

Devall, Bill and Sessions, George, *Deep Ecology: Living as if Nature Mattered* (Salt Lake City: Peregrine Smith Books, 1985).

Diamond, Irene and Orenstein, Gloria Feman (eds.), *Reweaving the World: The Emergence of Ecofeminism* (San Francisco: Sierra Club Books, 1990).

Dorrien, Gary, *Reconstructing the Common Good* (New York: Orbis, 1990).

Doyal, Len and Gough, Ian, 'Human Needs and Social Change', in Carolyn Merchant (ed.), *Ecology: Key Concepts in Critical Theory* (New Jersey: Humanities Press, 1994), pp. 107–11.

Drees, Willem B., *Religion, Science and Naturalism* (Cambridge University Press, 1996).

Dupré, Louis, *Passage to Modernity: An Essay in the Hermeneutics of Nature and Culture* (New Haven and London: Yale University Press, 1993).

'The Dissolution of the Union of Nature and Grace at the Dawn of the Modern Age', in Carl E. Braaten and Philip Clayton (eds.), *The Theology of Wolfhart Pannenberg* (Minneapolis: Augsburg, 1988), pp. 95–121.

'Nature and Grace: Fateful Separation and Attempted Reunion', in David L. Schindler (ed.), *Catholicism and Secularization in America* (Notre Dame, IN: Communio, 1990), pp. 52–73.

Eagleton, Terry, *The Body as Language: Outline of a 'New Left' Theology* (London: Sheed and Ward, 1970).

Eckersley, Robyn, *Environmentalism and Political Theory: Toward an Ecocentric Approach* (London: University College London Press, 1995).

Edwards, Denis, *Jesus the Wisdom of God: An Ecological Theology* (New York: Orbis, 1995).

Elkins, Stephan, 'The Politics of Mystical Ecology', *Telos* 82 (1989–90), 52–70.

Ely, John, 'Ernst Bloch, Natural Rights, and the Greens', in David Macauley (ed.), *Minding Nature: The Philosophers of Ecology* (New York: Guilford Press, 1996), pp. 134–66.

'Lukács's Construction of Nature', *Capitalism, Nature, Socialism* 1 (1998), 107–16.

Enzensberger, Hans Magnus, 'A Critique of Political Ecology', in Ted Benton (ed.), *The Greening of Marxism* (New York: Guilford Press, 1996), pp. 17–49.

Faricy, Robert, *Wind and Sea Obey Him: Approaches to a Theology of Nature* (London: SCM Press, 1982).

Farrow, Douglas B., 'In the End is the Beginning: A Review of Jürgen Moltmann's Systematic Contributions', *Modern Theology* 14:3 (1998), 425–47.

Ferry, Luc, *The New Ecological Order* (University of Chicago Press, 1995).

Ford, David F., *Self and Salvation: Being Transformed* (Cambridge University Press, 1999).

'What happens in the Eucharist?', *Scottish Journal of Theology* 8:3 (1995), 359–81.

Fox, Matthew, *Original Blessing* (Santa Fe: Bear & Co., 1983).

Fox, Warwick, *Toward a Transpersonal Ecology* (Dartington: Resurgence, 1995).

Gare, Allan A., *Postmodernism and the Environmental Crisis* (London and New York: Routledge, 1995).

Giddens, Anthony, *Beyond Left and Right: The Future of Radical Politics* (Oxford: Blackwell, 1994).

Glacken, Clarence, *Traces on the Rhodian Shore: Nature and Culture in Western Thought from Ancient Times to the End of the Eighteenth Century* (Berkeley, Los Angeles and London: University of California Press, 1967).

Goodpaster, Kenneth E., 'On Being Morally Considerable', *Journal of Philosophy* (1978), 308–25.

Grassie, William, 'Donna Haraway's Metatheory of Science and Religion: Cyborgs, Trickster, and Hermes', *Zygon* 31:2 (1996), 285–304.

Green, Clifford, *The Sociality of Christ and Humanity: Dietrich Bonhoeffer's Early Theology 1927–1933* (Missoula, MT: The Scholars' Press, 1972).

Gregorios, Paulos Mar, *The Human Presence: Ecological Spirituality and the Age of the Spirit* (New York: Amity House, 1987; orig. 1978).

Griffin, David, *God and Religion in the Postmodern World* (Albany: State University of New York Press, 1989).

Griffin, Roger (ed.), *Fascism* (Oxford University Press, 1995).

de Gruchy, John, *Christianity and Democracy* (Cambridge University Press, 1995).

Gruen, Lori, 'Revaluing Nature', in K. Warren (ed.), *Ecofeminism: Women, Culture, Nature* (Bloomington and Indianapolis: Indiana University Press, 1997), pp. 356–74.

'Toward an Ecofeminist Moral Epistemology', in Karen J. Warren (ed.), *Ecological Feminism* (London and New York: Routledge, 1994), pp. 120–38.

Grundmann, Reiner, *Marxism and Ecology* (Oxford: Clarendon Press, 1991).

'The Ecological Challenge to Marxism', *New Left Review* 187 (1991), 103–20.

Gundersen, Adolf G., *The Environmental Promise of Democratic Deliberation* (Madison: University of Wisconsin Press, 1995).

Gunn Allen, Paula, 'The Woman I Love is a Planet; the Planet I Love is a Tree,' in Irene Diamond and Gloria Feman Orenstein (eds.), *Reweaving the World: The Emergence of Ecofeminism* (San Francisco: Sierra Club Books, 1990), pp. 52–7.

Gunton, Colin E., *The Actuality of Atonement* (Edinburgh: T. & T. Clark, 1988).

The One, the Three and the Many: God, Creation and the Culture of Modernity (Cambridge University Press, 1993).

The Promise of Trinitarian Theology (Edinburgh: T. & T. Clark, 1991).

Theology through the Theologians (Edinburgh: T. & T. Clark, 1996).

Gustafson, James B., *A Sense of the Divine* (Edinburgh: T. & T. Clark, 1994).

Habermas, Jürgen, *The New Conservatism* (Cambridge: Polity Press pbk. edn., 1994).

Hall, Douglas John, *Imaging God: Dominion as Stewardship* (Grand Rapids: Eerdmans and New York: Friendship Press, 1986).

The Steward: A Biblical Symbol Comes of Age (Grand Rapids: Eerdmans and New York: Friendship Press, 1990).

Haraway, Donna, 'The Actors are Cyborg, Nature is Coyote, and the Geography is Elsewhere', in Constance Penley and Andrew Ross (eds.), *Technoculture* (Minnesota and London: University of Minnesota Press, 1991), pp. 21–6.

'A Cyborg Manifesto: Science, Technology, and Socialist-Feminism in the Late Twentieth Century', in *Simians, Cyborgs and Women: The Reinvention of Nature* (London: Free Association Books, 1991), pp. 149–81.

'Situated Knowledges: The Science Question in Feminism and the Privilege of Partial Perspective', in *Simians, Cyborgs and Women: The Reinvention of Nature* (London: Free Association Books, 1991), pp. 183–201.

Harding, Sandra, *The Science Question in Feminism* (Ithaca and London: Cornell University Press, 1986).

Hardy, Daniel W., *Finding the Church: The Dynamic Truth of Anglicanism* (London: SCM Press, 2001).

God's Ways with the World: Thinking and Practising Christian Faith (Edinburgh: T. & T. Clark, 1996).

Hardy, Daniel W. and Ford, David F., *Jubilate: Theology in Praise* (London: Darton, Longman and Todd, 1984).

Harvey, Barry, 'The Body Politic of Christ: Theology, Social Analysis and Bonhoeffer's Arcane Discipline', *Modern Theology* 13:3 (1997), 319–46.

Harvey, David, *The Condition of Postmodernity* (Oxford: Blackwell, 1989).

Justice, Nature and the Geography of Difference (Oxford: Blackwell, 1996).

Hauerwas, Stanley and Berkman, John, 'A Trinitarian Theology of the Chief End of all Flesh', in Stanley Hauerwas (ed.), *In Good Company: The Church as Polis* (University of Notre Dame Press, 1995), pp. 185–97.

Hayward, Tim, *Ecological Thought: an Introduction* (Cambridge: Polity Press, 1995).

Heidegger, Martin, *Being and Time* (Oxford: Blackwell, 1962).

An Introduction to Metaphysics (New Haven and London: Yale University Press, 1959).

'Modern Science, Metaphysics, and Mathematics', in D. F. Krell (ed.), *Basic Writings: Martin Heidegger* (London: Routledge, 1993), pp. 271–305.

Hendry, George S., *Theology of Nature* (Philadelphia: The Westminster Press, 1989).

Hewitt, Marsha, 'Cyborgs, Drag Queens, and Goddesses: Emancipatory–regressive Paths in Feminist Theory', *Method and Theory in the Study of Religion* 5:2 (1993), 135–54.

Hick, John, *Evil and the God of Love* (London: Macmillan, 1966).

Hodgson, Peter C., *Winds of the Spirit: A Constructive Christian Theology* (London: SCM Press, 1994).

Jackson, Celice, 'Radical Environmental Myths: A Gender Perspective', *New Left Review* 210 (1995), 124–40.

Jameson, Fredric, *The Political Unconscious: Narrative as a Socially Symbolic Act* (London: Routledge, 1981).

Jenson, Robert, *Systematic Theology*, vol. 2, *The Works of God* (Oxford and New York: Oxford University Press, 1999).

'Aspects of a Doctrine of Creation' in Colin Gunton (ed.), *The Doctrine of Creation* (Edinburgh: T. & T. Clark, 1997), pp. 17–28.

Johnson, Elizabeth A., *Women, Earth and Creator Spirit* (New York/Mahwah: Paulist Press, 1993).

Katz, Eric, Light, Andrew and Rothenberg, David (eds.), *Beneath the Surface: Critical Essays in the Philosophy of Deep Ecology* (Cambridge, MA and London: MIT Press, 2000).

Katz, Eric, 'Against the Inevitability of Anthropocentrism', in Eric Katz, Andrew Light and David Rothenberg (eds.), *Beneath the Surface: Critical Essays in the Philosophy of Deep Ecology* (Cambridge, MA and London: MIT Press, 2000), pp. 17–42.

Kaufman, Gordon D., *Theology for a Nuclear Age* (Manchester University Press, 1985).

'A Problem for Theology: The Concept of Nature', *Harvard Theological Review* 65 (1972), 337–66.

Kelsey, David H., 'Two Theologies of Death: Anthropological Gleanings', *Modern Theology* 13:3 (1997), 345–70.

Kheel, Marti, 'From Healing Drugs to Deadly Drugs', in Judith Plant (ed.), *Healing the Wounds: The Promise of Ecofeminism* (Philadelphia: New Society Publishors, 1989), pp. 96–111.

King, Ynestra, 'The Ecology of Feminism and the Feminism of Ecology', in J. Plant (ed.), *Healing the Wounds: The Promise of Ecofeminism* (Philadelphia: New Society Publishers, 1989), pp. 18–28.

'Feminism and the Revolt of Nature', *Heresies* 13 (1983), 12–16.

'Healing the Wounds: Feminism, Ecology and the Nature/Culture Dualism', in Irene Diamond and Gloria Feman Orenstein (eds.), *Reweaving the World: the Emergence of Ecofeminism* (San Francisco: Sierra Club Books, 1990), pp. 106–21.

Kovel, Joel, 'Commentary on Herbert Marcuse's "Ecology and the Critique of Modern Society"', *Capitalism, Nature, Socialism* 3:3 (1992), 40–2.

'Negating Bookchin', *Capitalism, Nature, Socialism* 8:1 (1997), 3–35.

'On the Notion of Human Nature: A Contribution toward a Philosophical Anthropology', in Stanley B. Messer, Louis A. Sass and Robert L. Woolfolk (eds.), *Hermeneutics and Psychological Theory: Interpretive Perspectives on Personality, Psychotherapy, and Psychopathology* (New Brunswick and London: Rutgers University Press, 1988), pp. 370–99.

Kretzmann, Norman, 'Trinity and Transcendentals', in Ronald J. Feenstra and Cornelius Plantinga (eds.), *Trinity, Incarnation and Atonement: Philosophical and Theological Essays* (University of Notre Dame Press, 1989), pp. 79–109.

LaCugna, Catherine Mowry, *God For Us: The Trinity and the Christian Life* (San Francisco: Harpers, 1991).

Lash, Nicholas, *The Beginning and the End of 'Religion'* (Cambridge University Press, 1996).

Latour, Bruno, 'To Modernise or Ecologise?' in B. Braun and N. Castree (eds.), *Remaking Reality: Nature at the Millennium* (London and New York: Routledge, 1998), pp. 221–42.

Lee, Martha F., *Earth First! Environmental Apocalypse* (Syracuse University Press, 1995).

'Environmental Apocalypse: The Millennial Ideology of "Earth First!"', in Thomas Robbins and Susan J. Palmer (eds.), *Millenium, Messiahs and Mayhem: Contemporary Apocalyptic Movements* (New York and London: Routledge, 1997), pp. 119–37.

Leiss, William, 'The Domination of Nature', in Caroline Merchant (ed.), *Ecology: Key Concepts in Critical Theory* (New Jersey: Humanities Press, 1994), pp. 55–64.

Lewis, C. S., *Studies in Words* (Cambridge University Press, 2nd edition 1967).

Light, Andrew, 'Bookchin as/and Social Ecology', in Andrew Light (ed.), *Social Ecology after Bookchin* (New York: Guilford Press, 1998), pp. 1–23.

Lindbeck, George, *The Nature of Doctrine* (Philadelphia: Westminster Press, 1984).

Lovelock, James, *Gaia: A Look at Life on Earth* (Oxford University Press, 1987).

Lukács, György, *History and Class Consciousness* (London: Merlin Press, 1972).

Macauley, David, 'Be-wildering Order: On Finding a Home for Domestication and the Domesticated Other', in R. S. Gottlieb (ed.), *The Ecological Community* (London and New York: Routledge, 1997), pp. 104–35.

'Evolution and Revolution: The Ecological Anarchism of Kropotkin and Bookchin', in Andrew Light (ed.), *Social Ecology after Bookchin* (New York: Guilford Press, 1998), pp. 298–342.

'On Critical Theory and Nature', *Capitalism, Nature, Socialism* 9:3 (1998), 32–4.

MacIntyre, John, *The Shape of Soteriology* (Edinburgh: T. & T. Clark, 1992).

MacKinnon, Donald, 'Objective and Subjective Conceptions of Atonement', in F. G. Healey (ed.), *Prospect for Theology* (Welwyn: James Nisbet, 1966), pp. 167–82.

'The Relation of the Doctrines of the Incarnation and Trinity', in Richard W. A. McKinney (ed.), *Creation, Christ and Culture: Studies in Honour of T. F. Torrance* (Edinburgh: T. & T. Clark, 1976), pp. 92–107.

Macquarrie, John, *Studies in Christian Existentialism* (London: SCM Press, 1966).

Markoff, John, 'Really Existing Democracy: Learning from Latin America in the late 1990s', *New Left Review* 223 (1997), 48–68.

Marsden, Jill, 'Virtual Sexes and Feminist Futures: The Philosophy of "Cyberfeminism"', *Radical Philosophy* 78 (1996), 6–16.

Marx, Karl and Engels, Friedrich, *The Communist Manifesto* (London: Verso, 1998 [originally published in 1848]).

'Marx and Engels on Ecology', in Carolyn Merchant (ed.), *Ecology: Key Concepts in Critical Theory* (New Jersey: Humanities Press, 1994), pp. 28–43.

Mathews, Freya, *The Ecological Self* (London: Routledge, 1993).

McDaniel, Jay B., *Of Gods and Pelicans: A Theology of Reverence for Life* (Westminster/John Knox Press, 1989).

McFadyen, Alistair, *Bound to Sin: Abuse, Holocaust and the Christian Doctrine of Sin* (Cambridge University Press, 2000).

McFague, Sallie, *The Body of God: An Ecological Theology* (London: SCM Press, 1993).

Models of God: Theology for an Ecological, Nuclear Age (London: SCM Press, 1987).

Super, Natural Christians: How we should Love Nature (London: SCM Press, 1997).

McKibben, Bill, *The End of Nature* (New York: Random House, 1989).

McLellan, David, 'Politics', in D. McLellan (ed.), *Marx: The First 100 Years* (London: Fontana, 1983), pp. 143–87.

McPherson, James, 'Ecumenical Discussion of the Environment 1966–1987', *Modern Theology* 7:4 (July 1991), 363–71.

Mellor, Mary, *Feminism and Ecology* (New York University Press, 1997).

'Myths and Realities: A Reply to Cecile Jackson', *New Left Review* 217 (1996), 132–7.

Merchant, Carolyn, *Radical Ecology* (New York and London: Routledge, 1992).

Merchant, Carolyn (ed.), *Ecology: Key Concepts in Critical Theory* (New Jersey: Humanities Press, 1994).

Mies, Maria and Shiva, Vandana, *Ecofeminism* (London and New Jersey: Zed Books, 1993).

Milbank, John, 'Postmodern Critical Augustinianism', *Modern Theology* 7:3 (1991), 224–37.

Moltmann, Jürgen, *The Coming of God: Christian Eschatology* (London: SCM Press, 1996).

God in Creation: An Ecological Doctrine of Creation (London: SCM Press, 1985).

The Spirit of Life: A Universal Affirmation (London: SCM Press, 1992).

The Trinity and the Kingdom of God (London: SCM Press, 1980).

The Way of Jesus Christ: Christology in Messianic Dimensions (London: SCM Press, 1990).

Naess, Arne, *Ecology, Community and Lifestyle* (Cambridge University Press, 1989).

'The Deep Ecological Movement: Some Philosophical Aspects' (1986), in George Sessions (ed.), *Deep Ecology for the 21st Century: Readings on the Philosophy and Practice of the New Environmentalism* (Boston and London: Shambhala, 1995), pp. 64–84.

'The Deep Ecology "Eight Points" Revisited', in George Sessions (ed.), *Deep Ecology for the 21st Century: Readings on the Philosophy and Practice of the New Environmentalism* (Boston and London: Shambhala, 1995), pp. 213–21.

'Deepness of Questions and the Deep Ecology Movement', in George Sessions (ed.), *Deep Ecology for the 21st Century: Readings on the Philosophy and Practice of the New Environmentalism* (Boston and London: Shambhala, 1995), pp. 204–12.

'Self-realization: an Ecological Approach to Being in the World', in George Sessions (ed.), *Deep Ecology for the 21st Century: Readings on the Philosophy and Practice of the New Environmentalism* (Boston and London: Shambhala, 1995), pp. 225–39.

'The Shallow and the Deep, Long Range Ecology Movements: A Summary' (1973), in George Sessions (ed.), *Deep Ecology for the 21st Century: Readings on the Philosophy and Practice of the New Environmentalism* (Boston and London: Shambhala, 1995), pp. 151–5.

Nash, James A., *Loving Nature: Ecological Integrity and Christian Responsibility* (Nashville: Abingdon Press, 1991).

Nash, Roderick Frazier, *The Rights of Nature: A History of Environmental Ethics* (Madison: The University of Wisconsin Press, 1989).

Nicholls, David, *Deity and Domination* (London: Routledge, 1989).

Northcott, Michael S., *The Environment and Christian Ethics* (Cambridge University Press, 1996).

'A Place of Our Own', in Peter Sedgwick (ed.), *God in the City* (London: Mowbray, 1995), pp. 119–38.

O' Connor, James, *Natural Causes: Essays in Ecological Marxism* (New York: Guilford Press, 1998).

O'Donovan, Oliver, *The Desire of the Nations: Rediscovering the Roots of Political Theology* (Cambridge University Press, 1996).

Oelschlaeger, Max, *Caring for Creation. An Ecumenical Approach to the Environmental Crisis* (London and New Haven: Yale University Press, 1994).

Oliver, Simon, 'The Eucharist before Nature and Culture', *Modern Theology* 15:3 (1999), 331–53.

Ollman, Bertell, *Dialectical Investigations* (London: Routledge, 1993).

Palmer, Clare, 'Stewardship', in Ian Ball, Margaret Goodall, Clare Palmer and John Reader (eds.), *The Earth Beneath: A Critical Guide to Green Theology* (London: SPCK, 1992), pp. 67–86.

Pannenberg, Wolfhart, *Introduction to Systematic Theology* (Edinburgh: T. & T. Clark, 1991).

Metaphysics and the Idea of God (Edinburgh: T. & T. Clark, 1990).

Systematic Theology, vol. 1 (Edinburgh: T. & T. Clark, 1991).

Systematic Theology, vol. 2 (Edinburgh: T. & T. Clark, 1994).

Systematic Theology, vol. 3 (Edinburgh: T. & T. Clark, 1998).

Toward a Theology of Nature (Louisville, KY: Westminster/John Knox Press, 1993).

Penley, Constance and Ross, Andrew, 'Cyborgs at Large: Interview with Donna Haraway', in Penley and Ross (eds.), *Technoculture* (Minnesota and London: University of Minnesota Press, 1991), pp. 1–20.

Pepper, David, *Eco-socialism: From Deep Ecology to Social Justice* (London: Routledge, 1993).

Modern Environmentalism: An Introduction (London: Routledge, 1996).

Petras, James, 'Latin America: The Resurgence of the Left', *New Left Review* 223 (1997), 17–47.

Plant, J. (ed.), *Healing the wounds: The Promise of Ecofeminism* (Philadelphia: New Society Publishers, 1989).

Plumwood, Val, *Feminism and the Mastery of Nature* (London: Routledge, 1993).

'Androcentrism and Anthropocentrism: Parallels and Politics', in Karen J. Warren (ed.), *Ecofeminism: Women, Culture, Nature* (Bloomington and Indianapolis: Indiana University Press, 1997), pp. 327–55.

'Deep Ecology, Deep Pockets and Deep Problems', in Eric Katz, Andrew Light and David Rothenberg (eds.), *Beneath the Surface: Critical Essays in the Philosophy of Deep Ecology* (Cambridge, MA and London: MIT Press, 2000), pp. 59–84.

'The Ecopolitics Debate and the Politics of Nature', in Karen J. Warren (ed.), *Ecological Feminism* (London and New York: Routledge, 1994), pp. 64–87.

'Nature, Self, and Gender: Feminism, Environmental Philosophy, and the Critique of Rationalism', in Robert Elliot (ed.), *Environmental Ethics* (Oxford University Press, 1995), pp. 155–64.

'Women, Humanity and Nature', *Radical Philosophy* 48 (1998), 16–24.

Race, Alan and Williamson, Roger (eds.), *True to this Earth* (Oxford: One World Publications, 1995).

Rahner, Karl, *Foundations of Christian Faith: An Introduction to the Idea of Christianity* (New York: Seabury Press, 1978).

'On the Theology of the Incarnation', *Theological Investigations* (New York: Crossroad, 1982), IV, pp. 105–20.

Rasmussen, Larry L., *Earth Community, Earth Ethics* (Maryknoll, NY: Orbis, 1996).

'Eco-Justice: Church and Community Together', in D. Hessel and L. Rasmussen (eds.), *Earth Habitat: Eco-Injustice and the Church's Response* (Philadelphia, PA: Fortress Press, 2001), pp. 1–19.

Roberts, Richard R., 'A Postmodern Church? Some Preliminary Reflections on Ecclesiology and Social Theory', in D. F. Ford and D. L. Stamps (eds.), *Essentials of Christian Community* (Edinburgh: T. & T. Clark, 1996), pp. 179–95.

Rodman, John, 'Four Forms of Ecological Consciousness Reconsidered', in George Sessions (ed.), *Deep Ecology for the 21st Century: Readings on the Philosophy and Practice of the New Environmentalism* (Boston and London: Shambhala, 1995), pp. 121–30.

Rolston III, Holmes, *Science and Religion: A Critical Survey* (New York: Random House, 1987).

Rossi-Landi, Ferruccio, *Marxism and Ideology* (Oxford University Press, 1990).

Rudy, Alan P., 'Ecology and Anthropology in the Work of Murray Bookchin', *Capitalism, Nature, Socialism* 9:1 (1998), 57–90.

Ruether, Rosemary Radford, *Gaia and God: An Ecofeminist Theology of Earth Healing* (London: SCM Press, 1994).

To Change the World: Christology and Cultural Criticism (London: SCM Press, 1981).

Salleh, Ariel, *Ecofeminism as Politics: Nature, Marx and the Postmodern* (London: Zed Books, 1997).

'Deeper than Deep Ecology: The Eco-feminist Connection', *Environmental Ethics* 6 (1984), 339–45.

'In Defense of Deep Ecology,' in Eric Katz, Andrew Light and David Rothenberg (eds.), *Beneath the Surface: Critical Essays in the Philosophy of Deep Ecology* (Cambridge, MA and London: MIT Press, 2000), pp. 107–24.

'The Ecofeminism/Deep Ecology Debate: A Reply to Patriarchal Reason', *Environmental Ethics* 14:3 (1992), 195–216.

'Nature, Women, Labor, Capital: Living the Deepest Contradiction', in Martin O'Connor (ed.), *Is Capitalism Sustainable? Political Economy and the Politics of Ecology* (New York and London: Guilford Press, 1994), pp. 106–24.

Santmire, H. Paul, *Nature Reborn: The Ecological and Cosmic Promise of Christian Theology* (Philadelphia: Fortress Press, 2000).

The Travail of Nature. The Ambiguous Ecological Promise of Christian Theology (Philadelphia: Fortress Press, 1985).

'Healing the Protestant Mind: Beyond the Theology of Human Dominion', in Dieter T. Hessel (ed.), *After Nature's Revolt: Eco-justice and Theology* (Minneapolis: Fortress Press, 1992), pp. 61–5.

'Toward a New Theology of Nature', *Dialog* 25:1 (1986), 43–50.

Scharper, Stephen Bede, *Redeeming the Time: A Political Theology of the Environment* (New York: Continuum, 1997).

Scott, Peter, *Theology, Ideology and Liberation* (Cambridge University Press, 1994).

'Christ, Nature, Sociality: Dietrich Bonhoeffer for an Ecological Age', *Scottish Journal of Theology*, 53:4 (2000), 413–30.

'Ecology: Religious or Secular?', *The Heythrop Journal* 38:1 (1997), 1–14.

'The Future of Creation: Ecology and Eschatology', in David S. Fergusson and Marcel Sarot (eds.), *The Future as God's Gift* (Edinburgh: T. & T. Clark, 2000), pp. 89–144.

'Imaging God: Creatureliness and Technology', *New Blackfriars* 79:928 (1998), 260–74.

'Nature in a "World come of Age"', *New Blackfriars* 78:919 (1997), 356–68.

'The Resurrection of Nature? Problems in the Theology of Nature', *Theology in Green*, 4:2 (1994), 23–35.

'"Return to the Vomit of 'legitimation'?" Scriptural Interpretation and the Authority of the Poor,' in Craig Bartholomew, Jonathan Chaplin, Robert Song and Al Wolters (eds.), *A Royal Priesthood: The Use of the Bible Ethically and Politically* (Paternoster and Zondervan, 2002).

'The Technological Factor: Redemption, Nature and the Image of God', *Zygon: Journal of Religion and Science* 35:2 (June 2000), 371–84.

'A Theology of Eucharistic Place: Pilgrimage as Sacramental', in C. Bartholomew and F. Hughes (eds.), *Explorations in a Christian Theology of Pilgrimage* (Aldershot: Ashgate, forthcoming).

Sessions, George (ed.), *Deep Ecology for the 21st Century: Readings on the philosophy and practice of the New Environmentalism* (Boston and London: Shambhala, 1995).

Shiva, Vandana, *Staying Alive: Women, Ecology and Development* (London: Zed Books, 1989).

'Development as a New Project of Western Patriarchy', in Irene Diamond and Gloria Fenan Orenstein (eds.), *Reweaving the World: The Emergence of Ecofeminism* (San Francisco: Sierra Club Books, 1990), pp. 189–200.

'The Greening of the Global Reach', in Wolfgang Sachs (ed.), *Global Ecology: A New Arena of Political Conflict* (London: Zed Books, 1993), pp. 149–56.

Sittler, Joseph, *The Ecology of Faith* (Philadelphia: Muhlenberg Press, 1961).

Essays on Nature and Grace (Philadelphia: Fortress Press, 1972).

Slicer, Deborah, 'Wrongs of Passage: Three Passages to the Maturing of Ecofeminism', in Karen J. Warren (ed.), *Ecological Feminism* (London and New York: Routledge, 1994), pp. 29–41.

Smith, Neil, 'Nature at the Millennium: Production and Re-enchantment', in B. Braun and N. Castree (eds.), *Remaking Reality: Nature at the Millennium* (London and New York: Routledge, 1998), pp. 271–85.

Soper, Kate, 'Greening Prometheus: Marxism and Ecology', in Ted Benton (ed.), *The Greening of Marxism* (New York: Guilford Press, 1996), pp. 81–99.

Spretnak, Charlene, 'Ecofeminism: Our Roots and Flowering', in Irene Diamond and Gloria Fenan Orenstein (eds.), *Reweaving the World: The Emergence of Ecofeminism* (San Francisco: Sierra Club Books, 1990), pp. 3–14.

Starhawk, 'Feminist, Earth-based Spirituality and Ecofeminism', in Judith Plant (ed.), *Healing the Wounds: The Promise of Ecofeminism* (Philadelphia: New Society, 1989), pp. 174–85.

Swimme, Brian, 'How to Heal a Lobotomy', in Irene Diamond and Gloria Fenan Orenstein (eds.), *Reweaving the World: The Emergence of Ecofeminism* (San Francisco: Sierra Club Books, 1990), pp. 15–22.

Sylvan, Richard, 'A Critique of Deep Ecology', part I, *Radical Philosophy* 40 (1985), 2–12.

'A Critique of Deep Ecology', part II, *Radical Philosophy* 41 (1985), 10–22.

Tanner, Kathryn, 'Creation, Environmental Crisis, and Ecological Justice', in Rebecca S. Chopp and Mark L. Taylor (eds.), *Reconstructing Christian Theology* (Minneapolis: Fortress, 1992), pp. 99–123.

Thomas, Keith, *Man and the Natural World* (Harmondsworth: Penguin, 1983).

Tillich, Paul, *Systematic Theology*, vol. 1 (London: SCM Press, 1987).

Torrance, Alan J., '*Creatio ex Nihilo* and the Spatio-temporal Dimensions, with Special Reference to Jürgen Moltmann and D. C. Williams', in Colin Gunton (ed.), *The Doctrine of Creation* (Edinburgh: T. & T. Clark, 1997), pp. 83–103.

Tracy, David, 'John Cobb's Theological Method', in David Ray Griffin and Thomas J. J. Altizer (eds.), *John Cobb's Theology in Process* (Philadelphia: Westminster Press, 1977), pp. 25–38.

'Models of God: Three Observations', in R. Gill (ed.), *Readings in Modern Theology* (London: SPCK, 1995), pp. 82–6.

Wainwright, Geoffrey, 'The Holy Spirit', in C. E. Gunton (ed.), *The Cambridge Companion to Christian Doctrine* (Cambridge University Press, 1997), pp. 273–96.

Wall, Derek, *Earth First and the Anti-Roads Movement* (London and New York: Routledge, 1999).

Wallace, Mark I., *Fragments of the Spirit: Nature, Violence and the Renewal of Creation* (New York: Continuum, 1997).

'The Wounded Spirit as the Basis for Hope in an Age of Radical Ecology', in Dieter T. Hessel and Rosemary Radford Ruether (eds.), *Christianity and Ecology: Seeking the Well-being of Earth and Humans* (Cambridge, MA: Harvard/CSWR, 2000), pp. 51–72.

Warren, Karen J., 'Feminism and Ecology: Making Connections', *Environmental Ethics* 9:1 (1987), 3–20.

'Introduction', to section on Ecofeminism, in Michael E. Zimmerman (ed.), *Environmental Philosophy: From Animal Rights to Radical Ecology* (Englewood Cliffs, NJ: Prentice-Hall, 1993), pp. 253–67.

'The Power and Promise of Ecological Feminism', *Environmental Ethics* 12:2 (1990), 125–46.

Warren, Karen J. (ed.), *Ecofeminism: Women, Culture, Nature* (Bloomington and Indianapolis: Indiana University Press, 1997).

Warren, Karen L. and Cheney, Jim, 'Ecological Feminism and Ecosystem Ecology,' *Hypatia* 6:1 (1991), 179–97.

Welker, Michael, *Creation and Reality* (Minneapolis: Fortress Press, 1999).

God the Spirit (Minneapolis: Fortress Press, 1994).

White, Lynn, 'Continuing the Conversation', in Ian Barbour (ed.), *Western Man and Environmental Ethics: Attitudes toward Nature and Technology* (Reading, MA: Addison-Wesley (1973), pp. 55–64.

'The Historical Roots of our Ecologic Crisis', *Science* 155 (1967), 1203–7.

Williams, Raymond, *Keywords* (London: Fontana, 1976).

Problems in Materialism and Culture (London: Verso, 1980).

Resources of Hope (London: Verso, 1989).

Williams, Rowan, *On Christian Theology* (Oxford: Blackwell, 2000).

'Between Politics and Metaphysics: Reflections in the Light of Gillian Rose', in L. Gregory Jones and Stephen Fowl (eds.), *Rethinking Metaphysics* (Oxford: Blackwell, 1995), pp. 3–22.

Worster, Donald, *Nature's Economy* (Cambridge University Press, 2nd pbk edition 1994).

Yoder, John Howard, 'Sacrament as Social Process', *Theology Today* 48 (1991), 33–44.

Zabinski, Catherine, 'Scientific Ecology and Ecological Feminism: the Potential for Dialogue', in Karen J. Warren (ed.), *Ecofeminism: Women, Culture, Nature* (Bloomington and Indianapolis: Indiana University Press, 1997), pp. 314–24.

Zimmerman, Michael E., 'Ecofascism: a Threat to American Environmentalism', in Roger Gottlieb (ed.), *The Ecological Community* (London and New York: Routledge, 1997), pp. 229–54.

'Possible Political Problems of an Earth-Based Religiosity', in Eric Katz, Andrew Light and David Rothenberg (eds.), *Beneath the Surface: Critical Essays in the Philosophy of Deep Ecology* (Cambridge, MA and London: MIT Press, 2000), pp. 151–94.

Zizioulas, John D., *Being as Communion: Studies in Personhood and the Church* (Crestwood, NY: St. Vladimir's Seminary Press, 1985).

Index

Allen, Paula Gunn 31
Anderson, Perry 6
anthropocentrism 63–6, 69, 85, 141, 221, 241
Arendt, Hannah 188

Barth, Karl 12, 43, 44, 253
Bauman, Zygmunt 12
Benton, Ted 138, 140, 142–3, 146, 147–8, 150, 154
Berger, Peter 27
Bewes, Timothy 76
Biehl, Janet 110
Birch, Thomas 65, 107
Bloch, Ernst 187
Bloch, Maurice 5
Boff, Leonardo 20, 227, 230
Bonhoeffer, Dietrich 7, 9, 10, 11, 12, 13–14, 16, 19, 22, 28, 44, 49, 53, 176, 178, 187, 193, 209, 226, 235, 236, 237, 241, 243–4, 250, 251, 258
Bookchin, Murray 67, 102, 103, 109, 110–35, 136, 138, 143, 177, 229
Borgmann, Albert 251
Bourdieu, Pierre 45
Brooke, John Hedley 9
Bruno, Giordano 71
Buckley, Michael J. 38

Camus, Albert 79
Castree, Noel and Braun, Bruce 137
Cavanaugh, William 246, 247, 248, 252, 253, 255, 257
Cheney, Jim 96, 97, 102–7, 197, 198, 228
Christ, Carol 31
Church, the 128, 133, 155, 169, 235, 243, 252–7
Clark, John 81, 103, 104, 110, 111, 114, 120, 122, 125, 128, 129, 162

Cobb, John B. 20, 39
common realm of God, nature and humanity 10, 13, 17, 19, 20, 30–2, 36, 38–40, 52, 55–6, 57, 63, 89, 103, 110, 131, 169, 172, 176, 179, 180, 182, 186, 199, 201–2, 242, 256
  ecosocial ontology 52–5, 56, 57, 58, 60, 104, 134, 169, 171, 172, 209
    sociality 26, 53–4, 132, 180, 187–90, 237
    spatiality 54, 108, 133, 176, 194–8, 212–14, 222, 237–8
    temporality 54–5, 108, 132, 184, 190, 238
  existence, categories of 52, 63
  historico-natural emergence, categories of (movement, structure, tendency) 59, 60, 63, 231
Commoner, Barry 70, 137, 151
creation, doctrine of 19, 20–5, 36, 63, 170, 174, 216
  creatio ex nihilo 21, 32, 170, 179, 181, 196, 198
  and incarnation 173–4, 194
creatureliness 30, 209, 234
  imago dei 46, 175, 210–13, 214–15
  in the middle of creation 15, 258
Cupitt, Don 18, 28

de Chardin, Teilhard 20
de Gruchy, John 226
deep ecology 143, 145, 150, 161, 176, 186, 238–9, 241
  and Christianity 71–2
  as cosmology 73–4, 85–6
  criticisms of 77–9, 80, 81–2, 85, 87
  and Earth First! 66–7
  and fascism 81–2
  formal method 68, 72
  history 66–7
  philosophical basis 67, 71, 73

deep ecology (*cont.*)
  platform 68–70, 72
  and transpersonal psychology 71, 74–80
Dell, Katherine 71, 72
Demeritt, David 6, 100
democracy 233
  of the commons 202, 222
  and deep ecology 80–1
  and difference 225–30
  and representation 229
  and social ecology 133
Derr, Thomas Sieger 19, 34, 214
Devall, Bill 68
Devall, Bill and Sessions, George 35, 71
Dorrien, Gary 223
Doyal, Len and Gough, Ian 53
Drees, Willem B. 34
Dupré, Louis 9, 11, 12, 13, 14, 15, 17, 24, 38,
    54

Eagleton, Terry 247
Eckersley, Robyn 114
ecocentrism 63–4, 66
ecofeminism 31, 239
  and the common realm 89, 90, 96, 105,
    107
  critique of deep ecology 89, 96–7
  cultural 93–4
  gendered relations of domination 92–3
  nature as agent, subject 89, 90, 107
  and reproduction 56, 89, 91, 94, 101, 104–5,
    177
  social/ist 93, 95, 177
  and standpoint epistemology 97, 98
ecological crisis 7, 8, 214
ecology 27, 28, 37, 139, 175
Edwards, Denis 237
Elkins, Stephan 91
Ely, John 130, 136, 138, 163, 187
environment, the 3, 27–8, 32
Enzensberger, Hans Magnus 145
epistemology 65, 83, 88, 134, 158, 170, 185
  and ideology 17, 103, 138
eschatology 176
eucharist 169, 235, 243–57
existence, categories of *see* common realm of
    God, nature and humanity

Farrow, Douglas B. 173
Faricy, Robert 19, 184
Ferry, Luc 81
Fichte 80
Ford, David 45, 248–9
Foreman, Dave 66, 67
Fox, Matthew 20, 76

Fox, Warwick 64, 67, 68, 71, 72, 73, 74–5,
    77–8, 79, 80, 82–3, 85, 86
Francis of Assisi 71, 227
freedom 26

Gaia 34
Gandhi, Mahatma 74, 80
Gare, Allan A. 52, 57
Giddens, Anthony 18
Glacken, Clarence 151
God
  as creator 32, 36, 38–41, 42
  displacement of 10, 13, 16, 35–6, 52
  See also triune God
Goodpaster, Kenneth E. 222
Gottwald, Norman 26
Grassie, William 100
Green, Clifford 44
Gregorios, Paulos Mar 10, 19
Griffin, David 20
Griffin, Roger 82
Gruen, Lori 102, 227, 228
Grundmann, Reiner 34, 145, 186
Gundersen, Adolf 229–30
Gunton, Colin E. 19, 44, 45, 53, 172, 181, 190,
    203, 205–6, 207–8, 209, 249
Gustafson, James B. 20

Habermas, Jürgen 6, 185
Hall, Douglas John 3, 19, 188, 212–16, 217, 218
Haraway, Donna 89, 99–100, 102, 107, 109,
    186, 190–2, 198, 240
Harding, Sandra 98, 99–100
Hardy, Daniel W. 22, 23, 43, 188, 193, 201,
    210–12, 227, 243, 257
Hardy, Daniel W. and Ford, David 248–9
Harvey, Barry 247, 257
Harvey, David 137, 149, 151–3, 156–60, 182,
    186, 224, 226, 234, 239, 247, 252, 253,
    255
Hauerwas, Stanley and Berkman, John 257
Hayward, Tim 146–7, 185
Heidegger, Martin 78, 79, 239–40
Hendry, George 38–41
Hewitt, Marsha 99
Hick, John 22
historico-natural emergence, categories of:
    see common realm of God, nature and
    humanity
Hodgson, Peter C. 25, 48, 172, 173, 235
Holy Spirit
  creator spiritus 203, 204, 207, 210–12
  doctrine of 203–12
  eschatological actions of 204–6, 209,
    222–4, 225

and un/natural fellowship 202, 203–4, 231,
    233, 234, 236, 252–6
see also democracy

Ignatieff, Michael 254, 255

Jameson, Fredric 226
Jenson, Robert 196–7, 198
Jesus Christ 4, 7, 9, 16, 43, 52, 143, 171, 179,
    199–200, 219, 221, 233, 234, 252
    career of 190–1, 194, 234
    and creation 19, 181, 200, 205
    crucifixion of 155, 235, 237
    and friendship 234, 235, 236, 256
    and incarnation 20, 21, 173, 179, 186, 201,
    212–14
    resurrection of 48, 49–50, 51, 171, 173, 176,
    179, 180, 182, 202, 208, 209, 236, 242,
    258
    and sacrifice 181, 184, 190–1, 193–4, 199,
    200, 250
Johnson, Elizabeth 205

Katz, Eric 88
Kaufman, Gordon D. 11, 20, 36, 37, 40, 179,
    218
Kelsey, David 254
Kheel, Marti 34
King, Ynestra 93, 101, 102, 105, 109
Kovel, Joel 57, 114, 189, 226
Kretzmann, Norman 43, 48
Kropotkin, Peter 113, 122

LaCugna, Catherine Mowry 172
Lash, Nicholas 203
Latour, Bruno 224
Lee, Martha F. 66
Leibniz, G. W. 158
Leiss, William 150
Lewis, C. S. 28, 33
Light, Andrew 111
Lindbeck, George 219
Lovelock, James 35
Lukács, György 138

Macauley, David 116, 226
MacKinnon, Donald 190–2, 199, 216
Macquarrie, John 39, 79
Malthus, T. R. 138, 147, 151–2
Markoff, John 80
Marsden, Jill 100
Marx, Karl 10, 137–9, 140, 144, 145, 147–8, 150,
    152, 187, 239, 255
Marx, Karl and Engels, Friedrich 138–9, 146,
    147, 150, 253, 255

Maslow, Abraham 74
materialism 26–7, 91, 96, 98, 101, 105, 135,
    139, 161, 162, 163, 165, 177, 182, 186, 188,
    200
Mathews, Freya 71, 73, 77–8, 81, 83–6
McDaniel, Jay B. 20
McFadyen, Alistair 45
McFague, Sallie 20, 24–6, 38, 39, 46–7, 56,
    179, 183, 193, 219–20, 221, 240–1
McIntyre, John 216, 217
McKibben, Bill 18, 34
McLean, Don 59
McLellan, David 163
McPherson, James 3
Mellor, Mary 90, 91, 93, 94, 95, 98, 101–6, 111
Merchant, Carolyn 28, 92, 95
Mies, Maria and Shiva, Vandana 95, 101–6
Milbank, John 44
Moltmann, Jürgen 19, 38, 49, 50, 175, 195–6,
    203–4, 207, 208, 237, 254

Naess, Arne 18, 65, 67, 68, 69, 70, 71, 72, 73,
    74, 81, 86, 87, 88, 217, 251
Nash, James A. 8, 19, 45–6, 47, 179
Nash, Roderick 227
nationalism 254
natural, the 12, 18, 30
natural law/laws 117, 124, 130–1, 134, 139, 145,
    146, 148, 151, 184
naturalism 32, 63, 106, 108, 117, 139, 146, 162,
    172, 178, 186, 200, 234
nature
    as agent, subject 132, 177, 187, 196, 198,
    210–13, 226
    as extra nos, in nobis, pro nobis see common
    realm of God, nature and humanity
    concept of 7, 11–12, 16, 18–20, 24, 38–42,
    105, 162, 163, 226, 250
    crucifixion of 235
    difference, otherness, independence of
    134, 137, 152, 162, 165, 176, 177, 185,
    189, 194, 196, 198, 199, 201, 212–14, 221,
    222, 233, 240
    disgracing of 8, 9, 10
    domestication/objectification of 16, 33, 182
    and grace 8–9, 10, 11, 12, 13, 14, 25
    mastery of 56, 134, 137, 139, 143–6, 161,
    238
    political–ideological interpretation of 5–8,
    25, 26, 27, 29, 32, 57, 90, 131
    politics of 20, 23, 47, 52, 178
    re-enchantment of 238
    separation from humanity 10, 52
    theology of 3, 13, 18, 19, 23, 25, 27, 30, 37
    value of 145, 202, 219–22, 225, 231

Nicholls, David 48, 49
Northcott, Michael 65, 73, 76, 79, 80, 187, 248, 251

O'Collins, Gerald 39
O'Connor, James 76, 137, 139–42, 149, 150, 154, 156, 161, 183, 186
O'Donovan, Oliver 245, 248, 249, 250, 251
Oelschlaeger, Max 3, 6, 22–3, 219–20
Ollman, Bertell 228
Oliver, Simon 250

Palmer, Clare 213
Pannenberg, Wolfhart 21, 23, 24, 38–40, 41, 173, 174, 175, 186, 192, 207, 208, 209, 231, 241, 244, 247
Penley, Constance and Ross, Andrew 198
Pepper, David 64, 65, 66, 68
personalism 32–8, 63, 106, 108, 234
Petras, James 78
Pickstock, Catherine 200
place 136, 156, 163, 235, 242–3, 245, 252
Plumwood, Val 14, 33, 35, 65, 68, 76, 80, 81, 82, 93, 94, 96, 97, 98, 105, 112, 113, 187, 227, 228
praxis 55
Przeworski, Adam 80, 223

Rahner, Karl 39, 174, 175, 186
Rasmussen, Larry 161, 213, 214, 228, 252
Roberts, Richard R. 129
Rodman, John 64, 65, 70–5
Rolston III, Holmes 34
Rossi-Landi, Ferruccio 30
Rousseau, J.-J. 80
Rudy, Alan P. 114, 119–20
Ruether, Rosemary Radford 13, 20, 23, 76

sacraments 7, 214, 218, 241, 243
Salleh, Ariel 90, 91, 94, 95, 96, 97, 98, 99, 101–7, 110–35
Santmire, H. Paul 11, 19, 40, 254
Sartre, Jean-Paul 79
Scharper, Stephen Bede 90, 92
Scott, Peter 48, 79, 98, 104, 105, 110, 111, 138, 181, 186, 187, 193, 204, 221, 255
Sessions, George 67, 68
Shiva, Vandana 31, 99, 102, 103, 106, 110, 163, 222–4, 225
Singer, Peter 85
Sittler, Joseph 28, 78
Slicer, Deborah 101–6
Smith, Neil 239, 240
social ecology 105, 112, 116, 123, 124, 177, 229
  as an anarchism 105, 113–14, 121, 125, 127

and the common realm 125, 130, 132
  criticisms of social ecology 118–22, 127–33
  critique of deep ecology 110, 114
  critique of hierarchy 115
  dialectical naturalism 113, 182–3
  domination of nature 104, 105, 111, 114
  free nature 116
  freedom and participation 116
  political theory: confederal municipalism 114, 119–20, 125–30
  reason as dialectical 124
socialist ecology 104, 111, 177
  conditions of production 140–55, 156, 161
  criticisms of 162–5
  natural limits 136, 143–6, 161
  place 136, 156–63
  production of nature 137, 138, 139, 140, 240
  reproduction of nature 142
  scarcity 136, 146–56, 161
sociality see common realm of God, nature and humanity
Soper, Kate 137
space 30, 156–60, 169–73, 194–243, 247, 252–3
spatiality see common realm of God, nature and humanity
Spinoza, B. 74, 80, 83
Spretnak, Charlene 239
Starhawk, 31
stewardship 19, 118, 144, 202, 210–18, 225, 231, 238–9
Sting 58
Swimme, Brian 38
Sylvan, Richard 64, 73, 76, 82

technology 14–15, 16, 113, 116
temporality see common realm of God, nature and humanity
Tanner, Kathryn 213, 214, 218
theology
  natural 38–9
  philosophical 38–42
theology of nature, political 4–5, 6, 7, 13, 16, 19, 20, 26, 38–40, 57–60, 88, 90, 102, 103, 109, 110, 130–1, 134, 136, 143, 150, 155, 156–60, 161, 163, 169–73, 231, 233, 235, 244
Thomas, Keith 10, 12, 37, 93
Tillich, Paul 39, 78
Torrance, Alan 195
totality 15, 38–40, 41, 52, 84–5, 96–8, 104, 134, 164, 176, 192, 240
Tracy, David 38, 180, 183
transcendentals 43–52, 55, 56, 57, 171, 172, 179
  becoming 44

openness 50, 169, 204, 210–18
sociality 48–51, 180, 188, 200
unity 50
see also common realm of God, nature and
    humanity, ecosocial antology
Triune God 5, 6, 7, 22, 51, 55, 90, 103, 110, 169,
    170, 172–3, 179, 187, 190–1, 199, 204,
    205, 210–13, 222, 231, 233

un/natural community 256
un/natural humanity 4, 7, 8, 13, 25, 29, 33, 36,
    57, 89, 169, 199, 200, 209, 210–12, 226,
    233, 235, 237
un/natural relations 58, 60, 64, 96, 104–5,
    108, 233, 234, 242–3, 250

van den Brom, Luco 34, 36, 214, 227
Van Gogh, Vincent 59

Wainwright, Geoffrey 203
Wall, Derek 67
Wallace, Mark 205–7
Warren, Karen J. 91, 92–3, 95, 98
Warren, Karen J. and Cheney, Jim 98
Welker, Michael 170, 179, 182, 203, 216
White, Lynn 8, 12, 27, 227
Whitehead, A. N. 158
Williams, Raymond 6, 21, 28, 59, 143, 224
Williams, Rowan 21, 179, 181, 195, 246, 255
work 56
Worster, Donald 28

Yoder, John Howard 246

Zabinski, Catherine 98
Zimmerman, Michael 81, 82
Zizioulas, John D. 172, 205